Multimedia Programming for Windows

Steve Rimmer

Warranty and information for included CD-ROM is contained on the last page of this book

Windcrest®/McGraw-Hill

New York San Francisco Washington, D.C. Auckland Bogotá
Caracas Lisbon London Madrid Mexico City Milan
Montreal New Delhi San Juan Singapore
Sydney Tokyo Toronto

FIRST EDITION
FIRST PRINTING

© 1994 by **Windcrest**.
Published by Windcrest, an imprint of McGraw-Hill, Inc.
The name "Windcrest" is a registered trademark of McGraw-Hill, Inc.

Library of Congress Cataloging-in-Publication Data

Rimmer, Steve.
    Multimedia programming for Windows / by Steve Rimmer.
        p.   cm.
    Includes index.
    ISBN 0-8306-4538-1 (hard)   ISBN 0-8306-4539-X (paper)
    1. Multimedia systems.   2. Windows (Computer programs) I. Title.
    QA76.575.R56   1993
    006.6—dc20   93-21596
                                                                     CIP

Editorial team: Brad Schepp, Acquisitions Editor
                          Kellie Hagan, Book Editor
Production team: Katherine G. Brown, Director
                          Rhonda E. Baker, Layout
                          Brenda M. Plasterer, Layout
                          Kelly Christman, Proofreading
Design team: Jaclyn J. Boone, Designer
                          Brian Allison, Associate Designer   4484
Cover design and illustration: Sandra Blair Design, Harrisburg, Pa.   WP1

For Ron, Beth, Sandy and Bryan,
and for Megan, who mixed the sound.

Contents

Introduction

"Entropy isn't what it used to be."

The hard part about designing computers—or about designing computer software—is in figuring out how the whole works will deal with the people who ultimately pay for it. Far more processor time is typically required to maintain a "user interface" than is tied up doing the sort of work a computer would consider to be respectable employment. The days when a computer the size of Nebraska could think for a week and a half and print out a single number to the cheers and adoration of a room full of people in lab coats ended several eons ago.

Even given mice and reasonably decent monitors, personal computers haven't really been able to communicate with people in something approaching human terms. Windows is arguably easier to work with than typing commands at a DOS prompt—if you have enough memory to run it—but it still insists on expressing itself using phenomena that are unique to computers.

Multimedia offers to let software authors achieve something a bit closer to a really human user interface for Windows applications. It will let you create singing software—a truly disturbing thought—or, in more useful terms, software that can speak, display graphics, and play music that doesn't sound like a backyard full of cats getting together to make more cats. While this is the sort of thing that happens all the time in science fiction movies, it hasn't been practical for most computers until recently.

Aside from simply providing hooks to perform these sorts of functions, the Windows multimedia extensions offer a standardized set of drivers and data formats to handle most of the things you'd probably want to do with multimedia. This means that pretty well anyone running Windows with a minimal level of multimedia hardware will be able to hear your software sing. As with most of the device-independent aspects of Windows, you'll be able to write applications that will support a wide selection of devices without ever seeing most of them.

When an aspect of multimedia turns up in a magazine article or as the filler at the end of "CNN Headline News," it often seems more like someone desperately searching for a new reason to sell you another card for your system than a genuinely useful extension of what a personal computer can do. It's really something you have to work with for a while to properly appreciate. The first time you watch a movie play in a window or listen to your system playing truly orchestral music through your stereo, you'll probably begin to get a feel for how bad computer user interfaces have been until now.

A pound of multimedia to go, please

The really exemplary aspect of multimedia under Windows is that it's about the most fun thing you can do with a computer that doesn't involve killing aliens. More to the point, it's very productive and leading edge. You can play with it for days and not have to feel even a bit guilty about doing so. It might involve just listening to sound bites from Monty Python movies and looking at pictures, but no one is likely to point out his or her own lack of sophistication by saying so.

Perhaps better still, when you finally do complete and ship your own multimedia applications, all sorts of other people will be able to have just as much fun and waste just as much time playing with them as you did creating them. In its most extreme sense, multimedia has the capability to bring joy to the entire western world—even to its lawyers—and to utterly cease all productive work for the foreseeable future.

While you've probably bought this book for a specific function—to learn how to play wave files or unpack Photo-CDs, for example—it's worth mentioning that multimedia is exceedingly open ended. It's probably best defined as that which could conceivably be contained in a box with the word *multimedia* printed on the outside. It's a blank canvas, upon which your imagination can splash whatever colors you like.

Think of this book as a stack of paint cans. It will provide you with the elemental functions to handle some of the most useful parts of multimedia under Windows. Because of the modular nature of these functions, you'll be able to assemble them into any application you can imagine. Multimedia is like that—there are all sorts of places to go where no human foot has thus far trodden. Or no mouse, if you prefer.

A choice of media

In writing this book, I've tried to select those aspects of multimedia for Windows that seem reasonably mainstream and useful. I've also tried to keep the depth of explanation commensurate with what most software authors are likely to want to do with them. This book won't tell you absolutely everything about any of the subjects it deals with, and if you're like most people, you won't want to know absolutely everything. Everything is a fairly large number.

As a final note, all books have a substantial lead time between when they're written and when they're read. As of this writing, much of the documentation for the development packages discussed in this book was a bit flaky, and contained a few errors. Microsoft's manuals for the Multimedia Development Kit, a central element of the applications in this book, contained several prize turkeys, each one guaranteed to frustrate you for hours if you happen to believe it.

All the code in this book works—you can find the compiled applications it generates in the \APPS directory of the companion CD-ROM, ready to run. In situations where this book seems to contradict the documentation from Microsoft and Kodak and such, you'll probably find that it's safer to trust the book.

The lead time inherent in this book might well mean that some of these problems will have been addressed by their respective owners by the time you read this. However, in most larger companies bugs have to become pretty hoary and carnivorous before they're dealt with.

Steve Rimmer
CIS: 70451,2734
BBS: (905) 729-4609

1

When one medium just isn't enough

"A black hole is what happens when the gods divide by zero."

There's a decided lack of certainty about multimedia. Ill-defined and infinitely expandable, it's whatever you want it to be as long as it doesn't rely too heavily on a keyboard and it doesn't run in text mode. It's *the* phrase to stamp on the boxes in which computer peripherals come, whether or not it's applicable.

Multimedia under Windows is arguably a little easier to define, in that Windows 3.1 was created with a number of specific multimedia "extensions"—hooks into Windows to facilitate several high-end features of the sort usually listed under the word *multimedia* on computer-peripheral boxes. Typically you'll find both in fluorescent orange or electric purple. (Multimedia is by its nature not tastefully refined.)

The Windows multimedia extensions offer programmers a standardized and relatively uncomplicated way to implement sound and graphics under Windows applications. In fact, these basic categories will break down into a number of more specific tasks. Sound is a singularly involved undertaking in Windows, with more options than most extraterrestrials have arms.

If you're uncomfortable with this comparison, never having had the opportunity to count the arms of an extraterrestrial, you're probably beginning to get a sense of the challenge awaiting anyone who wants to really work with multimedia under Windows at a programming level.

In fact, the multimedia facilities of Windows can be resolved into a number of fairly comprehensible functions. This book will deal with them—and with one or two other bits that you might find helpful—at a level that will allow you to integrate them into the applications you write. In many cases you might not be writing software that would come in boxes with the word *multimedia* plastered on the front, but the things discussed in this book can be applied to all sorts of applications.

Specifically, here's what the following chapters will give you access to:

- Playing wave files
- Displaying bitmapped graphic images
- Accessing Kodak Photo-CD images
- Playing compact disc audio
- Playing MIDI music
- Playing Video for Windows movies

This list probably deserves some elaboration. While you'll have to get into the chapters that deal with these subjects in detail to really understand them, here's a quick overview of what these media are up to:

Wave files   These are pieces of sampled sound stored as data, and have the extension .WAV under Windows. With suitable hardware—to be discussed in a moment—a wave file can reproduce sound with anything from telephone to compact disc quality, in monaural or stereo, under computer control. You can have your software speak, sing, emit sound effects, or plead piteously for you not to select Exit from the File menu.

Bitmapped graphics   These are probably among the more familiar Windows phenomena—they appear as icons and wallpaper, among other things. We'll look at how to create and display bitmapped images so they become an integral part of your applications.

Kodak Photo-CDs   Photo-CDs are, in a sense, a very sophisticated form of bitmapped graphics. A Photo-CD is a CD-ROM with meticulously scanned 35-millimeter pictures on it, which can be read from the disc and used in your software. You can have a Photo-CD made from your negatives by any Kodak photofinisher—most drugstores and camera shops will oblige you in this.

CD audio   If you have a CD-ROM drive in your computer, you also have a compact disc player. However, aside from being able to play "Thick As a Brick" from beginning to end with no interruptions, it will allow you to select and play portions of a compact disc under software control accurate to ⅟₇₅th of a second.

MIDI   This music standard defines instrumental music as data. It doesn't sample music, as wave files would, but rather specifies each note as a number. The MIDI standard also allows you to define how various voices will sound, how music with multiple voices will be played, and so on. Under Windows, MIDI can become even more useful, with a standardized set of instrument voices and such. You can use MIDI to play Pachelbel's Canon on equally tempered waterglasses or to have a fanfare sound every time your application opens a file, among other things.

Video for Windows   This is Microsoft's standard for displaying digitized television in a Windows application. You can play Video for Windows video bites from within your software, too. The results of doing so in an environment where not much usually moves save for your mouse cursor can be pretty eye catching.

Companion CD-ROM: The biggest disk I could find

If you have a look at the inside back cover of this book you'll find something that most computer books don't come with—a companion CD-ROM. As CD-ROMs are wont to do, it contains a huge amount of data. Among its directories you'll find:

- The source code for all the example applications in this book
- The executable files for all the applications in this book
- Graphic Workshop for Windows, to help you with the graphics
- About twenty megabytes worth of public-domain wave files
- About twenty megabytes worth of public-domain MIDI files
- About twenty megabytes worth of public-domain graphics
- Some Kodak Photo-CD images
- Several Video for Windows clips
- Half an hour with Loftus

This list, too, probably deserves some elaboration. In planning this book, I became aware fairly early on that the weight of the book would be dwarfed by the weight of the floppy disks required to hold a suitable number of example files. In fact, it's cheaper to supply one CD-ROM with a book than it is to include two floppies, and a CD-ROM can hold about 300 times more data than two disks. Of course, once I decided to use a CD-ROM, all sorts of other things to put on it turned up.

Clearly, you won't need twenty megabytes worth of wave files to use the code in this book. However, there was lots of space on the CD-ROM, and it seemed a shame to waste it. If you have an afternoon to kill, playing the wave and MIDI files can be an amusing time waster.

In creating applications that use sound effects, you'll probably find that having all these sounds to draw on is a very useful resource. The same can be said for much of the other data on the CD-ROM.

The rather mind-numbing amount of space on a CD-ROM can be pretty daunting in that when all the data in the foregoing list was assembled, the CD-ROM was well under half full. Once again, it seemed like a waste of real estate to leave a large portion of the disc blank. As such, it acquired the final item on the list (half an hour with Loftus), which also will require a bit of explanation.

The reason that a CD-ROM looks identical to an audio compact disc is because both do exactly the same thing in exactly the same way. In fact, a CD-ROM can contain both data and conventional music. This is very useful in some applications, because it will allow large interactive packages to store both files and sound bites—and the applications themselves, for that matter—on the same CD-ROM. One of the chapters in this book will show you how to access compact disc audio from a CD-ROM drive.

As there was a lot of space on hand—and as some sound bites seemed as if they'd be in keeping with the applications in this book—I decided to record some music in the unused space on the CD-ROM. If you put this disc in an audio compact disc player—or in a CD-ROM drive that's handled by the software explained in chapter 3—you'll find a selection of Celtic music by the band Loftus. There's a more detailed description of the audio portion of the disc in the \LOFTUS subdirectory on the CD-ROM.

One of the things you'll come to appreciate about multimedia is that as soon as it gets interesting, it gets big. Wave files, Photo-CD graphics, Video for Windows clips—all of them require phenomenal amounts of space. In a sense, CD-ROMs are one of the things that make whole classes of multimedia applications practical.

Software requirements

You can approach writing multimedia applications in a number of ways. The one that most developers have used to date is an *authoring language*. Authoring languages are high-level development environments that allow you to put together applications with a command structure somewhere between BASIC and English. As with all such languages, these things are relatively easy to use, but frequently produce software that's less than awe inspiring.

In addition, authoring languages are typically limited to whatever their creators thought you might want to do. Adding additional facilities—reading a Photo-CD, for example—can be difficult or impossible.

There are certainly applications in which an authoring language is a good way to deal with multimedia. However, for many of the things you'll probably think up to do with these new resources, an authoring language would constitute a decided compromise.

The alternative, of course, is to write multimedia applications in C. The extensibility and power of C will make it possible to do pretty well anything you can imagine and your hardware will handle. That's what this book is about. It will let you really tap the power of multimedia running under Windows.

The multimedia extensions of Windows 3.1 are accessible through libraries included with the Microsoft multimedia development kit. Before you can do much of anything with the code in this book, you must have this package. The lone exception to this is the example Photo-CD reader—it requires a development toolkit from Kodak, as will be described in chapter 4, but makes no use of the Microsoft multimedia development kit.

You can work with the source code provided in this book using pretty well any Windows C language-development environment. I've used Borland's C++ 3.1 for Windows, but Microsoft C compilers that generate Windows applications will be equally suitable. Users of Microsoft C will want to make a few changes to the source code in this book, however, which I'll discuss later in this chapter.

You'll also need Windows 3.1 or better—not Windows 3.0—to use most of the code in this book.

Hardware requirements

The hardware you'll need to support the code will vary a bit from chapter to chapter. This section contains a quick overview of the bits involved.

Sound card

The most elemental Windows multimedia device is a sound card. Let's begin exploring multimedia by looking at enhancing the sound facilities of Windows. Figure 1-1 illustrates a typical sound card. This is an Omni Labs AudioMaster. However, any number of other sound cards will do equally well for the applications in this book—you can use a SoundBlaster, an AdLib card, Microsoft's own sound board, and so on. Multimedia is like that.

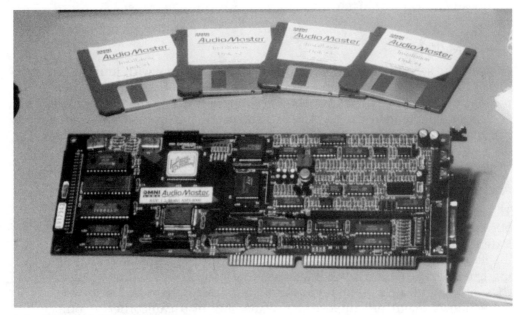

1-1   An Omni Labs AudioMaster card.

Having said this, for reasons that will become considerably more apparent as you work through this chapter, you'll need a Windows-compatible sound card of some sort to use much of the code in this book.

Deep in the heart of every PC is a speaker slightly larger than a quarter connected to a transistor about the size of the part of cat's brain that's actually involved in thinking. Going full blast, it's capable of about a tenth of a watt of sound, and on its best day it would make one of Thomas Edison's wax cylinder players seem like a source of high-fidelity sound. It's very likely that the same people responsible for the 640K memory limitation in PCs can also be blamed for the "squeaker speaker."

Over the years a lot has been done to try to make a PC's speaker do something more than beep when errors occur. Simple acoustical physics—or just plain common sense—will illustrate that this is somewhat futile. High-quality sound requires a high-quality sound system, something that's unlikely to fit in a PC no matter how small the motherboards get.

The best way to get good sound from a PC is to ignore the squeaker speaker entirely and install a better sound interface. That's what the sound card back in FIG. 1-1 is. It connects to a stereo system or other suitable amplifier and generates sound in much the same way that a compact disc player does. Not surprisingly, it's capable of generating sound with the same sort of enviable specifications as are attached to compact discs.

A sound card like the one in FIG. 1-1 implements PCM audio, which stands for pulse-coded modulation. While it requires a bit of an undertaking to understand (and is by no means necessary for the applications in this book), this means that your computer can generate sound in real time that's every bit as complex as real acoustic sound. In fact, it will allow you to digitally record and play back sounds with CD-quality audio.

CD-ROM drive

Perhaps the second most fundamental device for dealing with multimedia is a CD-ROM drive. There's an extensive discussion about the various capacities of these in chapter five. Somewhat more involved than they might seem, CD-ROM readers are an object lesson in why the phrase *open-ended specification* is a contradiction in terms. Figure 1-2 illustrates a CD-ROM drive of the sort that will be described in this book.

Additional hardware

The hardware you'll need beyond these two fundamental—if somewhat exotic—devices depends on exactly what you have in mind for multimedia. Extensive use of MIDI will probably require some additional MIDI toys. You might want a higher-end display card in your system, capable of displaying true-color graphics if you'll be spending your days looking at Photo-CDs, although this is by no means mandatory. Lengthy forays into Video for Windows might presuppose the availability of a camcorder or other

1-2 A Sony CDU-31A CD-ROM drive.

video source and the Video for Windows software. You'll also require a suitable video-capture board, something that's explained in the Video for Windows package.

It seems fair to note that while most of this hardware will run on nothing more sophisticated than an 80286-based computer, you won't get a lot of work done under these conditions. Video for Windows is perhaps the most hardware-intensive multimedia applications that's dealt with in this book, but they all require a significant amount of memory and processor capability. An 80386-based system will squeak by, but I highly recommend an 80486 machine. (You can use old PCs as plant stands, coffee tables, or wheel chocks for very light cars.)

Programming under Windows: Nothing is what it seems

If you've done some Windows programming in C you might not need much of this next section, but if you're new to creating Windows applications you'll do well to read it. The somewhat complex exterior of Windows is supported by a monumentally complex interior.

This book will teach you neither C programming in general nor the basics of writing a Windows application. There are all manner of well-written books on both subjects. If you're really new to C, you might want to start by writing some DOS applications first.

There are a few elements of C programming under Windows that do deserve some discussion here—they're a bit nasty, and are wont to sneak up on the unsuspecting, slip a cracker under them, and make them into a light lunch.

One of the things that makes Windows such a nice place to work, as opposed to DOS, is its memory management. Under DOS, there's conventional memory, extended memory, expanded memory, virtual memory, and any number of drivers to attempt to make sense of it all. Under Windows, all memory is the same, and your applications need not know where it resides.

All this notwithstanding, Windows runs on a computer with a processor that has very strange ideas indeed about memory. It's important to understand how the low-level memory structure of a PC affects Windows applications, although by definition great woe will betide you if you ever try to do anything practical with this knowledge.

A long time ago when the world was flat, the simple microprocessors of the day used linear memory addressing. This meant that the memory in a computer started at byte zero and went up to whatever the top of memory was, with simple numbers to address the space in between. This worked because, among other things, the numbers involved weren't very big. A really powerful computer of the late 1970s and a middle-of-the-road toaster of the early 1990s have about the same amount of memory on hand, although the toaster probably has a faster processor.

When the first 8086-series chips were created, ultimately to form the nexus of the first generation of IBM PC systems, their designers realized that there was an inherent drawback to perpetuating linear addressing on a chip that was intended to address more memory than was common at the time. Doing so required larger numbers. Specifically, a linear-memory 8086, if one existed, would require address registers 20 bits wide, as the chip can address one megabyte of memory. A megabyte, or 1,048,576 bytes, is 2^{20}. The architecture of an 8086 allows for only 16-bit registers, however. All other things being equal, wider registers would have made the processor slower.

If the aforementioned toasters were powered by first-generation 8086 processors, the interval between the moment when the processor decided that your toast was done and the time when it actually popped it out of the toaster would be sufficient to turn it from a golden brown offering of the new day to a charred, shapeless projectile of sufficient density to severely wound most household pets. The designers of the 8086 processors realized that their chips would be sufficiently slow without any further refinements.

To this end, they invented *segmented memory*. In a segmented processor, an absolute address in memory is handled by two 16-bit numbers, called the *segment* and the *offset*. The segment defines which paragraph of memory is involved, a paragraph being a 16-byte increment. The offset specifies which of the subsequent 65,535 bytes of memory is of interest, this being the largest number that will fit in a 16-bit register.

Although this sounds like an arrangement come up with by someone who'd eaten entirely too much burnt toast, it does offer a number of salient advantages over linear memory addressing. Among them, it means that while large programs must use 32-bit addresses to locate things in memory, small programs—those that will fit in 65,535 bytes of memory or less—can address everything they're interested in with 16-bit numbers. This means that small programs can run faster and be smaller still.

In creating complex PC applications—or complex PC-application environments, such as Windows—the segmented nature of PC memory can become an integral part of the works. Under Windows, differentiating between small objects and large objects—those that will fit in one 65,535-byte segment and those that won't—is one of the ways that Windows applications can improve their performance. Of course, it periodically drives Windows programmers to bash their heads against hard surfaces.

The first consequence of segmented memory for PC applications is the use of *memory models*. A memory model is a definition of how big things in your application are likely to get, and as such what sort of numbers are required to address them. The numbers involved are called *pointers*—they point to things in memory.

The simplest memory model under Windows is the *small model*. A small-model program is constrained to have all its code and all its data fit into a single memory segment. If a Windows application can do this, all its code addresses and pointers to data can be handled using 16-bit, or *near*, pointers. This is the most efficient way to write a Windows application, but it limits the size of what you can write.

The most common memory model for use with Windows applications is the *medium model*. A medium-model program is constrained to have its data fit in one memory segment but its code can expand to multiple segments. As such, the addresses in the code of a medium-model program will be 32-bit, or *far*, pointers.

There are two other memory models that appear in DOS applications, but are typically not called for directly in Windows applications. The first of these is the *large model*. Large-model programs use far addresses and far data pointers—32-bit numbers in all cases. Under DOS, a large-model program can in theory deal with a megabyte of code and a megabyte of data—admittedly, this is a bit tricky in an environment that supports only 640K of addressable memory in total.

Under a large-model program, a pointer consists of two 16-bit integers, one each for its segment and its offset. This has two serious consequences under Windows. The first is that there are multiple pointer values for every byte of memory in a computer under this arrangement—you can concoct pointers with differing component values that will point to the same absolute location in memory. For example, a pointer with a segment value of zero and an offset value of 16 would point to the 16th byte in memory. A pointer with a segment value of one and an offset value of zero would also point to the 16th byte in memory. If you compare these two pointers, they'll appear to be different, even though they really point to the same place.

The second catch to large-model programs is a bit nastier. Under C, you can only add integers to far pointers. You can't add long integers to far pointers. The actual mechanism for doing this pointer arithmetic involves adding integers to the offset part of a far pointer. There's no carrying or borrowing involved—if you increase the offset of a pointer so that it over-flows, it will just wrap back around past zero, and the segment will be un-changed. This means that large-model pointers can't address single objects larger than 65,535 bytes.

The final memory model, then, is one that speaks to this limitation. It's called the *huge model*. Huge-model pointers are also 32 bits wide, but when you go to work with one, it's "normalized" behind your back. This means that it's turned into a linear-memory value, a simple long integer. When you're done with it, it's turned back into a segment and offset value. Under C, all the normalization is handled transparently.

The meaningful aspect of huge-memory pointers is that you can add long integers to them, and as such they can address objects larger than 65,535 bytes.

Unless you ultimately come up with a very exotic reason for doing so, it's unlikely that you'll ever write Windows applications in the large- or huge-memory model. There's usually no call to do so, and fairly mean-ingful speed and space penalties lurking behind these models should you try.

Under Windows, it's quite acceptable to write *mixed-model* pro-grams—in fact, it's all but impossible not to. A mixed-model program is written in the medium model with far or huge pointers used when they're needed. This allows you have the speed and compact code of a small ap-plication with access to large-memory objects when you require them. It also offers to the unwary ways to crash Windows that were once the ex-clusive province of professional saboteurs.

It's not hard to understand how to work with mixed-model pro-grams—they get nasty only if you don't keep an eye on them. Here's a look at some pointer lore under Windows. In a medium-model program, this will create a near pointer:

```
char *p;
```

This will create a far pointer:

```
char far *p;
```

And this will create a huge pointer:

```
char huge *p;
```

To help protect you from yourself, Windows defines a dedicated data type for far pointers, called LPSTR, and one for huge pointers called HPSTR.

Memory in a Windows applications consists of local and global mem-ory. Every windows application has a local-memory segment, which is 65,535 bytes of space that must hold the program's stack, any static data that the program requires, and the local heap. The *local heap* is a place to allocate small memory objects. Objects in the local heap can be accessed by near pointers.

The local heap can be no larger than the memory in the local data segment left over by the stack and your static data. The stack and heap sizes are defined in the DEF file for a Windows application.

Note that because local variables in a function are actually allocated on the stack and because the stack is in the local data segment, you can address local variables with near pointers too.

On the brightest and sunniest of days, the local data segment will avail you of only a few tens of kilobytes of memory. Larger memory objects must be allocated from global memory. Under Windows, global memory is defined as being anything that isn't local memory. Windows manages all the conventional, extended, and expanded memory in your system so that it all appears as global memory to your applications.

Global memory objects must be addressed with either far or huge pointers, depending on their sizes. When you define a near pointer in a medium-model program, it doesn't have a segment value per se. By convention, it implicitly references something in the local data segment for the application it's part of. As such, you have to be really careful when you assign pointers in a Windows program. For example, this will work:

```
char *nearpointer;
char far *farpointer;
farpointer=nearpointer;
```

In this case, the farpointer object will assume the offset value of the nearpointer object and the segment value of the local data segment, and all will be well. Here's a second example that won't fare quite as well:

```
char *nearpointer;
char far *farpointer;
nearpointer=farpointer;
```

In this case, nearpointer will assume the offset value of farpointer. However, its segment value will be that of the common data segment no matter what the segment of farpointer was. Writing to nearpointer will probably fill your application's local data segment with something it won't like the taste of—perhaps overwriting the stack, for example, in the process.

Note that you can assign far and huge pointers to one another safely, but you must be sure to use a huge pointer when you're actually addressing things in a large allocated object.

You should be particularly careful about pointer models when you use type casts under C. In a sense, a cast is a way of telling C to shut off much of its type checking in a specific instance, and that you'll take responsibility for the results. Here's a good example of how this can get you into trouble:

```
GLOBALHANDLE objecthandle;
OBJECT far *objectpointer
objecthandle=GlobalAlloc(GMEM_MOVEABLE,100*(long)sizeof(OBJECT));
objectpointer=(OBJECT *)GlobalLock(objecthandle);
```

In this example, OBJECT is a data type of some sort, and objecthandle is being used to reference an allocated buffer of 100 of them. Having allocated the buffer, you must lock it so its memory can be accessed, the province of GlobalLock. In order to keep C happy, the pointer returned by GlobalLock must be cast to the type OBJECT. The bug in the foregoing code is that while the pointer itself is defined as being far, the cast is near. It should look like this:

```
objectpointer=(OBJECT far *)GlobalLock(objecthandle);
```

There's an even more insidious example of the problems that mixed-model pointers can cause—one that gets most Windows software authors from time to time. Here's a call to the wsprintf function, Windows' large-model implementation of the standard sprintf call:

```
char b[64],s[64];
lstrcpy(s,"dogs of war");
wsprintf(b,"Cry 'Havoc!' and let slip the %s.",s);
```

This bit of code should serve to correctly assemble a line from the play *Julius Caesar*. In fact, it won't. But this will:

```
wsprintf(b,"Cry 'Havoc!' and let slip the %s.",(LPSTR)s);
```

Notice that the third argument to wsprintf is cast to (LPSTR). This might seem a bit pointless, as it appears to be casting a pointer to a pointer. It is—sort of.

The wsprintf function is unusual because the types of its first two arguments are known and defined in prototypes, but all its subsequent arguments can be anything you like and no prototypes exist for them. For example, the first argument is defined as being of the type LPSTR, a far pointer, and the compiler knows to treat it as such. Left to its own devices, the argument b would, in this case, be handled as a near pointer, as it exists in the common data segment. The cast implied by the prototype for wsprintf sees to it that it's handled correctly.

The third and subsequent arguments to wsprintf cannot be prototyped, since their types can be whatever you want to print. It's up to you to make sure their types agree with the format string passed to wsprintf, of course. However, when you pass string arguments, you must also keep in mind that wsprintf expects far pointers to things. Local variables are allocated on the stack, which always resides in the common data segment of a Windows application in the small and medium models. By definition, then, pointers to such objects in a small- or medium-model program will be near unless you explicitly cast them far. This will confuse wsprintf. If wsprintf doesn't print what you expect, check this one.

There's a final consideration for mixed-model pointers that might turn up in your applications. This is one to watch out for as well, and if you find yourself enmired in it you'll probably not be pleased to know that it's without solution.

There are two sources of intrinsic functions available to someone programming under Windows. In this case, we'll assume that they're available to someone programming with one of Borland's compiler's under Windows—the specific function names might change a bit in other environments. The two sources are Windows and your C compiler.

Windows provides applications running under it with all sorts of useful calls to manage windows, open dialog boxes, make noise, delete atoms and, in short, do hundreds of things most people would never imagine wanting to do. They're all prototyped in windows.h and other Windows header files. When you pass pointers to these functions, their prototypes define them as far or huge pointers, which is what Windows functions expect. All this works absolutely seamlessly, and you can always pass pointers to Windows call with complete impunity. (Well, you pretty well always can, if you ignore that little contretemps with wsprintf I discussed a moment ago.)

The other source of functions are those provided by the libraries supplied with your compiler. The Borland C libraries are rich with useful functions that do a variety of things Windows itself doesn't provide for. It has buckets of string- and memory-manipulation functions, some nice sorting functions, numerical and mathematical functions, and so on. Most of them can be used successfully under Windows, but in some case they'll run into pointer problems if you don't watch them.

A typical problem of this type is that the memset function will fill a buffer with a fixed value. Here's an example of it in use:

```
char b[128];
memset(b,0,128);
```

This call will fill the buffer b with 128 zero bytes. The next call will probably trash your application's stack, or do something else equally as fatal:

```
GLOBALHANDLE h;
LPSTR p;
h=GlobalAlloc(GMEM_MOVEABLE,128L);
p=GlobalLock(h);
memset(p,0,128);
```

In theory, this should work. It won't, though—or at least, it won't work if your Windows application is compiled under the small or medium memory model. When you compile an application that makes calls to your compiler's libraries—where memset resides, in this case—the linker will select the library that matches the memory model of the program. In a medium-model program, then, the medium-model library will be linked in.

A medium-model version of memset will expect its first argument, a pointer, to be near. In the second application of memset, the pointer passed to it is far. The memset function will take its offset value as a near pointer and assume that it references memory in the local data segment of the application. By definition, it cannot, as it has been allocated from global memory. This will cause memset to reliably write 128 zero bytes to somewhere they shouldn't be.

There's no way to fix this problem—under a small- or medium-model Windows application you can't use your compiler's library functions in situations where they would have to work with objects referenced by far or huge pointers. In this example, you'd have to write a memset function of your own to deal with LPSTR pointers.

This doesn't mean that all the functions in your compiler's libraries are useless—it just means that you can't use them to work with far or huge pointers. In most cases, this won't prove to be a problem. It is, however, something to be very careful of.

Here's one more consideration to keep in mind about memory, pointers, and potential errors under Windows. Unlike DOS applications, Windows software runs in protected mode—at least it does unless you specifically run Windows in real mode or attempt to run Windows on an 80286 machine with a megabyte or less of memory.

Protected mode is so named because it protects applications residing in memory from unwarranted intrusions by other applications. Specifically, when a program runs in protected mode, it "owns" its memory. If it attempts to address memory outside the portion it owns, the processor will prevent it from doing so by throwing a protected-mode fault. Under Windows, this will call up a protected-mode fault dialog box and terminate the offending application.

Memory addresses in protected mode aren't quite what they seem. The segment value of a pointer under protected mode is really an index into the processor's address-selector table. A pointer to memory your application doesn't own, then, represents an invalid index into the selector table. Keep in mind that this is true of reading from as well as writing to memory.

It's especially important to keep this in mind if you actually write applications on a machine that's running Windows in real mode. Windows in real mode is a lot like DOS—your applications won't be prevented from addressing memory they don't own, and no harm will come from attempting to do so unless you write somewhere you shouldn't and damage another application or some part of Windows itself. However, most Windows users run in protected mode—getting away with sloppy pointer management in real mode might leave you with funky applications in protected mode.

Compiler harpies and header-file gremlins

One of the really laudable things about the C language is that it's portable. A C language program written under the auspices of one compiler can be successfully compiled on another. This, and the native ability of pigs to fly, are two of the more miraculous observations of the latter half of the twentieth century.

Experienced DOS programmers will appreciate that observing formations of pigs flying south for the winter is several orders of magnitude more likely than having two competing C compilers deal with more than eight lines of source code the same way. The morass of compiler standards under DOS is quite terrifying.

Things are much better under Windows. The calling convention of the intrinsic functions of Windows has largely defined how Windows languages must behave. As such, it's quite realistic to speak of writing Windows applications in Borland's C implementations and have them also compile successfully under Microsoft's languages.

The programs to be presented in this book are essentially portable between compilers. There are a few things to keep in mind, however. The first of these is the use of Borland's custom control library, the BWCC.DLL file included with Borland's languages. While used sparingly in the example programs herein, it does turn up. Users of Microsoft's languages should keep an eye out for it. The BWCC.DLL library provides programs with a particular style of three-dimensional controls, as is illustrated in FIG. 1-3.

1-3 The three-dimensional controls created by BWCC.DLL.

In fact, Microsoft has recently released its own custom control library. Aside from some of the Borland controls being a bit more colorful—or a bit more gaudy, depending on how you want to look at it—the Borland library integrates conveniently with Borland's Resource Workshop, making the creation of even large or complex dialogs painless and interactive.

If you're using one of Borland's languages with the code in this book, all you need do is to make sure that the BWCC.LIB file is in the WIN-DOWS\SYSTEM directory of your hard drive. It should be there, as it's installed when you install Borland's Windows development environments.

The Borland custom control library turns up only as decorations in the example applications in this book. For example, the window in FIG. 1-4 is the wave-file player application from the next chapter. The drop shadow around the list box is handled by a Borland custom control.

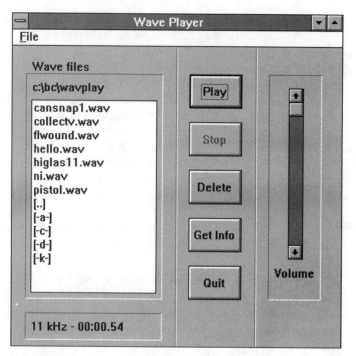

1-4 The wave-file player from chapter 2 of this book.

Clearly, the universe will continue to unfold as it should if this drop shadow isn't on hand. As such, if you're using a Microsoft C compiler, all you need do is remove the following line from the top of each of the example programs in this book:

```
#include <bwcc.h>
```

You should also delete this line from the WinMain functions of the example applications:

```
BWCCGetVersion();
```

The call to BWCCGetVersion serves to make sure the BWCC.DLL file is available when an application that uses it first boots up. Finally, you can delete the Borland controls from the various RC resource scripts for the example applications.

The code in this book is written in fairly standard ANSI C, which is the way Windows likes to see it. It uses the currently trendy Pascal function declaration style—while Windows doesn't much care about this, it makes the generation of prototypes somewhat easier. Most Windows C compilers are very interested in the use of prototypes, as they genuinely serve to displace whole phyla of bugs. As such, in simpler times a function might have been declared like this:

```
void AbortOnTuesdays(p,n)
    char *p;
    int n;
{
    /* some code goes here */
}
```

It's now considerably more fashionable to write it like this:

```
void AbortOnTuesdays(char *p,int n)
{
    /* some code goes here */
}
```

Neither style makes any difference to the code your compiler will ultimately generate, and you're free to choose the one you're most comfortable with.

The programs in this book all supply prototypes for the functions they contain, something that long-time DOS programmers might well look at with derision and contempt. Prototypes are a mechanism to protect you from yourself, and if you can't trust yourself there doesn't seem to be much point in living. However, under Windows you can do yourself some pretty subtle and nefarious injuries without half trying.

Prototypes address a fundamental assumption of the C language—that everything would rather be an integer, given the opportunity. C further tends to assume, in those cases in which the first assumption doesn't apply, that actually interchanging integers with other objects won't do them any serious harm, even if it really shouldn't be allowed. Under Windows, both of these assumptions can have some serious consequences. Here's a legal, if rather sloppy, C language declaration:

```
AbortOnTuesdays(n)
{
    /* some code goes here */
}
```

You'll note that this function conforms to neither of the forgoing programming styles. It's allowed because C assumes that everything is an integer unless you specifically tell it otherwise. Specifically, it assumes that n is an integer and that AbortOnTuesdays will return an integer value. If you call AbortOnTuesdays like this, nothing of any use is likely to happen:

```
AbortOnTuesdays("It's Wednesday");
```

In this case, the function AbortOnTuesdays has been passed a pointer to a string when it should have been passed an integer. In classic C, the compiler won't complain about this, because only AbortOnTuesdays knows what its arguments are supposed to be.

A prototype is a declaration of the number and type of arguments a function should expect and the type of the value it can be assumed to return. Function prototypes are typically ensconced at the top of an application file, or in a header file. The prototype for the foregoing function would be written like this:

```
void AbortOnTuesdays(int n);
```

This prototype tells C that AbortOnTuesdays expects an integer for an argument and that no functions that call AbortOnTuesdays should use the value it returns, as it's declared void, or meaningless.

In writing Windows applications, function prototypes also serve to iron out at least some of the pointer-model problems discussed in the previous section. For example, consider this variation of AbortOnTuesdays:

```
void AbortOnTuesdays(char far *p)
{
    /* some code goes here */
}
```

This would be a normal way of writing a Windows function to accept a string pointer as an argument, and you could substitute LPSTR for char far *. If you call AbortOnTuesdays like this, however, it will get into trouble if it hasn't been set up with a prototype:

```
AbortOnTuesdays("It's Wednesday");
```

The string "It's Wednesday" will be stored as static data, that is, in the local data segment for your application. As such, it will be referenced by a near pointer, which is what C will pass to AbortOnTuesdays. The resulting pointer will have the wrong data segment—the AbortOnTuesdays function will create one from whatever value happens to be on the stack—and dire things will probably happen. You should explicitly cast the pointer:

```
AbortOnTuesdays((char far *)"It's Wednesday");
```

or:

```
AbortOnTuesdays((LPSTR)"It's Wednesday");
```

With a prototype in place, Windows will perform the cast for you. If you really loath prototypes, you're free to turn prototype checking off for your compiler, and your compiler won't complain when it's confronted with functions that don't have them. However, in the complex environment of Windows you're really dancing with a dragon by doing so.

I mentioned earlier that the code in this book is written in ANSI C, which is distinguished from C++. As its name implies, C++ is a superset of C. While some of the C compilers you can use to compile the programs in this book are really C++ compilers, traditional C lurks within them. You can use C language code with a C++ compiler by simply ignoring the C++ extensions.

If you prefer to work in C++, you can add C++ trappings to the applications presented here, or mix the C language functions you abstract from the following chapters with your own C++ code. There's no penalty in doing so—C++ doesn't really allow you to do anything that C doesn't. It merely allows you to express your code in a different way, one that better lends itself to some programs—or to some programmers.

As a final note about the applications in this book, you'll find two macros in each one that are never used. Here's what they look like:

```
#define say(s) MessageBox(NULL,s,"Yo...",MB__OK ¦ MB__ICONSTOP);
#define saynumber(f,s) {char b[128]; \
    sprintf((LPSTR)b,(LPSTR)f,s); \
    MessageBox(NULL,b,"Debug Message",MB__OK ¦ MB__ICONSTOP); }
```

These are debugging tools—they don't expand into anything when they aren't used, and as such there's no penalty involved in their hanging around. The say macro will cause a message box to appear with whatever text has been passed to say as an argument. The saynumber argument will display a printf format string and a number—in fact, the second argument can be anything you like, as long as the format string agrees with it. You would display a value like this:

```
saynumber("The value is %d",value);
```

The say and saynumber macros are handy when you want to see what a value or other variable looks like at a particular place in your program while you try to find out why something isn't working. You can use a Windows debugger to do this, of course, but these bits of code are often quicker and simpler to use.

Using multimedia

Perhaps the most engaging aspect of multimedia is that very few people really have a clear idea of what it's there for. Unlike most areas of application programming, multimedia is more of a stone in a wall than a plan for the wall itself. You can make of it what you will.

This book will present you with the source code for a number of very simple multimedia applications—Windows programs to play wave files, display Photo-CD images, and so on. In reality, it's unlikely that you'll be writing these sorts of programs yourself. Except for itinerant file collectors and people who just like to play with computers for their own sake, there's little call for programs that just make noises or display pictures.

The real power of multimedia is in assembling these elements into more complex applications—a reference book that speaks and intersperses its text with pictures, an interactive computer game with stereo sound effects and graphics, large CD-ROM information bases with graphics and compact-disc audio are a few examples. Your own imagination will no doubt be the source of many others.

One of the reasons that Windows has proven far more popular as an operating environment than DOS ever was is that using it is a bit closer to interacting with a human being rather than a computer. At least it serves to express things with metaphors that human beings can easily relate to. The multimedia extensions of Windows allow you to have your applications speak to your users in a way they'll find comfortable, approachable, and easy to get along with.

For perhaps the first time in the history of personal computers, you can replace the classic C language program:

```
main()
{
    printf("Hello");
}
```

with a human voice.

2
Playing wave files

"Clones are people two."

Wave files are a Windows application's way of mouthing off at humans. In their simplest form they're short bites of sampled sound that can be played under software control. However, as was discussed in chapter 1, wave files have numerous controls that allow you to determine their audio quality—you can have wave file sounds played in mono or stereo, and at frequency ranges from telephone to compact-disc quality. Wave files can be stored as individual files on disk, or as elements in the resource file of an application.

In addition to allowing you to play wave files on command, Windows allows you to "attach" them to a limited number of system functions. Later in this chapter, we'll look at a program to attach wave files to a much larger group of events. With this application running you'll be able to have wave files play when you click on a button, pull down a menu, or open a window, among other things. (This is arguably one of the most loathsome things you can do to a computer, although quite a few Windows users do it. It's probably a cultural preference, like those Logitech mice with ears and faces.)

Despite their relatively simple appearance and function, wave files can be relatively complicated to work with for the same reason that most of Windows' other interesting data structures are—there are numerous ways to play a wave file, and it's often difficult to know which is the appropriate one to use in a particular application. We'll be looking at them all in this chapter.

You'll find several megabytes worth of example wave files on the CD-ROM accompanying this book. They have the extension WAV. If you work with the applications in this chapter, you might want to copy a few of them into the directory of your hard drive where you put the source code.

An overview

There are four broad classes of functions under Windows to deal with playing wave files. In a sense, each is somewhat lower level than the one before it. The lower-level functions are more capable, but also considerably more complicated to work with. The four classes are as follows:

- MessageBeep
- sndPlaySound
- MCI calls
- waveOut calls

One of the things you must work out for yourself when you write software that uses the sound facilities of Windows is which level of wave-file support you really need. Each of these four approaches involves some trade-offs in complexity and performance. The latter two are particularly difficult to choose between in many applications, being in some regards simply different interfaces to the same functions.

It's in the nature of Windows to provide numerous ways to achieve what would seem to be the same results.

Playing sounds with MessageBeep

The MessageBeep function will probably be familiar if you've done any Windows programming—it doesn't seem to be a multimedia call at all. Under normal circumstances, it simply causes the squeaker speaker of a PC, so maligned in chapter 1, to emit a beep. However, it does have an argument, which suggests that it's perhaps capable of greater things.

In fact, in normal Windows applications—without the multimedia extensions in place—the argument to MessageBeep is ignored, and it's used only as a place holder. However, if you have a sound card and suitable Windows drivers installed, you can use different arguments to Message-Beep. The arguments are defined as constants in the mmsystem.h. They are:

MB_OK   Plays the SystemDefault sound.

MB_ICONASTERISK   Plays the SystemAsterisk sound.

MB_ICONEXCLATION   Plays the SystemExclamation sound.

MB_ICONHAND   Plays the SystemHand sound.

MB__ICONQUESTION Plays the SystemQuestion sound.

The sounds that MessageBeep actually plays in response to these arguments are defined in the [sounds] section of your WIN.INI file. Here's what this looks like as Windows is first installed.

```
[sounds]
SystemAsterisk=chord.wav,Asterisk
SystemHand=chord.wav,Critical Stop
SystemDefault=ding.wav,Default Beep
SystemExclamation=chord.wav,Exclamation
SystemQuestion=chord.wav,Question
SystemExit=chimes.wav,Windows Exit
SystemStart=tada.wav,Windows Start
```

This means that if you were to issue the following command:

```
MessageBeep(MB__ICONEXCLAMATION)
```

the wave file CHORD.WAV would play. The [sounds] section of WIN.INI is actually used by Windows to define sounds to attach to certain system events—for the most part, to the appearance of certain icons in dialog boxes—and to Windows itself for booting up and shutting down. You can define these sounds and how they're used in the Sounds applet of the Windows control panel. It's shown in FIG. 2-1.

2-1 The Sounds applet of the Windows Control Panel.

The wave files initially defined in the [sounds] section of WIN.INI are the ones that are supplied with Windows. They're not very interesting, and you're free to change them for other sounds if you like. Having said this, there's a lot to be said for keeping these sounds short, and the files they reside in small. I'll say a lot more about this when we look at a program to augment the sound attachment facilities of Windows later in this chapter.

If you attempt to play a sound with MessageBeep that doesn't exist—or if Windows attempts to play a nonexistent wave file in response to a dialog box icon or other event—Windows will attempt to play the SystemDefault sound in its place. If this wave file also doesn't exist, it will generate the usual squeaker-speaker beep in protest. The wave files for Windows' internal use should be located in your WINDOWS directory.

There are two other possible arguments to MessageBeep. If you pass it the traditional zero value, it will play the SystemDefault sound, or it will beep the speaker if the designated wave file for this sound can't be located. If you run it as MessageBeep(-1), it will ignore the [sounds] section of WIN.INI entirely and just beep the speaker.

As an aside, when you're writing software that will use MessageBeep to attract attention you should keep all the foregoing in mind. If your software finds itself running on a system without a sound card, it won't matter what argument you pass to MessageBeep—the only sound available under these conditions is a speaker noise. On a system with a sound card, it's important to keep in mind that in many cases users will switch on the stereo or other output device their sound cards are driving only when they're required. As such, calling MessageBeep(0) might produce no sound at all if the amplifier it's driving is switched off, while MessageBeep(-1) will generate some noise under all conditions.

While this application of MessageBeep is interesting in its way, it offers access to a fairly limited range of sounds under less than ideal conditions. In practice, you probably won't find it all that useful as path to playing wave files from within your applications.

Playing sounds with sndPlaySound

The most elementary function to play wave files under program control is called sndPlaySound. It offers relatively few options, and is easy to implement. For the most part, you can hand it the path to a wave file or a pointer to one stashed in memory and let it get on with the problem of figuring out how to play it. Few things could be easier. There are some limitations to sndPlaySound, but if you'll be doing modest things with wave files you might never bump up against them.

There are two arguments to sndPlaySound: to wit, a pointer and a set of flags. Here's a simple example of this function in use:

```
sndPlaySound((LPSTR)"REDALERT.WAV",SND_ASYNC);
```

This will read a file called REDALERT.WAV from your hard drive and play it, or at least it will attempt to. As it's set up here, it will play the SystemDefault sound from your WIN.INI file, as discussed in the foregoing section, if REDALERT.WAV proves to be elusive. We'll look at how to change this in a moment.

The sndPlaySound function returns a true value if it has succeeded in playing something, and a false value otherwise.

In addition to passing a filename to sndPlaySound, you can also pass a sound key. A sound key is a string to be found in the [sounds] section of WIN.INI. For example, if you pass it the string "SystemStart" as its first argument, it will attempt to play the sound associated with the SystemStart line in WIN.INI—by default this is TADA.WAV. Like the permutations of MessageBeep, this is a facility with limited application.

The second argument to sndPlaySound offers a number of useful controls. You can OR multiple flags together to form it. The most common one, the SND_ASYNC flag used in the previous example, tells sndPlaySound to return immediately to the program that called it as soon as it has initiated sound playing. As such, a sound can be playing in the background after a call to sndPlaySound, and your application can get on with other things. Note that this can be a bit dangerous for the unwary, as you'll see in a moment.

The SND_ASYNC flag will be ignored if your Windows sound device can't play asynchronously—in this case, a call to sndPlaySound will put everything on hold until the sound being played has finished. In practice, the most common instance of this will be if your sound card is actually a Windows speaker driver.

You can insist that sndPlaySound not return to the program that called it until the sound it has initiated is complete. The flag for this is SND_SYNC.

In most cases you won't want sndPlaySound to play the SystemDefault sound if it can't find the sound you've specified. You can tell it not to attempt this by adding the flag SND_NODEFAULT to the second argument to sndPlaySound.

The SND_LOOP flag is particularly insidious. If sndPlaySound finds it in its flag argument, it will play the designated sound over and over again until you explicitly interrupt it. This is extremely useful for teaching parrots to speak—mine can do a variety of Python lines now—but it can make you want to take a shotgun to your speakers if you're in the room with them for more than a few minutes.

As an aside, it takes parrots a *long* time to get tired of a phrase once they've gone to the trouble of learning it. So before you use the SND_LOOP function in this application, consider carefully what you're prepared to listen to being shrieked at you at irregular intervals for the next six months.

By default, invoking sndPlaySound while a sound is playing will terminate the current sound and start a new sound going. However, you can add the SND_NOSTOP flag to the second argument of sndPlaySound if you like. In this case, attempting to play one sound while another is playing will cause sndPlaySound to return immediately with a false value, leaving the first sound untouched and the second sound unplayed.

The final flag option is SND_MEMORY. If this flag appears in the flags argument to sndPlaySound, the pointer argument will be assumed to point to a wave file that has been loaded into memory, rather than to a disk-file path.

Because wave files are typically large, they're always loaded into global memory. In fact, inasmuch as most of the interesting ones exceed

64 kilobytes of space, it's necessary to deal with them using huge pointers, rather than large ones.

Under Windows 3.1, the traditional LPSTR large-pointer object has been augmented by HPSTR, an equivalent huge pointer. Unlike large pointers, you can add long integers to HPSTR objects, and as such you can use one to address objects larger than 64K. An HPSTR object is equivalent to char huge *.

There are also some corresponding file functions to work with large files. While it's possible to load a file larger than 64K by using multiple calls to the conventional __lread function, you can load a whole file in one pass with __hread.

The following is a function to load a wave file into memory and return a global memory handle to it:

```
GLOBALHANDLE GetSound(LPSTR path)
{
    GLOBALHANDLE handle;
    HPSTR *p;
    unsigned long size;
    int fh;

    if((fh=__lopen(path,OF__READ)) != -1) {
        if((size=__llseek(fh,0L,2)) > 0) {
            __llseek(fh,0L,0);
            if((handle=GlobalAlloc(GMEM__MOVEABLE,size)) != NULL) {
                if((p=GlobalLock(handle)) != NULL) {
                    if(__hread(fh,p,size)==size) {
                        GlobalUnlock(handle);
                        __lclose(fh);
                        return(handle);
                    }
                    else {
                        GlobalUnlock(handle);
                        GlobalFree(handle);
                        __lclose(fh);
                        return(NULL);
                    }
                }
                else {
                    GlobalFree(handle);
                    __lclose(fh);
                    return(NULL);
                }
            }
        }
        else {
            __lclose(fh);
            return(NULL);
```

```
            }
        }
        else {
            __lclose(fh);
            return(NULL);
        }
    } else return(NULL);
}
```

This function should be pretty easy to work your way through. It attempts to open the file passed to it in its path argument with a call to __lopen. It then ascertains the file size by seeking to the end of the file, reading the file position returned by __lseek, and then seeking back to beginning of the file to prepare to actually read the data. The file size, in size, is used as an argument to GlobalAlloc. Assuming that enough memory is available to contain the file, a call to GlobalLock will return a pointer to it. The __hread function is used to actually load the data into memory.

It's important to make sure to unlock the file handle before it's returned by the GetSound function. The GetSound function will return NULL if the file you've asked for can't be found or if there isn't enough memory available to load it.

Once you have a wave file in memory, you can lock it in memory with GlobalLock and play it like this:

```
void PlayMemorySound(LPSTR p)
{
    sndPlaySound(p,SND_ASYNC | SND_MEMORY | SND_NOSTOP);
}
```

The SND_MEMORY flag in the foregoing call to sndPlaySound is essential— You can set the other flags in the second argument to suit your requirements.

This is one of the situations in which the multitasking nature of a sound card can do nasty things to you if you aren't careful. Because sndPlaySound will play the sound passed to it asynchronously, it will return before the sound is completely played. The sound driver assumes that the sound data in memory will remain valid until the sound is finished playing. If you were to unlock or deallocate the memory referenced by the handle passed to PlayMemorySound before the sound was complete, very nasty things could happen.

Windows expresses "very nasty things" as protected-mode faults most of the time. If you didn't read the section of chapter 1 that dealt with memory in protected mode, you might want to have a glance at it now. While wave data is really just a string of numbers and reading bad wave data should just generate a lot of white noise, Windows running in protected mode objects to an application attempting to address memory it doesn't own. This applies to reading as well as writing errant memory space.

The best way to make sure that sndPlaySound doesn't creep up from behind and throw a protected-mode fault is to explicitly shut off any sounds that are playing before you free up the memory they reside in. To do this, call sndPlaySound with NULL as its first argument, like this:

```
sndPlaySound(NULL,0);
```

This will immediately terminate the current sound, making it safe to deallocate its memory if you initially played it using the SND__MEMORY flag.

In writing applications that will use wave files, it's a good idea to call sndPlaySound this way to terminate any playing sounds when your application exits. If nothing is playing, sndPlaySound will simply return.

It's worth noting that if you call sndPlaySound to play a sound from a disk file, its first action will be to load it into memory, performing much the same task as the GetSound function does. There are a number of good reasons for you to handle loading the sound yourself, as you'll see in a moment. The important consideration, however, is that there must be enough physical memory available in your system for the wave file you want to play to be loaded. This must be real memory, not swap-file space.

Windows is empowered to juggle memory around to honor a GlobalAlloc memory request, something that will become more relevant when we look at an application to attach sounds to system events.

One of the very good reasons for loading a wave file yourself, rather than having sndPlaySound read it from a disk file, is the possibility that it might not exist as a disk file to begin with. You can store wave files as program resources and load them using the LoadResource call. In this way, a Windows application can have a number of canned sounds available for its own use without having to keep track of where a plethora of wave files have scurried off to.

As with other trackless binary information, a wave file can be stored in a Windows resource file as RCDATA. For example, this line in the RC resource script file for an application would include the contents of the wave file HELLO.WAV as a RCDATA resource called "Hello":

```
Hello RCDATA "HELLO.WAV"
```

You can see this in use in the wave-player application later in this chapter. Note that this assumes there actually will be a file called HELLO.WAV in the same directory as the resource script being compiled.

Windows gurus will observe that there is a dedicated resource type for wave files, predictably called WAVE. As such, you could accomplish the foregoing in a more politically correct way like this:

```
Hello WAVE "HELLO.WAVE"
```

In fact, there's no advantage in using WAVE rather than RCDATA. Not all resource compilers support the WAVE resource type, however, so the RCDATA type is likely to be less troublesome.

With this resource available, you can play the sound originally stored in HELLO.WAV by loading the resource "Hello" into memory and passing a pointer to it to sndPlaySound. This is how you'd handle it:

```
HANDLE sound;
LPSTR psound;
HANDLE handle;

if((handle=FindResource(hInst,"Hello",RT_RCDATA)) != NULL) {
    if((sound=LoadResource(hInst,handle)) != NULL) {
        if((psound=LockResource(sound)) != NULL)
            sndPlaySound(psound,SND_ASYNC | SND_MEMORY);
        }
    }
}

. . .

sndPlaySound(NULL,0);
if(psound != NULL) UnlockResource(sound);
if(sound != NULL) FreeResource(sound);
```

The FindResource function will return a handle to the "Hello" resource. The hInst argument is an instance handle for your application—the WinMain function that started your application will have been passed such a handle, which applications typically store in a global variable. The LoadResource call will inhale the wave data from the source file of your application and return a handle to it. Finally, LockResource will return a normal large pointer to the wave data in memory.

You can play the sound in memory with a call to sndPlaySound, just as if it had been loaded by the GetSound function discussed earlier in this chapter.

Having called sndPlaySound to play the foregoing file, the subsequent code should wait a while so the sound has a chance to play before executing the latter three lines to ensure that it has been shut down and the resource has been released. Exactly how you arrange this will be determined by your application. This code has actually been excised from the About box of the wave-player application to be discussed later in this chapter. It plays a wave-file resource when the box opens, and shuts it down when someone clicks on OK to close the box.

Limitations of sndPlaySound

There doesn't seem to be much about playing wave files that sndPlaySound won't do. With a bit of stealth you can use it to play sounds; investigate whether a sound is playing; use wave files stored on disk, in memory, and as resources; and so on. There would seem to be little reason to use anything more elaborate.

In fact, there is a major limitation to using sndPlaySound. It can work only with relatively small wave files. The Microsoft documentation suggests that this limit is somewhere around 100 kilobytes. In fact, it's usually rather higher than this if you have a reasonable amount of memory in your system, but it's probably not a good idea to assume that everyone will.

You can use sndPlaySound to reliably play short sound effects or other bits of acoustic regalia in your software. It would be unwise, however, to count on it for enacting long performances.

In addition, the structure of sndPlaySound doesn't lend itself to writing complex applications that use lots of sounds. You can determine whether a sound is playing with sndPlaySound by attempting to play another sound using the SND_NOSTOP flag— if the call returns FALSE, a sound is currently playing. As such, you can use sndPlaySound to string multiple sounds together.

At least, you can but you probably shouldn't. This approach to working with multiple sequential wave files is called *polling*. It essentially involves waiting in a loop, constantly rechecking the status of one sound until it's time to play the next one. This is a tremendous waste of processor time, and it's important to keep in mind that Windows is a multitasking environment. When you waste time in one application, it's not available for anything else running on the system.

The correct way to create an application that wants to string wave files together is to have the function that plays a file tell the application when it's ready to play another. In Windows terms, you want a message to appear somewhere when the first sound file is done. This would allow the application as a whole to do something else in the interval, and take notice of the sounds involved only when one is complete and it's time to play another.

This is a facility that sndPlaySound doesn't offer, and there's no way to trick it into doing so. It's one of the reasons you might want to abandon sndPlaySound for one of the two lower-level approaches to playing sounds available under the Windows multimedia extensions.

RIFF files: A major digression

As anyone who has done even a nominal amount of Windows programming will appreciate, one of the things that makes it tricky is the requirement that you learn about numerous things at once. Multimedia programming is no different—while it would have been handy to have discussed nothing but sound-playing functions in this chapter, doing so would not have left you with sufficient understanding of the various sound functions involved to do anything worthwhile. At least, it would not have been of much use for the latter approaches to playing wave files.

In order to play wave files using the MCI interface and especially with waveOut calls, you'll have to get within shouting distance of the actual structure of a wave file. Until now, this is a topic that hasn't really come up. Wave files are handled in their entirety by MessageBeep and sndPlaySound, which are both quite content to sort them out for you. The latter two sound-playing options under Windows won't prove to be quite as obliging.

A wave file is actually a particular case of a larger class of files used by various Windows multimedia functions, these being RIFF files. The acronym RIFF stands for *resource interchange file format*.

The RIFF format is "chunk" oriented, which is fundamental in understanding what the little beasts are up to. In theory, a RIFF file consists of one or more disparate chunks, in which each chunk points to the next chunk. Each chunk has a type followed by some data. An application that reads RIFF files can step through the chunks, read the ones it's interested in or recognizes, and skip over the ones that don't concern it. A RIFF file chunk is always preceded by the following header:

```
typedef struct {
    FOURCC ckID;
    DWORD ckSize;
    } CK;
```

A FOURCC data object is just a four-byte field. This identifies the type of the chunk. The field would contain WAVE for a wave file. In cases where a chunk type is identified with fewer than four characters, the rightmost ones are padded with blanks.

It's important to keep in mind that the characters in a FOURCC object are case sensitive. In fact, some functions that check the contents of a FOURCC object will do so by comparing it as a long integer, which is faster than doing a string comparison.

The ckSize object specifies the size of the data for the chunk in question. Following this header you would find ckSize bytes of data.

Chunks can contain subchunks. The actual structure a basic wave file is a WAVE chunk that contains an fmt chunk followed by a data chunk. There might be other chunks after the WAVE chunk—a wave-file player would ignore these. Figure 2-2 illustrates the structure of a RIFF file that contains wave data.

The modular nature of RIFF files allows applications to add things to wave files for their own use without necessarily interfering with the use of these files by other software. For example, you might want to add a text description to wave files created by your software to make it easier for users to know what they contain. There's actually a chunk type that handles this, called ZSTR, for *zero-terminated string*. In such a file, there would be a WAVE chunk with its fmt and data subchunks followed by a ZSTR chunk. Other packages, which probably wouldn't go looking for a ZSTR chunk, would ignore your text data and play just the WAVE chunk information.

2-2 The structure of a RIFF file containing wave information.

A RIFF file always begins with a chunk of the type RIFF. At least, it almost always does—Microsoft notes that there's a second possible sort of initial RIFF file chunk, this being RIFX. This type indicates that the file originated on a Motorola-based computer, and all the byte orders of the WORD and DWORD objects therein will be backwards. This isn't something that typically comes up in PC applications, and as such it's not something you need concern yourself with in the context of this chapter.

The two subchunks in a WAVE chunk specify information about a wave file's sound and then the sound data itself, respectively. The fmt chunk is a bit complicated. It's essentially a WAVEFORMAT object with some extra data tacked onto the end. This is what a WAVEFORMAT object looks like:

```
typedef struct waveformat__tag {
    WORD wFormatTag;
    WORD nChannels;
    DWORD nSamplesPerSec;
    DWORD nAvgBytesPerSec;
    WORD nBlockAlign;
    } WAVEFORMAT;
```

The wFormatTag element should contain the constant WAVE__FORMAT__ PCM, which is defined in MMSYSTEM.H, like this:

```
#define WAVE__FORMAT__PCM  1
```

The WAVE__FORMAT__PCM value tells software reading a wave file how the sound in it is encoded. At present, this represents the only way sound in a wave file can be encoded.

The nChannels element of a WAVEFORMAT object will be 1 for a monaural sound or 2 for a stereo sound. The nSamplesPerSec element tells a wave player the sampling rate of the original sound so it can play the samples back at the appropriate speed. The normal values for this field would be one of the following:

- 11025—11.025 kilohertz
- 22050—22.05 kilohertz
- 44100—44.1 kilohertz

The nAvgBytesPerSec field of a WAVEFORMAT object specifies the average number of bytes per second required to play back the wave data. As you'll see in a moment, this need not be the same as the nSamplesPerSec value, in that one sample need not occupy one byte.

The nBlockAlign value defines the number of bytes required to contain one sample. Samples with 8 or fewer bits of resolution can fit in one byte. Samples with between 9 and 16 bits of resolution require two bytes. Stereo samples require twice the number of bytes as monaural samples.

None of the previous information actually defines the number of bits per sample of a wave file's sound data, although you could roughly infer this information by making reference to the nBlockAlign and nChannels fields of a WAVEFORMAT object. In fact, a wave file does specify the exact number of bits of sampling data as a WORD object tacked onto the end of a WAVEFORMAT object. In C language notation, the resulting structure is defined like this:

```
typedef struct pcmwaveformat__tag {
    WAVEFORMAT wf;
    WORD wBitsPerSample;
    } PCMWAVEFORMAT;
```

In dealing with the fmt subchunk data of a WAVE chunk, you'll really be working with a PCMWAVEFORMAT object rather than a WAVEFORMAT. This will also be true when WAVEFORMAT objects turn up later in this chapter as objects to be passed to some of the multimedia extension functions. The wBitsPerSample element of a PCMWAVEFORMAT object defines the actual number of bits in a sample. Note that the sample data will still be stored in discrete bytes or words. A wave file with twelve bits of data per sample would have four bits of wasted data in each sample value, as the samples themselves would have to reside in 16-bit words.

It's hard to say whether the rather awkward structure of a PCMWAVEFORMAT object is the result of someone trying to allow for an open-ended file format, or of a late night at Microsoft when it was realized at the last minute that an essential bit of information had been omitted from the definition of a WAVEFORMAT.

The data subchunk of a wave file contains the raw sampled data for a sound. Sound data is actually very easy to understand. Figure 2-3 illustrates the relationship of the data in a monaural 8-bit sound file to the sound it will produce.

In 8-bit sounds, each sample can range from zero through 255. In 16-bit sounds, each sample can range from –32,768 to 32,767. This doesn't mean that 16-bit wave files play 256 times louder than 8-bit ones—the hardware of a sound card compensates for the sample depth accordingly. Rather, it means that 16-bit waveforms are represented with 256 times the accuracy of 8-bit ones, which is an audible distinction in most cases.

In an 8-bit monaural sample, the data chunk's data would consist of a long string of 1-byte sample values. Stereo samples are interleaved, with the first one being the left-channel sample and the second the right-channel sample. As such, in a stereo 8-bit sample, each sample would require two bytes, with all the even-numbered bytes being the left channel and the odd-numbered bytes being the right channel.

In a monaural 16-bit sound, each sample would be represented by one word, or two bytes. In a stereo 16-bit sound, the left and right words of each sample would be interleaved, with four actual bytes required for each sample.

While you won't have cause to read the data out of a sample to play it—this is something that can't be handled quickly enough in software to be of much use—you might want to deal with the individual sample values to graph, edit, or modify the sounds in a sample. We'll look at an example of doing so later in this chapter.

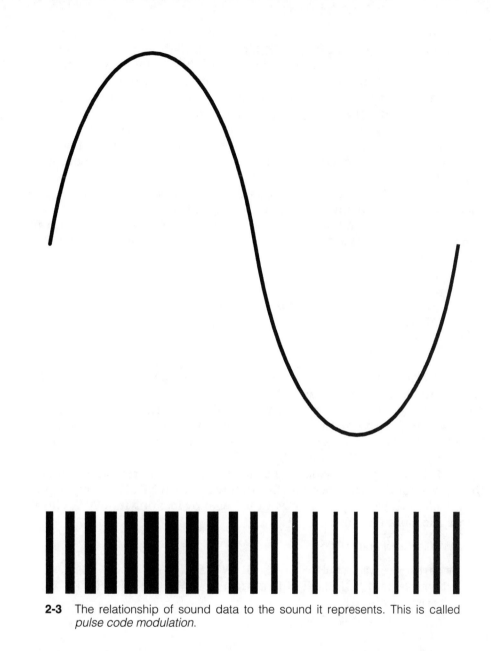

2-3   The relationship of sound data to the sound it represents. This is called *pulse code modulation*.

Reading RIFF files

The simple structure of RIFF files would make writing code to work through RIFF files pretty elementary. However, you need not do so—the multimedia extensions include a file package dedicated to handling RIFF files. While typically convoluted, as Windows functions usually are, they offer a bullet-proof approach to handling RIFF chunks. Presumably, these things would also take care of RIFX files, mentioned earlier, if any were to turn up.

In order to work with a RIFF file, you must open it and then "descend" into the chunks you're interested in. This really means locating a chunk of interest and positioning the file pointer at the beginning of its data. When you've finished with one chunk, you would "ascend" out of it and "descend" into the next one. You might think of a RIFF file as being a corridor with pits in it, each pit representing a chunk. The pits might in turn have pits within them, representing subchunks. You would descend into a pit to retrieve its contents and then ascend out of it to move on to the next pit.

This sounds a bit like a fantasy arcade game—one wonders what spells and sorcery might lurk in some of those RIFF file chunks.

The RIFF file functions all have the prefix mmio, and work with file handles of the type HMMIO. To begin with, here's how you'd open a RIFF file to read it:

```
HMMIO h;

if((h=mmioOpen(path,NULL,MMIO__READ)) == NULL) {
    /* say there was an error */
    return(0);
}
```

The path argument would contain a path to the wave file you wanted to open. The MMIO__READ flag tells mmioOpen to open the file for reading. You could also open it for writing with MMIO__WRITE or for both reading and writing with MMIO__READWRITE. You could then use the MMIO__CREATE flag to create a new RIFF file. There are a number of other, more esoteric flags available for this argument.

If it has successfully opened a file, mmioOpen will return a handle of the type HMMIO. If the open has failed, it will return NULL. Having opened a wave file, you would probably want to begin by locating its WAVE chunk. Here's the call to do this:

```
MMCKINFO mmParent;

mmParent.fccType=mmioFOURCC('W','A','V','E');
if(mmioDescend(h,(LPMMCKINFO)&mmParent,NULL,MMIO__FINDRIFF)) {
    mmioClose(h,0);
    /* say there was an error */
    return(0);
}
```

An MMCKINFO structure contains information about a chunk. It's defined in MMSYSTEM.H, and looks like this:

```
typedef struct {
    FOURCC ckid;
    DWORD cksize;
    FOURCC fccType;
```

```
    DWORD dwDataOffset;
    DWORD dwFlags;
    } MMCKINFO;
```

To descend into a chunk, you would set the ckid field of a MMCKINFO object to the type of the chunk you want to locate. There's a macro to handle this for you, mmioFOURCC. Having done this, you would call mmioDescend, as illustrated here. This call will return zero if the chunk you requested has been located. In this case, the MMCKINFO object passed to mmioDescend will have been filled in with information about the chunk in question.

The cksize field of an MMCKINFO object defines the size of the chunk in bytes. It's not a good idea to assume that this will be what you expect—always use the cksize value. For example, in reading the fmt subchunk of a WAVE chunk, the size of the data should be sizeof (PCMWAVEFORMAT). In theory, it could be sizeof(WAVEFORMAT), which would be two bytes smaller, or it could be larger if there's additional information tacked onto the end of the PCMWAVEFORMAT object for a custom application.

The third argument to mmioDescend is a flag. The MMIO_FINDRIFF flag instructs mmioDescend to look for a chunk with the ID RIFF and the chunk type specified by the ckid field of the MMCKINFO object passed to it. The other option you'll need to navigate RIFF files is MMIO_FINDCHUNK, which will look for a defined chunk.

Note that it's important to call mmioClose when you're done with a RIFF file handle, as was done in the error condition of mmioDescend previously. This frees the buffers and other memory objects associated with an HMMIO object, just as calling fclose closes a conventional C language FILE handle.

Having descended into a WAVE chunk, you would next descend into its fmt subchunk, like this:

```
    MMCKINFO mmSub;

    mmSub.ckid=mmioFOURCC('f','m','t',' ');
    if(mmioDescend(h,(LPMMCKINFO)&mmSub,
        (LPMMCKINFO)&mmParent,MMIO_FINDCHUNK)) {
        mmioClose(h,0);
        /* say there was an error */
        return(0);
    }
```

This call to mmioDescend instructs it to search for a subchunk of the type fmt within the chunk defined by the mmParent argument—that is, the MMCKINFO object returned by the earlier call to mmioDescend.

Having juggled and danced its way through the chunks of a RIFF file, a wave file reader would now be ready to actually read some data. This is how you'd read the PCMWAVEFORMAT object from a fmt chunk:

```
PCMWAVEFORMAT waveformat;
int n;

n=min((unsigned int)mmSub.cksize,sizeof(PCMWAVEFORMAT));
if(mmioRead(h,(LPSTR)&waveformat,(long)n) != (long)n) {
   mmioClose(h,0);
   /* say there was an error */
   return(0L);
}

if(waveformat.wf.wFormatTag != WAVE_FORMAT_PCM) {
   mmioClose(h,0);
   /* say there was an error */
   return(0L);
}
```

In calling mmioRead, the first argument is the HMMIO handle used to reference the file being read. The second argument is a far or huge pointer to the buffer where some data is expected to show up. The third argument is a long integer representing the number of bytes to be read. The mmioRead function will return the number of bytes it actually does read, which will agree with the value of its third argument if all is well.

Having read the contents of a chunk, you would ascend out of it in preparation for reading the next one.

```
mmioAscend(h,(LPMMCKINFO)&mmSub,0);
```

The first argument to mmioAscend is the HMMIO handle used to reference the file being read. The second is a pointer to the MMCKINFO object that defines the chunk to be ascended from. The third argument is a dummy—it would contain flags relevant to mmioAscend, if any existed.

The following is the remaining code required to read a wave file into memory. Specifically, this uses more calls to mmioDescend and mmioRead in order to locate and read the actual sample data. Note that the cksize value returned by mmioDescend has been used to specify the buffer size in a call to GlobalAlloc.

```
GLOBALHANDLE wavehandle;
HPSTR wavepointer;

mmSub.ckid=mmioFOURCC('d','a','t','a');
if(mmioDescend(h,(LPMMCKINFO)&mmSub,
   (LPMMCKINFO)&mmParent,MMIO_FINDCHUNK)) {
   mmioClose(h,0);
   /* say there was an error */
   return(0);
}

if((wavehandle=GlobalAlloc(GMEM_MOVEABLE | GMEM_SHARE,
   mmSub.cksize)) == NULL) {
```

```
    mmioClose(h,0);
    /* say there was an error */
    return(0);
}

if((wavepointer=(HPSTR)GlobalLock(wavehandle)) == NULL) {
    GlobalFree(wavehandle);
    mmioClose(h,0);
    /* say there was an error */
    return(0);
}

if(mmioRead(h,wavepointer,mmSub.cksize) != mmSub.cksize) {
    GlobalUnlock(wavehandle);
    GlobalFree(wavehandle);
    mmioClose(h,0);
    /* say there was an error */
    return(0);
}

GlobalUnlock(wavehandle);
```

With the wave data safely ensconced in memory, you would close the RIFF file being read like this:

```
mmioClose(h,0);
```

Once again, the first argument to mmioClose is an HMMIO handle, this time for the file being closed. The second argument contains flags, if any are applicable. While there's currently one flag defined for mmioClose, MMIO_FHOPEN, it's very unlikely that you'll want to use it in dealing with simple wave files. It's explained in the Microsoft multimedia development kit's programmer's reference book, should you be interested.

If you have cause to dig through the programmer's reference documentation, you'll probably notice that there are a lot more mmio calls than have been touched on here. There are all sorts of things you can do with a RIFF file that have little relevance to playing wave-file sounds. As with much of Windows, you can ignore these things—knowing which parts constitute the ignoreable elements, however, requires a keen eye.

Playing sounds with MCI calls

In most applications that use wave files, you can achieve the best balance of functionality and code complexity by using calls to the Windows media control interface, or MCI. MCI calls allow you to control a variety of media, including sound cards, compact disc players, laser discs, and so on.

The abstract concept of MCI is that it treats everything it communicates with as a device. It doesn't really know what a device is, save that one can accept commands and respond with information in various forms. Each device is handled by a device driver, and drivers are managed by the Drivers applet of the clipboard, as shown in FIG. 2-4.

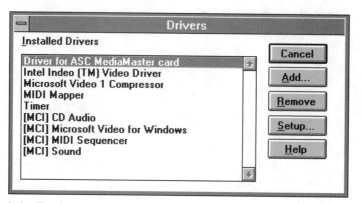

2-4 The Drivers applet of the Windows Control Panel.

Now, unbeknownst to MCI, all these devices are quite different. One would hardly ask a sound card to eject itself from your computer, for example, while such a command would make perfect sense to a CD-ROM player. In order to accommodate the wide range of multimedia devices that Windows can support, the expanse of MCI calls is pretty broad. Not all of them are applicable to all devices. Perhaps more to the point, it's not always obvious which calls should be used to support particular features of specific devices.

For example, you can pause an animation sequence, one of the things that MCI can control. You can't pause a compact disc, even though it would seem as if you should be able to. There's a lot of this sort of thing inherent in MCI.

Rather than discuss MCI as dedicated topic, I'll treat it as a way to play sounds in this chapter, as a way to play compact discs in the next, and so on. Some of the MCI calls dealt with in this section will turn up again in later chapters for other devices.

This is probably not quite what the creators of MCI had in mind when they created their device-independent approach to handling diverse peripherals. Unfortunately, if you try to work with MCI in the way it's expressed in the Microsoft documentation, you probably *will* see your sound card eject itself from your PC by the time you get a handle on the whole affair.

To begin with, there are two distinct ways to deal with MCI. The really elegant high-level interface allows you to pass text strings to a command interpreter, which will then make real MCI calls on your behalf. This is arguably handy for authoring languages, but represents severe overkill for a C language application. It also wastes a lot of time and system resources, as each string must be parsed and interpreted before it can be passed to

MCI. The more technical approach, and the one to be discussed in this section, involves making calls to the MCI functions themselves.

The multimedia extensions include a number of functions specific to calling MCI. For the applications discussed in this chapter, these are the relevant function calls:

mciSendCommand   Sends a command to MCI.

mciGetErrorString   Tells you what went wrong if mciSendCommand complains.

The wonderful thing about the MCI interface at a programming level is that there aren't a lot of function calls to keep track of. However, the arguments to mciSendCommand are legion.

To use MCI as a wave-file player, you must open the sound driver in your system as an MCI device, fetch the wave file you want to play, and then actually set it off playing. At this point, the overt involvement of MCI will be largely done with, and your sound player function can return to whatever called it to get on with the unfolding of the universe. However, unlike sndPlaySound, the MCI interface will send a message to the window of your choice when it's done playing a sound so you can do whatever should naturally follow the performance. One of these things will be to close the previously opened MCI sound driver.

This is a very handy arrangement. It means that you can play a sound and then think no more of it until it ceases playing. If you want to string multiple wave-file sounds together, you can do so by arranging to have the message that signals the conclusion of one sound initiate the playing of the next. While the applications in this chapter don't do this, you might want to have a look at the code that uses MCI calls to play audio tracks on compact discs in the next chapter. It handles playing multiple sequential tracks this way.

Let's begin by opening the sound device of MCI. This is a fairly typical call to mciSendCommand:

```
MCI_OPEN_PARMS mciopen;
DWORD rtrn;
char b[STRINGSIZE+1];
int id;

mciopen.lpstrDeviceType="waveaudio";
mciopen.lpstrElementName=path;
if((rtrn=mciSendCommand(0,MCI_OPEN,MCI_OPEN_TYPE | MCI_OPEN_ELEMENT,
    (DWORD)(LPVOID)&mciopen)) != 0L) {
        mciGetErrorString(rtrn,(LPSTR)b,STRINGSIZE);
        DoMessage(hwnd,b);
        return(0);
}

id=mciopen.wDeviceID;
```

The first argument to mciSendCommand is a device ID value—at present, there isn't one, as this is what opening a device will provide you with. As such, we'll pass a dummy value, zero, in this instance.

The second argument tells mciSendCommand what it's supposed to be doing. In this case, to open a device its argument will be MCI_OPEN. The third argument is a set of flags, which in this case tell mciSendCommand which elements of its fourth argument to look at. The flags in this argument will have different applications in different types of calls.

The fourth argument to mciSendCommand is a pointer to a parameter structure. There are numerous different parameter structures for use with this call, and some MCI devices support dedicated parameter objects as well. It's important to make sure you use the appropriate parameter structure, as neither your C compiler nor mciSendCommand will know if you don't—odd things might happen when you go to run your software, however.

The information that mciSendCommand requires to open the device in question is provided by the MCI_OPEN_PARMS object passed to it. In this case, it needs to know the driver it's intended to open, in this case waveaudio, and the name of the wave file it's to play, in this case path.

The return value from a call to mciSendCommand will be zero if all went well, or a return code. The return codes are defined in a long list of ineffable numeric constants, but you can deal with them in a much more civilized way. If you pass the return value from mciSendCommand to mciGetErrorString, it will in turn provide you with a text description of what went wrong. In fact, some of these are a bit questionable—if MCI fails to find a driver loaded, for example, it will tell you to contact the manufacturer of the hardware in question. Nonetheless, these messages are considerably more understandable than a clump of error codes. The calling sequence for mciGetErrorString is:

```
mciGetErrorString(rtrn,b,STRINGSIZE);
```

where the rtrn argument is a nonzero error code returned by mciSend Command, the b argument is a string buffer to hold the text message it returns, and the STRINGSIZE argument is the length of the buffer. In the example programs in this book, STRINGSIZE is a defined constant to specify buffers like this one:

```
#define STRINGSIZE 128
```

It's also worth noting that, in the programs in this book, the function DoMessage displays a text message. You could also use the Windows MessageBox function to handle this.

Assuming that the call to mciSendCommand to open the waveform device is successful, the wDeviceID of the MCI_OPEN_PARMS object will contain a device ID value for the waveform player. If MCI isn't involved in doing anything else at the moment, this will usually be 1, but it's unwise to count on it.

Having opened the wave-player device, all that's left to do is to play your wave file.

```
MCI__PLAY__PARMS mciplay;

mciplay.dwCallback=(DWORD)hwnd;
if((rtrn=mciSendCommand(id,MCI__PLAY,MCI__NOTIFY,
    (DWORD)(LPVOID)&mciplay)) != OL) {
        mciSendCommand(soundID,MCI__CLOSE,0,NULL);
        mciGetErrorString(rtrn,(LPSTR)b,STRINGSIZE);
        DoMessage(hwnd,b);
        return(0);
}
```

This call is a bit sneakier than it might seem. The first sneaky part is in the line that assigns a value to the dwCallback element of the MCI__PLAY__ PARMS object that will be passed to mciSendComamnd. This value is an HWND window handle. It tells MCI where to send a message indicating the end of the sound being played when the last notes finally fade to silence.

The MCI__NOTIFY flag in the third argument to mciSendCommand tells MCI that the value of dwCallback is a valid window handle, and to use it accordingly.

The second sneaky thing is that, like files, MCI devices must be closed when you're done with them. If the call to mciSendCommand to play the wave file fails, you must close the device immediately. If it's successful, you must close the device when the sound has been played. The command to close an MCI device is handled by another call to mciSendCommand:

```
mciSendCommand(id,MCI__CLOSE,0,NULL);
```

Having successfully executed these two MCI calls, all that's left to do is respond to the message MCI will send to the window you told it about when the sound is finished. The message it sends will be MM__ MCINOTIFY. Here's a typical case for it in the message switch of a window's message handling function:

```
case MM__MCINOTIFY:
    mciSendCommand(LOWORD(lParam),MCI__CLOSE,MCI__WAIT,NULL);
    break;
```

When an MM__MCINOTIFY message appears, the low-order word of the lParam value passed to the message handler will be the device ID for the device to be closed. You're free to do anything else you feel like in this case—in the wave-file player application to be discussed later in this chapter, various controls and menu items are modified when this message appears, setting the application up to play another wave file. In a program to play multiple wave files, you would initiate the next sound when everything else in this case had been done.

As will be dealt with in the next chapter, it's worth noting that there are several ways to go about this. The simplest one, including a call to the function that plays sounds, is not a terribly good idea. Neither is using SendMessage to send a message to the window handler case that makes the call. In both of these approaches, you will in effect have made your window message handler recursive—done often enough, it will cause your application to overflow its stack. The correct procedure would be to use PostMessage, which will allow the case for the MM_MCINOTIFY to be completed and for this instance of the call to your window message handler to return before the message to start playing the next sound is processed.

Keep in mind that SendMessage sends a message and doesn't return until it has been processed. By comparison, PostMessage places a message in the message queue and returns immediately, allowing the message to be processed when it makes its way to the head of the queue.

You might have cause to stop a sound prematurely—for example, if you attempt to play a sound and find that it goes on for a long time, or sounds like a lot of parrots attempting to speak. Here's how to tell MCI to shut up:

```
MCI_GENERIC_PARMS mcigen;

mcigen.dwCallback=hwnd;
mciSendCommand(id,MCI_STOP,MCI_NOTIFY | MCI_WAIT,
    (DWORD)(LPVOID)&mcigen);
```

This is a bit sneakier than it looks, too. To begin with, it's worth noting that the MCI_GENERIC_PARMS object is a set of MCI parameters for use when no obviously better parameter object comes quickly to mind. It provides only one element, this being dwCallback. It's probably the most elaborate expression Windows offers for what is, in reality, a single integer.

This call to mciSendCommand will stop the playing sound. However, because it has been told to notify a window of the event, it will also send an MM_MCINOTIFY message. This, in turn, will call the code in the MM_MCINOTIFY case to actually close the MCI wave-player device.

Some of the logistics of handling MCI calls might not be completely clear as yet—keeping track of the device ID values, for example, can require some forethought, as well as a few global variables. You'll see a real-world example of it in the wave-player program to be dealt with later in this chapter.

Playing sounds with waveOut calls

The lowest level of wave-playing functions available under the multimedia extensions is waveOut. Using the waveOut functions, you can control the playing of sounds to the limits of the functionality provided by your sound hardware. However, as you might expect, using these functions entails considerably more code.

The structure of a sound-playing function using waveOut calls is similar to that of the one based on MCI calls discussed in the previous section. It plays a sound and then signals the window of your choice when the wave has finished playing. However, using waveOut requires that the sound be loaded into memory, rather than passed as a path to a disk file. This involves working with the grotty details of RIFF files, as dealt with earlier in this chapter.

By using the waveOut calls, you can adjust several parameters of a sound being played back, including volume, playback speed, and pitch—at least you *might* be able to. These are parameters that sound cards can support and that the multimedia extensions provide access to. However, sound cards are not required to support them, and some don't. You'll have to ascertain the features supported by a particular sound card.

The wave player to be presented later in this chapter will illustrate how to control the playback volume of a sound, as this is a feature that most sound cards do support. If you want to implement pitch or playback speed control, you'll find them pretty easy to add based on the operation of the volume control.

In the following example of code to play sounds using waveOut calls, assume that the sound has been previously loaded into memory from its source RIFF file, and currently languishes in a buffer referenced by wavehandle. Its relevant format data is in a PCMWAVEFORMAT structure called waveformat. The code to get all this together was dealt with previously, in the section on RIFF files.

To begin with, let's open the wave-playing device for use with subsequent waveOut calls:

```
HWAVEOUT hwaveout;
char b[STRINGSIZE+1];

if((rtrn=waveOutOpen((LPHWAVEOUT)&hwaveout,WAVE_MAPPER,
    (LPWAVEFORMAT)&waveformat,(LONG)hwnd,0L,CALLBACK_WINDOW)) != 0) {
        waveOutGetErrorText(rtrn,(LPSTR)b,STRINGSIZE);
        DoMessage(hwnd,b);
        return(0);
}
```

The waveOutOpen function will attempt to open a sound-playing device. In sophisticated applications with several sound players available, you could actually specify which device you wanted to open—for most systems, it's much more practical to let Windows take care of this, as you'll probably have only one sound card in your computer. The second argument to waveOutOpen should be either the device ID of the sound device you want to open, or the constant WAVE_MAPPER, which tells Windows to find a suitable sound card.

As an aside, in a system with multiple sound players you would ascertain the device ID to use by figuring out how many devices there were and then testing each one to see if it had the characteristics you were after. The number of devices can be found like this:

```
int count;
count=waveOutGetNumDevices();
```

Having ascertained the number of sound players in your system, you can step through each one by calling waveOutGetDevCaps, which will return information about a specific wave player. There will be an an extensive look at working with waveOutGetDevCaps in the example wave-player application later in this chapter.

In theory, it's arguably practical to select a wave-player device algorithmically based on the information returned by waveOutGetDevCaps. In practice, you'd probably want to display a menu or a list of all the available wave players and allow your users to choose one—assuming that you feel using WAVE_MAPPER as a device ID and allowing Windows to choose a suitable device isn't sufficiently leading edge.

The waveformat argument passed to waveOutOpen is a far pointer to a PCMWAVEOUT object that will previously have been filled from the fmt chunk of the wave file to be played. The hwnd argument will be a handle to a window that waveOutOpen can send messages to. The CALLBACK_WINDOW flag tells it that it has been passed a window handle for this purpose. It's also possible to pass it a function address, in which case the flag would be CALLBACK_FUNCTION. However, this is a considerably more involved undertaking, as the function must reside in a dynamic link library, rather than in your application proper.

The fifth argument, passed as 0L here, is an instance handle for use if the callback is a function rather than a window handle. It's not applicable here.

If waveOutOpen is successful, it will fill the HWAVEOUT object pointed to by its first argument with information about the open device. This will serve as a handle for subsequent waveOut calls.

As with MCI calls, the waveOut functions will return zero if all's well or an error code. The waveOut functions include waveOutGetErrorText, which will return a text description of an error condition if a waveOut call runs into difficulties. Here's how you'd use it:

```
waveOutGetErrorText(rtrn,(LPSTR)b,STRINGSIZE);
```

The rtrn value is whatever was returned by a waveOut call. Having successfully opened a device for use with waveOut, it's necessary to prepare the wave header to be used in playing sounds through it. There's a call to handle this, perhaps not surprisingly waveOutPrepareHeader. The header is a WAVEHDR object. For reasons not adequately explained in the Microsoft documentation, waveOut would like this to reside in global memory, which means that it must be dynamically allocated, like this:

```
GLOBALHANDLE waveheader;
LPWAVEHDR pwaveheader;

if((waveheader=GlobalAlloc(GMEM_MOVEABLE | GMEM_SHARE,
    (long)sizeof(WAVEHDR))) == NULL) {
    DoMessage(hwnd,"Memory allocation error");
    return(0);
}

if((pwaveheader=(LPWAVEHDR)GlobalLock(waveheader))==NULL) {
    GlobalFree(waveheader);
    DoMessage(hwnd,"Memory locking error");
    return(0);
}
```

At this point, you should lock the wave data as well:

```
if((wavepointer=(HPSTR)GlobalLock(wavehandle)) == NULL) {
    GlobalFree(waveheader);
    DoMessage(hwnd,"Memory locking error");
    return(0);
}
```

The WAVEHDR object includes a number of fields you must set up prior to calling waveOutPrepareHeader. Specifically, you must tell waveOut where to find the wave data and how big it is—keep in mind that because wave data is just a long string of samples, it's impossible to know where the real samples end and random memory begins, unless you feel that reading until Windows generates a protected-mode fault is a workable test.

The size of the data will be the chunk size returned by mmioDescend when you descend into the data subchunk of the wave file to be played. Here's the call to waveOutPrepareHeader:

```
pwaveheader->lpData=(LPSTR)wavepointer;
pwaveheader->dwBufferLength=mmSub.cksize;
pwaveheader->dwFlags=0L;
pwaveheader->dwLoops=0L;
if((rtrn=waveOutPrepareHeader(hwaveout,
    pwaveheader,sizeof(WAVEHDR))) != 0) {
    waveOutUnprepareHeader(hwaveout,
        pwaveheader,sizeof(WAVEHDR));
    waveOutClose(hwaveout);
    waveOutGetErrorText(rtrn,(LPSTR)b,STRINGSIZE);
    DoMessage(hwnd,b);
    return(0);
}
```

As with the MCI calls, it's important to close a waveOut device in the event of an error condition. It's also important to call waveOutUnprepareHeader, as this will free up the memory previously allocated by waveOutPrepareHeader.

After all this dancing, waveOut is actually ready to make some noise. The function to set a wave file playing is waveOutWrite. In effect, you'll be writing the wave data to the wave-player device. Here's how it's called:

```
if((rtrn=waveOutWrite(hwaveout,pwaveheader,sizeof(WAVEHDR))) != 0) {
    waveOutUnprepareHeader(hwaveout,pwaveheader,sizeof(WAVEHDR));
    waveOutClose(hwaveout);
    waveOutGetErrorText(rtrn,(LPSTR)b,STRINGSIZE);
    DoMessage(hwnd,b);
    return(0L);
}
```

All the objects in the call to waveOutWrite should be familiar. The hwaveout object is the HWAVEOUT handle filled in by waveOutOpen. The pwaveheader object is the WAVEHDR object allocated previously and filled in by waveOutPrepareHeader. The third argument tells waveOutWrite how big the second argument is. If waveOutWrite returns a zero value, the sound is playing. As with the MCI calls, the waveOut driver will send a message to the window you indicated back in the call to waveOutOpen when the sound has finished—for the moment, you can return from this call and get on with whatever your application would normally do next.

When a sound initiated by waveOut calls finishes playing, it will send the message MM_WOM_DONE to the window you specified back in the waveOutOpen call. Here's what the message handler case for it might look like:

```
case MM_WOM_DONE:
    waveOutUnprepareHeader((HWAVEOUT)wParam,
        (LPWAVEHDR)lParam,sizeof(WAVEHDR));
    waveOutClose((HWAVEOUT)wParam);

    if(wavehandle != NULL) {
        GlobalUnlock(wavehandle);
        GlobalFree(wavehandle);
    }
    if(waveheader != NULL) {
        GlobalUnlock(waveheader);
        GlobalFree(waveheader);
    }
    break;
```

The global memory buffer that holds the wave data being played by waveOut must remain valid until the sound stops playing. This means you can't deallocate it until the MM_WOM_DONE message is sent. In practice, the easiest way to arrange this is to make the handle a global variable.

As with the other sound-playing functions discussed thus far, you can stop a sound being played by waveOut. The waveOutReset call will stop a sound and send a MM_WOM_DONE message to free up its buffers and such. Here's how it's used:

```
waveOutReset(hwaveout);
```

The hwaveout argument is the HWAVEOUT handle that indicates the opened waveOut device.

As was noted earlier, one of the reasons to use waveOut calls to manage playing wave files, rather than the arguably less involved MCI calls, is that you can use waveOut to modify several playback parameters, such as the volume. Setting the volume level for a sound using waveOut calls is agreeably uncomplicated. The function that does it is called waveOutSetVolume. Here's how you'd use it:

```
waveOutSetVolume(id,volume);
```

The id argument to waveOutSetVolume is the device ID value originally passed to waveOutOpen. If you used the WAVE_MAPPER constant, however, the actual device in use probably won't be known—all you'll have is an HWAVEOUT handle. There's another waveOut function to take care of this problem, waveOutGetID—it will derive a device ID from an HWAVEOUT object. Here's how you'd use it:

```
WORD id;
waveOutGetID(hwaveout,(LPWORD)&id);
```

Assuming waveOutGetID has returned zero, indicating that it liked the taste of the hwaveout argument you passed to it, the id argument will contain a valid device ID.

The volume argument to waveOutSetVolume is an unsigned long integer. The low-order word contains the left-channel volume and the high-order word contains the right-channel volume. If your sound card is a monaural device, the low-order word will control the volume and the high-order word will be ignored.

The volume values run from zero for silence to 65535—or FFFFH—for full blast. If you set the volume argument to waveOutSetVlume to 0xffffffffL, both channels will be turned up to full volume. As another example, setting the volume argument to 0x80008000L will set both channels to half volume.

There are a few things to keep in mind about using waveOutSetVolume. The first is that not all sound cards support it—you'll see how to determine whether a particular card allows for volume changes when you look at the waveOutGetCaps function later in this chapter. If you attempt to set the volume for a sound card that doesn't allow for volume changes, nothing will happen.

An application that allows for changes in volume and other playback parameters should probably disable its relevant controls if it finds itself playing through a card that doesn't support some or all of these parameters.

The second thing to keep in mind is that volume changes don't reset themselves when a sound stops playing. If you turn down the volume in the middle of one sound it will stay turned down until you explicitly turn it back up again.

The final consideration in using the volume control involves a bit of acoustic theory. You might want to skip this section if you don't want to get into a lot of grotty biological details.

A brief digression concerning acoustics

The human ear is a fairly remarkable organ as organic microphones go, the stuff of countless cut-away drawings in encyclopedias and other reference works. While in effect not much more complicated than an electrical microphone, it has arranged things in a way that you or I probably never would have thought of.

If you've used an electrical microphone, you'll probably have a sense of why ears are so clever. Should you turn up the gain on a conventional microphone sufficiently to have it pick up very soft sounds, a very loud sound will usually pin the needles on whatever the microphone is connected to, and very likely pop a few speakers. By comparison, the dynamic range of an ear—at least, of one that hasn't spent too much of its life listening to heavy metal at top volume—is enormous. Your ear can hear very quiet sounds and very loud sounds, making reasonable sense of both.

The reason the dynamic range of an ear is so much better than that of electrical microphones is because ears hear logarithmically. If you set up a speaker with one watt of sound playing through it and then double the amount of power to two watts, someone listening to the speaker will not perceive that the sound has become twice as loud. In fact, you'd have to crank the sound up to ten watts to arrive at this effect, and to 100 watts to do it again.

The volume setting of the waveOutSetVolume function is linear. This means that if you set the volume of your card with the argument 0x8000— that is, to half volume—the amount of sound power being generated by your speakers will be reduced to half of what it would have been at full volume. However, you won't perceive it as such. You'll probably perceive the sound level as being almost inaudible.

The wave-file player to be discussed shortly will sprout a volume control if you compile it to use waveOut calls—essentially a scroll bar connected to the waveOutSetVolume function. This does allow you to control the volume, but only about half the range of the slider is of much use. The bottom half seems to be silent—in fact, it works in a very linear portion of the dynamic range of your ear, which means that you'll perceive almost no change in volume in this area.

If you write multimedia applications in which you allow your users to set the volume of a sound card, you might want to see about implementing logarithmic controls.

As a final note, you might well ask why the volume controls of conventional amplifiers and other audio equipment appear to behave in a linear manner, since they're confronted with much the same problem that sound controlled by data would be. In fact, they cheat—the controls themselves are logarithmic.

Getting information about wave files

The PCMWAVEFORMAT data structure has appeared informally earlier in this chapter. In this section, we'll look at how you can use the information in it to find out about the structure of a particular wave file—how long it will play, how many bits of sampling resolution it supports, and so on. This information will turn up in a practical application in the wave-file player to be discussed later in this chapter.

Figure 2-5 illustrates the Get Info dialog of the wave player. The numerical information about a wave file, as seen in the left half of FIG. 2-5, can all be derived from the file's fmt chunk, essentially a PCMWAVEFORMAT data structure. Some of the numbers are a bit complex to come up with, however. (While the graph on the right side of FIG. 2-5 looks a bit complex, it's pretty easy to create based on the sound data of a wave file itself. We'll look at that presently, too.)

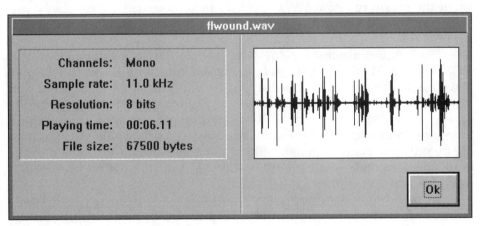

2-5 The Get Info dialog of the wave player.

In the following example, we'll allow that there's a PCMWAVEFORMAT object laying about and that it has been previously filled with the data from the fmt chunk of a wave file. It would be declared like this:

```
PCMWAVEFORMAT waveformat;
```

Let's walk through the procedures used to derive the information presented in the dialog box in FIG. 2-3. To begin with, deciding whether a wave file is in monaural or stereo is pretty simple:

```
if(waveformat.wf.nChannels==1) /* it's monaural */
else /* it's stereo */
```

It's probably worth noting that the present definition of wave files does not allow for four-channel sound. However, it seems inevitable that, when all other options to sell more feature-laden sound cards have been exhausted, someone will create hardware capable of reproducing them should they ever turn up.

The sample rate in kilohertz can be displayed using the following bit of code:

```
char b[STRINGSIZE+1];

wsprintf(b,"%u.%1.1u kHz",
    (int)(waveformat.wf.nSamplesPerSec / 1000L),
    (int)(fi->waveformat.wf.nSamplesPerSec % 1000L)/100);
```

The string b will contain some text that indicates the sampling rate. The number of bits of sample data resolution is actually stored in a PCMWAVEWFORMAT object in a pretty simple format—the number of bits is just represented by a number, and no recourse to bit shifting, masking, or complex calculations need be undertaken. Here's how you'd display it. Note that this value is not part of a WAVEFORMAT structure, but is tacked on at the end in the PCMWAVEFORMAT definition:

```
wsprintf(b,"%u bits",waveformat.wBitsPerSample);
```

The really mind-numbingly complex calculation to be derived from a PCMWAVFORMAT structure is figuring out how long a sound will play for. This is calculated by figuring out how big the wave-data chunk is, how big a sample is, and then how many actual samples are contained in the wave data. You'll recall that one sample can require anywhere from one to four bytes of information. Having worked this out, you can figure out how many samples will play in a second, and thus derive the number of seconds—and fractions thereof—that the sound in question will play.

In this calculation, we'll allow that there's a long integer called datasize, which contains the chunk size of the data chunk of the wave file being investigated:

```
double pt;
int min,sec,hun;

pt=(double)datasize/
    ((double)waveformat.wf.nSamplesPerSec
*    (double)waveformat.wf.nBlockAlign);
```

```
min=(int)(pt/60);
sec=(int)(pt-60*(double)min);
hun=(int)((pt-floor(pt))*100);
wsprintf(b,"%02.2u:%02.2u.%02.2u",min,sec,hun);
```

You might well ask if it's really important to know exactly how long a sound will play for, down to the nearest hundredth of a second. This could be regarded as information that's presented largely because it's available, rather than because it's essential. To be sure, if you're playing a wave file from disk, the time it takes to load will certainly make the playing time value inaccurate to some degree.

Getting information about wave-player devices

It's often important to be able to ascertain the characteristics of the devices available to play wave files. Once again, I touched on this briefly earlier in this chapter.

The wave-player application you'll find later in this chapter includes the dialog shown here in FIG. 2-6. If you write an application to play wave files, this is arguably a good thing to include, as it will be of great help if a user of your software wants to figure out why something is misbehaving. For example, someone who found that there didn't seem to be any stereo separation in the samples being played could find the reason in FIG. 2-6— this wave-player device is monaural.

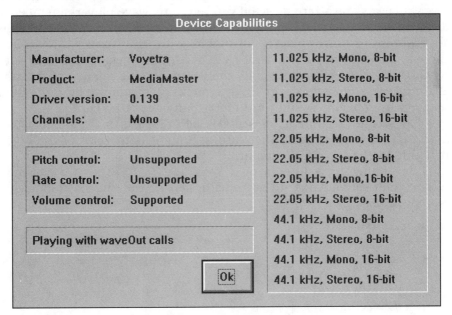

2-6 The Capabilities dialog of the wave player.

In addition to displaying information about a particular device, you can use the information on which FIG. 2-6 is based to automatically configure applications that play wave files. You could check to see if things like volume, playback speed, and playback pitch adjustments are supported by the current wave player, and disable the relevant controls in your software if it turns out that they aren't.

It's worth noting that you don't have to check for the ability to play stereo files per se. Attempting to play a two-channel wave file on a one-channel device will not upset anything—the two channels will simply be combined into one.

Wave-player device information is fetched by the function waveOutGetDevCaps, and stored in an object of the type WAVEOUTCAPS. Here's how you'd use it:

```
WAVEOUTCAPS wc;
char b[STRINGSIZE+1];
int rtrn;

if((rtrn=waveOutGetDevCaps(0,&wc,sizeof(WAVEOUTCAPS)) != 0) {
    waveOutGetErrorText(rtrn,(LPSTR)b,STRINGSIZE);
    DoMessage(hwnd,b);
    return(0L);
}
```

The first argument to waveOutGetDevCaps is the device ID for the wave-player device you'd like information about. This example cheats a bit. Because wave-player devices are installed and numbered consecutively, there will always be a zero device if you have any wave players installed at all. To be grindingly thorough about this, however, you should ascertain the number of wave players available with the waveOutGetNumDevs function, allocate an array of WAVEOUTCAPS objects, and then call waveOutGetDevCaps repeatedly to fill each of them. This will allow for people with multiple sound cards in their systems. It's admittedly difficult to imagine why someone would want more than one sound card.

The second argument to waveOutGetDevCaps is a far pointer to a WAVEOUTCAPS object, and the third argument is the size of the object pointed to by the second argument.

Interpreting the contents of a WAVEOUTCAPS object is far more involved than fetching one. To begin with, here's what one looks like when it's under glass:

```
typedef struct {
    unsigned int wMid;
    unsigned int wPid;
    VERSION vDriverVersion;
    char szPname[32];
    DWORD dwFormats;
    unsigned int wChannels;
```

```
    DWORD dwSupport;
    } WAVEOUTCAPS;
```

The first element in a WAVEOUTCAPS object is wMid, which specifies the manufacturer of the output device. This value will be one of a number of defined constants—the number increases from time to time. The constants are defined in the header file MMREG.H. As of this writing, the following is the list:

Manufacturer	Value
#define MM__MICROSOFT	1
#define MM__CREATIVE	2
#define MM__MEDIAVISION	3
#define MM__FUJITSU	4
#define MM__ARTISOFT	20
#define MM__TURTLE__BEACH	21
#define MM__IBM	22
#define MM__VOCALTEC	23
#define MM__ROLAND	24
#define MM__DIGISPEECH	25
#define MM__NEC	26
#define MM__ATI	27
#define MM__WANGLABS	28
#define MM__TANDY	29
#define MM__VOYETRA	30
#define MM__ANTEX	31
#define MM__ICL__PS	32
#define MM__INTEL	33
#define MM__GRAVIS	34
#define MM__VAL	35
#define MM__INTERACTIVE	36
#define MM__YAMAHA	37
#define MM__EVEREX	38
#define MM__ECHO	39
#define MM__SIERRA	40
#define MM__CAT	41
#define MM__APPS	42
#define MM__DSP__GROUP	43
#define MM__MELABS	44
#define MM__COMPUTER__FRIENDS	45

The MMREG.H file is not part of the Microsoft multimedia development kit, but you can find it in the Microsoft Media Developer Registration Kit. While this package is primarily for use by developers who want to be added to the previous list, it also includes a list of the existing developers in the form of this header file. There's a version of this package on the companion

CD-ROM for this book in the \SOURCE directory as MDRK.ZIP. You can get the current one by writing:

> Microsoft Corporation
> Multimedia Systems Group
> Product Marketing
> One Microsoft Way
> Redmond, WA 98052-6399

As of this writing, you can also download it from CompuServe. Type GO WINSDK and download MDRK.ZIP from library one. You'll find MMREG.H by itself in the \SOURCE directory on the CD-ROM included with this book, as well.

In displaying the manufacturer of a sound card based on the wMid element of a WAVEOUTCAPS structure, you'll need a way to associate these constants with the text strings they represent. Here's how it's done. First, this is a data structure to contain one manufacturer:

```
typedef struct {
    int id;
    char name[33];
    } MANUFACTURER;
```

And this is an array of MANUFACTURER objects with all the currently defined names in it:

```
static MANUFACTURER manufacturer[]= {
    MM_MICROSOFT,"Microsoft",
    MM_CREATIVE,"Creative Labs Inc.",
    MM_MEDIAVISION,"Media Vision Inc",
    MM_FUJITSU,"Fujitsu",
    MM_ARTISOFT, "Artisoft Inc.",
    MM_TURTLE_BEACH,"Turtle Beach",
    MM_IBM,"IBM",
    MM_VOCALTEC,"Vocaltec Ltd.",
    MM_ROLAND,"Roland",
    MM_DIGISPEECH,"Digispeech Inc.",
    MM_NEC,"NEC",
    MM_ATI,"ATI",
    MM_WANGLABS,"Wang Laboratories Inc.",
    MM_TANDY,"Tandy Corporation",
    MM_VOYETRA,"Voyetra",
    MM_ANTEX,"Antex",
    MM_ICL_PS,"ICL",
    MM_INTEL,"Intel",
    MM_GRAVIS,"Gravis",
    MM_VAL,"Video Associates Labs",
```

```
        MM__INTERACTIVE,"InterActive, Inc.",
        MM__YAMAHA,"Yamaha Corp. of America ",
        MM__EVEREX,"Everex Systems, Inc.",
        MM__ECHO,"Echo Speech Corporation",
        MM__SIERRA,"Sierra Semiconductor",
        MM__CAT,"Computer Aided Technologies",
        MM__APPS,"APPS Software International",
        MM__DSP__GROUP,"DSP Group Inc.",
        MM__MELABS,"microEngineering Labs",
        MM__COMPUTER__FRIENDS,"Computer Friends, Inc",
        -1,"Unknown",
    };
```

The final element serves as a marker for the end of the list. Here's a bit of code to search the list for a manufacturer that matches the constant found in the wMid element of a WAVEOUTCAPS object filled in by waveOutGetDevCaps:

```
char b[STRINGSIZE+1];
int i;

wsprintf(b,"Unknown (#%u)",wc.wMid);

for(i=0;manufacturer[i].id != -1;++i) {
    if(manufacturer[i].id==wc.wMid) {
        lstrcpy(b,manufacturer[i].name);
        break;
    }
}
```

When this loop terminates, the string b will either contain the name of the manufacturer corresponding to the value in wMid, or be unknown.

The wPid element of a WAVEOUTCAPS object is a rather more complicated thing to make sense of, and one with which you might not want to bother unless your application for wave files really does involve knowing exactly what is about to play them. This value should be interpreted based on which manufacturer constant is found in the wMid element. For example, here are the current valid constants for wPid if wMid holds the value MM__MICROSOFT:

```
#define MM__WAVE__MAPPER              2  // Wave Mapper
#define MM__SNDBLST__SYNTH            5  // Sound Blaster internal synthesizer
#define MM__SNDBLST__WAVEOU          6  // Sound Blaster waveform output
#define MM__ADLIB                     9  // Ad Lib-compatible synthesizer
#define MM__PCSPEAKER__WAVEOUT       13  // PC Speaker waveform output
#define MM__MSFT__WSS__WAVEOUT       15  // MS audio board waveform output
#define MM__MSFT__WSS__FMSYNTH__STEREO  16  // MS audio board stereo FM synthesizer
#define MM__MSFT__WSS__OEM__WAVEOUT  19  // MS OEM audio board waveform output
```

```
#define MM__MSFT__WSS__OEM__FMSYNTH__STEREO  20 // MS OEM audio board stereo FM synthesizer
#define MM__MSFT__WSS__AUX                    21 // MS audio board auxiliary port
#define MM__MSFT__WSS__OEM__AUX               22 // MS OEM audio auxiliary port
#define MM__MSFT__GENERIC__WAVEOUT            24 // MS vanilla driver waveform output
```

If the value of wMid were something else, say MM__ROLAND, none of these constants would mean very much. Note also that some of the constants for wMid don't have any corresponding values for wPid.

You can find a complete list of the applicable wPid constants in MMREG.H, should you be curious about what they all mean. Plan on writing a lot of nested switch statements or long lookup tables if you decide to fully implement this feature, however.

The vDriverVersion of a WAVEOUTCAPS structure defines the driver version. The high-order byte is the major version number and the low-order byte is the minor version number. Here's how you'd format it up to display it:

```
wsprintf(b,"%u.%u",
    (wc.vDriverVersion>>8) & 0xff,
    wc.vDriverVersion & 0xff);
```

The pzPname is a C language null-terminated string that specifies the name of the manufacturer of your sound card—in theory, this should duplicate the information found in the wMid element. In practice, the list of constants stored in wMid will continue to expand, and your application won't be able to make sense of the new ones until you get an updated copy of MMREG.H and recompile your program. The information in pzPname doesn't require any interpretation, and as such should always make sense.

The dwFormats value of a WAVEOUTCAPS object is a set of flags that define the wave-file formats the sound card in question can reproduce. The flags are defined as a set of constants in MMSYSTEM.H, like this:

```
#define WAVE__FORMAT__1M08 0x00000001 // 11.025 kHz, monaural, 8-bit
#define WAVE__FORMAT__1S08 0x00000002 // 11.025 kHz, stereo, 8-bit
#define WAVE__FORMAT__1M16 0x00000004 // 11.025 kHz, monaural, 16-bit
#define WAVE__FORMAT__1S16 0x00000008 // 11.025 kHz, stereo, 16-bit
#define WAVE__FORMAT__2M08 0x00000010 // 22.05 kHz, monaural, 8-bit
#define WAVE__FORMAT__2S08 0x00000020 // 22.05 kHz, stereo, 8-bit
#define WAVE__FORMAT__2M16 0x00000040 // 22.05 kHz, monaural, 16-bit
#define WAVE__FORMAT__2S16 0x00000080 // 22.05 kHz, stereo, 16-bit
#define WAVE__FORMAT__4M08 0x00000100 // 44.1 kHz, monaural, 8-bit
#define WAVE__FORMAT__4S08 0x00000200 // 44.1 kHz, stereo, 8-bit
#define WAVE__FORMAT__4M16 0x00000400 // 44.1 kHz, monaural, 16-bit
#define WAVE__FORMAT__4S16 0x00000800 // 44.1 kHz, stereo, 16-bit
```

If, for example, wc.dwFormats & WAVEFORMAT__2M08 is true, the sound card being investigated can play 22.05-kilohertz, 8-bit, monaural sound.

The wChannels element of a WAVEOUTCAPS object defines the number of channels the sound card in your system can play—this will be either 1 or 2. This need not have much to do with the dwFormats value, as a monaural sound card can still play stereo wave files by combining the two channels, as was mentioned earlier.

It's also worth noting that what this value really defines is the number of channels handled by the driver for your card, rather than by your card itself. In some cases, such as with the version of the Voyetra drivers used to create FIG. 2-6, the drivers are monaural while the card itself can handle stereo sound.

Finally, the dwSupport element of a WAVEOUTCAPS object is another set of flags. This one defines whether several optional parameters of a wave output device can be modified on the card in question. At present, the following flags are defined:

```
#define WAVECAPS_PITCH        0x0001 // supports pitch control
#define WAVECAPS_PLAYBACKRATE 0x0002 // supports playback rate control
#define WAVECAPS_VOLUME       0x0004 // supports volume control
#define WAVECAPS_LRVOLUME     0x0008 // separate left-right volume control
```

For example, if wc.dwSupport & WAVECAPS_VOLUME is true, the sound card being investigated will respond to changes in volume using waveOutSetVolume, as discussed earlier in this chapter.

In most applications, save for displaying the information in a WAVEOUTCAPS object in something like FIG. 2-6, you won't have to go into quite this much detail in decoding one. It's relatively easy to fetch a WAVEOUTCAPS object and test it for a specific characteristic of interest.

The wave player, at last

You've probably experienced enough theory about wave files by now to write a wave player in your sleep. As with much of the software to be explored in this book, a wave player is mostly a fairly conventional Windows application with a few multimedia calls scattered about. If you're familiar with Windows programming in general, you probably won't find too much about the wave player that looks wholly alien. Figure 2-7 illustrates the main window of WAVEPLAY.

The WAVEPLAY application was written with several things in mind. It serves to exercise the various functions discussed thus far, and as you'll see, you can compile it to use any one of the latter three approaches you looked at to play wave files. I also used it to weed out the wave files included on the CD-ROM for this book—hence the Delete button.

You'll find a compiled .EXE file for WAVEPLAY in the APPS directory of the CD-ROM, should you want to try it out as it stands.

To use WAVEPLAY, select a wave file from its main list box and click on Play. The sound will start playing, and if WAVEPLAY is using either MCI or waveOut calls, the Play button and the list box will be disabled. When the sound runs out, or if you click on Stop to terminate it early, the Play button and the list box will be re-enabled.

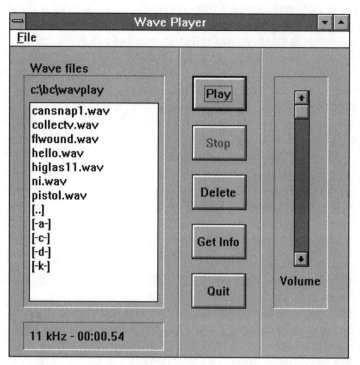

2-7 The main window of the wave player.

The Get Info button will display a dialog like the one back in FIG. 2-5. The File menu of WAVEPLAY duplicates the functions of its buttons. It also allows you to have a look at the Capabilities dialog box from FIG. 2-6.

Figure 2-8 is the complete C language source code for WAVE-PLAY.CPP. Note that WAVEPLAY.CPP expects to find MMREG.H when it compiles, as discussed earlier in this chapter.

2-8 The C language source listing for the wave player, WAVEPLAY.CPP.

```
/*
    Wave Player
    Copyright (c) 1993 Alchemy Mindworks Inc.
*/
#include <windows.h>
#include <stdio.h>
#include <stdlib.h>
#include <dir.h>
#include <ctype.h>
#include <alloc.h>
```

```
#include <string.h>
#include <io.h>
#include <bwcc.h>
#include <dos.h>
#include <errno.h>
#include <math.h>
#include <mmsystem.h>
#include <mmreg.h>
```

/* note: MMREG.H is not part of the Multimedia Developer's kit. It's
available in the Multimedia Registraion kit, and can be found on the
CDROM for Windows Multimedia Programming. */

```
#define    USE_SOUNDPLAYSOUND    0 /* true to use sndPlaySound */
#define    USE_MCICALLS          0 /* true to use MCI calls — better choice */
#define    USE_WAVEOUT           1 /* true to use waveOut calls */

#define    say(s)    MessageBox(NULL,s,"Yo...",MB_OK | MB_ICONSTOP);
#define    saynumber(f,s)    {char b[128]; sprintf((LPSTR)b,(LPSTR)f,s); \
           MessageBox(NULL,b,"Debug Message",MB_OK | MB_ICONSTOP); }

#define    ItemName(item,string)    { dlgH=GetDlgItem(hwnd,item); \
                                     SetWindowText(dlgH,(LPSTR)string); }
#define    ItemOn(item)    { dlgH=GetDlgItem(hwnd,item); \
                            EnableWindow(dlgH,TRUE); }
#define    ItemOff(item)    { dlgH=GetDlgItem(hwnd,item); \
                            EnableWindow(dlgH,FALSE); }

#define    STRINGSIZE    129          /* how big is a string? */

#define    MAIN_LIST     201          /* objects in the main window */
#define    MAIN_TEXT     202
#define    MAIN_PATH     203

#define    MAIN_PLAY     101          /* buttons and main menu items */
#define    MAIN_STOP     102
#define    MAIN_GETINFO  103
#define    MAIN_DELETE   104
#define    MAIN_ABOUT    105
#define    MAIN_CAPS     106
#define    MAIN_EXIT     107

#define    INFO_CHANNELS 101          /* objects in the Get Info box */
#define    INFO_SAMPLES  102
#define    INFO_SAMPLING 103
#define    INFO_PLAYTIME 104
```

```
#define    INFO_FILESIZE    105


#define    INFO_WAVELEFT    288         /* where the wave diagram goes */
#define    INFO_WAVETOP     16
#define    INFO_WAVEWIDE    248
#define    INFO_WAVEDEEP    128


#define    MESSAGE_STRING   101         /* message box object */


#define    FILE_EXTENSION   "WAV"        /* file extension? Could be... */


#define    GET_FILE_SIZE    0x0001        /* flag to get the file size */


#define    MAIN_VOLUME      401
#define    MAIN_VTEXT       501


#define    SCROLL_RANGE     256


#define    CAPS_MANUF       101
#define    CAPS_PRODUCT     102
#define    CAPS_VERSION     103
#define    CAPS_CHANNELS    104
#define    CAPS_PITCH       201
#define    CAPS_RATE        202
#define    CAPS_VOLUME      203
#define    CAPS_MODEBASE    301
#define    CAPS_PLAYTYPE    401


#ifndef max
#define max(a,b)          (((a)>(b))?(a):(b))
#endif
#ifndef min
#define min(a,b)          (((a)<(b))?(a):(b))
#endif

typedef struct {              /* what we need to know about a wave file */
    PCMWAVEFORMAT waveformat;
    unsigned long datasize;
    unsigned long filesize;
    char filename[128];
    } FILEINFO;

typedef struct {
    int id;
    char name[33];
```

```
        } MANUFACTURER;

/* prototypes */
DWORD FAR PASCAL CapsDlgProc(HWND hwnd,WORD message,WORD wParam,LONG lParam);
DWORD FAR PASCAL SelectProc(HWND hwnd,WORD message,WORD wParam,LONG lParam);
DWORD FAR PASCAL AboutDlgProc(HWND hwnd,WORD message,WORD wParam,LONG lParam);
DWORD FAR PASCAL MessageDlgProc(HWND hwnd,WORD message,WORD wParam,LONG lParam);
DWORD FAR PASCAL InfoDlgProc(HWND hwnd,WORD message,WORD wParam,LONG lParam);
DWORD PlaySound(LPSTR path,HWND hwnd);

void ShowCaps(HWND hwnd);
void SetCurrentVolume(unsigned int n);
void ShowCurrentStats(HWND hwnd,unsigned int listbox,unsigned int textbox);
void ResetSelectorList(HWND hwnd,unsigned int listbox,unsigned int pathstring);
void DoMessage(HWND hwnd,LPSTR message);
void ShowInfo(HWND hwnd,FILEINFO far *fi);
void lmemset(LPSTR s,int n,unsigned int size);

int DrawWave(HDC hdc,unsigned int x,unsigned int y,LPSTR filepath);
int GetInfo(FILEINFO far *fi,LPSTR path,unsigned int flags);
int testdisk(int n);
int lmemcmp(LPSTR d,LPSTR s,unsigned int size);
int YesNo(HWND hwnd,LPSTR message);

/* globals */

LPSTR messagehook;
char szFileSpec[145];

char szAppName[] = "WavePlayer";
HANDLE hInst;

#if USE_MCICALLS
int soundID=-1;
#endif

#if USE_WAVEOUT
HWAVEOUT hwaveout=NULL;
GLOBALHANDLE wavehandle=NULL;
GLOBALHANDLE waveheader=NULL;
HPSTR wavepointer=NULL;
LPWAVEHDR pwaveheader=NULL;
unsigned int currentvolume=SCROLL_RANGE;
#endif

#pragma warn -par
```

2-8 Continued.

```
int PASCAL WinMain(HANDLE hInstance,HANDLE hPrevInstance,
                   LPSTR lpszCmdParam,int nCmdShow)
{
    FARPROC dlgProc;
    int r=0;

    BWCCGetVersion();

    hInst=hInstance;

    dlgProc=MakeProcInstance((FARPROC)SelectProc,hInst);
    r=DialogBox(hInst,"MainScreen",NULL,dlgProc);

    FreeProcInstance(dlgProc);

    return(r);
}

DWORD FAR PASCAL SelectProc(HWND hwnd,WORD message,WORD wParam,LONG lParam)
{
    FILEINFO fi;
    PAINTSTRUCT ps;
    HICON hIcon;
    FARPROC lpfnDlgProc;
    POINT point;
    char b[STRINGSIZE+1],s[STRINGSIZE+1];
    unsigned long l;
    unsigned int i;

    #if USE_WAVEOUT
    HWND dlgH;
    HMENU hmenu;
    int vpos;
    #endif

    #if USE_MCICALLS
    MCI_GENERIC_PARMS mcigen;
    HMENU hmenu;
    HWND dlgH;
    RECT rect;
    #endif

    #if USE_SOUNDPLAYSOUND
    RECT rect;
    #endif
```

```
switch(message) {
    #if USE_WAVEOUT
    case MM_WOM_DONE:
        waveOutUnprepareHeader((HWAVEOUT)wParam,
            (LPWAVEHDR)lParam,sizeof(WAVEHDR));
        waveOutClose((HWAVEOUT)wParam);
        hwaveout=NULL;

        if(wavehandle != NULL) {
            GlobalUnlock(wavehandle);
            GlobalFree(wavehandle);
            wavehandle=NULL;
        }
        if(waveheader != NULL) {
            GlobalUnlock(waveheader);
            GlobalFree(waveheader);
            waveheader=NULL;
        }
        ItemOn(MAIN_LIST);
        ItemOn(MAIN_PLAY);
        ItemOff(MAIN_STOP);
        hmenu=GetMenu(hwnd);
        EnableMenuItem(hmenu,MAIN_LIST,MF_ENABLED);
        EnableMenuItem(hmenu,MAIN_PLAY,MF_ENABLED);
        EnableMenuItem(hmenu,MAIN_STOP,MF_GRAYED);
        break;
    case WM_VSCROLL:
        vpos = GetScrollPos(HIWORD(lParam),SB_CTL);
        switch(wParam) {
            case SB_LINEUP:
                vpos-=1;
                break;
            case SB_LINEDOWN:
                vpos+=1;
                break;
            case SB_PAGEUP:
                vpos-=SCROLL_RANGE/64;
                break;
            case SB_PAGEDOWN:
                vpos+=SCROLL_RANGE/64;
                break;
            case SB_THUMBPOSITION:
                vpos=LOWORD(lParam);
                break;
        }
```

```
        if(vpos < 0) vpos=0;
        else if(vpos > SCROLL_RANGE) vpos=SCROLL_RANGE;

        if(vpos != GetScrollPos(HIWORD(lParam),SB_CTL)) {
            SetScrollPos(HIWORD(lParam),SB_CTL,vpos,TRUE);
            if(GetDlgCtrlID(HIWORD(lParam))== MAIN_VOLUME)
                SetCurrentVolume(vpos);
        }
        break;
    #endif
    #if USE_MCICALLS
    case MM_MCINOTIFY:
        mciSendCommand(LOWORD(lParam),MCI_CLOSE,MCI_WAIT,NULL);
        soundID=-1;
        ItemOn(MAIN_LIST);
        ItemOn(MAIN_PLAY);
        ItemOff(MAIN_STOP);
        hmenu=GetMenu(hwnd);
        EnableMenuItem(hmenu,MAIN_LIST,MF_ENABLED);
        EnableMenuItem(hmenu,MAIN_PLAY,MF_ENABLED);
        EnableMenuItem(hmenu,MAIN_STOP,MF_GRAYED);
        break;
    #endif
    case WM_CTLCOLOR:
        if(HIWORD(lParam)==CTLCOLOR_STATIC ||
           HIWORD(lParam)==CTLCOLOR_DLG) {
            SetBkColor(wParam,RGB(192,192,192));
            SetTextColor(wParam,RGB(0,0,0));

            ClientToScreen(hwnd,&point);
            UnrealizeObject(GetStockObject(LTGRAY_BRUSH));
            SetBrushOrg(wParam,point.x,point.y);

            return((DWORD)GetStockObject(LTGRAY_BRUSH));

        }
        if(HIWORD(lParam)==CTLCOLOR_BTN) {
            SetBkColor(wParam,RGB(192,192,192));
            SetTextColor(wParam,RGB(0,0,0));

            ClientToScreen(hwnd,&point);
            UnrealizeObject(GetStockObject(BLACK_BRUSH));
            SetBrushOrg(wParam,point.x,point.y);

            return((DWORD)GetStockObject(BLACK_BRUSH));
```

```
        }
        break;
case WM_SYSCOMMAND:
    switch(wParam & 0xfff0) {
        case SC_CLOSE:
            SendMessage(hwnd,WM_COMMAND,MAIN_EXIT,0L);
            break;
    }
    break;
case WM_INITDIALOG:
    hIcon=LoadIcon(hInst,szAppName);
    SetClassWord(hwnd,GCW_HICON, (WORD)hIcon);
    ResetSelectorList(hwnd,MAIN_LIST,MAIN_PATH);
    ShowCurrentStats(hwnd,MAIN_LIST,MAIN_TEXT);
    waveOutSetVolume(0,0xffffffffL);
    #if USE_WAVEOUT
    ItemOn(MAIN_VOLUME);
    ItemOn(MAIN_VTEXT);
    SetScrollRange(GetDlgItem(hwnd,MAIN_VOLUME),
        SB_CTL,0,SCROLL_RANGE,FALSE);
    SetScrollPos(GetDlgItem(hwnd,MAIN_VOLUME),
        SB_CTL,0,TRUE);
    SetCurrentVolume(0);
    ItemOff(MAIN_STOP);
    hmenu=GetMenu(hwnd);
    EnableMenuItem(hmenu,MAIN_STOP,MF_GRAYED);
    #endif
    #if USE_MCICALLS
    ItemOff(MAIN_STOP);
    hmenu=GetMenu(hwnd);
    EnableMenuItem(hmenu,MAIN_STOP,MF_GRAYED);
    GetWindowRect(hwnd,&rect);
    SetWindowPos(hwnd,NULL,0,0,(rect.right-rect.left)-104,
        rect.bottom-rect.top,SWP_NOMOVE);
    #endif
    #if USE_SOUNDPLAYSOUND
    GetWindowRect(hwnd,&rect);
    SetWindowPos(hwnd,NULL,0,0,(rect.right-rect.left)-104,
        rect.bottom-rect.top,SWP_NOMOVE);
    #endif
    break;
case WM_PAINT:
    BeginPaint(hwnd,&ps);
    EndPaint(hwnd,&ps);
    break;
case WM_COMMAND:
```

```
        switch(wParam) {
          case MAIN_LIST:
            switch(HIWORD(lParam)) {
              case LBN_DBLCLK:
                if(DlgDirSelect(hwnd,b,MAIN_LIST)) {
                    i=lstrlen(b);
                    if(b[i-1]=='\\') {
                        b[i-1]=0;
                        chdir(b);
                    }
                    else {
                        if(!testdisk(b[0]-'A'))
                            setdisk(toupper(b[0])-'A');
                        else DoMessage(hwnd,
                          "That drive is off line. Please"
                          " check to see that there's a disk in it.");
                    }
                    ResetSelectorList(hwnd,MAIN_LIST,MAIN_PATH);
                    ShowCurrentStats(hwnd,MAIN_LIST,MAIN_TEXT);
                }
                else {
                    SendMessage(hwnd,WM_COMMAND,MAIN_PLAY,0L);
                }
                break;
              case LBN_SELCHANGE:
                ShowCurrentStats(hwnd,MAIN_LIST,MAIN_TEXT);
                break;

            }
            break;
          case MAIN_STOP:
            #if USE_WAVEOUT
            if(wavehandle != NULL) {
                waveOutReset(hwaveout);
                SetCurrentVolume(0);
            }
            #endif
            #if USE_MCICALLS
            if(soundID != -1) {
                mcigen.dwCallback=hwnd;
                mciSendCommand(soundID,MCI_STOP,MCI_NOTIFY |
                    MCI_WAIT,(DWORD)(LPVOID)&mcigen);
            }
            #endif
            #if USE_SOUNDPLAYSOUND
```

```
                sndPlaySound(NULL,SND_SYNC);
                #endif
                break;
        case MAIN_DELETE:
                if((l=SendDlgItemMessage(hwnd,MAIN_LIST,
                  LB_GETCURSEL,0,0L)) != LB_ERR) {
                    SendDlgItemMessage(hwnd,MAIN_LIST,LB_GETTEXT,
                      (unsigned int)l,(DWORD)b);
                    if(b[0] != '[') {
                        wsprintf(s,"Do you want to delete %s?",(LPSTR)b);
                            if(YesNo(hwnd,s)) {
                            remove(b);
                            SendDlgItemMessage(hwnd,MAIN_LIST,LB_DELETESTRING,
                                (unsigned int)l,0L);
                            }
                    }
                }
                break;
        case MAIN_PLAY:
                if((l=SendDlgItemMessage(hwnd,MAIN_LIST,
                  LB_GETCURSEL,0,0L)) != LB_ERR) {
                    SendDlgItemMessage(hwnd,MAIN_LIST,
                      LB_GETTEXT,(unsigned int)l,(DWORD)b);
                    if(b[0] != '[') {
                        if(PlaySound((LPSTR)b,hwnd)) {
                            #if USE_WAVEOUT || USE_MCICALLS
                            ItemOff(MAIN_LIST);
                            ItemOff(MAIN_PLAY);
                            ItemOn(MAIN_STOP);
                            hmenu=GetMenu(hwnd);
                            EnableMenuItem(hmenu,MAIN_LIST,MF_GRAYED);
                            EnableMenuItem(hmenu,MAIN_PLAY,MF_GRAYED);
                            EnableMenuItem(hmenu,MAIN_STOP,MF_ENABLED);
                            #endif
                        }
                    }
                }
                break;
        case MAIN_GETINFO:
                if((l=SendDlgItemMessage(hwnd,MAIN_LIST,
                  LB_GETCURSEL,0,0L)) != LB_ERR) {
                    SendDlgItemMessage(hwnd,MAIN_LIST,
                      LB_GETTEXT,(unsigned int)l,(DWORD)b);
                    if(b[0] != '[') {
                        if(GetInfo(&fi,b,GET_FILE_SIZE)) {
                            ShowInfo(hwnd,&fi);
```

```
                              } else DoMessage(hwnd,"Error reading file");
                          }
                      }
                      break;
                  case MAIN_ABOUT:
                      if((lpfnDlgProc=MakeProcInstance((FARPROC)AboutDlgProc,
                         hInst)) != NULL) {
                          DialogBox(hInst,"AboutBox",hwnd,lpfnDlgProc);
                          FreeProcInstance(lpfnDlgProc);
                      }
                      break;
                  case MAIN_CAPS:
                      ShowCaps(hwnd);
                      break;
                  case MAIN_EXIT:
                      SendMessage(hwnd,WM_COMMAND,MAIN_STOP,0L);
                      PostQuitMessage(0);
                      break;
              }
              break;

      }

      return(FALSE);
}

#if USE_WAVEOUT
DWORD PlaySound(LPSTR path,HWND hwnd)
{
      PCMWAVEFORMAT waveformat;
      HMMIO h;
      MMCKINFO mmParent,mmSub;
      char b[STRINGSIZE+1];
      int n,rtrn;

      if((h=mmioOpen(path,NULL,MMIO_READ)) == NULL) {
          DoMessage(hwnd,"Error opening file");
          return(0L);
      }

      mmParent.fccType=mmioFOURCC('W','A','V','E');
      if(mmioDescend(h,(LPMMCKINFO)&mmParent,NULL,MMIO_FINDRIFF)) {
          mmioClose(h,0);
          DoMessage(hwnd,"Error descending file");
          return(0L);
```

```
    }

mmSub.ckid=mmioFOURCC('f','m','t',' ');
if(mmioDescend(h,(LPMMCKINFO)&mmSub,(LPMMCKINFO)&mmParent,MMIO_FINDCHUNK)) {
    mmioClose(h,0);
    DoMessage(hwnd,"Error descending file");
    return(0L);
}

n=min((unsigned int)mmSub.cksize,sizeof(PCMWAVEFORMAT));
if(mmioRead(h,(LPSTR)&waveformat,n) != n) {
    mmioClose(h,0);
    DoMessage(hwnd,"Error reading file");
    return(0L);
}

if(waveformat.wf.wFormatTag != WAVE_FORMAT_PCM) {
    mmioClose(h,0);
    DoMessage(hwnd,"Error int file structure");
    return(0L);
}

mmioAscend(h,&mmSub,0);

mmSub.ckid=mmioFOURCC('d','a','t','a');
if(mmioDescend(h,(LPMMCKINFO)&mmSub,(LPMMCKINFO)&mmParent,MMIO_FINDCHUNK)) {
    mmioClose(h,0);
    DoMessage(hwnd,"Error descending file");
    return(0L);
}

if((wavehandle=GlobalAlloc(GMEM_MOVEABLE | GMEM_SHARE,mmSub.cksize)) == NULL) {
    mmioClose(h,0);
    DoMessage(hwnd,"Memory allocation error");
    return(0L);
}

if((wavepointer=(HPSTR)GlobalLock(wavehandle)) == NULL) {
    GlobalFree(wavehandle);
    mmioClose(h,0);
    wavehandle=NULL;
    DoMessage(hwnd,"Memory locking error");
    return(0L);
}

if(mmioRead(h,wavepointer,mmSub.cksize) != mmSub.cksize) {
```

```
      GlobalUnlock(wavehandle);
      GlobalFree(wavehandle);
      mmioClose(h,0);
      wavehandle=NULL;
      DoMessage(hwnd,"Error reading file");
      return(0L);
}

if((waveheader=GlobalAlloc(GMEM_MOVEABLE | GMEM_SHARE,
  (long)sizeof(WAVEHDR))) == NULL) {
      GlobalUnlock(wavehandle);
      GlobalFree(wavehandle);
      mmioClose(h,0);
      wavehandle=NULL;
      DoMessage(hwnd,"Memory allocation error");
      return(0L);
}

if((pwaveheader=(LPWAVEHDR)GlobalLock(waveheader))==NULL) {
      GlobalFree(waveheader);
      GlobalUnlock(wavehandle);
      GlobalFree(wavehandle);
      mmioClose(h,0);
      wavehandle=NULL;
      DoMessage(hwnd,"Memory locking error");
      return(0L);
}

if((rtrn=waveOutOpen((LPHWAVEOUT)&hwaveout,
  WAVE_MAPPER,(LPWAVEFORMAT)&waveformat,
      (LONG)hwnd,0L,CALLBACK_WINDOW)) != 0) {
      GlobalUnlock(waveheader);
      GlobalFree(waveheader);
      GlobalUnlock(wavehandle);
      GlobalFree(wavehandle);
      mmioClose(h,0);
      wavehandle=NULL;
      waveOutGetErrorText(rtrn,(LPSTR)b,STRINGSIZE);
      DoMessage(hwnd,b);
      return(0L);
}

pwaveheader->lpData=(LPSTR)wavepointer;
pwaveheader->dwBufferLength=mmSub.cksize;
pwaveheader->dwFlags=0L;
```

```
    pwaveheader->dwLoops=OL;
    if((rtrn=waveOutPrepareHeader(hwaveout,pwaveheader,sizeof(WAVEHDR))) != 0) {
        GlobalUnlock(waveheader);
        GlobalFree(waveheader);
        waveOutUnprepareHeader(hwaveout,pwaveheader,sizeof(WAVEHDR));
        waveOutClose(hwaveout);
        GlobalUnlock(wavehandle);
        GlobalFree(wavehandle);
        mmioClose(h,0);
        wavehandle=NULL;
        waveOutGetErrorText(rtrn,(LPSTR)b,STRINGSIZE);
        DoMessage(hwnd,b);
        return(OL);
    }

    SetCurrentVolume(currentvolume);
    if((rtrn=waveOutWrite(hwaveout,pwaveheader,sizeof(WAVEHDR))) != 0) {
        GlobalUnlock(waveheader);
        GlobalFree(waveheader);
        waveOutUnprepareHeader(hwaveout,pwaveheader,sizeof(WAVEHDR));
        waveOutClose(hwaveout);
        GlobalUnlock(wavehandle);
        GlobalFree(wavehandle);
        mmioClose(h,0);
        wavehandle=NULL;
        waveOutGetErrorText(rtrn,(LPSTR)b,STRINGSIZE);
        DoMessage(hwnd,b);
        return(OL);
    }

    mmioClose(h,0);

    return(1L);
}
#endif

#if USE_MCICALLS
DWORD PlaySound(LPSTR path,HWND hwnd)
{
    MCI_OPEN_PARMS mciopen;
    MCI_PLAY_PARMS mciplay;
    MCI_GENERIC_PARMS mcigen;
    DWORD rtrn;
    char b[STRINGSIZE+1];

    if(soundID != -1) {
```

```
        mcigen.dwCallback=hwnd;
        mciSendCommand(soundID,MCI_STOP,0,(DWORD)(LPVOID)&mcigen);
        soundID=-1;
    }

    mciopen.lpstrDeviceType="waveaudio";
    mciopen.lpstrElementName=path;
    if((rtrn=mciSendCommand(0,MCI_OPEN,MCI_OPEN_TYPE | MCI_OPEN_ELEMENT,
        (DWORD)(LPVOID)&mciopen)) != 0L) {
        mciGetErrorString(rtrn,(LPSTR)b,STRINGSIZE);
        DoMessage(hwnd,b);
        return(0L);
    }

    soundID=mciopen.wDeviceID;

    mciplay.dwCallback=(DWORD)hwnd;
    if((rtrn=mciSendCommand(soundID,MCI_PLAY,MCI_NOTIFY,
      (DWORD)(LPVOID)&mciplay)) != 0L) {
        mciSendCommand(soundID,MCI_CLOSE,0,NULL);
        mciGetErrorString(rtrn,(LPSTR)b,STRINGSIZE);
        DoMessage(hwnd,b);
        return(0L);
    }

    return(1L);
}
#endif


#if USE_SOUNDPLAYSOUND
DWORD PlaySound(LPSTR path,HWND hwnd)
{
    if(!sndPlaySound(path,SND_ASYNC | SND_NOSTOP)) {
        DoMessage(hwnd,"Error playing sound");
    }
    return(1L);
}
#endif

DWORD FAR PASCAL AboutDlgProc(HWND hwnd,WORD message,WORD wParam,LONG lParam)
{
    static HANDLE sound;
    static LPSTR psound;
    HANDLE handle;
    POINT point;
```

```
switch(message) {
    case WM_INITDIALOG:
        if((handle=FindResource(hInst,"Hello",RT_RCDATA)) != NULL) {
            if((sound=LoadResource(hInst,handle)) != NULL) {
                if((psound=LockResource(sound)) != NULL)
                    sndPlaySound(psound,SND_ASYNC | SND_MEMORY | SND_NOSTOP);
            }
        }
        return(TRUE);
    case WM_CTLCOLOR:
        if(HIWORD(lParam)==CTLCOLOR_STATIC ||
           HIWORD(lParam)==CTLCOLOR_DLG) {
            SetBkColor(wParam,RGB(192,192,192));
            SetTextColor(wParam,RGB(0,0,0));

            ClientToScreen(hwnd,&point);
            UnrealizeObject(GetStockObject(LTGRAY_BRUSH));
            SetBrushOrg(wParam,point.x,point.y);

            return((DWORD)GetStockObject(LTGRAY_BRUSH));

        }
        if(HIWORD(lParam)==CTLCOLOR_BTN) {
            SetBkColor(wParam,RGB(192,192,192));
            SetTextColor(wParam,RGB(0,0,0));

            ClientToScreen(hwnd,&point);
            UnrealizeObject(GetStockObject(BLACK_BRUSH));
            SetBrushOrg(wParam,point.x,point.y);

            return((DWORD)GetStockObject(BLACK_BRUSH));
        }
        break;
    case WM_COMMAND:
        switch(wParam) {
            case IDOK:
                if(psound != NULL) UnlockResource(sound);
                if(sound != NULL) FreeResource(sound);
                sndPlaySound(NULL,SND_SYNC);
                EndDialog(hwnd,wParam);
                return(TRUE);
        }
        break;
}

return(FALSE);
```

```
}

int YesNo(HWND hwnd,LPSTR message)
{
     FARPROC lpfnDlgProc;
    int r;

    messagehook=message;

    if((lpfnDlgProc=MakeProcInstance((FARPROC)MessageDlgProc,hInst)) != NULL) {
        r=DialogBox(hInst,"YesNoBox",hwnd,lpfnDlgProc);
        FreeProcInstance(lpfnDlgProc);
    }
    if(r==IDYES) return(1);
    else return(0);
}

void DoMessage(HWND hwnd,LPSTR message)
{
    FARPROC lpfnDlgProc;

    messagehook=message;

    if((lpfnDlgProc=MakeProcInstance((FARPROC)MessageDlgProc,hInst)) != NULL) {
        DialogBox(hInst,"MessageBox",hwnd,lpfnDlgProc);
        FreeProcInstance(lpfnDlgProc);
    }
}

void ShowCaps(HWND hwnd)
{
     FARPROC lpfnDlgProc;

    if((lpfnDlgProc=MakeProcInstance((FARPROC)CapsDlgProc,hInst)) != NULL) {
        DialogBox(hInst,"CapsBox",hwnd,lpfnDlgProc);
        FreeProcInstance(lpfnDlgProc);
    }
}

DWORD FAR PASCAL MessageDlgProc(HWND hwnd,WORD message,WORD wParam,LONG lParam)
{
    POINT point;
    HWND dlgH;

    switch(message) {
```

```
        case WM_INITDIALOG:
            dlgH=GetDlgItem(hwnd,MESSAGE_STRING);
            SetWindowText(dlgH,messagehook);
            return(TRUE);
        case WM_CTLCOLOR:
            if(HIWORD(lParam)==CTLCOLOR_STATIC ||
               HIWORD(lParam)==CTLCOLOR_DLG) {
                SetBkColor(wParam,RGB(192,192,192));
                SetTextColor(wParam,RGB(0,0,0));

                ClientToScreen(hwnd,&point);
                UnrealizeObject(GetStockObject(LTGRAY_BRUSH));
                SetBrushOrg(wParam,point.x,point.y);

                return((DWORD)GetStockObject(LTGRAY_BRUSH));

            }
            if(HIWORD(lParam)==CTLCOLOR_BTN) {
                SetBkColor(wParam,RGB(192,192,192));
                SetTextColor(wParam,RGB(0,0,0));

                ClientToScreen(hwnd,&point);
                UnrealizeObject(GetStockObject(BLACK_BRUSH));
                SetBrushOrg(wParam,point.x,point.y);

                return((DWORD)GetStockObject(BLACK_BRUSH));
            }
            break;
        case WM_COMMAND:
            switch(wParam) {
                case IDCANCEL:
                case IDOK:
                case IDYES:
                case IDNO:
                    EndDialog(hwnd,wParam);
                    return(TRUE);
            }
            break;
    }

    return(FALSE);
}

DWORD FAR PASCAL CapsDlgProc(HWND hwnd,WORD message,WORD wParam,LONG lParam)
{
static  MANUFACTURER manufacturer[]= {
```

```
        MM_MICROSOFT,"Microsoft",
        MM_CREATIVE,"Creative Labs Inc.",
        MM_MEDIAVISION,"Media Vision Inc",
        MM_FUJITSU,"Fujitsu",
        MM_ARTISOFT, "Artisoft Inc.",
        MM_TURTLE_BEACH,"Turtle Beach",
        MM_IBM,"IBM",
        MM_VOCALTEC,"Vocaltec Ltd.",
        MM_ROLAND,"Roland",
        MM_DIGISPEECH,"Digispeech Inc.",
        MM_NEC,"NEC",
        MM_ATI,"ATI",
        MM_WANGLABS,"Wang Laboratories Inc.",
        MM_TANDY,"Tandy Corporation",
        MM_VOYETRA,"Voyetra",
        MM_ANTEX,"Antex",
        MM_ICL_PS,"ICL",
        MM_INTEL,"Intel",
        MM_GRAVIS,"Gravis",
        MM_VAL,"Video Associates Labs",
        MM_INTERACTIVE,"InterActive, Inc.",
        MM_YAMAHA,"Yamaha Corp. of America ",
        MM_EVEREX,"Everex Systems, Inc.",
        MM_ECHO,"Echo Speech Corporation",
        MM_SIERRA,"Sierra Semiconductor",
        MM_CAT,"Computer Aided Technologies",
        MM_APPS,"APPS Software International",
        MM_DSP_GROUP,"DSP Group Inc.",
        MM_MELABS,"microEngineering Labs",
        MM_COMPUTER_FRIENDS,"Computer Friends, Inc",
        -1,"Unknown",
        };

    WAVEOUTCAPS wc;
    POINT point;
    HWND dlgH;
    char b[STRINGSIZE+1];
    int rtrn,i;

    switch(message) {
        case WM_INITDIALOG:
            if((rtrn=waveOutGetDevCaps(0,&wc,sizeof(WAVEOUTCAPS))) == 0) {

                wsprintf(b,"Unknown (#%u)",wc.wMid);

                for(i=0;manufacturer[i].id != -1;++i) {
```

```
        if(manufacturer[i].id==wc.wMid) {
            lstrcpy(b,manufacturer[i].name);
            break;
        }
}

ItemName(CAPS_MANUF,(LPSTR)b);

wsprintf(b,"%u.%u",(wc.vDriverVersion>>8) & 0xff,
    wc.vDriverVersion & 0xff);
ItemName(CAPS_VERSION,(LPSTR)b);

ItemName(CAPS_PRODUCT,(LPSTR)wc.szPname);

if(wc.wChannels==1) lstrcpy(b,"Mono");
else lstrcpy(b,"Stereo");
ItemName(CAPS_CHANNELS,(LPSTR)b);

if(wc.dwSupport & WAVECAPS_PITCH) lstrcpy(b,"Supported");
else lstrcpy(b,"Unsupported");
ItemName(CAPS_PITCH,(LPSTR)b);

if(wc.dwSupport & WAVECAPS_PLAYBACKRATE) lstrcpy(b,"Supported");
else lstrcpy(b,"Unsupported");
ItemName(CAPS_RATE,(LPSTR)b);

if(wc.dwSupport & WAVECAPS_VOLUME) lstrcpy(b,"Supported");
else lstrcpy(b,"Unsupported");
ItemName(CAPS_VOLUME,(LPSTR)b);

if(wc.dwFormats & WAVE_FORMAT_1M08) ItemOn(CAPS_MODEBASE+0);
if(wc.dwFormats & WAVE_FORMAT_1S08) ItemOn(CAPS_MODEBASE+1);
if(wc.dwFormats & WAVE_FORMAT_1M16) ItemOn(CAPS_MODEBASE+2);
if(wc.dwFormats & WAVE_FORMAT_1S16) ItemOn(CAPS_MODEBASE+3);
if(wc.dwFormats & WAVE_FORMAT_2M08) ItemOn(CAPS_MODEBASE+4);
if(wc.dwFormats & WAVE_FORMAT_2S08) ItemOn(CAPS_MODEBASE+5);
if(wc.dwFormats & WAVE_FORMAT_2M16) ItemOn(CAPS_MODEBASE+6);
if(wc.dwFormats & WAVE_FORMAT_2S16) ItemOn(CAPS_MODEBASE+7);
if(wc.dwFormats & WAVE_FORMAT_4M08) ItemOn(CAPS_MODEBASE+8);
if(wc.dwFormats & WAVE_FORMAT_4S08) ItemOn(CAPS_MODEBASE+9);
if(wc.dwFormats & WAVE_FORMAT_4M16) ItemOn(CAPS_MODEBASE+10);
if(wc.dwFormats & WAVE_FORMAT_4S16) ItemOn(CAPS_MODEBASE+11);

#if USE_SOUNDPLAYSOUND
ItemName(CAPS_PLAYTYPE,(LPSTR)"Playing with sndPlaySound");
#endif
#if USE_MCICALLS
```

```
                ItemName(CAPS_PLAYTYPE,(LPSTR)"Playing with MCI calls");
                #endif
                #if USE_WAVEOUT
                ItemName(CAPS_PLAYTYPE,(LPSTR)"Playing with waveOut calls");
                #endif


            }
            else {
                waveOutGetErrorText(rtrn,(LPSTR)b,STRINGSIZE);
                DoMessage(hwnd,b);
            }
            return(TRUE);
        case WM_CTLCOLOR:
            if(HIWORD(lParam)==CTLCOLOR_STATIC ||
               HIWORD(lParam)==CTLCOLOR_DLG) {
                SetBkColor(wParam,RGB(192,192,192));
                SetTextColor(wParam,RGB(0,0,0));

                ClientToScreen(hwnd,&point);
                UnrealizeObject(GetStockObject(LTGRAY_BRUSH));
                SetBrushOrg(wParam,point.x,point.y);

                return((DWORD)GetStockObject(LTGRAY_BRUSH));

            }
            if(HIWORD(lParam)==CTLCOLOR_BTN) {
                SetBkColor(wParam,RGB(192,192,192));
                SetTextColor(wParam,RGB(0,0,0));

                ClientToScreen(hwnd,&point);
                UnrealizeObject(GetStockObject(BLACK_BRUSH));
                SetBrushOrg(wParam,point.x,point.y);

                return((DWORD)GetStockObject(BLACK_BRUSH));
            }
            break;
        case WM_COMMAND:
            switch(wParam) {
                case IDOK:
                    EndDialog(hwnd,wParam);
                    return(TRUE);
            }
            break;
    }
```

```
    return(FALSE);
}

int testdisk(int n)
{
    FILE *fp;
    char b[32];
    int r;

    SetErrorMode(1);
    sprintf(b,"%c:\\TEMP.DAT",n+'A');
    if((fp=fopen(b,"r")) != NULL) fclose(fp);

    if(_doserrno==ENOPATH) r=1;
    else r=0;

    SetErrorMode(0);
    return(r);
}

void lmemset(LPSTR s,int n,unsigned int size)
{
    unsigned int i;

    for(i=0;i<size;++i) *s++=n;
}

int lmemcmp(LPSTR d,LPSTR s,unsigned int size)
{
    unsigned int i;

    for(i=0;i<size;++i) {
        if(*d++ != *s++) return(1);
    }
    return(0);
}

void ResetSelectorList(HWND hwnd,unsigned int listbox,unsigned int pathstring)
{
    HWND dlgH;
    HCURSOR hSaveCursor,hHourGlass;
    char b[145];

    hHourGlass=LoadCursor(NULL,IDC_WAIT);
    hSaveCursor=SetCursor(hHourGlass);
```

```
    dlgH=GetDlgItem(hwnd,listbox);

    SendDlgItemMessage(hwnd,listbox,LB_RESETCONTENT,0,0L);
    getcwd(b,64);
    AnsiLower(b);
    SetDlgItemText(hwnd,pathstring,b);

    SendMessage(dlgH,WM_SETREDRAW,FALSE,0L);

    lstrcpy(b,"*.");
    lstrcat(b,FILE_EXTENSION);
    SendDlgItemMessage(hwnd,listbox,LB_DIR,0x0000,(long )b);

    lstrcpy(b,"*.*");
    SendDlgItemMessage(hwnd,listbox,LB_DIR,0xc010,(long )b);

    SendDlgItemMessage(hwnd,listbox,LB_SETCURSEL,0,0L);

    SendMessage(dlgH,WM_SETREDRAW,TRUE,0L);

    SetCursor(hSaveCursor);
}


int GetInfo(FILEINFO far *fi,LPSTR path,unsigned int flags)
{
    HMMIO h;
    MMCKINFO mmParent,mmSub;
    unsigned int n;

    lmemset((LPSTR)fi,0,sizeof(FILEINFO));

    lstrcpy(fi->filename,path);

    if((h=mmioOpen(path,NULL,MMIO_READ)) == NULL) return(0);

    if(flags & GET_FILE_SIZE) {
        fi->filesize=mmioSeek(h,0L,SEEK_END);
        mmioSeek(h,0L,SEEK_SET);
    }

    mmParent.fccType=mmioFOURCC('W','A','V','E');
    if(mmioDescend(h,(LPMMCKINFO)&mmParent,NULL,MMIO_FINDRIFF)) {
        mmioClose(h,0);
        return(0);
    }
```

```
    mmSub.ckid=mmioFOURCC('f','m','t',' ');
    if(mmioDescend(h,(LPMMCKINFO)&mmSub,(LPMMCKINFO)&mmParent,MMIO_FINDCHUNK)) {
        mmioClose(h,0);
        return(0);
    }

    n=min((unsigned int)mmSub.cksize,sizeof(PCMWAVEFORMAT));
    if(mmioRead(h,(LPSTR)&fi->waveformat,n) != n) {
        mmioClose(h,0);
        return(0);
    }

    if(fi->waveformat.wf.wFormatTag != WAVE_FORMAT_PCM) {
        mmioClose(h,0);
        return(0);
    }

    mmioAscend(h,&mmSub,0);

    mmSub.ckid=mmioFOURCC('d','a','t','a');

    if(mmioDescend(h,(LPMMCKINFO)&mmSub,(LPMMCKINFO)&mmParent,MMIO_FINDCHUNK)) {
        mmioClose(h,0);
        return(0);
    }

    fi->datasize=mmSub.cksize;

    mmioClose(h,0);
    return(1);
}

void ShowInfo(HWND hwnd,FILEINFO far *fi)
{
    FARPROC lpfnDlgProc;

    messagehook=(LPSTR)fi;
    if((lpfnDlgProc=MakeProcInstance((FARPROC)InfoDlgProc,hInst)) != NULL) {
        DialogBox(hInst,"InfoBox",hwnd,lpfnDlgProc);
        FreeProcInstance(lpfnDlgProc);
    }
}

DWORD FAR PASCAL InfoDlgProc(HWND hwnd,WORD message,WORD wParam,LONG lParam)
{
    FILEINFO *fi;
```

```
     HWND dlgH;
     POINT point;
     HDC hdc;
     PAINTSTRUCT ps;
     char b[STRINGSIZE+1];
     double pt;
     int min,sec,hun;

     switch(message) {
         case WM_INITDIALOG:
             fi=(FILEINFO *)messagehook;

             if(fi->waveformat.wf.nChannels==1) lstrcpy(b,"Mono");
             else lstrcpy(b,"Stereo");
             ItemName(INFO_CHANNELS,b);

             wsprintf(b,"%u.%1.1u kHz",
                 (int)(fi->waveformat.wf.nSamplesPerSec / 1000L),
                 (int)(fi->waveformat.wf.nSamplesPerSec % 1000L)/100);
             ItemName(INFO_SAMPLES,b);

             wsprintf(b,"%u bits",fi->waveformat.wBitsPerSample);
             ItemName(INFO_SAMPLING,b);

             pt=(double)fi->datasize/
                 ((double)fi->waveformat.wf.nSamplesPerSec*
                 (double)fi->waveformat.wf.nBlockAlign);

             min=(int)(pt/60);
             sec=(int)(pt-60*(double)min);
             hun=(int)((pt-floor(pt))*100);
             wsprintf(b,"%02.2u:%02.2u.%02.2u",min,sec,hun);
             ItemName(INFO_PLAYTIME,b);

             wsprintf(b,"%lu bytes",fi->filesize);
             ItemName(INFO_FILESIZE,b);

             SetWindowText(hwnd,(LPSTR)fi->filename);

             return(TRUE);
         case WM_CTLCOLOR:
             if(HIWORD(lParam)==CTLCOLOR_STATIC ||
                 HIWORD(lParam)==CTLCOLOR_DLG) {
                 SetBkColor(wParam,RGB(192,192,192));
                 SetTextColor(wParam,RGB(0,0,0));
```

```
                ClientToScreen(hwnd,&point);
                UnrealizeObject(GetStockObject(LTGRAY_BRUSH));
                SetBrushOrg(wParam,point.x,point.y);

                return((DWORD)GetStockObject(LTGRAY_BRUSH));

            }
            if(HIWORD(lParam)==CTLCOLOR_BTN) {
                SetBkColor(wParam,RGB(192,192,192));
                SetTextColor(wParam,RGB(0,0,0));

                ClientToScreen(hwnd,&point);
                UnrealizeObject(GetStockObject(BLACK_BRUSH));
                SetBrushOrg(wParam,point.x,point.y);

                return((DWORD)GetStockObject(BLACK_BRUSH));
            }
            break;
        case WM_PAINT:
            hdc=BeginPaint(hwnd,&ps);
            fi=(FILEINFO *)messagehook;

            DrawWave(hdc,INFO_WAVELEFT,INFO_WAVETOP,(LPSTR)fi->filename);
            EndPaint(hwnd,&ps);
            break;
        case WM_COMMAND:
            switch(wParam) {
                case IDOK:
                    EndDialog(hwnd,wParam);
                    return(TRUE);
            }
            break;
    }

    return(FALSE);
}

int DrawWave(HDC hdc,unsigned int x,unsigned int y,LPSTR path)
{
    HMMIO h;
    MMCKINFO mmParent,mmSub;
    GLOBALHANDLE gh;
    PCMWAVEFORMAT waveformat;
    char huge *p;
    unsigned long nextsample;
```

```
long afactor;
unsigned int i,n,amp;
int huge *ip;

SelectObject(hdc,GetStockObject(BLACK_PEN));
SelectObject(hdc,GetStockObject(WHITE_BRUSH));
Rectangle(hdc,x,y,x+INFO_WAVEWIDE,y+INFO_WAVEDEEP);

if((h=mmioOpen(path,NULL,MMIO_READ)) == NULL) return(0);

mmParent.fccType=mmioFOURCC('W','A','V','E');
if(mmioDescend(h,(LPMMCKINFO)&mmParent,NULL,MMIO_FINDRIFF)) {
    mmioClose(h,0);
    return(0);
}

mmSub.ckid=mmioFOURCC('f','m','t',' ');
if(mmioDescend(h,(LPMMCKINFO)&mmSub,(LPMMCKINFO)&mmParent,MMIO_FINDCHUNK)) {
    mmioClose(h,0);
    return(0);
}

n=min((unsigned int)mmSub.cksize,sizeof(PCMWAVEFORMAT));
if(mmioRead(h,(LPSTR)&waveformat,n) != n) {
    mmioClose(h,0);
    return(0);
}

if(waveformat.wf.wFormatTag != WAVE_FORMAT_PCM) {
    mmioClose(h,0);
    return(0);
}

mmioAscend(h,&mmSub,0);

mmSub.ckid=mmioFOURCC('d','a','t','a');
if(mmioDescend(h,(LPMMCKINFO)&mmSub,(LPMMCKINFO)&mmParent,MMIO_FINDCHUNK)) {
    mmioClose(h,0);
    return(0);
}

if(waveformat.wBitsPerSample==8 && waveformat.wf.nChannels==1) {
    nextsample=mmSub.cksize/(long)INFO_WAVEWIDE;
    afactor=2L*(255L/(long)INFO_WAVEDEEP);
}
```

```
        else if(waveformat.wBitsPerSample==8 && waveformat.wf.nChannels==2) {
            nextsample=2L*((mmSub.cksize/2L)/(long)INFO_WAVEWIDE);
            afactor=2L*(255L/(long)INFO_WAVEDEEP);
        }
        else if(waveformat.wBitsPerSample > 8 && waveformat.wf.nChannels==1) {
            nextsample=2L*((mmSub.cksize/(long)INFO_WAVEWIDE)) & 0xfffffffeL;
            afactor=2L*(65535L/(long)INFO_WAVEDEEP);
        }
        else {
            nextsample=4L*((mmSub.cksize/4L)/(long)INFO_WAVEWIDE) & 0xfffffffeL;
            afactor=2L*(65535L/(long)INFO_WAVEDEEP);
        }

        if((gh=GlobalAlloc(GMEM_MOVEABLE,mmSub.cksize)) != NULL) {
            if((p=(char huge *)GlobalLock(gh)) != NULL) {
                if(mmioRead(h,p,mmSub.cksize)==mmSub.cksize) {
                    for(i=0;i<INFO_WAVEWIDE;++i) {
                        ip=(int huge *)p;
                        if(waveformat.wBitsPerSample==8 && waveformat.wf.nChannels==1)
                            amp=(unsigned int)max(labs(((long)p[0]-128L) / afactor),1L);
                        else if(waveformat.wBitsPerSample==8 &&
                            waveformat.wf.nChannels==2)
                            amp=(unsigned int)max(labs(((long)p[0]-128L+
                            (long)p[1]-128L)/2)/afactor,1L);
                        else if(waveformat.wBitsPerSample > 8 &&
                          waveformat.wf.nChannels==1)
                            amp=(unsigned int)max(labs((long)ip[0]/afactor),1L);
                        else
                            amp=(unsigned int)max(labs((((long)ip[0]+
                            (long)ip[1])/2)/afactor),1L);

                        MoveTo(hdc,x+i,y+(INFO_WAVEDEEP/2)-amp);
                        LineTo(hdc,x+i,y+(INFO_WAVEDEEP/2)+amp);
                            p+=nextsample;
                    }
                }
                GlobalUnlock(gh);
            }
            GlobalFree(gh);
        }

    mmioClose(h,0);
    return(1);
}

void ShowCurrentStats(HWND hwnd,unsigned int listbox,unsigned int textbox)
```

```
{
    FILEINFO fi;
    HWND dlgH;
    double pt;
    char b[STRINGSIZE+1];
    long l;
    int min,sec,hun;

    b[0]=0;
    if((l=SendDlgItemMessage(hwnd,listbox,LB_GETCURSEL,0,0L)) != LB_ERR) {
        SendDlgItemMessage(hwnd,listbox,LB_GETTEXT,(unsigned int)l,(DWORD)b);
        if(b[0] != '[') {
            if(GetInfo(&fi,b,0)) {

                pt=(double)fi.datasize/
                    ((double)fi.waveformat.wf.nChannels*
                     (double)fi.waveformat.wf.nSamplesPerSec*
                     (double)fi.waveformat.wf.nBlockAlign);

                min=(int)(pt/60);
                sec=(int)(pt-60*(double)min);
                hun=(int)((pt-floor(pt))*100);

                wsprintf(b,"%u kHz - %02.2u:%02.2u.%02.2u",
                    (int)(fi.waveformat.wf.nSamplesPerSec / 1000L),
                    min,sec,hun);
            }
        }
    }
    ItemName(textbox,b);
}

#if USE_WAVEOUT
void SetCurrentVolume(unsigned int n)
{
    unsigned int i;
    currentvolume=n;

    if(!waveOutGetID(hwaveout,(unsigned int far *)&i)) {
        waveOutSetVolume(i,(long)(SCROLL_RANGE-n)*(0xffffL/(long)SCROLL_RANGE));
    }
}
#endif
```

In addition to WAVEPLAY.CPP, you'll also need WAVEPLAY.RC, which is the resource script definition. This is almost the complete resource definition for the program—it expects to find HELLO.WAV in the same directory as itself. This is the wave file that plays when you open the About box of WAVEPLAY. You can use any wave file you like in this capacity—there are hundreds to choose from on the CD-ROM. The WAVEPLAY.RC file is illustrated in FIG. 2-9. Finally, you'll need the WAVEPLAY.DEF file, shown below:

```
NAME          WAVEPLAY
DESCRIPTION   'Wave Player'
EXETYPE       WINDOWS
CODE          PRELOAD MOVEABLE
DATA          PRELOAD MOVEABLE MULTIPLE
SEGMENTS      WM__TEXT LOADONCALL
HEAPSIZE      8192
STACKSIZE     8192
```

and a project file, shown in FIG. 2-10, to put the whole works together. Note that these files assume you'll be compiling WAVEPLAY using Borland C++ for Windows, running with the integrated development environment. If you use a different compiler, you'll probably have to create a MAKE file and modify the DEF file somewhat. You can find all the files to compile WAVEPLAY in the SOURCES subdirectory of the CDROM that accompanies this book.

2-9 The resource script for the wave player, WAVEPLAY.RC.

```
MainScreen DIALOG 9, 24, 200, 176
STYLE WS_POPUP | WS_CAPTION | WS_SYSMENU | WS_MINIMIZEBOX | WS_MAXIMIZEBOX
CAPTION "Wave Player"
MENU MainMenu
BEGIN
  CONTROL "", 201, "LISTBOX", LBS_STANDARD | WS_CHILD | WS_VISIBLE, 12, 32, 76, 112
  LTEXT " Wave files", -1, 8, 8, 84, 8, WS_CHILD | WS_VISIBLE | WS_GROUP
  CONTROL "", -1, "BorShade", BSS_GROUP | WS_CHILD | WS_VISIBLE, 8, 16, 84, 132
  CONTROL "", -1, "BorShade", BSS_GROUP | WS_CHILD | WS_VISIBLE, 8, 156, 84, 16
  LTEXT "", 202, 12, 160, 76, 8, WS_CHILD | WS_VISIBLE | WS_GROUP
  LTEXT "", 203, 12, 20, 75, 8, WS_CHILD | WS_VISIBLE | WS_GROUP
  CONTROL "", 204, "BorShade", 3 | WS_CHILD | WS_VISIBLE, 100, 0, 2, 176
  DEFPUSHBUTTON "Play", 101, 108, 16, 32, 20, WS_CHILD | WS_VISIBLE | WS_TABSTOP
  PUSHBUTTON "Stop", 102, 108, 44, 32, 20, WS_CHILD | WS_VISIBLE | WS_TABSTOP
  PUSHBUTTON "Delete", 104, 108, 72, 32, 20, WS_CHILD | WS_VISIBLE | WS_TABSTOP
  PUSHBUTTON "Get Info", 103, 108, 100, 32, 20, WS_CHILD | WS_VISIBLE | WS_TABSTOP
  PUSHBUTTON "Quit", 107, 108, 128, 32, 20, WS_CHILD | WS_VISIBLE | WS_TABSTOP
  CONTROL "", 204, "BorShade", 3 | WS_CHILD | WS_VISIBLE, 148, 0, 2, 176
  CONTROL "", -1, "BorShade", BSS_GROUP | WS_CHILD | WS_VISIBLE, 156, 16, 32, 132
  SCROLLBAR 401, 168, 24, 9, 100, SBS_VERT | WS_CHILD | WS_VISIBLE | WS_DISABLED
  CONTROL "Volume", 501, "STATIC", SS_CENTER | WS_CHILD | WS_VISIBLE |
    WS_DISABLED | WS_GROUP, 160, 128, 24, 8
```

2-9 Continued.
```
END

MainMenu MENU
BEGIN
    POPUP "&File"
    BEGIN
        MENUITEM "&Play", 101
        MENUITEM "&Stop", 102
        MENUITEM "&Get Info", 103
        MENUITEM "&Delete", 104
        MENUITEM "&About", 105
        MENUITEM "&Capabilities", 106
        MENUITEM SEPARATOR
        MENUITEM "E&xit", 107
    END

END

AboutBox DIALOG 18, 18, 156, 104
STYLE WS_POPUP | WS_CAPTION
CAPTION "About Wave Player..."
BEGIN
    CONTROL "", 102, "BorShade", BSS_GROUP | WS_CHILD | WS_VISIBLE | WS_TABSTOP,
        8, 8, 140, 68
    LTEXT "Wave Player 1.0\nCopyright (c) 1993\nAlchemy Mindworks Inc.\n"
        "This program is part of the book Multimedia Programming for Windows "
        "by Steven William Rimmer, published by Windcrest (Book 4484).",
        -1, 12, 12, 128, 60, WS_CHILD | WS_VISIBLE | WS_GROUP
    DEFPUSHBUTTON "Ok", IDOK, 116, 80, 32, 20, WS_CHILD | WS_VISIBLE | WS_TABSTOP
END

WavePlayer ICON
BEGIN
    '00 00 01 00 01 00 20 20 10 00 00 00 00 00 E8 02'
    '00 00 16 00 00 00 28 00 00 00 20 00 00 00 40 00'
    '00 00 01 00 04 00 00 00 00 00 80 02 00 00 00 00'
    '00 00 00 00 00 00 00 00 00 00 00 00 00 00 00 00'
    '00 00 00 00 80 00 00 80 00 00 00 80 80 00 80 00'
    '00 00 80 00 80 00 80 80 00 00 80 80 80 00 C0 C0'
    'C0 00 00 00 FF 00 00 FF 00 00 00 FF FF 00 FF 00'
    '00 00 FF 00 FF 00 FF FF 00 00 FF FF FF 00 44 44'
    '44 44 44 44 44 F4 4E 44 E4 4E 44 E4 4E 44 44 44'
    '44 44 44 44 44 4E 44 E4 4E 44 E4 4E 44 E4 44 44'
    '44 44 44 44 4F 44 E4 4E 44 E4 4E 44 E4 4E 44 44'
    '44 44 44 44 44 E4 4E 44 E4 4E 44 E4 4E 44 44 44'
```

```
          '44 44 44 44 F4 4E 44 E4 4E 44 E4 4E 44 E4 44 44'
          '44 44 44 44 4E 44 E4 4E 44 E4 4E 44 E4 4E 44 44'
          '44 44 44 4F 44 E4 4E 44 E4 4E 44 E4 4E 44 44 44'
          '44 44 44 44 E4 4E 44 E4 4E 44 E4 4E 44 E4 44 44'
          '44 44 44 F4 4E 44 E4 4E 44 E4 4E 44 E4 4E 44 44'
          '44 44 44 4E 44 E4 4E 44 E4 4E 44 E4 4E 44 44 44'
          '44 44 4F 44 4E 44 E4 4E 44 E4 4E 44 E4 44 44 44'
          '77 44 44 E7 7E 44 E4 7E 77 E4 4E 44 E4 4E 44 44'
          'FF 77 77 FF FF 77 77 FF FF 77 74 E4 4E 44 44 44'
          '44 FF FF 44 44 FF FF 44 44 FF F7 4E 44 E4 44 44'
          '44 44 44 77 77 44 44 77 77 44 4E 44 E4 4E 44 44'
          '44 44 77 FF FF 77 77 FF FF 77 74 E4 4E 44 44 44'
          '44 44 FF 44 44 FF FF 44 44 FF F7 4E 44 E4 44 44'
          '44 44 44 77 77 44 44 77 77 44 4E 44 E4 4E 44 44'
          '44 44 44 FF FF 77 77 FF FF 77 74 E4 4E 44 44 44'
          '44 44 44 44 44 FF FF 44 44 FF F7 4E 44 E4 44 44'
          '44 44 44 44 77 44 44 77 77 44 4E 44 E4 4E 44 44'
          '44 44 44 44 FF 77 77 FF FF 77 74 E4 4E 44 44 44'
          '44 44 44 44 44 FF FF 44 44 FF F7 4E 44 E4 44 44'
          '44 44 44 44 44 44 44 77 77 44 4E 44 E4 4E 44 44'
          '44 44 44 44 44 47 77 FF FF 77 74 E4 4E 44 44 44'
          '44 44 44 44 44 4F FF 44 44 FF F7 4E 44 E4 44 44'
          '44 44 44 44 44 44 44 44 44 44 4E 44 E4 4E 44 44'
          '44 44 44 44 44 44 44 44 44 44 E4 4E 44 44 44'
          '44 44 44 44 44 44 44 44 44 44 4E 44 E4 4E 44 44'
          '44 44 44 44 44 44 44 44 44 44 44 E4 4E 44 44 44'
          '44 44 44 44 44 44 44 44 44 44 44 44 4E 44 44 44'
          '44 44 44 44 44 44 44 44 44 44 44 44 44 E4 00 00'
          '00 00 00 00 00 00 00 00 00 00 00 00 00 00 00 00'
          '00 00 00 00 00 00 00 00 00 00 00 00 00 00 00 00'
          '00 00 00 00 00 00 00 00 00 00 00 00 00 00 00 00'
          '00 00 00 00 00 00 00 00 00 00 00 00 00 00 00 00'
          '00 00 00 00 00 00 00 00 00 00 00 00 00 00 00 00'
          '00 00 00 00 00 00 00 00 00 00 00 00 00 00 00 00'
          '00 00 00 00 00 00 00 00 00 00 00 00 00 00 00 00'
          '00 00 00 00 00 00 00 00 00 00 00 00 00 00 00 00'
END

InfoBox DIALOG 11, 36, 273, 104
STYLE DS_MODALFRAME | WS_POPUP | WS_CAPTION
CAPTION "Information"
BEGIN
    CONTROL "", 201, "BorShade", BSS_GROUP | WS_CHILD | WS_VISIBLE, 4, 8, 124, 64
    LTEXT "", 101, 68, 12, 56, 8, WS_CHILD | WS_VISIBLE | WS_GROUP
    LTEXT "", 102, 68, 24, 56, 8, WS_CHILD | WS_VISIBLE | WS_GROUP
    LTEXT "", 103, 68, 36, 56, 8, WS_CHILD | WS_VISIBLE | WS_GROUP
```

```
  CONTROL "", 104, "STATIC", SS_LEFTNOWORDWRAP | WS_CHILD | WS_VISIBLE | WS_GROUP,
      68, 48, 56, 8
  CONTROL "", 105, "STATIC", SS_LEFTNOWORDWRAP | WS_CHILD | WS_VISIBLE | WS_GROUP,
      68, 60, 56, 8
  RTEXT "Channels:", -1, 8, 12, 52, 8,
      SS_RIGHT | WS_CHILD | WS_VISIBLE | WS_GROUP
  RTEXT "Sample rate:", -1, 8, 24, 52, 8,
      SS_RIGHT | WS_CHILD | WS_VISIBLE | WS_GROUP
  RTEXT "Resolution:", -1, 8, 36, 52, 8,
      SS_RIGHT | WS_CHILD | WS_VISIBLE | WS_GROUP
  RTEXT "Playing time:", -1, 8, 48, 52, 8,
      SS_RIGHT | WS_CHILD | WS_VISIBLE | WS_GROUP
  RTEXT "File size:", -1, 8, 60, 52, 8,
      SS_RIGHT | WS_CHILD | WS_VISIBLE | WS_GROUP
  DEFPUSHBUTTON "Ok", IDOK, 236, 80, 32, 20,
      WS_CHILD | WS_VISIBLE | WS_TABSTOP
  CONTROL "", 106, "BorShade", 3 | WS_CHILD | WS_VISIBLE, 136, 0, 1, 104
END
YesNoBox DIALOG 72, 72, 144, 64
STYLE DS_MODALFRAME | WS_POPUP | WS_CAPTION
CAPTION "Message"
BEGIN
  CONTROL "", 102, "BorShade", BSS_GROUP | WS_CHILD | WS_VISIBLE, 4, 8, 136, 28
  CTEXT "", 101, 8, 12, 128, 20, WS_CHILD | WS_VISIBLE | WS_GROUP
  DEFPUSHBUTTON "Yes", IDYES, 108, 40, 32, 20, WS_CHILD | WS_VISIBLE | WS_TABSTOP
  PUSHBUTTON "No", IDNO, 68, 40, 32, 20, WS_CHILD | WS_VISIBLE | WS_TABSTOP
END
CapsBox DIALOG 18, 18, 264, 164
STYLE WS_POPUP | WS_CAPTION
CAPTION "Device Capabilities"
BEGIN
  DEFPUSHBUTTON "Ok", IDOK, 116, 136, 32, 20, WS_CHILD | WS_VISIBLE | WS_TABSTOP
  LTEXT "Manufacturer:", -1, 12, 12, 52, 8, WS_CHILD | WS_VISIBLE | WS_GROUP
  LTEXT "Product:", -1, 12, 24, 52, 8, WS_CHILD | WS_VISIBLE | WS_GROUP
  LTEXT "Driver version:", -1, 12, 36, 52, 8, WS_CHILD | WS_VISIBLE | WS_GROUP
  LTEXT "Channels:", -1, 12, 48, 52, 8, WS_CHILD | WS_VISIBLE | WS_GROUP
  CONTROL "", -1, "BorShade", BSS_GROUP | WS_CHILD | WS_VISIBLE, 8, 8, 140, 52
  LTEXT "", 101, 72, 12, 68, 8, WS_CHILD | WS_VISIBLE | WS_GROUP
  LTEXT "", 102, 72, 24, 68, 8, WS_CHILD | WS_VISIBLE | WS_GROUP
  LTEXT "", 103, 72, 36, 68, 8, WS_CHILD | WS_VISIBLE | WS_GROUP
  LTEXT "", 104, 72, 48, 68, 8, WS_CHILD | WS_VISIBLE | WS_GROUP
  LTEXT "Pitch control:", -1, 12, 72, 52, 8, WS_CHILD | WS_VISIBLE | WS_GROUP
  LTEXT "Rate control:", -1, 12, 84, 52, 8, WS_CHILD | WS_VISIBLE | WS_GROUP
  LTEXT "Volume control:", -1, 12, 96, 52, 8, WS_CHILD | WS_VISIBLE | WS_GROUP
```

```
  CONTROL "", -1, "BorShade", BSS_GROUP | WS_CHILD | WS_VISIBLE, 8, 68, 140, 40
  LTEXT "", 201, 72, 72, 68, 8, WS_CHILD | WS_VISIBLE | WS_GROUP
  LTEXT "", 202, 72, 84, 68, 8, WS_CHILD | WS_VISIBLE | WS_GROUP
  LTEXT "", 203, 72, 96, 68, 8, WS_CHILD | WS_VISIBLE | WS_GROUP
  CONTROL "", -1, "BorShade", BSS_GROUP | WS_CHILD | WS_VISIBLE, 156, 8, 100, 148
  CONTROL "11.025 kHz, Mono, 8-bit", 301, "STATIC",
      SS_LEFT | WS_CHILD | WS_VISIBLE | WS_DISABLED | WS_GROUP, 160, 12, 88, 8
  CONTROL "11.025 kHz, Stereo, 8-bit", 302, "STATIC",
      SS_LEFT | WS_CHILD | WS_VISIBLE | WS_DISABLED | WS_GROUP, 160, 24, 88, 8
  CONTROL "11.025 kHz, Mono, 16-bit", 303, "STATIC",
      SS_LEFT | WS_CHILD | WS_VISIBLE | WS_DISABLED | WS_GROUP, 160, 36, 88, 8
  CONTROL "11.025 kHz, Stereo, 16-bit", 304, "STATIC",
      SS_LEFT | WS_CHILD | WS_VISIBLE | WS_DISABLED | WS_GROUP, 160, 48, 88, 8
  CONTROL "22.05 kHz, Mono, 8-bit", 305, "STATIC",
      SS_LEFT | WS_CHILD | WS_VISIBLE | WS_DISABLED | WS_GROUP, 160, 60, 88, 8
  CONTROL "22.05 kHz, Stereo, 8-bit", 306, "STATIC",
      SS_LEFT | WS_CHILD | WS_VISIBLE | WS_DISABLED | WS_GROUP, 160, 72, 88, 8
  CONTROL "22.05 kHz, Mono,16-bit", 307, "STATIC",
      SS_LEFT | WS_CHILD | WS_VISIBLE | WS_DISABLED | WS_GROUP, 160, 84, 88, 8
  CONTROL "22.05 kHz, Stereo, 16-bit", 308, "STATIC",
      SS_LEFT | WS_CHILD | WS_VISIBLE | WS_DISABLED | WS_GROUP, 160, 96, 88, 8
  CONTROL "44.1 kHz, Mono, 8-bit", 309, "STATIC",
      SS_LEFT | WS_CHILD | WS_VISIBLE | WS_DISABLED | WS_GROUP, 160, 108, 88, 8
  CONTROL "44.1 kHz, Stereo, 8-bit", 310, "STATIC",
      SS_LEFT | WS_CHILD | WS_VISIBLE | WS_DISABLED | WS_GROUP, 160, 120, 88, 8
  CONTROL "44.1 kHz, Mono, 16-bit", 311, "STATIC",
      SS_LEFT | WS_CHILD | WS_VISIBLE | WS_DISABLED | WS_GROUP, 160, 132, 88, 8
  CONTROL "44.1 kHz, Stereo, 16-bit", 312, "STATIC",
      SS_LEFT | WS_CHILD | WS_VISIBLE | WS_DISABLED | WS_GROUP, 160, 144, 88, 8
  CONTROL "", -1, "BorShade", BSS_GROUP | WS_CHILD | WS_VISIBLE, 8, 116, 140, 16
  LTEXT "", 401, 12, 120, 128, 8, WS_CHILD | WS_VISIBLE | WS_GROUP
END

Hello RCDATA "HELLO.WAV"

MessageBox DIALOG 72, 72, 144, 72
STYLE DS_MODALFRAME | WS_POPUP | WS_CAPTION
CAPTION "Message"
BEGIN
  CONTROL "", 102, "BorShade", BSS_GROUP | WS_CHILD | WS_VISIBLE, 4, 8, 136, 36
  CTEXT "", 101, 8, 12, 128, 28, WS_CHILD | WS_VISIBLE | WS_GROUP
  DEFPUSHBUTTON "Ok", IDOK, 108, 48, 32, 20, WS_CHILD | WS_VISIBLE | WS_TABSTOP
END
```

```
  -                                Borland C++                              ▼ ▲
 File  Edit  Search  Run  Compile  Project  Browse  Options  Window              Help
 ? ►→ ☑ 🖉 ⊕ ⊟ 🗏 🔓 🔊
```

```
  ⊖                             Project: waveplay                            ▼ ▲
 File Name       Lines    Code    Data    Location
 waveplay.cpp    1260     9046    1938    .
 waveplay.rc     n/a      n/a     n/a     .
 waveplay.def    n/a      n/a     n/a     .
 bwcc.lib        n/a      n/a     n/a     ..\lib
 mmsystem.lib    n/a      n/a     n/a     ..\lib
```

2-10   The project file for the wave player, WAVEPLAY.PRJ.

The first thing to note about WAVEPLAY.CPP is the three defines at the top of the source listing. You should set one of them true to specify the functions you want to use for playing wave files. The characteristics of the resulting application will vary somewhat, depending on which one you choose. Specifically, if USE_SOUNDPLAYSOUND is true, WAVEPLAY will be limited to playing wave files no larger than about 100 kilobytes. Its Play button and list box won't be disabled during play, as sndPlaySound doesn't inform the function that called it when it has finished playing. If you define USE_MCI-CALLS true, the WAVEPLAY application will play wave files of any size.

Finally, if you define USE_WAVEOUT true, the WAVEPLAY application will be limited to playing wave files that fit in the available memory of your system. However, it will support setting the playback volume, and the main WAVEPLAY window will expand somewhat to include a scroll-bar volume control.

The WAVEPLAY main window is actually a dialog box, as defined in WAVEPLAY.RC, rather than a conventional window summoned forth by CreateWindow. The WinMain function illustrates how this is handled. Creating modestly-sized applications this way eliminates a lot of the head-scratching involved in defining a window in C.

The main message handler in WAVEPLAY, the SelectProc function, is where most of the interesting things happen. Its contents will change slightly, depending on the wave player functions you define for WAVEPLAY. Much of this can be seen in the first message cases of the main switch statement. These handle the messages sent back by the wave-player function when a sound terminates, as was discussed earlier in this chapter.

If USE_WAVEOUT is defined, a case to handle WM_VSCROLL messages will be added to SelectProc. This deals with the scroll bar that serves as a volume control. There's a slight cosmetic inconsistency in this application of scroll bars—this one is upside down. In most cases you'd want a vertical scroll bar's value to increase as you drag its thumb down. In a conventional analog sliding volume control, you'd expect the opposite to happen—the level of the sound should increase as the slider of the control moves up. Since Windows doesn't provide for a way to invert a scroll bar, however, the one in WAVEPLAY is used in the normal manner and its value is fiddled after the fact. The actual fiddling is handled in the SetCurrentVolume function, down at the end of WAVEPLAY.CPP.

You should keep in mind that, for this reason, passing zero to SetCurrentVolume will tell it to turn the sound full on. This corresponds to the top of the scroll bar's travel.

If you define USE_MCICALLS as true, the case added to SelectProc will be significantly simpler, as MCI calls don't assume you'll buffer the wave file being played yourself. All you have to do in this case is close down the MCI sound device when an MM_MCINOTIFY message shows up.

The case that deals with WM_CTLCOLOR messages is wholly cosmetic. It causes the background of the main window to be gray, rather than white, by returning the handle to the stock LTGRAY_BRUSH object when the window is first being constructed. You can achieve much the same result by using the BorDlg class in dialogs created with Resource Workshop—this will cause your dialog boxes to have a gray, textured background. I've handled the problem of getting things grayed out this way to allow the code to be used with Microsoft's languages as well, which don't support the Borland custom controls.

In addition, of course, you can change the dialog background to some other color this way, that is, by passing pen and brush handles that are something other than gray.

You might well ask why dialog boxes and application windows should be gray. I can't say that I know, although most of them are at the moment. By comparison, the traditional white backgrounds of older Windows software look a bit dated.

The WM_INITDIALOG case in SelectProc deals with setting up the dialog before its window is actually drawn. There are a number of things handled by this case. The call to LoadIcon and SetClassWord defines the icon for this application, something you must do explicitly if your application's main window is actually a dialog box. The icon will appear when the application is minimized.

The ResetSelectorList call fetches the names and other entries for the main list box. It also selects the first filename in the list. Having done so, the ShowCurrentStats function will display the playing time of the selected file under the list box. The call to waveOutSetVolume will establish the default volume level at maximum, something applications that use multimedia wave-player calls probably should do, lest it have been turned down and left that way by a previous application. Once again, this assumes that the wave player to be used will be the "zero'th" wave-player device in the system.

Additional items will be added to the WM__INITDIALOG case, depending on which of the wave player options you compile WAVEPLAY to use. For the USE__WAVEOUT and USE__MCICALLS options, several menu and dialog items will be enabled or disabled. The USE__WAVEOUT calls must set up the volume-control scroll bar. The USE__MCICALLS and USE__SOUNDPLAYSOUND options adjust the size of the WAVEPLAY window so that the volume control area won't be visible, as these configurations don't allow for controlling the playback volume.

The WM__COMMAND case handles messages generated by the menu items and buttons in the main window. The buttons duplicate menu items—it's arguably easier to use the buttons, but omitting a menu interface from a Windows application is almost certain to call down the wrath of Windows purists. In order to avoid duplicating the cases for functions that are handled by both buttons and menu items, the buttons and menu items in question have duplicate resource ID numbers. As such, clicking on the Play button or selecting the Play item from the File menu of the WAVEPLAY main window will both generate the same wParam value for the message they result in.

The MAIN__LIST case of the the WM__COMMAND message handler takes care of clicks in the main list box. Whenever an item is selected, indicated by LBN__SELCHANGE in the high-order word of lParam, this case will call ShowCurrentStats to display the playing time of the selected wave file. If you double click on an item, the DlgDirSelect function will decide whether it's a filename or a drive or directory entry. Double clicking on a filename will cause a WM__COMMAND message to be sent with MAIN__PLAY as its wParam value, essentially pushing the Play button for you. Double clicking on a drive or a directory entry will cause WAVEPLAY to change to wherever you've told it and reinitialize its main list box.

The aforementioned Windows purists—or Windows "thought police," depending on how pure you feel about Windows—will probably argue that this all could have been handled using the File Open common dialog. This sort of argument is usually put forth on the premise that Windows applications should seek to maintain a consistent user interface. The main list box in WAVEPLAY is, after all, just a way to open files.

In designing WAVEPLAY, I decided that having to open a dialog box every time I wanted to play a ten-second sound bite seemed a bit excessive. You are, of course, free to disagree with this premise. Source code is infinitely malleable.

The MAIN_STOP case deals with requests to tell the currently playing sound to shut up and go home. As has been touched on earlier in this chapter, the mechanics of shutting off a sound vary with the procedure used to initiate it. Note that for both the USE_MCICALLS and USE_WAVEOUT options, shutting down the sound will generate the appropriate message—either MM_MCINOTIFY or MM_WOM_DONE—to tell SelectProc that silence has returned. In effect, this is what would have happened if the sound had been allowed to terminate normally—it just happens a little sooner. This being the case, there's no need to explicitly close the drivers or free up any buffers in MAIN_STOP.

The MAIN_DELETE case handles deleting the currently selected wave file, should you find that it's rude, badly recorded, or merely not worthy of your speakers. It uses the YesNo function to ask whether you really have it in for the sound in question. We'll discuss YesNo in a moment.

The MAIN_PLAY case of the WM_COMMAND handler deals with requests to play a wave file—either by clicking on the Play button, selecting the Play item from the file menu, or double clicking on a filename in the main list box. It retrieves the currently selected filename and passes it to PlaySound, which actually does all the work. The contents of PlaySound will vary depending on the playing function you've selected at the top of WAVE-PLAY.CPP. We'll look at the mechanics of the PlaySound function presently, although you're probably familiar with most of it by now.

If PlaySound successfully starts a wave file playing, the Play button and Play item in the File menu and the main list box will be disabled and the Stop button and Stop item of the File menu will be enabled. These calls are compiled only if you've selected the USE_MCICALLS or USE_WAVE-OUT options.

The MAIN_GETINFO case fetches the file to get information about in much the same way that MAIN_PLAY does, and passes it to the GetInfo function.

The PlaySound functions

There are three distinct variations on the PlaySound function in WAVE-PLAY, to be compiled based on the settings of the three defines at the top of the source code. All three embody the principles discussed throughout the first part of this chapter. The first handles playing wave files using waveOut calls.

The steps involved in playing a wave file with waveOut calls can be seen pretty clearly in the first of the PlaySound functions. The file is opened for reading with mmioOpen, and its fmt and data chunks are read. The data chunk contents are stored in a global buffer referenced by wavehandle. A suitable wave-player device is opened with waveOutOpen, in this case using the WAVE_MAPPER constant to allow Windows to find an appropriate device. The wave header is prepared with waveOutPrepareHeader and the wave is played by a call to waveOutWrite.

You'll note that the hwnd argument to PlaySound is passed to wave-OutOpen. This represents the window that waveOut will notify when the sound about to be played has finished so the header can be unprepared, the sound driver closed, and any buffers involved deallocated.

The PlaySound function for use with MCI calls is predictably simpler, as most of what was done explicitly in the waveOut version of the function is handled behind your back by MCI. The whole function consists of one call to mciSendCommand to open the waveaudio driver, and a second call to actually play the wave file. The MCI drivers will fetch the wave-file data, buffer it as it's read into memory, and so on. The hwnd window handle to notify is passed to mciSendMessage when the wave file is played, which is how MCI tells the SelectProc window when the sound being played is done. The version of PlaySound for use with sndPlaySound is all but nonexistent, of course.

The support functions

The AboutDlgProc function is the message handler for the WAVEPLAY About box, and in most cases it would be pretty pedestrian. However, it serves to illustrate some real-world code for fetching and playing wave files that have been stored as program resources. I discussed the details of handling wave files in this way earlier in this chapter—the AboutDlgProc function illustrates how to actually work with them.

The DoMessage and YesNo functions implement message boxes—the former to display a message and the latter to prompt for a decision. These could have been handled with the Windows MessageBox call, and users of Microsoft's development languages might want to modify the WAVE-PLAY.CPP file to do so. They're implemented as custom dialogs here to keep their appearance consistent with that of the rest of the WAVEPLAY application.

The ShowCaps and CapsDlgProc functions will display the wave-player device capabilities for the first audio device in your system, as discussed earlier in this chapter. Virtually all its work is done in its WM__INITDIA-LOG case, reading a WAVEOUTCAPS object with waveOutGetDevCaps and formatting the data found therein.

The testdisk function makes sure that the drive specified in its argument is actually on line. It's used by SelectProc to make sure someone hasn't attempted to access a floppy drive with no floppy in it, for example. As an aside, if you'll be writing applications using the Borland custom controls to provide bitmapped buttons for your dialog boxes, you might want to see what happens if you supply the constants IDABORT, IDRETRY, and IDIGNORE as resource ID values for Borland buttons. The IDRETRY button, a slot machine, and IDIGNORE button, a 55 mph speed-limit sign, are particularly well done. While WAVEPLAY as it stands simply complains that a drive is off line using DoMessage, you can implement these buttons for a more useful message box.

The ResetSelectorList function deletes the contents of the list box passed to it—typically the list box in the WAVEPLAY main window—and loads it up with the wave files and drive and directory entries for the current directory. It's called when WAVEPLAY first starts up, and whenever the current drive or directory changes.

The GetInfo function gets the fmt chunk of a wave file and displays information about it, something else I expounded upon earlier in this chapter. The InfoDlgProc illustrates how the information in a PCMWAVEFORMAT chunk can be displayed.

If you've been working through the code in WAVEPLAY, you'll have noticed the use of messagehook to communicate with some of the dialog box message handlers. This is simply a far pointer defined as a global variable. Windows does not provide a particularly elegant way to pass a pointer to a dialog box's message handler from the function that instigates the dialog box, hence this somewhat elementary approach to the problem. While intended to pass strings to the dialog handler for DoMessage and YesNo, it has also been pressed into service to pass a pointer to a PCMWAVEFORMAT object to InfoDlgProc, an analogous situation.

The DrawWave code is among the more visually interesting functions of WAVEPLAY. It was responsible for generating the envelope graph back in FIG. 2-5. In fact, the procedure for doing so is quite simple if you understand the structure of wave-data samples, as discussed earlier in this chapter. The DrawWave code simply draws a vertical line representing the relative amplitude of selected samples along the sampled sound.

There's a bit of fudging involved in DrawWave, as the absolute magnitude of 16-bit samples will be 256 times that of 8-bit samples, for example, and stereo samples must be averaged into a single line. As it's implemented here, DrawWave is pretty elementary. It displays selected samples, rather than integrating all the samples it skips over into a single value, something that would create a "fatter" and perhaps more accurate display. You might want to look at enhancing DrawWave if you'll be using it in your software.

The ShowCurrentStats function uses the GetInfo function to fetch information about the currently selected file and displays it in the text control below the list box in the main window of WAVEPLAY. SetCurrentVolume finally sets the playback level if you're playing wave files using the waveOut calls.

Attaching wave files to system events

One of the popular applications in which wave files have appeared, in the wake of Windows 3.1, are gadgets to make user-defined noises when dialog boxes are opened, menus popped up, things minimized or maximized, and so on. These creatures are an acquired taste, and one that I confess I've never acquired. Fully loaded with sounds, these gadgets can make a Windows session take on a carnival atmosphere, sort of a Mardi Gras in phosphor.

Mardi Gras means "fat Tuesday," suggesting a touch of vulgarity amidst the dancing and revelry. This seems an appropriate metaphor for this application of wave file sounds. You're not constrained to agree with my perception of wave files appearing throughout your Windows sessions, and to be sure, many users would not.

Windows itself offers only the most limited facilities for attaching sounds to system events, as touched on at the beginning of this chapter in the discussion of making noise with MessageBeep. If you'd like to be able to have sounds sprouting from your every mouse click and system event, you'll require a way to add this facility to Windows externally.

While it might not be immediately obvious, Windows does offer you a path to handle this. It's a bit tricky to implement, but it promises a world of opportunities for customizing the Windows environment as a whole. This section will look at an application called ATTACH, which will allow you to add wave file sounds to 18 common Windows system events. Once you understand what it's up to, you'll be able to expand this list to whatever degree you like.

To understand how to attach a sound to a system event, you should begin by understanding what a system event really means to Windows. The system event I'll discuss here is clicking on an OK button, although all the events applicable to this application will work in the same way.

When you click on a button in a Windows application, a message appears at the message-handler procedure for the window that owns the button. The message is of the type WM_COMMAND, and will have the resource ID of the button in its wParam field. By convention, OK buttons will have the constant IDOK for their resource IDs.

Messages under Windows are handled by the message *queue*. The best way to think of this is as a long tube stretching from the Windows kernel itself through all the applications running at the moment. Keep in mind that the Program Manager is itself a Windows application. Whenever an application wants to communicate with another part of itself, it places a message with the HWND of the window it wants to communicate with in the message queue, and the message makes its way to the message handler for the designated window.

If you send a message with its HWND value set to NULL, it will be received by whichever is the top window at the moment. If you send a message with its HWND set to −1, it will be received by all the open windows. When you click on an OK button, then, this is in effect what happens:

```
SendMessage(hwnd,WM_COMMAND,IDOK,0L);
```

The hwnd argument is the window handle for the window that will interpret the button click.

If you'd like to have Windows play a wave file every time an OK button is clicked, then, you must interrupt the message queue and watch the messages going by. If the foregoing message appears, the code that's reading everyone's mail should initiate the playing of its wave file and then send the message on its way.

You can interrupt the message queue in this way by having Windows install a message *filter*. A filter is a function that's passed each message in the queue and given the opportunity to modify or respond to it. Filters are typically a bit onerous to write, as a poorly thought-out filter can have some fairly nasty global consequences. Windows' message queue is central to its existence.

The message filter to play wave files is arguably among the more relaxed examples of the craft. Here's a simplified one—this filter deals only with clicking on an OK button.

```
DWORD FAR PASCAL __export MessageHook(int iCode,WORD wParam,LONG lParam)
{
    FILTERMSG far *msg;

    msg = (FILTERMSG far *)lParam;

    if(msg->message==WM_COMMAND && msg->wParam==IDOK) {
        /* play the sound */
    }

    if(iCode >= 0) return(1);
    else return(DefHookProc(iCode,wParam,lParam,&lpfnOldHook));
}
```

The MessageHook function is added to the current windows filter chain. The filter chain is a list of functions that are called to have a shot at responding to or modifying messages before they get into the message queue. The form of MessageHook is defined by Windows, as it knows what sort of arguments it will pass to MessageHook each time it's called.

The iCode argument is a flag. If it's greater than or equal to zero, MessageHook should do whatever it wants to do and return the value one. If it's less than zero, MessageHook should call the DefHookProc function, which will process the message as it normally would have been handled if the filter wasn't installed. It should then return the value returned by DefHookProc. The lpfnOldHook argument passed to DefHookProc in the foregoing example is the address of the original filter chain hook, as we'll get to in a moment.

The lParam value passed to MessageHook is a far pointer to a FILTERMSG object, which defines the message for MessageHook to work with. The message, wParam, and lParam elements of a FILTERMSG object correspond the arguments passed by Windows to a message handler function, such as the SelectProc function in the WAVEPLAY application discussed earlier in this chapter.

The wParam argument to MessageHook is a NULL value, and serves only as a place holder. You can set a number of different sorts of filters under Windows—some of the other options use the wParam argument.

Here's how you would install the MessageHook function as a Windows message filter. To begin with, you must define two FARPROC objects—one to hold the address of the new hook and one to store the address of the old one. The old address is used by DefHookProc, as noted earlier, and to restore the filter chain to its previous state when your application quits, or it will otherwise no longer be around to filter messages. Here are the two FARPROC objects:

```
FARPROC FAR lpfnKeyHook;
FARPROC FAR lpfnOldHook;
```

and here's how to actually install the new message filter:

```
lpfnKeyHook = MakeProcInstance((FARPROC)MessageHook,hInst);
lpfnOldHook = SetWindowsHook(WH__CALLWNDPROC,lpfnKeyHook);
```

The MakeProcInstance function returns a FARPROC address for the function passed to it. The hInst argument is the instance handle for your application, as was passed to its WinMain function.

The SetWindowsHook function sets the new hook into the filter chain and returns a FARPROC to the old hook. The first argument is a constant to tell it what sort of filter to install. The WH__CALLWNDPROC filter type gets to peek at all the messages of interest to this application—you might want to have a look at the complete discussion of the SetWindowsHook function in the Windows software development kit reference to get a better idea of the range of uses for this function.

Until it's explicitly removed, MessageHook will get to peek at all the messages in the message queue. You must make certain to remove it when your application quits, lest Windows find itself calling thin air, rather than a function, and crashing rather colorfully as a result. Here's how to remove a filter:

```
UnhookWindowsHook(WH__CALLWNDPROC,lpfnKeyHook);
```

The second argument to UnhookWindowsHook is the original filter chain FARPROC value, as returned by SetWindowsHook.

In the complete ATTACH application, to be presented in a moment, the MessageHook function will actually look through a list of canned messages and associate a sound with those messages passed to it that match an entry in its table. Playing a sound isn't particularly onerous, as seen in this chapter. On the assumption that most users who want sounds attached to their system events at all will be content with relatively short ones, we'll use sndPlaySound to handle making noise in this situation.

In fact, this presents a bit of a problem. The most obvious way to actually load and play the sounds in question—the one that will actually be used once all the Zen and platonic dialogs are over with—is to pass snd-PlaySound paths to the wave file in question on disk and let it load them when it needs them. This seems as if it should be a very bad approach, as it will cause the system to pause for a disk access every time one of the system events takes place. In reality, the pause involved will be exceedingly short for wave files of modest size, and if you have a reasonable disk cache installed it will be shorter still after the first time a sound is used, as it will have been cached.

The salient aspect of this is making sure that you use short wave files as noises for system events. This is a good idea in any case—most people won't want an entire Shakespearean sonnet read to them every time they pull down a menu.

There are alternatives to leaving your wave files on disk, but they all turn out to have unpleasant catches associated with them. One fairly obvious approach would be to load them into memory, and then to use sndPlaySound to play them in this form. This does work, and it certainly seems as if it should eliminate the pause involved in loading a file from your hard drive to play it.

Unfortunately, this doesn't prove to be the case, although the reason for it is rather obtuse. When applications call for memory under Windows—something that also happens when an application is run, when a Window is opened, and so on—Windows attempts to satisfy the memory request from the current memory pool. If there doesn't prove to be sufficient memory on hand, Windows will "spill" some of the existing allocated global buffers in memory to disk, and free up the space they were occupying. When an application calls for a spilled buffer—typically by calling GlobalLock—Windows will reverse the procedure, spilling something else to disk so it can reload the buffer in question.

What this means is that if you load an assortment of wave files into memory and then get on with your Windows session, the buffers will very likely be spilled to disk in time to free up their memory. As such, when ATTACH wants to play one in response to a system event, it will have to ask Windows to reload it from its spill file. The result is to play the sound from disk whether you wanted to or not.

You could get around this by simply loading the wave files in question into memory and keeping them locked. This is a very bad idea, as it will place a number of immovable objects in memory, which will in turn cripple Windows' memory management, and generally slow your system down considerably.

The ATTACH application

Figure 2-11 illustrates the main window of ATTACH. In fact, this isn't what you'd normally see when ATTACH runs, as it starts up minimized. In normal use, it would be placed in the Startup group of the Windows program Manager so it could come on line when Windows boots up and begin making a nuisance of itself without any further prompting.

The items in the list box of the ATTACH window are the system events the program knows how to trap and the wave files associated with them. The associations are defined in a file called ATTACH.INI, which ATTACH expects to find in the WINDOWS directory of your hard drive. Here's a typical one:

```
ButtonHelp=c:\sounds\castle.wav
ButtonNo=c:\sounds\collectv.wav
Enable=c:\sounds\g'day.wav
HorizontalScroll=c:\sounds\hello.wav
Maximize=c:\sounds\ni.wav
Menu=c:\sounds\notkeen.wav
Minimize=c:\sounds\violence.wav
Resize=c:\sounds\yellowal.wav
SelectMenuItem=c:\sounds\zap.wav
VerticalScroll=c:\sounds\yourtype.wav
```

You'll find all these sounds on the CD-ROM for this book if you'd like to duplicate this list, and hundreds of others as well.

The words to the left of the equal signs in each of the previous lines are the events to which the sounds to the right are attached. Here's a complete list of the recognized key words and the messages they look for:

Key word	Message	Resource ID
ButtonOk	WM_COMMAND	IDOK
ButtonCancel	WM_COMMAND	IDCANCEL
ButtonHelp	WM_COMMAND	IDHELP
ButtonAbort	WM_COMMAND	IDABORT
ButtonRetry	WM_COMMAND	IDRETRY
ButtonIgnore	WM_COMMAND	IDIGNORE
ButtonYes	WM_COMMAND	IDYES
ButtonNo	WM_COMMAND	IDNO
Maximize	WM_SYSCOMMAND	SC_MAXIMIZE
Minimize	WM_SYSCOMMAND	SC_MINIMIZE
Enable	WM_ENABLE	None
Dialog	WM_INITDIALOG	None
Menu	WM_INITMENU	None
HorizontalScroll	WM_HSCROLL	SB_THUMBPOSITION
VerticalScroll	WM_VSCROLL	SB_THUMBPOSITION
Resize	WM_SIZE	None
SelectMenuItem	WM_MENUSELECT	None
Activate	WM_ACTIVATE	None

These messages are the Windows messages peeked at in the message queue. The resource ID values are what is in the wParam value of the message being perused. Not all the key words have specific resource IDs associated with them.

A table to associate these keywords and messages will appear in the source code for ATTACH. Once you understand what it's up to, you'll be able to add more events to it.

2-11 The main window of the wave attacher application.

Figure 2-12 is the C language source code for ATTACH. In addition to the C language source listing for ATTACH, you'll need ATTACH.RC, its resource file, as shown in FIG. 2-13. Finally, you'll need a DEF file (ATTACH.DEF), shown here:

```
NAME            Attach
DESCRIPTION     'Wave Attacher'
EXETYPE         WINDOWS
CODE            PRELOAD MOVEABLE
DATA            PRELOAD MOVEABLE MULTIPLE
SEGMENTS        WM__TEXT LOADONCALL
HEAPSIZE        24576
STACKSIZE       8192
```

and a project file to compile and link ATTACH. The project file is shown in FIG. 2-14. It assumes you'll be using the Borland C++ for Windows integrated development environment—if you're working with another compiler, you'll require a suitable MAKE file.

2-12 The C language source listing for the wave attacher, ATTACH.CPP.

```
/*
    Wave Attacher
    Copyright (c) 1992, 1993 Alchemy Mindworks Inc.
*/
#include <windows.h>
#include <stdio.h>
#include <stdlib.h>
#include <dir.h>
#include <ctype.h>
#include <alloc.h>
#include <string.h>
```

2-12 Continued.
```
#include <io.h>
#include <bwcc.h>
#include <dos.h>
#include <mmsystem.h>
#include <errno.h>

#define     say(s)      MessageBox(NULL,s,"Yo...",MB_OK | MB_ICONSTOP);
#define     saynumber(f,s)      {char b[128]; sprintf((LPSTR)b,(LPSTR)f,s); \
            MessageBox(NULL,b,"Debug Message",MB_OK | MB_ICONSTOP); }

#define CheckOn(item)      SendDlgItemMessage(hwnd,item,BM_SETCHECK,1,0L);
#define CheckOff(item)      SendDlgItemMessage(hwnd,item,BM_SETCHECK,0,0L);
#define ItemOn(item)    { dlgH=GetDlgItem(hwnd,item); EnableWindow(dlgH,TRUE); }
#define ItemOff(item)     { dlgH=GetDlgItem(hwnd,item); EnableWindow(dlgH,FALSE); }
#define IsItemChecked(item)      SendDlgItemMessage(hwnd,item,BM_GETCHECK,0,0L)
#define ItemName(item,string)     { dlgH=GetDlgItem(hwnd,item); \
                SetWindowText(dlgH,(LPSTR)string); }
#define GetItemName(item,string){ dlgH=GetDlgItem(hwnd,item); \
            GetWindowText(dlgH,(LPSTR)string,STRINGSIZE); }
#define GetSelectedItem(hwnd,item,string) SendDlgItemMessage(hwnd,item,LB_GETTEXT, \
    (unsigned int)SendDlgItemMessage(hwnd,item,LB_GETCURSEL,0,0L),(long )string)

#ifndef max
#define max(a,b)        (((a)>(b))?(a):(b))
#endif
#ifndef min
#define min(a,b)        (((a)<(b))?(a):(b))
#endif

#define     SEPARATOR         187

#define     MAXSOUNDEVENTS         24

#define     STRINGSIZE         128

#define     HOOKTYPE         WH_CALLWNDPROC

#define     INIFILE         "ATTACH.INI"

#define     MESSAGE_STRING    101
#define     MAIN_EVENTS       101
#define     SYS_ABOUT         1

#define     DoSilence()       --silence
```

```c
#define    DoSound()          ++silence

typedef struct {
    WORD hlParam;
    WORD llparam;
    WORD wParam;
    WORD message;
    WORD hWnd;
    } FILTERMSG;

typedef struct {
    char filename[STRINGSIZE+1];
    unsigned int message;
    unsigned int condition;
    } SOUNDEVENT;

typedef struct {
    char name[33];
    unsigned int message;
    unsigned int condition;
    } EVENTNAME;

#define    MAXEVENTNAMES    18

EVENTNAME eventname[MAXEVENTNAMES] = {
    "ButtonOk",         WM_COMMAND,IDOK,
    "ButtonCancel",     WM_COMMAND,IDCANCEL,
    "ButtonHelp",       WM_COMMAND,IDHELP,
    "ButtonAbort",      WM_COMMAND,IDABORT,
    "ButtonRetry",      WM_COMMAND,IDRETRY,
    "ButtonIgnore",     WM_COMMAND,IDIGNORE,
    "ButtonYes",        WM_COMMAND,IDYES,
    "ButtonNo",         WM_COMMAND,IDNO,
    "Maximize",         WM_SYSCOMMAND,SC_MAXIMIZE,
    "Minimize",         WM_SYSCOMMAND,SC_MINIMIZE,
    "Enable",           WM_ENABLE,0,
    "Dialog",           WM_INITDIALOG,0,
    "Menu",             WM_INITMENU,0,
    "HorizontalScroll", WM_HSCROLL,SB_THUMBPOSITION,
    "VerticalScroll",   WM_VSCROLL,SB_THUMBPOSITION,
    "Resize",           WM_SIZE,0,
    "SelectMenuItem",   WM_MENUSELECT,0,
    "Activate",         WM_ACTIVATE,0,
    };

/* prototypes */
```

2-12 Continued.

```
DWORD FAR PASCAL SelectProc(HWND hwnd,WORD message,WORD wParam,LONG lParam);
DWORD FAR PASCAL AboutDlgProc(HWND hwnd,WORD message,WORD wParam,LONG lParam);
DWORD FAR PASCAL MessageDlgProc(HWND hwnd,WORD message,WORD wParam,LONG lParam);

DWORD FAR PASCAL _export MessageHook(int iCode,WORD wParam,LONG lParam);

unsigned long FindMessageType(LPSTR b);

void ResetAttachSelectorList(HWND hwnd);
void DoMessage(HWND hwnd,LPSTR message);
void _export PlaySound(LPSTR path);
void InitializeSounds(void);
void lmemset(LPSTR s,int n,unsigned int size);
void lstrlwr(LPSTR s);
void InitializeLists(HWND hwnd,unsigned int list);

int testdisk(int n);
int lmemcmp(LPSTR d,LPSTR s,unsigned int size);
int FindSoundName(char *string);
int FindSoundEvent(char *string);

/* globals */

char szFileSpec[145];

LPSTR messagehook;

char szAppName[] = "WaveAttacher";
char allCatagories[] = "[ All Categories ]";
HANDLE hInst;

FARPROC FAR lpfnKeyHook;
FARPROC FAR lpfnOldHook;

SOUNDEVENT soundevent[MAXSOUNDEVENTS];

unsigned int soundindex=0;
int silence=1;

unsigned int usernumber=87;

#pragma warn -par
int PASCAL WinMain(HANDLE hInstance,HANDLE hPrevInstance,
        LPSTR lpszCmdParam,int nCmdShow)
{
```

```
    FARPROC dlgProc;
    int r=0;

    BWCCGetVersion();

    hInst=hInstance;

    dlgProc=MakeProcInstance((FARPROC)SelectProc,hInst);
    r=DialogBox(hInst,"MainScreen",NULL,dlgProc);

    FreeProcInstance(dlgProc);

    return(r);
}

DWORD FAR PASCAL _export MessageHook(int iCode,WORD wParam,LONG lParam)
{
    FILTERMSG far *msg;
    int i;

    msg = (FILTERMSG far *)lParam;

    if(silence > 0) {
        for(i=0;i<soundindex;++i) {
            if(soundevent[i].message==msg->message) {
                if(soundevent[i].condition==0 ||
                    soundevent[i].condition==msg->wParam) {
                    PlaySound(soundevent[i].filename);
                    break;
                }
            }
        }
    }

    if(iCode >= 0) return(1);
    else return(DefHookProc(iCode,wParam,lParam,&lpfnOldHook));
}

DWORD FAR PASCAL SelectProc(HWND hwnd,WORD message,WORD wParam,LONG lParam)
{
    POINT point;
    FARPROC lpfnDlgProc;
    PAINTSTRUCT ps;
    HICON hIcon;
    HMENU hmenu;
    char b[STRINGSIZE+1];
```

```
    long l;
    int i;

    DoSilence();
    switch(message) {
        case WM_DESTROY:
        break;
        case WM_SYSCOMMAND:
            if((wParam & 0xfff0)==SC_CLOSE) {
                sndPlaySound(NULL,SND_SYNC);
                UnhookWindowsHook(HOOKTYPE,lpfnKeyHook);
                PostQuitMessage(0);
            }
            else if(wParam == SYS_ABOUT) {
                DoSilence();
        if((lpfnDlgProc=MakeProcInstance((FARPROC)
          AboutDlgProc,hInst)) != NULL) {
                    DialogBox(hInst,"AboutBox",hwnd,lpfnDlgProc);
                    FreeProcInstance(lpfnDlgProc);
                }
                DoSound();
            }
            break;
        case WM_INITDIALOG:
                DoSilence();
            for(i=0;i<MAXSOUNDEVENTS;++i)
                lmemset((LPSTR)&soundevent,0,sizeof(SOUNDEVENT));
            hmenu=GetSystemMenu(hwnd,FALSE);
            AppendMenu(hmenu,MF_SEPARATOR,NULL,NULL);
            AppendMenu(hmenu,MF_STRING,SYS_ABOUT,(LPSTR)"About Sound Player");

            InitializeSounds();
            InitializeLists(hwnd,MAIN_EVENTS);
            hIcon=LoadIcon(hInst,szAppName);
            SetClassWord(hwnd,GCW_HICON,(WORD)hIcon);

            lpfnKeyHook = MakeProcInstance((FARPROC)MessageHook,hInst);
            lpfnOldHook = SetWindowsHook(HOOKTYPE,lpfnKeyHook);

            SendMessage(hwnd,WM_SYSCOMMAND,SC_MINIMIZE,0L);

            DoSound();
            break;
        case WM_CTLCOLOR:
            if(HIWORD(lParam)==CTLCOLOR_STATIC ||
```

```
        HIWORD(lParam)==CTLCOLOR_DLG) {
         SetBkColor(wParam,RGB(192,192,192));
         SetTextColor(wParam,RGB(0,0,0));

         ClientToScreen(hwnd,&point);
         UnrealizeObject(GetStockObject(LTGRAY_BRUSH));
         SetBrushOrg(wParam,point.x,point.y);

         return((DWORD)GetStockObject(LTGRAY_BRUSH));

        }
       if(HIWORD(lParam)==CTLCOLOR_BTN) {
         SetBkColor(wParam,RGB(192,192,192));
         SetTextColor(wParam,RGB(0,0,0));

         ClientToScreen(hwnd,&point);
         UnrealizeObject(GetStockObject(BLACK_BRUSH));
         SetBrushOrg(wParam,point.x,point.y);

         return((DWORD)GetStockObject(BLACK_BRUSH));
       }

       break;
    case WM_PAINT:
       BeginPaint(hwnd,&ps);
       EndPaint(hwnd,&ps);
       break;
    case WM_COMMAND:
       switch(wParam) {
          case MAIN_EVENTS:
             switch(HIWORD(lParam)) {
                case LBN_SELCHANGE:
                   if((l=SendDlgItemMessage(hwnd,MAIN_EVENTS,
                      LB_GETCURSEL,0,0L)) != LB_ERR) {
                      SendDlgItemMessage(hwnd,MAIN_EVENTS,
                         LB_GETTEXT,(int)l,(DWORD)(LPSTR)b);
                      i=FindSoundEvent(b);
                      PlaySound(soundevent[i].filename);
                   }
                   break;
             }
          }
       break;
    }
DoSound();
return(FALSE);
```

2-12 Continued.
```
}

void InitializeLists(HWND hwnd,unsigned int list)
{
    char b[145],name[16],ext[6];
    int i,j;

    sndPlaySound(NULL,SND_SYNC);
    SendDlgItemMessage(hwnd,list,LB_RESETCONTENT,0,0L);

    for(i=0;i<MAXEVENTNAMES;++i) {
        sprintf(b,"%s %c [ Nothing ]",eventname[i].name,SEPARATOR);
        for(j=0;j<soundindex;++j) {
            if(soundevent[j].message==eventname[i].message &&
                soundevent[j].condition==eventname[i].condition) {
                fnsplit(soundevent[j].filename,NULL,NULL,name,ext);
                lstrcat(name,ext);
                sprintf(b,"%s %c %s",eventname[i].name,SEPARATOR,name);
                break;
            }
        }

        SendDlgItemMessage(hwnd,list,LB_ADDSTRING,0,(long)&b);
    }
}

void _export PlaySound(LPSTR path)
{
    sndPlaySound(path,SND_ASYNC | SND_NODEFAULT | SND_NOSTOP);
}

DWORD FAR PASCAL AboutDlgProc(HWND hwnd,WORD message,WORD wParam,LONG lParam)
{
    POINT point;

    switch(message) {
        case WM_INITDIALOG:
            return(TRUE);
        case WM_CTLCOLOR:
            if(HIWORD(lParam)==CTLCOLOR_STATIC ||
                HIWORD(lParam)==CTLCOLOR_DLG) {
                SetBkColor(wParam,RGB(192,192,192));
                SetTextColor(wParam,RGB(0,0,0));

                ClientToScreen(hwnd,&point);
```

```
                    UnrealizeObject(GetStockObject(LTGRAY_BRUSH));
                    SetBrushOrg(wParam,point.x,point.y);

                    return((DWORD)GetStockObject(LTGRAY_BRUSH));

                }
                if(HIWORD(lParam)==CTLCOLOR_BTN) {
                    SetBkColor(wParam,RGB(192,192,192));
                    SetTextColor(wParam,RGB(0,0,0));

                    ClientToScreen(hwnd,&point);
                    UnrealizeObject(GetStockObject(BLACK_BRUSH));
                    SetBrushOrg(wParam,point.x,point.y);

                    return((DWORD)GetStockObject(BLACK_BRUSH));
                }

                break;
            case WM_COMMAND:
                switch(wParam) {
                    case IDOK:
                        EndDialog(hwnd,wParam);
                        return(TRUE);
                }
                break;
        }

    return(FALSE);
}


void DoMessage(HWND hwnd,LPSTR message)
{
    FARPROC lpfnDlgProc;

    DoSilence();
    messagehook=message;

    if((lpfnDlgProc=MakeProcInstance((FARPROC)MessageDlgProc,hInst)) != NULL) {
        DialogBox(hInst,"MessageBox",hwnd,lpfnDlgProc);
        FreeProcInstance(lpfnDlgProc);
    }
    DoSound();
}

DWORD FAR PASCAL MessageDlgProc(HWND hwnd,WORD message,WORD wParam,LONG lParam)
{
```

2-12 Continued.

```
    POINT point;
    HWND dlgH;

    switch(message) {
        case WM_INITDIALOG:
            dlgH=GetDlgItem(hwnd,MESSAGE_STRING);
            SetWindowText(dlgH,messagehook);
            return(TRUE);
        case WM_CTLCOLOR:
            if(HIWORD(lParam)==CTLCOLOR_STATIC ||
               HIWORD(lParam)==CTLCOLOR_DLG) {
                SetBkColor(wParam,RGB(192,192,192));
                SetTextColor(wParam,RGB(0,0,0));

                ClientToScreen(hwnd,&point);
                UnrealizeObject(GetStockObject(LTGRAY_BRUSH));
                SetBrushOrg(wParam,point.x,point.y);

                return((DWORD)GetStockObject(LTGRAY_BRUSH));

            }
            if(HIWORD(lParam)==CTLCOLOR_BTN) {
                SetBkColor(wParam,RGB(192,192,192));
                SetTextColor(wParam,RGB(0,0,0));

                ClientToScreen(hwnd,&point);
                UnrealizeObject(GetStockObject(BLACK_BRUSH));
                SetBrushOrg(wParam,point.x,point.y);

                return((DWORD)GetStockObject(BLACK_BRUSH));
            }
            break;
        case WM_COMMAND:
            switch(wParam) {
                case IDCANCEL:
                case IDOK:
                case IDYES:
                case IDNO:
                    EndDialog(hwnd,wParam);
                    return(TRUE);
            }
            break;
    }

    return(FALSE);
```

```
}

void lmemset(LPSTR s,int n,unsigned int size)
{
    unsigned int i;

    for(i=0;i<size;++i) *s++=n;
}

int lmemcmp(LPSTR d,LPSTR s,unsigned int size)
{
    unsigned int i;

    for(i=0;i<size;++i) {
        if(*d++ != *s++) return(1);
    }
    return(0);
}

void lstrlwr(LPSTR s)
{
    while(*s) {
        *s=tolower(*s);
        ++s;
    }
}

unsigned long FindMessageType(LPSTR b)
{
    char s[33];
    int i;

    lstrlwr(b);

    for(i=0;i<MAXEVENTNAMES;++i) {
        lstrcpy(s,eventname[i].name);
        lstrlwr(s);
        if(!lstrcmp((LPSTR)s,b))
            return((unsigned long)eventname[i].message |
                ((unsigned long)eventname[i].condition<< 16));
    }
    return(-1L);
}

void InitializeSounds(void)
{
```

```
    HCURSOR hSaveCursor,hHourGlass;
    FILE *fp;
    char *p,*pr,b[145];
    unsigned long l;
    int i;

    hHourGlass=LoadCursor(NULL,IDC_WAIT);
    hSaveCursor=SetCursor(hHourGlass);

    sndPlaySound(NULL,SND_SYNC);
    for(i=0;i<MAXSOUNDEVENTS;++i)
        lmemset((LPSTR)&soundevent[i],0,sizeof(SOUNDEVENT));
    soundindex=0;

    GetWindowsDirectory(b,128);
    if(b[lstrlen(b)-1] != '\\') lstrcat(b,"\\");
    lstrcat(b,INIFILE);

    if((fp=fopen(b,"ra")) != NULL) {
        do {
            if((p=fgets(b,144,fp)) != NULL) {
                if((pr=strchr(b,13)) != NULL) *pr=0;
                if((pr=strchr(b,10)) != NULL) *pr=0;
                if((pr=strchr(b,32)) != NULL) *pr=0;
                if((pr=strchr(b,';')) != NULL) *pr=0;

                for(i=0;i<144 && p[i] != '=' && p[i] != 0;++i);
                p[i]=0;
                p+=(i+1);
                while(*p==32 || *p=='=') ++p;

                if((l=FindMessageType(b)) != -1L) {
                    lstrcpy(soundevent[soundindex].filename,(LPSTR)p);
                    lstrlwr(soundevent[soundindex].filename);
                    soundevent[soundindex].message=LOWORD(l);
                    soundevent[soundindex].condition=HIWORD(l);
                    if(access(p,0)==0) ++soundindex;
                    else {
                        wsprintf(b,"Can't find %s",
                            (LPSTR)soundevent[soundindex].filename);
                        DoMessage(NULL,b);
                    }
                }
            }
        } while(p != NULL && soundindex < MAXSOUNDEVENTS);
```

```
            fclose(fp);
        }

        SetCursor(hSaveCursor);
    }

    int FindSoundEvent(char *string)
    {
        char b[STRINGSIZE+1],*pr;
        int i,j;

        lstrcpy(b,string);

        if((pr=strchr(b,32)) == NULL) return(-1);
        *pr=0;

        for(i=0;i<MAXEVENTNAMES;++i) {
            if(!lstrcmp(b,eventname[i].name)) {
                for(j=0;j<soundindex;++j) {
                    if(eventname[i].message==soundevent[j].message &&
                        (eventname[i].condition==0 ||
                            eventname[i].condition==soundevent[j].condition)) return(j);
                }
                return(-1);
            }
        }
        return(-1);
    }
```

2-13   The resource script for the wave attacher, ATTACH.RC.

```
MainScreen DIALOG 35, 15, 164, 113
STYLE WS_POPUP | WS_CAPTION | WS_SYSMENU | WS_MINIMIZEBOX | WS_MAXIMIZEBOX
CAPTION "Wave Attacher"
BEGIN
  CONTROL "", 101, "LISTBOX", LBS_STANDARD | WS_CHILD | WS_VISIBLE, 12, 20, 140, 83
  CONTROL "", 102, "BorShade", 1 | WS_CHILD | WS_VISIBLE, 8, 16, 148, 88
  LTEXT "Sound events", -1, 8, 8, 148, 8, WS_CHILD | WS_VISIBLE | WS_GROUP
END


AboutBox DIALOG 18, 18, 156, 104
STYLE WS_POPUP | WS_CAPTION
CAPTION "About Wave Attacher..."
BEGIN
  CONTROL "", 102, "BorShade", BSS_GROUP | WS_CHILD | WS_VISIBLE | WS_TABSTOP,
      8, 8, 140, 68
```

```
     LTEXT "Wave Attacher 1.0\nCopyright (c) 1993\nAlchemy Mindworks Inc.\n"
       "This program is part of the book Multimedia Programming for "
       "Windows by Steven William Rimmer, published by Windcrest (Book 4484).",
       -1, 12, 12, 128, 60, WS_CHILD | WS_VISIBLE | WS_GROUP
     DEFPUSHBUTTON "Ok", IDOK, 116, 80, 32, 20, WS_CHILD | WS_VISIBLE | WS_TABSTOP
END


MessageBox DIALOG 72, 72, 144, 72
STYLE DS_MODALFRAME | WS_POPUP | WS_CAPTION
CAPTION "Message"
BEGIN
     CONTROL "", 102, "BorShade", BSS_GROUP | WS_CHILD | WS_VISIBLE, 4, 8, 136, 36
     CTEXT "", 101, 8, 12, 128, 28, WS_CHILD | WS_VISIBLE | WS_GROUP
     DEFPUSHBUTTON "Ok", IDOK, 108, 48, 32, 20, WS_CHILD | WS_VISIBLE | WS_TABSTOP
END


WaveAttacher ICON
BEGIN
       '00 00 01 00 01 00 20 20 10 00 00 00 00 00 E8 02'
       '00 00 16 00 00 00 28 00 00 00 20 00 00 00 40 00'
       '00 00 01 00 04 00 00 00 00 00 80 02 00 00 00 00'
       '00 00 00 00 00 00 00 00 00 00 00 00 00 00 00 00'
       '00 00 00 00 80 00 00 80 00 00 00 80 80 00 80 00'
       '00 00 80 00 80 00 80 80 00 00 80 80 80 00 C0 C0'
       'C0 00 00 00 FF 00 00 FF 00 00 00 FF FF 00 FF 00'
       '00 00 FF 00 FF 00 FF FF 00 00 FF FF FF 00 00 00'
       '00 00 00 00 00 00 00 00 00 00 00 00 00 00 00 00'
       '00 00 00 00 00 00 00 00 00 00 00 00 00 00 00 00'
       '00 00 00 00 00 00 00 00 00 00 00 00 00 00 00 00'
       '00 00 00 00 00 00 00 00 00 00 00 00 00 00 00 00'
       '00 00 33 33 33 33 33 33 33 33 30 00 00 00 00 00'
       '00 03 33 33 33 33 33 33 33 33 33 00 00 00 00 00'
       '00 33 33 33 33 33 33 33 33 33 33 30 00 00 00 00'
       '03 33 33 33 33 33 33 33 33 33 33 33 00 00 00 00'
       '33 33 33 33 33 00 00 03 33 33 33 33 30 00 00 00'
       '33 33 33 33 33 00 00 03 33 33 33 33 30 00 00 03'
       '33 33 33 33 33 00 00 03 33 33 33 33 33 00 00 03'
       '33 33 33 33 33 00 00 03 33 33 33 33 33 00 00 33'
       '33 33 33 33 33 30 00 33 33 33 33 33 33 30 00 33'
       '33 33 33 33 33 33 33 33 33 33 33 33 33 30 00 33'
       '33 33 33 33 33 33 33 33 33 33 33 33 33 30 00 33'
       '33 33 33 33 33 33 33 33 33 33 33 33 33 30 00 33'
       '33 33 33 00 03 33 33 33 00 03 33 33 33 30 00 33'
       '33 33 33 00 03 33 33 33 00 03 33 33 33 30 00 33'
       '33 33 33 00 03 33 33 33 00 03 33 33 33 30 00 33'
```

```
'33 33 33 00 03 33 33 33 00 03 33 33 33 30 00 03'
'33 33 33 00 03 33 33 33 00 03 33 33 33 00 00 03'
'33 33 33 00 03 33 33 33 00 03 33 33 33 00 00 00'
'33 33 33 00 03 33 33 33 00 03 33 33 30 00 00 00'
'33 33 33 00 03 33 33 33 00 03 33 33 30 00 00 00'
'03 33 33 33 33 33 33 33 33 33 33 33 00 00 00 00'
'00 33 33 33 33 33 33 33 33 33 33 30 00 00 00 00'
'00 03 33 33 33 33 33 33 33 33 33 00 00 00 00 00'
'00 00 33 33 33 33 33 33 33 33 30 00 00 00 00 00'
'00 00 00 00 00 00 00 00 00 00 00 00 00 00 00 00'
'00 00 00 00 00 00 00 00 00 00 00 00 00 00 00 00'
'00 00 00 00 00 00 00 00 00 00 00 00 00 00 00 00'
'00 00 00 00 00 00 00 00 00 00 00 00 00 00 FF FF'
'FF FF FF FF FF FF FF FF FF FF FF FF FF FF FF 00'
'00 7F FE 00 00 3F FC 00 00 1F F8 00 00 0F F0 00'
'00 07 F0 00 00 07 E0 00 00 03 E0 00 00 03 C0 00'
'00 01 C0 00 00 01 C0 00 00 01 C0 00 00 01 C0 00'
'00 01 C0 00 00 01 C0 00 00 01 C0 00 00 01 E0 00'
'00 03 E0 00 00 03 F0 00 00 07 F0 00 00 07 F8 00'
'00 0F FC 00 00 1F FE 00 00 3F FF 00 00 7F FF FF'
'FF FF FF FF FF FF FF FF FF FF FF FF FF FF'
END
```

Despite its using some fairly exotic Windows calls, the source code for ATTACH is quite a bit simpler than the WAVEPLAY application discussed earlier in this chapter. It requires relatively little interaction with its users—as a rule, maintaining user-interface elements under Windows takes much more work than actually getting something done.

The eventname table at the top of the ATTACH.CPP source listing illustrates how the key words in ATTACH.INI are associated with messages. This table, in turn, is used to construct a second one, called soundevent, from the contents of ATTACH.INI.

The InitializeSounds function toward the end of ATTACH.CPP in FIG. 2-12 illustrates how the soundevents table is set up. The ATTACH.INI file is opened and each line is parsed to extract its key word and a path to the sound associated with the event in question. The eventname table is then searched to find the message constant associated with the key word, and the resulting values are stored in the current soundevents entry.

Having ascertained which message is to be used for a particular soundevent entry, the InitializeSounds function will then determine whether or not the wave file in question exists.

Once all the sounds have been loaded, ATTACH can begin processing messages. If you have a look at the implementation of the MessageHook function in ATTACH.CPP, you'll see how the soundevents table is used. When a message appears at MessageHook, the eventname table is scanned

File   Edit   Search   Run   Compile   Project   Browse   Options   Window   Help

? |⊢→| |▨| |⊡| |⊞| |⊟| |⊫| |▨| |▥|

Project: attach

File Name	Lines	Code	Data	Location
attach.cpp	526	3177	4154	.
attach.res	n/a	n/a	n/a	.
attach.def	n/a	n/a	n/a	.
bwcc.lib	n/a	n/a	n/a	..\lib
mmsystem.lib	n/a	n/a	n/a	..\lib

2-14   The project file for the wave attacher, ATTACH.PRJ.

to see if the message type and the wParam value match any of its entries. If a match is found, MessageHook calls PlaySound, which is really just snd-PlaySound.

The main window of ATTACH will appear only if you unminimize it. You can see what the various wave files sound like by clicking on the items in the list. Finally, you can shut ATTACH down by double clicking on its System menu. After ten or fifteen minutes of life with ATTACH, you might find this to be its best trick.

More sounds

There are a number of obvious classes of Windows applications to use wave files, of which the two discussed in detail in this chapter are pretty well representative. In a sense, they use wave files for their own sake, however. A wave-file browser like WAVEPLAY is really useful only if you feel like hearing noises squawk and cough and bark from your speakers. It has little application beyond this.

Most of the serious applications of wave files involve using them as part of a larger package, in which case you'll probably want to extract parts of the applications dealt with in this chapter. Having a program speak, for example, is arguably a more profound use of Windows multimedia sound resources than having your speaker perform all or part of a Python sketch every time you click on OK.

As a final note, it seems fair to observe that there are whole tracts of the multimedia extensions as they pertain to wave files that I haven't gotten within a light year of in this chapter. In fact, this entire book could have dealt with little else than wave files. If you're of a mind to go exploring, you'll find that there's plenty of untouched jungle still to be found.

3
Playing audio compact discs

"Eagles may fly but weasels don't get sucked into jets."

A decade from now there will probably be a whole generation of people who'll look at old vinyl records at garage sales and wonder, disinterestedly, what they're for. While there are probably a few luddites left who regard the demise of mechanical recording as the passing of a great age, for most of the western world, compact discs represent a stunning innovation. It hasn't been all that long since the notion of hearing sound as it was actually recorded was something like science fiction, only harder to believe.

Consider that prior to the introduction of compact discs, the basic technology for recording sound on phonograph records hadn't changed appreciably since 1877. By comparison, the basis of compact disc technology dates back to the mid-seventies, a development project of Philips with some additional error-correction techniques from Sony. The first compact discs were available in North America in 1983, which makes the technology about a decade old as I write this.

A compact disc can store up to 74 minutes of 44.1-kilohertz two-channel audio encoded as digital information. The maximum playing time, as legend has it, was decided by asking the German conductor Herbert von Karajan for his opinion of a suitable playing time for a new audio medium. He decided that a single compact disc should be able to play his performance of Beethoven's Ninth Symphony uninterrupted.

The information on a compact disc is encoded as a string of 16-bit words stored as variable-length pits in an aluminum surface. The pits are about half a micrometer wide. They're arranged in a spiral track, much as phonograph records were made back in the dark ages. The track of a compact disc is about three miles long and can contain something on the order of two billion pits.

A compact disc is read by a semiconductor laser—the edges of the pits don't reflect light well, and represent binary ones. The bottoms of the pits and the areas outside the pits do reflect light, and represent binary zeros. In fact, the mechanics of how information is encoded in a compact disc doesn't really matter to a compact disc player or reader, as long as the result of playing one is to generate ones and zeros at the reading laser. The Kodak Photo-CD process, which will be discussed in greater detail later in this book, replaces physical pits with variable dye densities, but the result is the same. Figure 3-1 illustrates the laser in a compact disc player passing over one track in a compact disc.

The information on an audio compact disc is stored using pulse-code modulation. It's beyond the scope of this book to deal with how audio is actually handled between a compact disc and your speakers—it's

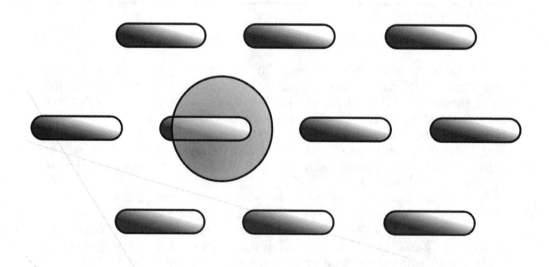

Disc moves this way ⟶

3-1　How the laser in a compact disc player tracks the pits of a disc.

arguably sufficient to know that the whole complicated circus actually works.

In fact, what comes off a compact disc is raw binary information. While its most common form is as encoded sound, it's equally applicable to storing other sorts of data. Perhaps the second most common application of compact disc technology is CD-ROMs.

A CD-ROM is physically structured just like an audio compact disc. In fact—as you'll have discovered if you investigated the CD-ROM that came with this book before you read this chapter—a CD-ROM can hold both data and audio tracks. I'll get into this in greater detail later in this chapter. The 74 minutes of music on an audio compact disc works out to about 600 megabytes of file data on a CD-ROM.

A CD-ROM in a suitable CD-ROM drive can appear to your computer like a conventional DOS volume. Typically, if you add a CD-ROM drive to your computer, it will show up with the letter of the next free drive in your system. For example, my computer has drive C as a hard drive, drive D as a RAM drive, drive E as a Syquest removable drive, and drive F as the CD-ROM drive.

A CD-ROM drive can be physically mounted in a drive bay of your computer or as an external box. The former is less expensive and generally easier to use—the latter is handy if you have no more free drive bays available.

CD-ROM hardware: Attack of the scuzzies

If you haven't installed a CD-ROM drive in your computer, or if you find that the one you have isn't adequate for what you have in mind, you might want to read this section. While ostensibly pretty simple, CD-ROM technology actually embodies a few catches at the moment that are worth knowing about.

I'll also discuss the suitability of CD-ROM drives. This primarily affects Kodak Photo-CDs and applications in which you'll want to read CD-ROMs fairly quickly.

Figure 3-2 illustrates a typical CD-ROM drive. This is a Sony CDU-31A drive, state-of-the-art hardware. While it deals with fairly exotic technology, the drive in FIG. 3-2 looks to DOS like just another hard drive. In order for it to do so, however, you must add several components to the computer that supports this drive. Aside from the drive itself, there's an interface card that connects it to the computer's expansion bus, a low-level driver to allow the interface card to be communicated with in a standard format, and then a higher-level driver to make the drive look like a DOS volume. The higher-level driver is called MSCDEX, something else created by Microsoft.

3-2 A Sony CDU-31A CD-ROM drive.

In theory, a PC knows about only two types of drives: floppy drives and hard drives. Both are controlled by dedicated boards that interface with their electronics. Other sorts of drives—such as CD-ROMs, floptical drives, removable hard drives, tape streamers, and such—must be interfaced to your computer so they look like conventional hard drives.

Back at the dawn of time, every one of these devices would have come with its own proprietary interface card. In most cases, these sorts of cards worked well enough in a system with no other unusual devices installed, but they often ran into problems when they were combined with other dedicated controllers. They also ate a lot of slots if you wanted to have several different drives in your system.

To deal with this problem, a number of manufacturers of peripheral devices adopted a standard of sorts, called SCSI, for *small computer systems interface*. A somewhat unpronounceable acronym as it stands, it's usually verbalized as "scuzzy."

The idea behind SCSI adapters was uncharacteristically brilliant, marred only slightly by how it was later implemented. A SCSI interface card, or *host adapter*, can support up to seven SCSI devices. This can include various sorts of storage devices and some other types of peripherals, such as scanners. Using a SCSI host adapter will both free up numerous slots in a computer with a large helping of peripherals and eliminate the potential for conflict between multiple cards by eliminating the cards themselves.

Ideas like this almost never work quite right in the real world, and so it has been for the SCSI interface. The SCSI specification was left a bit open ended to allow for a variety of different devices. Sadly, many of the designers of SCSI cards took the opportunity to cheat on things a bit. As a result, most devices that come with SCSI host adapters include a recommendation that you not attempt to drive multiple SCSI devices with them. If you have a SCSI hard drive, a SCSI CD-ROM, and a SCSI floptical drive in your computer, for example, you'll probably have to install three SCSI host adapters to support them.

In fact, this isn't quite as chaotic as it used to be, as multiple SCSI adapters are more likely to get along with each other than four or five wholly disparate cards made to no one's specifications but their own. There are still some considerations in making these things coexist, however.

A SCSI host adapter consists of some hardware to do the actual interfacing with your computer and your SCSI device—or devices, should you be fortunate enough to get one that can deal with more than one device at a time—and an extension BIOS that will hook into your system when it boots up and make your SCSI device accessible by other software. An extension BIOS lives in the memory space above your computer's video buffer. Typically the first one in memory will be your VGA card BIOS, at location C000:0000H. Other BIOS extensions will show up after this.

The amount of real estate in high memory in which to locate BIOS extensions is finite—in fact, it's pretty limited. If you install enough devices that want to put an extension in high memory, you can run out of room.

Finding some free space in high memory for a new peripheral's extension BIOS can be quite frustrating. While a few devices I've encountered have come with analyzer utilities that scout around for free space and tell you how to configure the card in question before it's installed, most just tell you to try the beast with the factory settings and play hop-scotch with some board jumpers if things don't work out.

Typically, the segment address of a BIOS extension is defined with jumpers or DIP switches on a SCSI interface card. If you install the card and you can't access your new drive, chances are the BIOS in the SCSI card has been installed on top of an existing BIOS, and as such must be moved. Most SCSI host adapters offer four or more potential locations for their extension BIOSs. In practice, figuring out what's wrong with a SCSI device that refuses to behave itself usually requires a lot of screwdriver action.

It's worth noting that other devices might also locate extension BIOSs or other bits of firmware code in high memory, which can also get in the way of installing new cards. For example, the system that supports the CD-ROM drive in FIG. 3-2, as well as several other devices, has its high-memory space effectively full. When I went to install the AudioMaster card from the previous chapter in it, I found that there was no place to park, and no amount of juggling was going to change that. The AudioMaster went to live in a different computer.

An extension BIOS always starts with the two bytes 55H and AAH, that is, one byte with every other bit set and then the inverse of it. You can reduce the mean time between failures of your screwdriver when you install a SCSI device by running DEBUG from the DOS prompt and looking to see if there's an extension BIOS located where your new card intends to put one. For example, if you run DEBUG and issue this command:

```
DC000:0000
```

you should see the extension BIOS for your VGA card, assuming that's what's in your computer. A few unusual VGA cards don't locate their extensions at C000:0000.

If you find the bytes 55H and AAH at the location at which your new SCSI card is configured to position its BIOS before you install the card, change the configuration of the SCSI card. While not finding evidence of an extension BIOS at a particular place in high memory doesn't guarantee that your card won't run into difficulties if it uses the space in question, attempting to use space that does have something already in residence pretty well guarantees that it will.

After all this consideration of SCSI devices, it's worth noting that some of the more recent CD-ROM drives, like the Sony CDU-31A back in FIG. 3-2, have abandoned SCSI cards for proprietary interfaces of their own. In most cases, this has allowed the interfaces for these drives to be quite a bit faster than comparable SCSI host adapters would have been. With the general confusion surrounding SCSI interfaces, "proprietary bus" interfaces as they're usually called, are certainly no more likely to cause conflict problems than SCSI cards are.

There are a few other considerations to keep in mind about using a CD-ROM drive with the applications in this book, and especially about buying one. The specification for CD-ROM drives was defined quite a while ago, but as is the case with many specifications designed to standardize PC hardware, it has become somewhat more refined as it has matured. First-generation CD-ROM drives will still read contemporary CD-ROMs, but they do have a few catches. There's one illustrated in FIG. 3-3. This is a Sony Laser Library CD-ROM drive from a few years back.

3-3 An ancient, dusty, antique of a CD-ROM drive, the Sony Laser Library.

There are a number of characteristics inherent in the drive in FIG. 3-3 that are typical of older CD-ROM drives. To begin with, it's slower than two lawyers waiting for each other. State-of-the-art drives will read data from a CD-ROM several times faster than this creature can. Secondly, it uses disc "caddies"—little plastic drawers that hold a disc and are then pushed into the drive. Easy to misplace and infuriating to use, they serve as one of the more compelling reasons to upgrade an old CD-ROM drive if you switch discs frequently. Contemporary drives use disc trays, just like an audio compact disc player.

Finally, these old first-generation drives won't read Kodak Photo-CDs, which are based on elements of the CD-ROM specification that have been defined fairly recently. The real antiques, like the one in FIG. 3-3, won't read them at all. Slightly less dusty drives, called *single-session* drives, will read only those images stored on a Photo-CD on its first pass, and will ignore any images added to it after the fact. This will be discussed in detail when we deal with the Photo-CD interface later in this book.

As a final note about buying a new CD-ROM drive, you can buy a drive with its interface card and drivers, a healthy supply of packing peanuts, and a box to ship it all in. Alternately, you can buy the drive and such along with a bundle of CD-ROM titles for somewhat more. This will typically get you an encyclopedia on disc, a catalog of aquatic mammals or something equally educational, and a few interactive games. There's a much higher profit margin on CD-ROM titles than there is on CD-ROM drives, and as such most computer stores would like to sell you one of these bundles. While they're useful in their own right, you should be aware that CD-ROM drives are available without any bundled discs, should you know enough about aquatic mammals as it is.

Of drives and drivers

There are two levels of drivers involved in accessing a CD-ROM drive. The simplest of the two is a device driver to make the particular hardware of your CD-ROM drive look like a standard, accessible CD-ROM. Drivers of this type typically live in your CONFIG.SYS file. The second level of drivers is something called MSCDEX, which is Microsoft's standard CD-ROM access package. With MSCDEX successfully loaded and running, your CD-ROM drive will look like just another hard drive, save that you won't be able to write to it.

The MSCDEX driver is a fascinating and fairly complex entity that allows you to access a CD-ROM as both a DOS volume and an audio disc, that is, by recorded tracks or portions thereof. One of its best features, however, is that you'll never have to get within a light year of it from within a Windows application. All CD-ROM access under Windows is handled by much more civilized means.

Accessing data from a CD-ROM that's been structured as a DOS volume is exceedingly easy under Windows—you can treat CD-ROM files just like hard-drive files, and read them just as you would any other file. There are two catches to this, although they're pretty mild as catches go. The first one is that if you have an application that likes to write temporary files, maintain a database index, update a time or date stamp, or otherwise create or modify data on the drive it's reading, you'll have to come up with a way to have it make an exception when it's confronted with a CD-ROM.

This is usually pretty easy to manage under Windows, actually. Configuration settings can be stored in your \WINDOWS directory, for example, and Windows can help you find out what sort of drive you're working with. Be particularly careful about this if you write applications that will be run from a CD-ROM.

The second catch is a bit more subtle, and some forethought can help you minimize its effects. Even with the newer high-speed CD-ROM drives, a CD-ROM is still a very slow device as compared to a hard drive. This, coupled with the nature of things on CD-ROMs tending to be very big, can make reading data from one particularly time consuming. In many cases, the things that programmers do to speed up data access from a hard drive might be dead wrong for applications designed to read data from a CD-ROM.

Here's an example. Graphic files, of the sorts I'll discuss later in this book, can be stored in a variety of file formats. One of the things that characterizes these different file formats is a trade-off of compression versus access time. A Windows BMP file is essentially uncompressed. It takes up a lot of space, but it can be read very quickly because the computer doing so doesn't need to spend meaningful amount of time running an algorithm to unpack the data. Perhaps the antithesis of this, GIF files use a very elaborate compression method that results in the smallest possible files. However, the procedure for unpacking this data is time-consuming, making GIF files fairly slow to read.

At least, all this is true if you're reading the source data from a fairly fast medium, such as a hard drive. Quite the opposite is true on a CD-ROM drive, where the speed at which data can be read is very much slower than the speed at which a computer can process it. A GIF file, because it's compressed and requires that less actual data be read, can be quicker to read and unpack than a BMP file, which involves little processing but very much more reading.

Data types that typically create large files, such as databases, graphics, and AutoCAD drawings, can impose some serious speed penalties on applications that propose to read them from a CD-ROM.

Playing compact disc audio

With the exception of the foregoing digression into CD-ROM files, this chapter is primarily concerned with playing audio tracks. Most CD-ROM drives include a headphone jack in front and an audio jack on their interface cards to allow you to play compact discs through an amplifier or a stereo. Figure 3-4 illustrates the headphone jack on a Sony CD-ROM drive. You can plug any set of standard 8-ohm headphones into this jack to listen to compact discs played in a CD-ROM drive.

For the sake of this discussion, let's look at playing a typical audio compact disc under software control. You can use a disc of your own choosing, or, if you don't have one handy, you can use the CD-ROM that comes with this book. Aside from the files, you'll find about half an hour of traditional celtic music on it, recorded in various living rooms and churches in the months before the publication of this book. In all respects save one, this can be treated as a normal compact disc. The one exception is that you should not attempt to play track one, as this appears to a disc player as an audio track but is in fact computer data. It will play as random noise.

An audio compact disc, or the audio portion of a CD-ROM with both data and audio on it, is organized as tracks, where one track is typically one song. This has nothing to do with disk tracks and sectors, and is really a bit of jargon left over from the heyday of vinyl phonograph records. A track can be any length you want it to be, as long as it fits in the length of the disc.

The length of a compact disc track is measured in minutes, seconds, and frames, where one frame is ⅟₇₅ of a second. It's possible to play portions of a track, starting and stopping with the accuracy of a single frame, that is, accurate to the nearest ⅟₇₅ of a second. Having said this, remember that while a CD-ROM drive can play partial tracks in real time, the amount of time required to seek from one track to another and locate the starting frame in question can be substantial; even worse, it could vary depending on where you're starting from. Applications that play canned sounds from a CD-ROM drive this way should keep the potential seek times in mind. If your application calls for playing numerous sound bites from a CD-ROM with precise timing, make sure they're located physically close together on the disc.

Playing sound from a compact disc under Windows is handled through MCI calls, which were introduced in the previous chapter. The compact disc interface is, if anything, even less complicated than the one for wave files. The basic structure of using MCI calls works in much the same way for a compact disc—you open the appropriate device, start playing the track you're interested in, and then get on with something else. The MCI driver will send a message to the window of your choice when the track is complete.

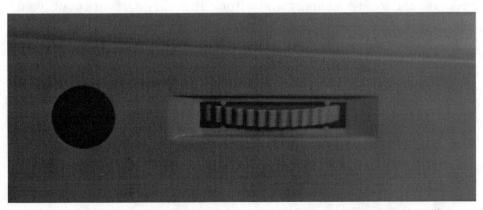

3-4   The headphone jack of a CD-ROM drive, shown here somewhat larger than life.

In the CDPLAY application to be discussed later in this chapter—perhaps predictably, an example compact disc player—we'll look at how you can use the end of track message from one track to start playing the next track in a list.

In addition to playing tracks, MCI calls allow you to find out things about a compact disc, such as how many tracks it contains and how long each track is. It's worth noting that when you use these calls to read a compact disc that also contains computer data, MCI will completely ignore the computer data and will present the disc to you as an audio-only device.

Finally, if you read through this chapter and then have a look at the corresponding parts of the Microsoft Multimedia Programmer's Workbook that accompanies the multimedia software development kit, you'll find that a few things are handled differently here. There are a few pretty hoary errors in the Microsoft book. One of the ones to watch out for in the examples is the Microsoft approach to playing an entire track on a compact disc. They handle it by playing from the start of one track to the start of the next. This works flawlessly unless you attempt to play the last track on a disc—as you might imagine, there's no next track in this case, and the request will fail.

MCI calls and compact discs

The MCI interface will allow you to turn a $5,000 computer into a $100 compact disc player with a minimum of complicated software. Perhaps more to the point, it will let you use the resulting $5,000 compact disc player to do things that a conventional consumer disc player could never imagine.

Figure 3-5 illustrates the main window of CDPLAY, the application discussed later in this chapter. It will generate a list of the tracks on a compact disc, displaying the playing time of each, and allow you to select one, some, or all of them to play. It will keep a running count of what's being played while it's in the process of doing something else. It will also eject your current compact disc from the CD-ROM drive of your computer on command, one of the ancillary things that MCI knows how to handle.

In creating an application like CDPLAY, which merely plays tracks from a compact disc, it's worth keeping in mind that the software will use almost no system resources while it's running. Its big moment comes when it's time to end one track and start another, which might occur a dozen times an hour if you use it to play entire discs. You can run CDPLAY, have it start a disc playing, and minimize it, letting it manage the CD-ROM drive in the background while you get on with other things.

Let's start with something simple. We'll fetch a list of the tracks on a compact disc and store them somewhere. In the case of CDPLAY, they're stored in a list box—you're free to do whatever you like with this information.

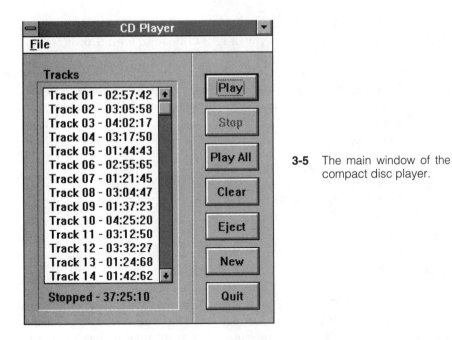

3-5 The main window of the compact disc player.

To begin with, as with the code to play wave files in the last chapter, you must start by opening a suitable device to play a compact disc. The device in question is called cdaudio. Here's the MCI call to handle it. If you haven't read the discussion of MCI calls in general in chapter 2, you should probably do so now, so all this can make a degree of sense.

```
MCI__OPEN__PARMS mciOpen;
char b[STRINGSIZE+1];
int id;

mciOpen.lpstrDeviceType="cdaudio";
if((rtrn=mciSendCommand(NULL,MCI__OPEN,MCI__OPEN__TYPE,
    (DWORD)(LPVOID)&mciOpen)) != 0) {
        mciGetErrorString(rtrn,(LPSTR)b,STRINGSIZE);
        DoMessage(hwnd,b);
        SendMessage(dlgH,WM__SETREDRAW,TRUE,0L);
        SetCursor(hSaveCursor);
        return(0);
}

id=mciOpen.wDeviceID;
```

As in the examples of MCI calls that were used to play wave files, the mciSendCommand function will either open the device you've asked for and return a handle to it in the wDeviceID element of the MCI_OPEN_PARMS object passed to it—and a zero value as its function return—or it will return an error code. One common error is attempting to open the cdaudio device with MSCDEX not loaded. Because the MSCDEX driver eats a substantial amount of memory, you might choose to load it only when it's required.

Once you've opened the cdaudio device, you can set it up to provide you with the information you require. To begin with, let's put it in the format that will have it provide the aforementioned information in the most useful way:

```
MCI__SET__PARMS mciSet;

mciSet.dwTimeFormat=MCI__FORMAT__TMSF;
if((rtrn=mciSendCommand(id,MCI__SET,MCI__SET__TIME__FORMAT,
    (DWORD)(LPVOID)&mciSet)) != 0) {
        mciGetErrorString(rtrn,(LPSTR)b,STRINGSIZE);
        DoMessage(hwnd,b);
        mciSendCommand(id,MCI__CLOSE,0,NULL);
        return(0);
}
```

This call to mciSendCommand tells the cdaudio driver to return track information in the TMSF format—this stands for track, minutes, seconds, and frames. As you'll see in a moment, the multimedia development kit offers a number of macros to make these numbers dead easy to turn into human-readable information.

The next thing we'd like to know is the number of tracks on the compact disc in question. Here's how to have the cdaudio driver count them:

```
MCI__STATUS__PARMS mciStat;
unsigned int tracks;

mciStat.dwItem=MCI__STATUS__NUMBER__OF__TRACKS;
if((rtrn=mciSendCommand(id,MCI__STATUS,MCI__STATUS__ITEM,
    (DWORD)(LPVOID)&mciStat)) != 0) {
        mciGetErrorString(rtrn,(LPSTR)b,STRINGSIZE);
        DoMessage(hwnd,b);
        mciSendCommand(id,MCI__CLOSE,0,NULL);
        return(0);
}

tracks=(unsigned int)mciStat.dwReturn;
```

The value of tracks represents the number of the last track on the compact disc about to be played. The first track is one, however, not zero. Here's how to actually retrieve the playing time of each track:

```
unsigned int i;

for(i=1;i<=tracks;++i) {

    mciStat.dwItem=MCI__STATUS__LENGTH;
```

```
    mciStat.dwTrack=i;
    if((rtrn=mciSendCommand(id,MCI__STATUS,MCI__STATUS__ITEM | MCI__TRACK,
        (DWORD)(LPVOID)&mciStat)) != 0) {
        mciGetErrorString(rtrn,(LPSTR)b,STRINGSIZE);
        DoMessage(hwnd,b);
        mciSendCommand(id,MCI__CLOSE,0,NULL);
        return(0);
    }

    wsprintf(b," Track %02u - %02u:%02u:%02u",i,
        MCI__MSF__MINUTE(mciStat.dwReturn),
        MCI__MSF__SECOND(mciStat.dwReturn),
        MCI__MSF__FRAME(mciStat.dwReturn)
        );

    SendDlgItemMessage(hwnd,LIST__BOX,LB__ADDSTRING,0,(DWORD)(LPSTR)b);
}
```

The foregoing bit of code will step through each track on a compact disc and
fetch its track length. The call to mciSendCommand will cause the track length
to be returned in the dwReturn element of the MCI__STATUS__PARMS object
passed to it. This value will be encoded into the MSF format—minutes, seconds, frames—because of the earlier mciSendCommand call that asked that it
be so. You can extract the actual number of minutes, seconds, and frames
required to play each track by using three macros defined in MMSYSTEM.H:

```
#define MCI__MSF__MINUTE(msf)  ((BYTE)(msf))
#define MCI__MSF__SECOND(msf)  ((BYTE)(((WORD)(msf)) >> 8))
#define MCI__MSF__FRAME(msf)   ((BYTE)((msf)>>16))
```

In each case, the msf argument is a packed time value of the sort returned
by the call to mciSendCommand in the previous example. There's also a
macro to reassemble the three resulting numbers into an MSF value:

```
#define MCI__MAKE__MSF(m,s,f)  ((DWORD)(((BYTE)(m) | \
                               ((WORD)(s)<<8)) | \
                               (((DWORD)(BYTE)(f))<<16)))
```

In this case, the arguments m, s, and f represent the number of minutes,
seconds, and frames involved. The code to step through each of the tracks
will retrieve the track length, format it into a text string, and add it to a
hypothetical list box, with the resource ID LIST__BOX. You're free to use
this information in some other form, of course.

When you're done with the compact disc for the time being, you
should close its MCI driver, like this:

```
mciSendCommand(id,MCI__CLOSE,0,NULL);
```

It's rather unfortunate that, along with the audio information on compact
discs, the tracks don't carry some text to represent them—the name of the

song or performance in question would be useful to applications like this one. In fact, there's quite a bit of unused capacity on any compact disc— even the ones with a full 74 minutes of sound—in the form of six unspoken-for subcode bits on each word of stored data. This amounts to about twenty megabytes of left-over free space on a full disc.

Actually playing a track from a compact disc isn't much more involved than figuring out how long it runs for, and the calls involved are almost the same. Once again, you must begin by opening the cdaudio MCI device to access the compact disc to be played. Also as in the example of fetching track information, the time format should be set to MCI_FORMAT_TMSF. Unfortunately, there isn't a practical way to tell MCI to just go ahead and play a whole track. Rather, you must find out how long the track in question and then hand the number back to MCI as the length of time to play for—which sounds a bit like what consultants do for a living. The code is as follows:

```
MCI_OPEN_PARMS mciOpen;
MCI_SET_PARMS mciSet;
DWORD rtrn;
char b[STRINGSIZE+1];
int id;

mciOpen.lpstrDeviceType="cdaudio";
if((rtrn=mciSendCommand(NULL,MCI_OPEN,MCI_OPEN_TYPE,
    (DWORD)(LPVOID)&mciOpen)) != 0) {
        mciGetErrorString(rtrn,(LPSTR)b,STRINGSIZE);
        DoMessage(hwnd,b);
        return(-1);
}

id=mciOpen.wDeviceID;

mciSet.dwTimeFormat=MCI_FORMAT_TMSF;
if((rtrn=mciSendCommand(id,MCI_SET,MCI_SET_TIME_FORMAT,
    (DWORD)(LPVOID)&mciSet)) != 0) {
        mciGetErrorString(rtrn,(LPSTR)b,STRINGSIZE);
        DoMessage(hwnd,b);
        mciSendCommand(id,MCI_CLOSE,0,NULL);
        return(-1);
}
```

Now that the MCI cdaudio driver knows what it's supposed to be doing, you can get the length of the track in question. In this example, the number of the track to be played is in the value tracknumber:

```
MCI_STATUS_PARMS mciStat;
unsigned long time;

mciStat.dwItem=MCI_STATUS_LENGTH;
mciStat.dwTrack=tracknumber;
```

```
if((rtrn=mciSendCommand(id,MCI_STATUS,MCI_STATUS_ITEM | MCI_TRACK,
    (DWORD)(LPVOID)&mciStat)) != 0) {
    mciGetErrorString(rtrn,(LPSTR)b,STRINGSIZE);
    DoMessage(hwnd,b);
    mciSendCommand(id,MCI_CLOSE,0,NULL);
    return(-1);
}

time=mciStat.dwReturn;
```

Finally, with all the preamble over, the track can actually be played:

```
lmemset(((LPSTR)&mciPlay,0,sizeof(MCI_PLAY_PARMS));

mciPlay.dwFrom=MCI_MAKE_TMSF(track,
    MCI_MSF_MINUTE(0),
    MCI_MSF_SECOND(0),
    MCI_MSF_FRAME(0));
mciPlay.dwTo=MCI_MAKE_TMSF(track,
    MCI_MSF_MINUTE(time),
    MCI_MSF_SECOND(time),
    MCI_MSF_FRAME(time));

mciPlay.dwCallback=(DWORD)hwnd;
if((rtrn=mciSendCommand(id,MCI_PLAY,MCI_FROM | MCI_TO | MCI_NOTIFY,
    (DWORD)(LPVOID)&mciPlay)) != 0) {
    mciGetErrorString(rtrn,(LPSTR)b,STRINGSIZE);
    DoMessage(hwnd,b);
    mciSendCommand(id,MCI_CLOSE,0,NULL);
    return(0);
}

return(id);
```

The call to mciSendCommand that plays a compact disc track expects to see
a number of parameters in the MCI_SET_PARMS object passed to it. The
dwFrom element should contain the start time for the sound to be played,
relative to the beginning of the track, and the track number—all packed
up into the TMSF format, a variation on the earlier MSF format in that it
includes the track number to be played. The macro MCI_MAKE_TMSF,
defined in MMSYSTEM.H, allows you to pack the discrete elements of a
TMSF value into the proper format, as illustrated in the foregoing example.

The dwTo element of the MCI_SET_PARMS object tells the MCI
driver where to stop playing the compact disc. The dwCallback element of
the MCI_SET_PARMS object should contain an HWND window handle
for the MCI driver to send a message to when the track that has been requested is finished playing. This works pretty much like it did in the last
chapter, where MCI calls were used to play wave files. The message, once
again, will be MM_MCINOTIFY. Here's a typical case to handle it:

```
    case MM__MCINOTIFY:
       mciSendCommand(LOWORD(lParam),MCI__CLOSE,MCI__WAIT,NULL);
       break;
```

The low-order word of the lParam argument passed to the message handler
for the window in question will hold the ID value for the MCI device that
was opened back at the beginning of the discussion of playing wave files.
As there are no buffers to free up in this example, all the handler for this
message really has to do is close the driver.

Finally, let's look at one more bit of the mysteries of playing compact
discs under software control. In most cases, you can eject the disc tray
from your drive by physically pushing the eject button. However, there's
also a function that can manage this under software control. You might
want to use it if the software you write isn't given the disc it expects, or if
it finds itself playing rap or elevator music—it's up to you to come up with
a way for it to know this, of course.

Here's a function to eject the current compact disc from your CD-
ROM drive. The hwnd argument is a window handle, and is used to hang
the message dialog on only if something goes wrong. You can pass NULL
for this argument if you like.

```
int EjectCD(HWND hwnd)
{
    MCI__OPEN__PARMS mciOpen;
    MCI__SET__PARMS mciSet;
    DWORD rtrn;
    int id;
    char b[STRINGSIZE+1];

    mciOpen.lpstrDeviceType="cdaudio";
    if((rtrn=mciSendCommand(NULL,MCI__OPEN,MCI__OPEN__TYPE,
        (DWORD)(LPVOID)&mciOpen)) != 0) {
            mciGetErrorString(rtrn,(LPSTR)b,STRINGSIZE);
            DoMessage(hwnd,b);
            return(0);
    }

id=mciOpen.wDeviceID;

if((rtrn=mciSendCommand(id,MCI__SET,MCI__SET__DOOR__OPEN,
    (DWORD)(LPVOID)&mciSet)) != 0) {
        mciGetErrorString(rtrn,(LPSTR)b,STRINGSIZE);
        DoMessage(hwnd,b);
        mciSendCommand(id,MCI__CLOSE,0,NULL);
        return(0);
}

mciSendCommand(id,MCI__CLOSE,0,NULL);
```

```
        return(1);
    }
```

The EjectCD function is pretty easy to understand, as it uses largely the same MCI calls as the previous examples in this chapter. It opens the cdaudio driver and then sends it the command MCI_SET_DOOR_OPEN. It then closes the driver and returns a true value to indicate that the disc was ejected.

Note that there's also an MCI command called MCI_SET_DOOR_CLOSED, which will predictably load a compact disc back into your CD-ROM drive. At least, it will if your drive actually has the mechanics to do this. Many CD-ROM drives don't, and as such it's probably a good idea not to count on this command being usable in all cases. The Sony CDU-31A drive illustrated earlier, for example, has a spring-loaded drive tray that must be pushed into the drive by hand. When you issue an MCI_SET_DOOR_OPEN command, the spring releases and the drive tray launches itself from the drive. Being a moderately priced drive, the Sony CDU-31A lacks a mechanical hand that can reach out and push its drive tray back in.

Casual observers of technology might well speculate why it is that a $300 CD-ROM drive has a much more primitive mechanism than a $100 consumer compact disc player, especially considering that in this case the same manufacturer makes both.

The compact disc player application

An application to play compact discs through a CD-ROM drive need be little more than the foregoing code put in a convenient package. In fact, with a few additional functions, you can add some worthwhile features to it. The MCI interface for compact disc audio is unusually elegant, and allows a reasonable degree of seamless integration with very little code.

The CDPLAY application, illustrated back in FIG. 3-5, can play all or part of a compact disc. It will allow you to select the tracks you'd like to listen to from its list box, click on Play, and forget it's there until the disc runs out. It will also play partial tracks, and it has a button to eject the current disc under software control.

The C language source code for CDPLAY is illustrated in FIG. 3-6. In addition to CDPLAY.CPP, you'll need the CDPLAY.RC file, as shown in FIG. 3-7. This, in turn, requires two medium-sized blue parrots to compile, the usefulness of which will become apparent in a moment. The parrots are stored in a file called CDPLAY.BMP, which should be located in the same directory as CDPLAY.RC. All the source files for CDPLAY, including the parrots, are available on the companion CD-ROM for this book.

3-6 The C language source listing for the compact disc player, CDPLAY.CPP.

```
/*
    CD Player
    Copyright (c) 1993 Alchemy Mindworks Inc.
*/

#include <windows.h>
#include <stdio.h>
#include <stdlib.h>
#include <dir.h>
#include <ctype.h>
#include <alloc.h>
#include <string.h>
#include <io.h>
#include <bwcc.h>
#include <dos.h>
#include <errno.h>
#include <math.h>
#include <mmsystem.h>

#define say(s)      MessageBox(NULL,s,"Yo...",MB_OK | MB_ICONSTOP);
#define saynumber(f,s)    {char b[128]; sprintf((LPSTR)b,(LPSTR)f,s);\
        MessageBox(NULL,b,"Debug Message",MB_OK | MB_ICONSTOP); }

#define ItemName(item,string)   { dlgH=GetDlgItem(hwnd,item); \
                                  SetWindowText(dlgH,(LPSTR)string); }
#define ItemOn(item)    { dlgH=GetDlgItem(hwnd,item); EnableWindow(dlgH,TRUE); }
#define ItemOff(item)   { dlgH=GetDlgItem(hwnd,item); EnableWindow(dlgH,FALSE); }

#define STRINGSIZE          129         /* how big is a string? */

#define MAIN_LIST           201         /* objects in the main window */

#define MAIN_PLAY           101         /* buttons and main menu items */
#define MAIN_STOP           102
#define MAIN_EJECT          103
#define MAIN_NEW            104
#define MAIN_ABOUT          105
#define MAIN_PLAYPART       106
#define MAIN_EXIT           107
#define MAIN_CLEAR          108
#define MAIN_PLAYALL        109
#define MAIN_STATUS         202

#define PLAYPART_FROM       101         /* partial play dialog items */
```

```
#define PLAYPART_TO           102
#define PLAYPART_FTEXT        201
#define PLAYPART_TTEXT        202


#define THETIMER              1              /* timer number */


#define MESSAGE_STRING        101            /* message box object */

#ifndef max
#define max(a,b)              (((a)>(b))?(a):(b))
#endif
#ifndef min
#define min(a,b)              (((a)<(b))?(a):(b))
#endif


#define    SECONDS(n)    (MCI_MSF_SECOND(n)+MCI_MSF_MINUTE(n)*60)
#define    SAYFRAMES(b,n)    wsprintf(b,"%02u:%02u:%02u",MCI_MSF_MINUTE(n),\
                         MCI_MSF_SECOND(n),MCI_MSF_FRAME(n))


typedef struct{
    DWORD from;
    DWORD to;
    DWORD total;
    int track;
    } TRACK;

/* prototypes */
long FAR PASCAL WaitProc(HWND hwnd,unsigned int message,
                         unsigned int wParam,LONG lParam);
DWORD FAR PASCAL SelectProc(HWND hwnd,WORD message,WORD wParam,LONG lParam);
DWORD FAR PASCAL AboutDlgProc(HWND hwnd,WORD message,WORD wParam,LONG lParam);
DWORD FAR PASCAL MessageDlgProc(HWND hwnd,WORD message,WORD wParam,LONG lParam);
DWORD FAR PASCAL PartialDlgProc(HWND hwnd,WORD message,WORD wParam,LONG lParam);
int GetTrackLength(HWND hwnd,TRACK *track);
int PlayTrack(HWND hwnd,TRACK *track);
int GetNextSelection(HWND hwnd,int listbox);

void DoMessage(HWND hwnd,LPSTR message);
void lmemset(LPSTR s,int n,unsigned int size);

int GetPartial(HWND hwnd,TRACK *track);
int ResetSelectorList(HWND hwnd,unsigned int listbox,TRACK *track);
int EjectCD(HWND hwnd);

HWND ShowWaitWindow(HWND hwnd);
```

```
/* globals */
FARPROC waitDlgProc;

LPSTR messagehook;

char stopped[]=" Stopped - %02u:%02u:%02u";
char szAppName[] = "CDPlayer";
HANDLE hInst;

int soundID=-1;

#pragma warn -par
int PASCAL WinMain(HANDLE hInstance,HANDLE hPrevInstance,
                LPSTR lpszCmdParam,int nCmdShow)
{
    FARPROC dlgProc;
    int r=0;

    BWCCGetVersion();

    hInst=hInstance;

    dlgProc=MakeProcInstance((FARPROC)SelectProc,hInst);
    r=DialogBox(hInst,"MainScreen",NULL,dlgProc);

    FreeProcInstance(dlgProc);

    return(r);
}

DWORD FAR PASCAL SelectProc(HWND hwnd,WORD message,WORD wParam,LONG lParam)
{
    MCI_GENERIC_PARMS mcigen;
    PAINTSTRUCT ps;
    static HICON hIcon;
    FARPROC lpfnDlgProc;
    POINT point;
    HWND dlgH,hwait;
    HMENU hmenu;
    static TRACK track;
    char b[STRINGSIZE+1];
    unsigned int minutes,seconds,frames;
    int n;

    switch(message) {
```

```
case MM_MCINOTIFY:
    mciSendCommand(LOWORD(lParam),MCI_CLOSE,MCI_WAIT,NULL);
    soundID=-1;
    ItemOn(MAIN_LIST);
    ItemOn(MAIN_PLAY);
    ItemOn(MAIN_PLAYALL);
    ItemOff(MAIN_STOP);
    ItemOn(MAIN_EJECT);
    ItemOn(MAIN_NEW);
    ItemOn(MAIN_CLEAR);
    hmenu=GetMenu(hwnd);
    EnableMenuItem(hmenu,MAIN_PLAY,MF_ENABLED);
    EnableMenuItem(hmenu,MAIN_PLAYALL,MF_ENABLED);
    EnableMenuItem(hmenu,MAIN_STOP,MF_GRAYED);
    EnableMenuItem(hmenu,MAIN_EJECT,MF_ENABLED);
    EnableMenuItem(hmenu,MAIN_PLAYPART,MF_ENABLED);
    EnableMenuItem(hmenu,MAIN_NEW,MF_ENABLED);
    EnableMenuItem(hmenu,MAIN_CLEAR,MF_ENABLED);
    KillTimer(hwnd,THETIMER);
    wsprintf(b,stopped,MCI_MSF_MINUTE(track.total),
        MCI_MSF_SECOND(track.total),
        MCI_MSF_FRAME(track.total));
    ItemName(MAIN_STATUS,b);

    if((n=GetNextSelection(hwnd,MAIN_LIST)) != -1) {
        if(SendDlgItemMessage(hwnd,MAIN_LIST,LB_SETSEL,0,
          (long)n) != LB_ERR) {
            PostMessage(hwnd,WM_COMMAND,MAIN_PLAY,0L);
        }
    }
    break;
case WM_CTLCOLOR:
    if(HIWORD(lParam)==CTLCOLOR_STATIC ||
        HIWORD(lParam)==CTLCOLOR_DLG) {
        SetBkColor(wParam,RGB(192,192,192));
        SetTextColor(wParam,RGB(0,0,0));

        ClientToScreen(hwnd,&point);
        UnrealizeObject(GetStockObject(LTGRAY_BRUSH));
        SetBrushOrg(wParam,point.x,point.y);

        return((DWORD)GetStockObject(LTGRAY_BRUSH));

    }
    if(HIWORD(lParam)==CTLCOLOR_BTN) {
        SetBkColor(wParam,RGB(192,192,192));
```

```
                SetTextColor(wParam,RGB(0,0,0));

            ClientToScreen(hwnd,&point);
            UnrealizeObject(GetStockObject(BLACK_BRUSH));
            SetBrushOrg(wParam,point.x,point.y);

            return((DWORD)GetStockObject(BLACK_BRUSH));
        }
        break;
    case WM_SYSCOMMAND:
        switch(wParam & 0xfff0) {
            case SC_CLOSE:
                SendMessage(hwnd,WM_COMMAND,MAIN_EXIT,0L);
                break;
        }
        break;
    case WM_INITDIALOG:
        hwait=ShowWaitWindow(hwnd);
        hIcon=LoadIcon(hInst,szAppName);
        SetClassWord(hwnd,GCW_HICON,(WORD)hIcon);
        ResetSelectorList(hwnd,MAIN_LIST,&track);

        ItemOff(MAIN_STOP);
        hmenu=GetMenu(hwnd);
        EnableMenuItem(hmenu,MAIN_STOP,MF_GRAYED);

        wsprintf(b,stopped,MCI_MSF_MINUTE(track.total),\
            MCI_MSF_SECOND(track.total),MCI_MSF_FRAME(track.total));
        ItemName(MAIN_STATUS,b);

        DestroyWindow(hwait);
        if(waitDlgProc != NULL) FreeProcInstance(waitDlgProc);
        break;
    case WM_PAINT:
        BeginPaint(hwnd,&ps);
        EndPaint(hwnd,&ps);
        break;
    case WM_TIMER:
        minutes=MCI_MSF_MINUTE(track.from);
        seconds=MCI_MSF_SECOND(track.from)+1;
        if(seconds >=60) {
            ++minutes;
            seconds=0;
        }
        frames=MCI_MSF_FRAME(track.from);
```

```
        track.from=MCI_MAKE_MSF(minutes,seconds,frames);

    wsprintf(b,"#%u - %02u:%02u  -  %02u:%02u ",
        track.track,
        MCI_MSF_MINUTE(track.from),
        MCI_MSF_SECOND(track.from),
        MCI_MSF_MINUTE(track.to),
        MCI_MSF_SECOND(track.to)
        );
    ItemName(MAIN_STATUS,b);

    break;
case WM_COMMAND:
    switch(wParam) {
        case MAIN_NEW:
            SendMessage(hwnd,WM_COMMAND,MAIN_STOP,0L);
            if(ResetSelectorList(hwnd,MAIN_LIST,&track)) {
                ItemOn(MAIN_LIST);
                ItemOn(MAIN_PLAY);
                ItemOff(MAIN_PLAYALL);
                ItemOn(MAIN_CLEAR);
                ItemOff(MAIN_STOP);
                hmenu=GetMenu(hwnd);
                EnableMenuItem(hmenu,MAIN_PLAY,MF_ENABLED);
                EnableMenuItem(hmenu,MAIN_PLAYALL,MF_ENABLED);
                EnableMenuItem(hmenu,MAIN_STOP,MF_GRAYED);
                EnableMenuItem(hmenu,MAIN_PLAYPART,MF_ENABLED);
                EnableMenuItem(hmenu,MAIN_CLEAR,MF_ENABLED);
            }
            break;
        case MAIN_STOP:
            if(soundID != -1) {
                SendMessage(hwnd,WM_COMMAND,MAIN_CLEAR,0L);
                mcigen.dwCallback=hwnd;
                mciSendCommand(soundID,MCI_STOP,\
                    MCI_NOTIFY | MCI_WAIT,(DWORD)(LPVOID)&mcigen);
            }
            break;
        case MAIN_CLEAR:
            SendDlgItemMessage(hwnd,MAIN_LIST,LB_SETSEL,0,-1L);
            break;
        case MAIN_PLAYALL:
            SendDlgItemMessage(hwnd,MAIN_LIST,LB_SETSEL,1,-1L);
            SendMessage(hwnd,WM_COMMAND,MAIN_PLAY,0L);
            break;
        case MAIN_PLAYPART:
```

```
            if((track.track=GetNextSelection(hwnd,MAIN_LIST)) != -1) {
                ++track.track;
                if(GetTrackLength(hwnd,&track)) {
                    if(GetPartial(hwnd,&track)) {
                        if((soundID=PlayTrack(hwnd,&track)) != -1) {
                            SetTimer(hwnd,THETIMER,1000,NULL);
                            ItemOff(MAIN_LIST);
                            ItemOff(MAIN_PLAY);
                            ItemOff(MAIN_PLAYALL);
                            ItemOff(MAIN_CLEAR);
                            ItemOn(MAIN_STOP);
                            ItemOff(MAIN_EJECT);
                            ItemOff(MAIN_NEW);
                            hmenu=GetMenu(hwnd);
                            EnableMenuItem(hmenu,MAIN_PLAY,MF_GRAYED);
                            EnableMenuItem(hmenu,MAIN_PLAYALL,MF_GRAYED);
                            EnableMenuItem(hmenu,MAIN_STOP,MF_ENABLED);
                            EnableMenuItem(hmenu,MAIN_PLAYPART,MF_GRAYED);
                            EnableMenuItem(hmenu,MAIN_EJECT,MF_GRAYED);
                            EnableMenuItem(hmenu,MAIN_NEW,MF_GRAYED);
                            EnableMenuItem(hmenu,MAIN_CLEAR,MF_GRAYED);
                        }
                    }
                }
            }
            break;
        case MAIN_PLAY:
            if((track.track=GetNextSelection(hwnd,MAIN_LIST)) != -1) {
                ++track.track;
                if(GetTrackLength(hwnd,&track)) {
                    if((soundID=PlayTrack(hwnd,&track)) != -1) {
                        SetTimer(hwnd,THETIMER,1000,NULL);
                        ItemOff(MAIN_PLAY);
                        ItemOff(MAIN_PLAYALL);
                        ItemOff(MAIN_CLEAR);
                        ItemOn(MAIN_STOP);
                        ItemOff(MAIN_EJECT);
                        ItemOff(MAIN_NEW);
                        hmenu=GetMenu(hwnd);
                        EnableMenuItem(hmenu,MAIN_LIST,MF_GRAYED);
                        EnableMenuItem(hmenu,MAIN_PLAY,MF_GRAYED);
                        EnableMenuItem(hmenu,MAIN_PLAYALL,MF_GRAYED);
                        EnableMenuItem(hmenu,MAIN_STOP,MF_ENABLED);
                        EnableMenuItem(hmenu,MAIN_PLAYPART,MF_GRAYED);
                        EnableMenuItem(hmenu,MAIN_EJECT,MF_GRAYED);
```

```
                            EnableMenuItem(hmenu,MAIN_NEW,MF_GRAYED);
                            EnableMenuItem(hmenu,MAIN_CLEAR,MF_GRAYED);
                        }
                    }
                }
                break;
            case MAIN_EJECT:
                SendMessage(hwnd,WM_COMMAND,MAIN_STOP,0L);
                if(EjectCD(hwnd)) {
                    SendDlgItemMessage(hwnd,MAIN_LIST,LB_RESETCONTENT,0,0L);
                    ItemOff(MAIN_LIST);
                    ItemOff(MAIN_PLAY);
                    ItemOff(MAIN_PLAYALL);
                    ItemOff(MAIN_STOP);
                    hmenu=GetMenu(hwnd);
                    EnableMenuItem(hmenu,MAIN_PLAY,MF_GRAYED);
                    EnableMenuItem(hmenu,MAIN_PLAYALL,MF_GRAYED);
                    EnableMenuItem(hmenu,MAIN_STOP,MF_GRAYED);
                    EnableMenuItem(hmenu,MAIN_PLAYPART,MF_GRAYED);
                }
                break;
            case MAIN_ABOUT:
                if((lpfnDlgProc=MakeProcInstance((FARPROC)
                   AboutDlgProc,hInst)) != NULL) {
                    DialogBox(hInst,"AboutBox",hwnd,lpfnDlgProc);
                    FreeProcInstance(lpfnDlgProc);
                }
                break;
            case MAIN_EXIT:
                SendMessage(hwnd,WM_COMMAND,MAIN_STOP,0L);
                FreeResource(hIcon);
                PostQuitMessage(0);
                break;
        }
        break;

    }

    return(FALSE);
}

int PlayTrack(HWND hwnd,TRACK *track)
{
    MCI_OPEN_PARMS mciOpen;
    MCI_SET_PARMS mciSet;
    MCI_PLAY_PARMS mciPlay;
```

```
    DWORD rtrn;
    int id=-1;
    char b[STRINGSIZE+1];

    mciOpen.lpstrDeviceType="cdaudio";
    if((rtrn=mciSendCommand(NULL,MCI_OPEN,MCI_OPEN_TYPE,
      (DWORD)(LPVOID)&mciOpen)) != 0) {
        mciGetErrorString(rtrn,(LPSTR)b,STRINGSIZE);
        DoMessage(hwnd,b);
        return(-1);
    }

    id=mciOpen.wDeviceID;

    mciSet.dwTimeFormat=MCI_FORMAT_TMSF;
    if((rtrn=mciSendCommand(id,MCI_SET,MCI_SET_TIME_FORMAT,
      (DWORD)(LPVOID)&mciSet)) != 0) {
        mciGetErrorString(rtrn,(LPSTR)b,STRINGSIZE);
        DoMessage(hwnd,b);
        mciSendCommand(id,MCI_CLOSE,0,NULL);
            return(-1);
    }

    lmemset((LPSTR)&mciPlay,0,sizeof(MCI_PLAY_PARMS));

    mciPlay.dwFrom=MCI_MAKE_TMSF(track->track,MCI_MSF_MINUTE(track->from),
      MCI_MSF_SECOND(track->from),MCI_MSF_FRAME(track->from));

    mciPlay.dwTo=MCI_MAKE_TMSF(track->track,MCI_MSF_MINUTE(track->to),
      MCI_MSF_SECOND(track->to),MCI_MSF_FRAME(track->to));

    mciPlay.dwCallback=(DWORD)hwnd;
    if((rtrn=mciSendCommand(id,MCI_PLAY,MCI_FROM | MCI_TO | MCI_NOTIFY,
      (DWORD)(LPVOID)&mciPlay)) != 0) {
        mciGetErrorString(rtrn,(LPSTR)b,STRINGSIZE);
        DoMessage(hwnd,b);
        mciSendCommand(id,MCI_CLOSE,0,NULL);
        return(-1);
    }

    return(id);
}

int GetPartial(HWND hwnd,TRACK *track)
{
```

```
        FARPROC lpfnDlgProc;
        int r;

        messagehook=(LPSTR)track;

        if((lpfnDlgProc=MakeProcInstance((FARPROC)PartialDlgProc,hInst)) != NULL) {
            r=DialogBox(hInst,"PlayPartialBox",hwnd,lpfnDlgProc);
            FreeProcInstance(lpfnDlgProc);
        }

        return(r);
}

DWORD FAR PASCAL PartialDlgProc(HWND hwnd,WORD message,WORD wParam,LONG lParam)
{
        static TRACK *track;
        static unsigned int seconds;
        POINT point;
        HWND dlgH;
        char b[STRINGSIZE+1];
        long pos;

        switch(message) {
            case WM_INITDIALOG:
                        track=(TRACK *)messagehook;
                seconds=SECONDS(track->to);

                SAYFRAMES(b,track->from);
                ItemName(PLAYPART_FTEXT,(LPSTR)b);

                SAYFRAMES(b,track->to);
                ItemName(PLAYPART_TTEXT,(LPSTR)b);

                dlgH=GetDlgItem(hwnd,PLAYPART_FROM);
                SetScrollRange(dlgH,SB_CTL,0,seconds,FALSE);
                SetScrollPos(dlgH,SB_CTL,0,TRUE);

                dlgH=GetDlgItem(hwnd,PLAYPART_TO);
                SetScrollRange(dlgH,SB_CTL,0,seconds,FALSE);
                SetScrollPos(dlgH,SB_CTL,seconds,TRUE);

                return(TRUE);
            case WM_CTLCOLOR:
                if(HIWORD(lParam)==CTLCOLOR_STATIC ||
                    HIWORD(lParam)==CTLCOLOR_DLG) {
                    SetBkColor(wParam,RGB(192,192,192));
```

```
            SetTextColor(wParam,RGB(0,0,0));

            ClientToScreen(hwnd,&point);
            UnrealizeObject(GetStockObject(LTGRAY_BRUSH));
            SetBrushOrg(wParam,point.x,point.y);

            return((DWORD)GetStockObject(LTGRAY_BRUSH));

        }
        if(HIWORD(lParam)==CTLCOLOR_BTN) {
            SetBkColor(wParam,RGB(192,192,192));
            SetTextColor(wParam,RGB(0,0,0));

            ClientToScreen(hwnd,&point);
            UnrealizeObject(GetStockObject(BLACK_BRUSH));
            SetBrushOrg(wParam,point.x,point.y);

            return((DWORD)GetStockObject(BLACK_BRUSH));
        }
        break;
    case WM_HSCROLL:
        dlgH=HIWORD(lParam);
        pos=(long)GetScrollPos(dlgH,SB_CTL);
        switch(wParam) {
            case SB_LINEUP:
                pos-=1L;
                break;
            case SB_LINEDOWN:
                pos+=1L;
                break;
            case SB_PAGEUP:
                pos-=(seconds/60);
                break;
            case SB_PAGEDOWN:
                pos+=(seconds/60);
                break;
            case SB_THUMBPOSITION:
                pos=(long)LOWORD(lParam);
                break;
        }

        if(pos < 0L) pos=0L;
        else if(pos > seconds) pos=seconds;

        if(pos != GetScrollPos(dlgH,SB_CTL)) {
```

```
                SetScrollPos(dlgH,SB_CTL,(unsigned int)pos,TRUE);

                switch(GetDlgCtrlID(dlgH)) {
                    case PLAYPART_FROM:
                        SAYFRAMES(b,MCI_MAKE_MSF(pos/60,pos % 60,0));
                        ItemName(PLAYPART_FTEXT,(LPSTR)b);
                        break;
                    case PLAYPART_TO:
                        SAYFRAMES(b,MCI_MAKE_MSF(pos/60,pos % 60,0));
                        ItemName(PLAYPART_TTEXT,(LPSTR)b);
                        break;
                }
            }
            return(FALSE);
        case WM_COMMAND:
            switch(wParam) {
                case IDCANCEL:
                    EndDialog(hwnd,FALSE);
                    return(TRUE);
                case IDOK:
                    dlgH=GetDlgItem(hwnd,PLAYPART_FROM);
                    pos=GetScrollPos(dlgH,SB_CTL);
                    track->from=MCI_MAKE_MSF(pos/60,pos % 60,0);

                    dlgH=GetDlgItem(hwnd,PLAYPART_TO);
                    pos=GetScrollPos(dlgH,SB_CTL);
                    track->to=MCI_MAKE_MSF(pos/60,pos % 60,0);

                    EndDialog(hwnd,TRUE);
                    return(TRUE);
            }
            break;
    }

    return(FALSE);
}

DWORD FAR PASCAL AboutDlgProc(HWND hwnd,WORD message,WORD wParam,LONG lParam)
{
    POINT point;

    switch(message) {
        case WM_INITDIALOG:
            return(TRUE);
        case WM_CTLCOLOR:
            if(HIWORD(lParam)==CTLCOLOR_STATIC ||
```

```
                HIWORD(lParam)==CTLCOLOR_DLG) {
                 SetBkColor(wParam,RGB(192,192,192));
                 SetTextColor(wParam,RGB(0,0,0));

                 ClientToScreen(hwnd,&point);
                 UnrealizeObject(GetStockObject(LTGRAY_BRUSH));
                 SetBrushOrg(wParam,point.x,point.y);

                 return((DWORD)GetStockObject(LTGRAY_BRUSH));

            }
            if(HIWORD(lParam)==CTLCOLOR_BTN) {
                 SetBkColor(wParam,RGB(192,192,192));
                 SetTextColor(wParam,RGB(0,0,0));

                 ClientToScreen(hwnd,&point);
                 UnrealizeObject(GetStockObject(BLACK_BRUSH));
                 SetBrushOrg(wParam,point.x,point.y);

                 return((DWORD)GetStockObject(BLACK_BRUSH));
            }
            break;
        case WM_COMMAND:
            switch(wParam) {
                case IDOK:
                    EndDialog(hwnd,wParam);
                    return(TRUE);
            }
            break;
    }

    return(FALSE);
}


void DoMessage(HWND hwnd,LPSTR message)
{
    FARPROC lpfnDlgProc;

  messagehook=message;

  if((lpfnDlgProc=MakeProcInstance((FARPROC)MessageDlgProc,hInst)) != NULL) {
      DialogBox(hInst,"MessageBox",hwnd,lpfnDlgProc);
      FreeProcInstance(lpfnDlgProc);
  }
}
```

```
DWORD FAR PASCAL MessageDlgProc(HWND hwnd,WORD message,WORD wParam,LONG lParam)
{
    POINT point;
    HWND dlgH;

    switch(message) {
        case WM_INITDIALOG:
            dlgH=GetDlgItem(hwnd,MESSAGE_STRING);
            SetWindowText(dlgH,messagehook);
            return(TRUE);
        case WM_CTLCOLOR:
            if(HIWORD(lParam)==CTLCOLOR_STATIC ||
               HIWORD(lParam)==CTLCOLOR_DLG) {
                SetBkColor(wParam,RGB(192,192,192));
                SetTextColor(wParam,RGB(0,0,0));

                ClientToScreen(hwnd,&point);
                UnrealizeObject(GetStockObject(LTGRAY_BRUSH));
                SetBrushOrg(wParam,point.x,point.y);

                return((DWORD)GetStockObject(LTGRAY_BRUSH));

            }
            if(HIWORD(lParam)==CTLCOLOR_BTN) {
                SetBkColor(wParam,RGB(192,192,192));
                SetTextColor(wParam,RGB(0,0,0));

                ClientToScreen(hwnd,&point);
                UnrealizeObject(GetStockObject(BLACK_BRUSH));
                SetBrushOrg(wParam,point.x,point.y);

                return((DWORD)GetStockObject(BLACK_BRUSH));
            }
            break;
        case WM_COMMAND:
            switch(wParam) {
                case IDCANCEL:
                case IDOK:
                case IDYES:
                case IDNO:
                    EndDialog(hwnd,wParam);
                    return(TRUE);
            }
            break;
    }
```

```
    return(FALSE);
}

void lmemset(LPSTR s,int n,unsigned int size)
{
    unsigned int i;

    for(i=0;i<size;++i) *s++=n;
}

int ResetSelectorList(HWND hwnd,unsigned int listbox,TRACK *track)
{
    HWND dlgH;
    HCURSOR hSaveCursor,hHourGlass;
    MCI_OPEN_PARMS mciOpen;
    MCI_SET_PARMS mciSet;
    MCI_STATUS_PARMS mciStat;
    DWORD rtrn;
    char b[STRINGSIZE+1];
    unsigned int i,tracks,minutes=0,seconds=0,frames=0;
    int id;

    hHourGlass=LoadCursor(NULL,IDC_WAIT);
    hSaveCursor=SetCursor(hHourGlass);

    dlgH=GetDlgItem(hwnd,listbox);
    EnableWindow(dlgH,TRUE);
    SendDlgItemMessage(hwnd,listbox,LB_RESETCONTENT,0,0L);

    SendMessage(dlgH,WM_SETREDRAW,FALSE,0L);

    mciOpen.lpstrDeviceType="cdaudio";
    if((rtrn=mciSendCommand(NULL,MCI_OPEN,MCI_OPEN_TYPE,
      (DWORD)(LPVOID)&mciOpen)) != 0) {
        mciGetErrorString(rtrn,(LPSTR)b,STRINGSIZE);
        DoMessage(hwnd,b);
        SendMessage(dlgH,WM_SETREDRAW,TRUE,0L);
        SetCursor(hSaveCursor);
        return(0);
    }

    id=mciOpen.wDeviceID;

    mciSet.dwTimeFormat=MCI_FORMAT_TMSF;
    if((rtrn=mciSendCommand(id,MCI_SET,MCI_SET_TIME_FORMAT,
```

```
    (DWORD)(LPVOID)&mciSet)) != 0) {
      mciGetErrorString(rtrn,(LPSTR)b,STRINGSIZE);
      DoMessage(hwnd,b);
      mciSendCommand(id,MCI_CLOSE,0,NULL);
      SendMessage(dlgH,WM_SETREDRAW,TRUE,0L);
      SetCursor(hSaveCursor);
      return(0);
}

mciStat.dwItem=MCI_STATUS_NUMBER_OF_TRACKS;
if((rtrn=mciSendCommand(id,MCI_STATUS,MCI_STATUS_ITEM,
  (DWORD)(LPVOID)&mciStat)) != 0) {
    mciGetErrorString(rtrn,(LPSTR)b,STRINGSIZE);
    DoMessage(hwnd,b);
    mciSendCommand(id,MCI_CLOSE,0,NULL);
    SendMessage(dlgH,WM_SETREDRAW,TRUE,0L);
    SetCursor(hSaveCursor);
    return(0);
}

tracks=(unsigned int)mciStat.dwReturn;

for(i=1;i<=tracks;++i) {

    mciStat.dwItem=MCI_STATUS_LENGTH;
    mciStat.dwTrack=i;
    if((rtrn=mciSendCommand(id,MCI_STATUS,MCI_STATUS_ITEM | MCI_TRACK,
        (DWORD)(LPVOID)&mciStat)) != 0) {
        mciGetErrorString(rtrn,(LPSTR)b,STRINGSIZE);
        DoMessage(hwnd,b);
        mciSendCommand(id,MCI_CLOSE,0,NULL);
        SendMessage(dlgH,WM_SETREDRAW,TRUE,0L);
        SetCursor(hSaveCursor);
        return(0);
    }

    wsprintf(b," Track %02u - %02u:%02u:%02u",i,
        MCI_MSF_MINUTE(mciStat.dwReturn),
        MCI_MSF_SECOND(mciStat.dwReturn),
        MCI_MSF_FRAME(mciStat.dwReturn)
        );

    SendDlgItemMessage(hwnd,listbox,LB_ADDSTRING,0,(DWORD)(LPSTR)b);

    frames+=MCI_MSF_FRAME(mciStat.dwReturn);
```

```
        if(frames >= 75) {
            seconds+=(frames/75);
            frames=frames%75;
        }
        seconds+=MCI_MSF_SECOND(mciStat.dwReturn);
        if(seconds >= 60) {
            minutes+=(seconds/75);
            seconds=seconds%60;
        }
        minutes+=MCI_MSF_MINUTE(mciStat.dwReturn);

    }

    track->total=MCI_MAKE_MSF(minutes,seconds,frames);

    mciSendCommand(id,MCI_CLOSE,0,NULL);

    SendMessage(dlgH,WM_SETREDRAW,TRUE,OL);
    SetCursor(hSaveCursor);

    return(1);
}

int EjectCD(HWND hwnd)
{
    MCI_OPEN_PARMS mciOpen;
    MCI_SET_PARMS mciSet;
    DWORD rtrn;
    int id;
    char b[STRINGSIZE+1];

    mciOpen.lpstrDeviceType="cdaudio";
    if((rtrn=mciSendCommand(NULL,MCI_OPEN,MCI_OPEN_TYPE,
      (DWORD)(LPVOID)&mciOpen)) != 0) {
        mciGetErrorString(rtrn,(LPSTR)b,STRINGSIZE);
        DoMessage(hwnd,b);
        return(0);
    }

    id=mciOpen.wDeviceID;

    if((rtrn=mciSendCommand(id,MCI_SET,MCI_SET_DOOR_OPEN,
      (DWORD)(LPVOID)&mciSet)) != 0) {
        mciGetErrorString(rtrn,(LPSTR)b,STRINGSIZE);
        DoMessage(hwnd,b);
```

```
            mciSendCommand(id,MCI_CLOSE,0,NULL);
                return(0);
        }

        mciSendCommand(id,MCI_CLOSE,0,NULL);

        return(1);
}

int GetTrackLength(HWND hwnd,TRACK *track)
{
        MCI_OPEN_PARMS mciOpen;
        MCI_SET_PARMS mciSet;
        MCI_STATUS_PARMS mciStat;
        DWORD rtrn;
        char b[STRINGSIZE+1];
        int id,minutes,seconds,frames;

        mciOpen.lpstrDeviceType="cdaudio";
        if((rtrn=mciSendCommand(NULL,MCI_OPEN,MCI_OPEN_TYPE,
          (DWORD)(LPVOID)&mciOpen)) != 0) {
            mciGetErrorString(rtrn,(LPSTR)b,STRINGSIZE);
            DoMessage(hwnd,b);
            return(0);
        }

        id=mciOpen.wDeviceID;

        mciSet.dwTimeFormat=MCI_FORMAT_TMSF;
        if((rtrn=mciSendCommand(id,MCI_SET,MCI_SET_TIME_FORMAT,
          (DWORD)(LPVOID)&mciSet)) != 0) {
            mciGetErrorString(rtrn,(LPSTR)b,STRINGSIZE);
            DoMessage(hwnd,b);
            mciSendCommand(id,MCI_CLOSE,0,NULL);
            return(0);
        }

        mciStat.dwItem=MCI_STATUS_NUMBER_OF_TRACKS;
        if((rtrn=mciSendCommand(id,MCI_STATUS,MCI_STATUS_ITEM,
          (DWORD)(LPVOID)&mciStat)) != 0) {
            mciGetErrorString(rtrn,(LPSTR)b,STRINGSIZE);
            DoMessage(hwnd,b);
            mciSendCommand(id,MCI_CLOSE,0,NULL);
            return(0);
        }
```

3-6 Continued.

```
     if(track->track < 1 || track->track > mciStat.dwReturn) {
          DoMessage(hwnd,"Bad track number");
          mciSendCommand(id,MCI_CLOSE,0,NULL);
          return(0);
     }

     mciStat.dwItem=MCI_STATUS_LENGTH;
     mciStat.dwTrack=track->track;
     if((rtrn=mciSendCommand(id,MCI_STATUS,MCI_STATUS_ITEM | MCI_TRACK,
          (DWORD)(LPVOID)&mciStat)) != 0) {
          mciGetErrorString(rtrn,(LPSTR)b,STRINGSIZE);
          DoMessage(hwnd,b);
          mciSendCommand(id,MCI_CLOSE,0,NULL);
          return(0);
     }

     mciSendCommand(id,MCI_CLOSE,0,NULL);

     track->from=0L;

     minutes=MCI_MSF_MINUTE(mciStat.dwReturn);
     seconds=MCI_MSF_SECOND(mciStat.dwReturn);
     frames=MCI_MSF_FRAME(mciStat.dwReturn);

     if(frames)--frames;
     else {
          frames=74;
          --seconds;
     }

     track->to=MCI_MAKE_MSF(minutes,seconds,frames);

     return(1);
}

HWND ShowWaitWindow(HWND hwnd)
{
     if((waitDlgProc=MakeProcInstance((FARPROC)WaitProc,hInst)) != NULL)
          return(CreateDialog(hInst,"WaitBox",hwnd,waitDlgProc));
     else return(NULL);
}

long FAR PASCAL WaitProc(HWND hwnd,unsigned int message,
  unsigned int wParam,LONG lParam)
{
```

```
HDC hMemoryDC;
HBITMAP hBitmap,hOldBitmap;
HDC hdc;
PAINTSTRUCT ps;
BITMAP bitmap;
RECT rect;
int x,y;

switch(message) {
    case WM_INITDIALOG:
        if((hBitmap=LoadBitmap(hInst,"CDPlayerBitmap")) != NULL) {
            GetObject(hBitmap,sizeof(BITMAP),(LPSTR)&bitmap);
            x=(GetSystemMetrics(SM_CXSCREEN)-bitmap.bmWidth)/2;
            y=(GetSystemMetrics(SM_CYSCREEN)-bitmap.bmHeight)/2;
            SetWindowPos(hwnd,NULL,x,y,bitmap.bmWidth,
              bitmap.bmHeight,SWP_NOZORDER);
            DeleteObject(hBitmap);
        }
        return(TRUE);
    case WM_PAINT:
        hdc=BeginPaint(hwnd,&ps);
        GetClientRect(hwnd,&rect);
        if((hBitmap=LoadBitmap(hInst,"CDPlayerBitmap")) != NULL) {
            if((hMemoryDC=CreateCompatibleDC(hdc)) != NULL) {
                hOldBitmap=SelectObject(hMemoryDC,hBitmap);
                if(hOldBitmap) {
                    GetObject(hBitmap,sizeof(BITMAP),(LPSTR)&bitmap);
                    BitBlt(hdc,
                            0,
                            rect.bottom-bitmap.bmHeight,
                            bitmap.bmWidth,
                            bitmap.bmHeight,
                            hMemoryDC,
                            0,
                            0,
                            SRCCOPY);
                    SelectObject(hMemoryDC,hOldBitmap);
                }
                DeleteDC(hMemoryDC);
            }
            FreeResource(hBitmap);
        }

        EndPaint(hwnd,&ps);
        return(FALSE);
}
```

3-6 Continued.

```
    return(FALSE);
}

int GetNextSelection(HWND hwnd,int listbox)
{
    long count;
    int i,n;

    if((count=SendDlgItemMessage(hwnd,listbox,LB_GETCOUNT,0,0L)) != LB_ERR) {
        for(i=0;i<(int)count;++i) {
            n=(int)SendDlgItemMessage(hwnd,MAIN_LIST,LB_GETSEL,i,0L);
            if(n==LB_ERR) return(-1);
            if(n > 0) return(i);
        }
    }
    return(-1);
}
```

3-7 The resource script for the compact disc player, CDPLAY.RC.

```
MainScreen DIALOG 117, 55, 148, 156
STYLE WS_POPUP | WS_CAPTION | WS_SYSMENU | WS_MINIMIZEBOX
CAPTION "CD Player"
MENU MainMenu
BEGIN
  CONTROL "", 201, "LISTBOX", LBS_NOTIFY | LBS_MULTIPLESEL | WS_CHILD | WS_VISIBLE |
      WS_BORDER | WS_VSCROLL, 12, 20, 76, 112
  LTEXT " Tracks", -1, 8, 8, 84, 8, WS_CHILD | WS_VISIBLE | WS_GROUP
  CONTROL "", -1, "BorShade", BSS_GROUP | WS_CHILD | WS_VISIBLE, 8, 16, 84, 132
  DEFPUSHBUTTON "Play", 101, 108, 12, 32, 16, WS_CHILD | WS_VISIBLE | WS_TABSTOP
  PUSHBUTTON "Stop", 102, 108, 32, 32, 16, WS_CHILD | WS_VISIBLE | WS_TABSTOP
  PUSHBUTTON "Eject", 103, 108, 92, 32, 16, WS_CHILD | WS_VISIBLE | WS_TABSTOP
  PUSHBUTTON "Quit", 107, 108, 132, 32, 16, WS_CHILD | WS_VISIBLE | WS_TABSTOP
  CONTROL "", -1, "BorShade", BSS_VDIP | WS_CHILD | WS_VISIBLE, 100, 0, 1, 156
  PUSHBUTTON "New", 104, 108, 112, 32, 16, WS_CHILD | WS_VISIBLE | WS_TABSTOP
  LTEXT "", 202, 12, 136, 76, 8, WS_CHILD | WS_VISIBLE | WS_GROUP
  PUSHBUTTON "Clear", 108, 108, 72, 32, 16, WS_CHILD | WS_VISIBLE | WS_TABSTOP
  PUSHBUTTON "Play All", 109, 108, 52, 32, 16, WS_CHILD | WS_VISIBLE | WS_TABSTOP
END

MainMenu MENU
BEGIN
    POPUP "&File"
    BEGIN
        MENUITEM "&Play", 101
```

```
                MENUITEM "P&lay All", 109
                MENUITEM "&Clear", 108
                MENUITEM "Pla&y partial", 106
                MENUITEM "&Stop", 102
                MENUITEM "&Eject", 103
                MENUITEM "&New", 104
                MENUITEM "&About", 105
                MENUITEM SEPARATOR
                MENUITEM "E&xit", 107
        END

END

AboutBox DIALOG 18, 18, 156, 104
STYLE WS_POPUP | WS_CAPTION
CAPTION "About CD Player..."
BEGIN
    CONTROL "", 102, "BorShade", BSS_GROUP | WS_CHILD | WS_VISIBLE | WS_TABSTOP,
        8, 8, 140, 68
    LTEXT "CD Player 1.0\nCopyright (c) 1993\nAlchemy Mindworks Inc.\n"
        "This program is part of the book Multimedia Programming for Windows by "
        "Steven William Rimmer, published by Windcrest (Book 4484).",
        -1, 12, 12, 128, 60, WS_CHILD | WS_VISIBLE | WS_GROUP
    DEFPUSHBUTTON "Ok", IDOK, 116, 80, 32, 20, WS_CHILD | WS_VISIBLE | WS_TABSTOP
END

MessageBox DIALOG 72, 72, 144, 80
STYLE DS_MODALFRAME | WS_POPUP | WS_CAPTION
CAPTION "Message"
BEGIN
    CONTROL "", 102, "BorShade", BSS_GROUP | WS_CHILD | WS_VISIBLE, 4, 8, 136, 44
    CTEXT "", 101, 8, 12, 128, 36, WS_CHILD | WS_VISIBLE | WS_GROUP
    DEFPUSHBUTTON "Ok", IDOK, 108, 56, 32, 20, WS_CHILD | WS_VISIBLE | WS_TABSTOP
END

CDPlayer ICON
BEGIN
    '00 00 01 00 01 00 20 20 10 00 00 00 00 00 E8 02'
    '00 00 16 00 00 00 28 00 00 00 20 00 00 00 40 00'
    '00 00 01 00 04 00 00 00 00 00 80 02 00 00 00 00'
    '00 00 00 00 00 00 00 00 00 00 00 00 00 00 00 00'
    '00 00 00 00 80 00 00 80 00 00 00 80 80 00 80 00'
    '00 00 80 00 80 00 80 80 00 00 80 80 80 00 C0 C0'
    'C0 00 00 00 FF 00 00 FF 00 00 00 FF FF 00 FF 00'
    '00 00 FF 00 FF 00 FF FF 00 00 FF FF FF 00 00 00'
    '00 00 00 00 00 00 00 00 00 00 00 00 00 00 00 00'
```

```
'00 00 00 00 88 87 33 AA 00 00 00 00 00 00 00 00'
'00 00 08 8F 88 87 33 AA 88 70 00 00 00 00 00 00'
'00 0F F8 F8 88 87 33 AA 88 C7 60 00 00 00 00 00'
'00 FF FF 8F 88 87 33 AA 87 C6 66 00 00 00 00 00'
'0F FF FF F8 88 87 37 A8 8C 76 66 60 00 00 00 00'
'88 FF FF 8F 88 87 38 A8 7C 66 66 88 00 00 00 08'
'78 8F FF F8 F8 87 38 A8 C7 66 68 88 80 00 00 07'
'87 88 FF FF 88 87 3A A7 C6 66 88 88 E0 00 00 78'
'78 78 8F FF F8 87 3A AC 76 68 88 EE EE 00 00 87'
'87 87 88 FF 8F 87 3A 7C 66 88 EE EE BB 00 08 78'
'78 78 78 8F F8 87 3A C7 68 8E EB BB BA A0 07 87'
'87 87 87 88 F7 77 77 C6 8E BB BB AA AA A0 08 78'
'78 78 78 78 77 00 00 77 BB BA AA A3 33 30 07 87'
'87 87 87 87 70 70 07 07 33 33 33 DD DD D0 07 77'
'77 77 77 77 70 00 00 07 5D 5D 5D 5D 5D 50 05 D5'
'D5 D5 D5 D5 70 00 00 07 77 77 77 77 77 70 0D DD'
'DD 33 33 33 70 70 07 07 78 78 78 78 78 70 03 33'
'3A AA AB BB 77 00 00 77 87 87 87 87 87 80 0A AA'
'AA BB BB E8 6C 77 77 7F 88 78 78 78 78 70 0A AB'
'BB BE E8 86 7C A3 78 8F F8 87 87 87 87 80 00 BB'
'EE EE 88 66 C7 A3 78 F8 FF 88 78 78 78 00 00 EE'
'EE 88 86 67 CA A3 78 8F FF F8 87 87 87 00 00 0E'
'88 88 66 6C 7A A3 78 88 FF FF 88 78 70 00 00 08'
'88 86 66 7C 8A 83 78 8F 8F FF F8 87 80 00 00 00'
'88 66 66 C7 8A 83 78 88 F8 FF FF 88 00 00 00 00'
'06 66 67 C8 8A 73 78 88 8F FF FF F0 00 00 00 00'
'00 66 6C 78 AA 33 78 88 F8 FF FF 00 00 00 00 00'
'00 06 7C 88 AA 33 78 88 8F 8F F0 00 00 00 00 00'
'00 00 07 88 AA 33 78 88 F8 80 00 00 00 00 00 00'
'00 00 00 00 AA 33 78 88 00 00 00 00 00 00 00 00'
'00 00 00 00 00 00 00 00 00 00 00 00 00 00 FF F0'
'0F FF FF 80 01 FF FE 00 00 7F FC 00 00 3F F8 00'
'00 1F F0 00 00 0F E0 00 00 07 C0 00 00 03 C0 00'
'00 03 80 00 00 01 80 00 00 01 00 00 00 00 00 00'
'00 00 00 00 00 00 00 01 80 00 00 03 C0 00 00 03'
'C0 00 00 01 80 00 00 00 00 00 00 00 00 00 00 00'
'00 00 80 00 00 01 80 00 00 01 C0 00 00 03 C0 00'
'00 03 E0 00 00 07 F0 00 00 0F F8 00 00 1F FC 00'
'00 3F FE 00 00 7F FF 80 01 FF FF F0 0F FF'
END

PlayPartialBox DIALOG 79, 70, 168, 84
STYLE DS_MODALFRAME | WS_POPUP | WS_CAPTION | WS_SYSMENU
CAPTION "Play Partial"
BEGIN
```

```
SCROLLBAR 101, 8, 16, 112, 9
SCROLLBAR 102, 8, 40, 112, 9
LTEXT "From", -1, 8, 8, 112, 8, WS_CHILD | WS_VISIBLE | WS_GROUP
LTEXT "To", -1, 8, 32, 112, 8, WS_CHILD | WS_VISIBLE | WS_GROUP
DEFPUSHBUTTON "Ok", IDOK, 128, 60, 32, 20, WS_CHILD | WS_VISIBLE | WS_TABSTOP
PUSHBUTTON "Cancel", IDCANCEL, 88, 60, 32, 20, WS_CHILD | WS_VISIBLE | WS_TABSTOP
CONTROL "", 103, "BorShade", 1 | WS_CHILD | WS_VISIBLE, 4, 4, 156, 48
LTEXT "", 201, 124, 16, 32, 8, WS_CHILD | WS_VISIBLE | WS_GROUP
LTEXT "", 202, 124, 40, 32, 8, WS_CHILD | WS_VISIBLE | WS_GROUP
END

WaitBox DIALOG 18, 18, 96, 116
STYLE WS_POPUP | WS_VISIBLE | WS_BORDER
BEGIN
END

CDPlayerBitmap BITMAP cdplay.bmp
```

Finally, you'll need a project file, shown in FIG. 3-8, and a DEF file, CDPLAY.DEF, as follows:

```
NAME          CDPLAY
DESCRIPTION   'CD Player'
EXETYPE       WINDOWS
CODE          PRELOAD MOVEABLE
DATA          PRELOAD MOVEABLE MULTIPLE
SEGMENTS      WM__TEXT LOADONCALL
HEAPSIZE      8192
STACKSIZE     8192
```

to complete the CDPLAY application—you can replace the project file with a suitable MAKE file if you're not using the Borland C++ for Windows integrated development environment. These files are illustrated in FIG. 3-8.

The structure of CDPLAY.CPP is substantially similar to that of WAVEPLAY from the previous chapter, save that all the wave-file regalia has been replaced by compact disc regalia. The somewhat device-independent nature of MCI calls means that much the same things will be happening in both applications.

One thing you'll certainly have noticed about the WAVEPLAY application is a general absence of parrots, although they were mentioned briefly in chapter 2. Parrots have crept into CDPLAY to deal with a peculiar characteristic of this application, to wit, that it takes a fair bit of time to boot up, as it must begin by opening the cdaudio driver and reading the track list from your compact disk. This would typically cause absolutely nothing to happen for quite a while after you click CDPLAY into existence. As this is arguably not a good way to create software, the

CDPLAY application begins by displaying a somewhat elaborate wait box. It then loads its track list and opens its main window. The wait box is illustrated in FIG. 3-9.

The idea for the graphic wait box was borrowed from Borland C++ itself, which has much the same problem when it first boots up—and it solves it in much the same way. The graphic wait box has absolutely nothing to do with playing compact discs, of course, and a complete discussion of what it's up to will have to wait 'til the next chapter, when we deal with displaying bitmapped graphics.

When CDPLAY first boots up, the message handler for its main window, SelectProc, will receive a WM__INITDIALOG message. The case for this message illustrates how the compact disc player gets itself ready to face the world. It begins by calling ShowWaitWindow to display the parrots in FIG. 3-10. It then calls LoadIcon and SetClassWord to set the icon for the CDPLAY application. The icon in this case, a compact disc, was drawn from the MOREICON.DLL that comes with Windows.

The ResetSelectorList function fetches the tracks from the current compact disc, as was discussed earlier in this chapter, and stores their track numbers and playing times in the list box of the main window. The third

File Name	Lines	Code	Data	Location
cdplay.cpp	902	7467	320	.
cdplay.def	n/a	n/a	n/a	.
cdplay.rc	n/a	n/a	n/a	.
bwcc.lib	n/a	n/a	n/a	..\lib
mmsystem.lib	n/a	n/a	n/a	..\lib

3-8 The project file for the compact disc player, CDPLAY.PRJ.

3-9 The compact disc player's wait box. Not dead . . . merely restin'.

argument to ResetSelectorList is an object of the type TRACK, which CD-PLAY uses to represent the current track to be played. It's defined like this:

```
typedef struct{
    DWORD from;
    DWORD to;
    DWORD total;
    int track;
    } TRACK;
```

The ResetSelectorList fills in the total element of a TRACK object with the total playing time of all the tracks on the disc about to be played. The MAIN_STATUS control in the main window is a text field. It's initially set to display the total playing time of the current compact disc. This will change to a running status of the track being played when something's actually happening.

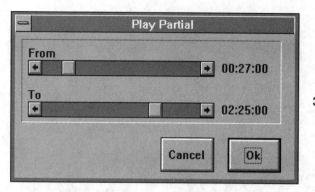

3-10 The Play Partial box.

If you click on the Play button of CDPLAY or select the Play item of its File menu, the code in the MAIN__PLAY case of SelectProc will deal with actually playing the track you've selected. In fact, what it does is a bit more complicated than it might seem, as it can be invoked in a number of ways. It begins by calling GetNextSelection, which returns the index of the first selected item in the list box, or −1 if no items are selected. Because compact disc tracks begin with number one, rather than number zero, the return value must be incremented by one.

The next call in playing a track is to GetTrackLength, which will fill in a TRACK object with values that reflect the entire length of the specified track. Having read through the earlier discussion of retrieving track information with MCI calls, you can probably work out what it's up to.

The PlayTrack function actually initiates playing the requested track. It looks a lot like the example code presented earlier to play compact disc audio, save that it finds the track length to be played in the TRACK object passed to it. If it successfully initiates playing the requested track, the various menu items and buttons that deal with sending instructions to the CD-ROM drive will have their states adjusted accordingly. For example, the Play button will be disabled because once you're playing a tune there's very little more the Play button can be used for.

You'll also notice a call to SetTimer in the code after PlayTrack. This will cause one of the Windows timers to send a WM_TIMER message to SelectProc once every 1,000 milliseconds, or once a second. The message is handled by the WM_TIMER case of SelectProc, and is responsible for keeping a running count of the length of time the current track has been playing. The MCI interface itself offers no way to update a status display— while using WM_TIMER messages is a bit artificial because the actual timing mechanism has nothing to do with the compact disc being played, it does work reliably.

Having the MAIN__PLAY case find the track to be played by scanning through the list box for a selected entry does actually have a purpose. You can see why it's done this way if you look at the MM__MCINOTIFY case of SelectProc. As was dealt with in the previous section of this chapter, the MCI interface will send an MM__MCINOTIFY message to this window when the current compact disc track stops playing. This allows the MCI cdaudio driver to be closed at the appropriate time. However, it also allows the CDPLAY application to arrange to play multiple tracks consecutively. If you look at the code at the bottom of this case, you'll note that the GetNextSelection function is again called to locate the first selected entry in the list box. There must be one, as it was used to play the track that has just ended. It unselects this entry and posts a WM__COMMAND message to the SelectProc message handler with MAIN__PLAY as its wParam argument.

When this MAIN__PLAY instruction is received by SelectProc, it will look like someone has clicked on the Play button. Because the previous track has been unselected, the call to GetNextSelection will find the next track in the list and PlayTrack will play it. In this way, the end of each track sets the next track in the list up to play, until no more selected tracks exist in the list box.

Note that this is a multiple-selection list box. You can select more than one entry at a time. Clicking on the Select All button will set up the whole disc to be played.

The MAIN__PLAYPART case handles clicks on the Play Partial button. It works pretty much like the MAIN__PLAY case, save that it calls the GetPartial function to modify the from and to elements of the TRACK object being passed around. The Play Partial dialog box is illustrated in FIG. 3-10.

The facility to play partial tracks in CDPLAY is more illustrative of the techniques used to do so than it is a practical application of this facility. Selecting the start and play times with scroll bars is less than ideally accurate, but it makes it easy to see what everything's doing.

The other functions of note in SelectProc are MAIN__EJECT, which ejects the current disc, as I've discussed, and MAIN__NEW, which handles clicks on the New button. This latter case will cause SelectProc to call ResetSelectorList, in case you're changing the disc in your CD-ROM drive.

Compact disc applications

You probably won't want to write a Windows application anything like CD-PLAY, unless you merely want to become familiar with the nuances of using compact disc audio. There are numerous shareware compact disc players like this one—some considerably more sophisticated—but they all suffer from much the same drawback. A conventional audio compact disc player is a lot easier to use than even the most well-written Windows application. I have a normal stereo in my office and a Sony Discman for those occasions when my choice in music would set the dogs howling. Needless to say, I don't use my CD-ROM drive to listen to the Grateful Dead.

There are exceptions to this observation, of course. You can listen to compact discs at work without it being obvious what you're doing by using a CD-ROM drive and CDPLAY—because the CDPLAY application merely sits idle and waits for messages most of the time, it can stay running under Windows and consume virtually no system resources. In addition, it's worth noting that a Discman can be made off with pretty effortlessly if left unguarded on your desk in an office with more fingers than hands to contain them. By comparison, purloining a CD-ROM drive requires the availability of a screwdriver. If the climate of your office is such that someone is likely to make off with your CD-ROM drive, they'll have long since stolen all the screwdrivers, effectively safeguarding it.

With the growing availability of relatively low-cost compact disc recorders, it's increasingly more realistic to create custom compact discs, or more useful still, hybrid discs with audio and CD-ROM data on them. This is an ideal medium for authoring interactive multimedia applications, of course, and you can use the MCI compact disc audio calls to have them speak, sing, croak, trumpet, burp, cough, squeak, roar, howl, bark, or recite the complete pagan calendar in Gaelic, all with impeccable stereo sound quality any time you like.

In a sense, a compact disc used this way can be regarded as a 74-minute wave file, although it's one that doesn't require the respectable portion of a gigabyte of memory such a structure would entail if you were to attempt to play it.

4
Displaying and animating bitmaps

"The more people I meet, the more I like my dog."

Somehow, it seems that one of the media that multimedia offers ought to be visual. In fact, while the Windows multimedia extensions don't really have much to do with low-level visual displays, Windows itself has some fairly sophisticated—if monumentally confusing—facilities to handle pictures.

In fact, the code to be discussed in this chapter has nothing to do with the Windows multimedia development kit. Everything it will deal with is part of Windows itself, and can be accessed with the basic Borland or Microsoft Windows development environments.

While having your computer talk or sing—or do both at the same time if you're adventurous—will certainly get it noticed, having text and images appear on the screen is more likely to make it good for something. Human beings are very visual creatures. You might want to think of a pair of eyes and the brain they're connected to as being the most sophisticated image-processing computer in the known universe. It would be a shame to let all that state-of-the-art software go to waste.

In fact, aside from this somewhat philosophical justification for using graphics in your applications, people deal with visual information much more readily and effectively than they do with, say, sound. For example, there's a lot more news in a newspaper than there is on the tube at eleven o'clock. Television might be visual, but the news on television is essentially radio with a slide show in the background.

Windows, of course, is very much a visual environment for just this reason. People have been expressing themselves pictorially since they came down out of the trees.

Displaying graphics in your Windows applications is surprisingly easy once you know how to do it. There are actually two catches hidden in the preceding sentence—you have to understand which of the numberless Windows graphics facilities will actually suit the sort of image you want to display, and you have to understand and live with Windows' somewhat draconian use of color and display characteristics.

This chapter will deal with both these issues—illustrating code to display simple bitmapped graphics, multiple bitmapped graphics in the same window, and, finally, code to make a 150-pound Labrador retriever run across your screen and eat your mouse. No foolin'.

Bitmapped graphics

A computer monitor is a bitmapped device. This means that while you might see lines and circles and pictures on it—largely thanks to the assistance of that sophisticated image-processing software touched on a few paragraphs ago—the structure of everything on your monitor is really a matrix of colored dots. Given a matrix with sufficiently small dots, turning on the appropriate ones will create the illusion of recognizable figures on your tube.

A matrix of dots—or *pixels*—is called a *bitmap*. In fact, this is a misnomer under Windows, wherein one pixel is usually not represented by a single bit. In fact, this is somewhat irrelevant, as Windows insulates you from the internal structure of bitmapped graphics when you're using them at the level to be discussed in this chapter.

Perhaps the simplest way to think of bitmapped graphics is to regard them as that which comes out of a scanner. Bitmapped graphics are analogous to photographs. A bitmapped image is a rectangular area that contains colored bits that represent a photorealistic image—or anything else you might take a picture of.

In a bitmapped image, each pixel is stored as a value, with the value representing a color. The simplest way to look at this is to consider FIG. 4-1. The picture is a bitmapped graphic. Because this book is printed in black and white, it's a gray-scale graphic, rather than a color one. Gray-scale images are just color images in which all the colors are gray.

The band along the bottom of FIG. 4-1 is called a *palette*. Its tiles represent all the colors in the graphic itself. In this case, there are sixteen discrete levels of gray, from pure black to pure white. All the colors in the picture have been drawn from this palette. As such, each pixel in the picture can be represented by a number from zero through fifteen, specifying the palette entry that holds the color the pixel in question is supposed to be. The image in FIG. 4-1, then, can be represented in data as a matrix of numbers from zero through fifteen.

4-1 A bitmapped image and its palette. More than compilers and microprocessors, caffeine is what actually makes contemporary Windows applications possible.

When you first install Windows on a system with a VGA card, it will be set up with a 16-color screen driver. You can see the 16 colors involved if you open the Windows Paintbrush application. In fact, for practical purposes, these are the only 16 colors you can use in a 16-color Windows environment. While you can change the way the available colors are assigned—for example, by selecting a color set in the Windows control panel—you can't change the actual colors involved.

There's a good reason for this limitation. In the 16-color VGA graphics mode that Windows defaults to using, you can in theory choose among a quarter of a million discrete colors. You can have only 16 different ones on the screen at a time, however. The 16 colors in use at the moment are referred to as the *system palette*.

Windows is a cooperative multitasking environment. Multiple applications can run on the same physical screen at the same time. If each application were empowered to make off with the screen palette and change it for its own use, Windows could get very confusing very quickly. You might start seeing white dialog boxes with white text in them, for example, something that can be fairly tricky to make sense of.

There is a reserved palette of 20 colors under Windows, which are constrained not to change. In a 16-color environment, this is comprised of 16 real colors and 4 *dithered* colors, that is, colors synthesized by alternating dots of the first 16 colors. In a 256-color environment, there will be 20 genuine colors in the reserved palette, with the remaining 236 colors available for use by the foreground application if need be.

One of the tenets of Windows is that it tries very hard not to refuse to do things. It tries not to run out of memory, for example, by spilling things to disk, as I've touched on earlier in this book. It also tries not to outright refuse to display bitmaps. Confronted with a bitmap that's awkward to display, it will play tricks with its colors.

It's not hard to imagine bitmaps that are awkward for Windows to display, given the foregoing discussion of Windows' use of color. For example, consider a 16-color Windows environment that finds itself confronted with a 16-color bitmap using a different color palette. In this case, Windows will display the picture, but it will "remap" its colors. In effect, it will replace each color in the bitmap with the closest match in the reserved Windows palette. This can cause a fairly substantial color shift in some graphics.

If you attempt to display a 256-color bitmap under Windows with a 16-color driver, the same thing will happen, although the color shift will typically be a lot more radical. Pictures displayed this way often look pretty dreadful. Figure 4-2 illustrates an example of the graphic outrage of Windows image remapping.

4-2 Windows remaps a color graphic.

Something similar to this will happen if you attempt to display a 256-color bitmap under Windows running with a 256-color driver, although you'll probably never notice it. A 256-color picture requires that the device it's to be displayed on be able to support the 256 colors of its choosing, as defined by the palette used by the picture. Windows has only 236 free colors, as twenty of the colors are reserved. In this case, Windows will actually remap twenty of the colors in the graphic to be displayed. However, the range of colors available to a 256-color picture usually makes this unnoticeable.

Figure 4-3 illustrates the color palette of a 256-color graphic before and after Windows has adjusted it for display. Notice that the colors at the ends of the palette have changed—these are the twenty reserved colors of the Windows palette. In fact, Windows has juggled the remaining colors so there's no perceptible color shift when the graphic this palette came from is displayed.

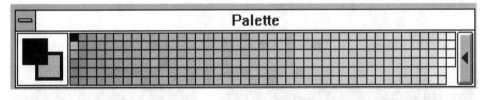

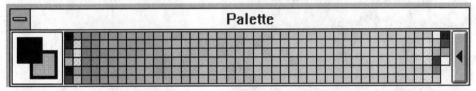

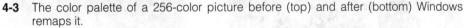

4-3 The color palette of a 256-color picture before (top) and after (bottom) Windows remaps it.

Windows can also support high-color and true-color display drivers, which don't have color palettes—or, at least, their effective color palettes are so large as to make virtually any colors available in whatever quantities you require. If you attempt to display a bitmapped graphic on such a display, no remapping will take place.

Thus far I've talked about bitmapped graphic images abstractly, and the number of colors available to them might seem somewhat arbitrary. In fact, the color "depth" of a graphic is defined by the data that represents it. Under Windows, bitmapped graphics are said to have 1, 4, 8, or 24 bits of colors, representing maximum color values of 2, 16, 256, and 16,777,216, respectively.

Bitmapped graphics tend to require a lot of real estate to store them, and as such are structured to make the most effective use of memory and disk space. These color depths fit comfortably into the structure of eight-bit bytes. In a two-color picture, each pixel is represented by one bit, and eight pixels fit into a byte. In a 16-color picture, each pixel is represented by four bits, and two pixels fit in a byte. A 256-color picture requires eight bits to store one pixel, and each pixel is represented by one byte. A picture with 16 million colors requires three bytes per pixel— these images are typically serious memory pigs. While they'll turn up in the next chapter when we look at Kodak Photo-CDs, they aren't all that applicable to this discussion.

Dithering: The fine art of cheating

If you ran the compact disc player from the previous chapter, you'll have encountered the parrots that turned up as its opening screen. Figure 4-4 illustrates the parrots as they began life and as they were used in the compact disc player. A bit of investigation of the graphic compiled into the compact disc player program will reveal that it supports only 16 colors.

4-4 The parrots from the compact disc player in the previous chapter, before (left) and after (right) dithering.

The compact disc player opening screen can be displayed correctly—with no remapping—by both 16- and 256-color Windows screen drivers. It has two important characteristics. To begin with, it uses a 16-color palette in which all the colors match Windows' reserved colors, and as such it will exhibit no color shift when it's displayed. However, even though it started life as a picture with rather more colors, it won't suffer the fate of remapped pictures, as it has been dithered.

In dealing with photorealistic images, dithering is a fairly involved procedure that uses patterns of alternating dots to simulate colors that aren't available in the image, using colors that are. The algorithm to perform dithering is complex, and you won't have to get involved with it here. You can find more detailed discussions of dithering in my books *Bitmapped Graphics, second edition*, *Supercharged Bitmapped Graphics*, and *Windows Bitmapped Graphics*, all published by Windcrest/McGraw-Hill. This chapter will deal only with creating and using dithered images.

Now, dithering is by no means a perfect process. The dithered parrots back in FIG. 4-4 are mere shadows of their former selves. In effect, dithering allows you to trade apparent color depth for resolution. The dithered parrots have the correct image colors—more or less—but they appear considerably coarser and more "grainy" than the original scanned image.

In an application that calls for optimum graphic quality, no matter what sort of display adapter it turns out to be running on, you'd probably want to have two versions of each color picture to be displayed—an undithered one for 256 colors and a second dithered one for 16 colors. You could have your software work out the number of colors available to the display it's running on and select an image to display accordingly.

Here's how to ascertain the number of bits of color supported by the current screen driver. The hwnd object is a window handle. The value of bits will be the color depth of your driver. Note that bits might be 15 or 16, in addition to the standard color depths of 1, 4, 8, and 24 bits. These intermediate values will turn up if Windows is running with a high-color driver.

```
HDC hdc
int bits;

hdc=GetDC(hwnd);
bits=(GetDeviceCaps(hdc,PLANES) * GetDeviceCaps(hdc,BITSPIXEL));
ReleaseDC(hwnd,hdc);
```

The applications to be discussed in this chapter more or less assume that they'll be working with a 256-color display. All of them will run correctly on a system supporting only 16 colors, but in many cases they won't look very good. All the cheating in the world won't make a 256-color graphic displayed on a 16-color display device look that attractive. If the software you ultimately write to use the functions in this chapter can display photorealistic images, you might consider how best to handle users who are limited to 16 colors. If your software simply refuses to run on a machine supporting fewer than 256 display colors, it certainly won't be the first.

It's probably worth noting that 256-color photorealistic images are also dithered. As they first come from a scanner, color graphics have 24 bits of color. Somewhat more elaborate color dithering is used to reduce them to 256-color pictures. In most cases, the result of doing so is hard to detect visually. You'll encounter 256-color dithering in a moment.

Creating dithered images with Graphic Workshop

One of the things on the companion CD-ROM for this book is the Graphic Workshop for Windows application. You can find it in the \GWSWIN subdirectory. If you install it and boot it up, it will look something like the top image in FIG. 4-5. Before you use it you'll probably want to turn off the the thumbnail mode—toggle Use Thumbnails in the Thumbnails menu—so it looks more like the bottom image in FIG. 4-5.

Graphic Workshop will allow you to do pretty well everything there is to do with bitmapped graphics. A number of applications for it will turn up in this chapter. To begin with, let's look at how you can use it to create dithered images. For this example, we'll work with the PARROTS.TGA file from the \GRAPHICS directory of the companion CD-ROM. (This will probably look familiar.) The PARROTS.TGA file is a 24-bit graphic of the sort that a color scanner would produce.

Begin by copying PARROTS.TGA to the \GWSWIN directory on your hard drive, or to wherever you had Graphic Workshop install itself.

You can have Graphic Workshop show you what the PARROTS.TGA file looks like by double-clicking on its filename. However, unless you have a high-color or true-color display driver in your system, Graphic Workshop will run into a problem similar to the one discussed in the foregoing section of this chapter. It will have to display a 24-bit image on a display device having only four or eight bits of color. And it will solve this problem in much the same way, too—by dithering.

Graphic Workshop dithers pictures having too many colors using a very crude eight-color dither. While not much to look at, it's exceedingly fast. If you see a coarse, grainy representation of the parrots in PARROTS.TGA when you go to view them, keep in mind that the actual graphic looks a lot better than this.

Let's begin by creating a 256-color version of PARROTS.TGA. To do this, select the PARROTS.TGA file by clicking on it and then click on the Effects button at the top of the Graphic Workshop window. A dialog like the one in FIG. 4-6 will appear. Select the following options from the Effects dialog:

- Color reduction
- 256-color orthogonal palette
- Floyd-Steinberg dither

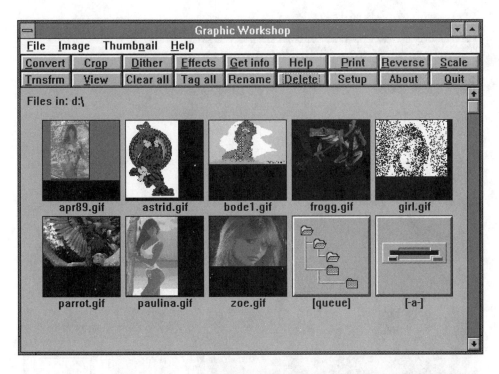

4-5 Graphic Workshop for Windows, in its default thumbnail mode (top) and in its list box mode (right).

When you click on OK, Graphic Workshop will ask you for a destination format type—the destination format dialog is shown in FIG. 4-7. Select the BMP format, as this the native graphic standard for Windows. It will then process PARROTS.TGA and create a file called X_PARROT.BMP.

If you have a 256-color Windows screen driver installed in your system, you'll be able to view X_PARROT.BMP without Graphic Workshop dithering it. You can also open this file with Windows Paintbrush and edit it, or use it as wallpaper.

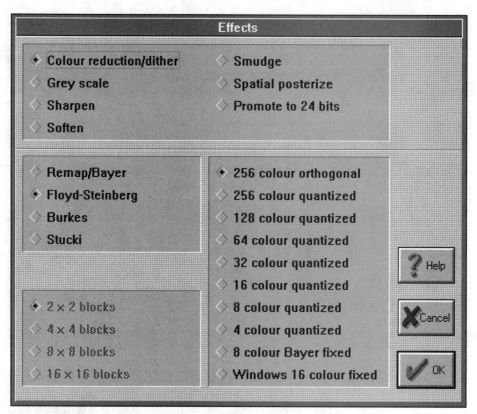

4-6 The Graphic Workshop for Windows Effects dialog, set up here to do color reduction.

This process probably deserves a bit of elaboration. The Colour Reduction function reduces images to lower color depths. The dithering options are ordered by increasing image quality—remapping produces very ugly, posterized images. Floyd-Steinberg dithering produces intermediate-quality images. Stucki dithering arguably produces somewhat better dithered images, but with a substantial speed penalty.

The 256-color orthogonal palette option is somewhat peculiar, and will require a brief explanation. A 24-bit image, such as PARROTS.TGA, has a theoretical palette of 16 million colors. In reducing this to a 256-color image, a 256-color palette for the new picture must be created. There are several ways to go about this, each with its advantages and drawbacks. The most obvious approach is to *quantize* the palette.

Quantizing a color graphic is a process that derives a smaller palette based on the dispersal of colors in the source image. In a real scanned image, not all 16 million possible colors will be used—for one thing, graphics of reasonable dimensions don't have 16 million pixels. In practice, a considerably smaller number of colors will turn out to appear in the picture.

4-7 The Graphic Workshop for Windows destination file format dialog.

Quantization works out which colors are used most frequently, and assembles a 256-color palette based on the best mix of colors. There's a more complete discussion of quantization in my book *Supercharged Bitmapped Graphics*, published by Windcrest/McGraw-Hill.

There are two arguable drawbacks to quantization. The first is that if you quantize multiple images, each picture will have a different 256-color palette. As you'll see later in this chapter, having a constant palette can be very useful.

The second drawback to quantization is a bit more subtle. In theory, it should produce the best possible palette for each picture being reduced, as the destination palette is derived from the source image itself. In practice, however, this isn't always the case. It's not all that hard to fool the quantization algorithm into selecting a palette in which there are insufficient colors to represent certain details of a graphic. Small details having colors radically different from the rest of the picture might find themselves assigned relatively few colors by a quantization function, even though they're important to the picture as a whole.

The alternative to quantization is to use a fixed palette with an even dispersal of colors, ranging from pure black to pure white. In theory, this should not produce dithered images with as faithful a color reproduction as a quantized palette would. In practice, the results are often more attractive.

You might want to experiment with the 256-color quantized and orthogonal palette options in the Graphic Workshop Effects box and observe the results of each. Note in doing so, however, that when Graphic Workshop creates a destination image, it will overwrite an existing file with the same name if one exists. Use the Rename button to change the names of the files you create.

Creating 16-color dithered images, such as the parrot wait screen for the compact disc player, involves pretty much the same procedure as creating 256-color dithers, save that you should select the 16-color Windows palette option.

Windows bitmap structures

Some of the confusion over displaying bitmapped graphics under Windows stems from the level of backward compatibility Windows seeks to maintain with former incarnations of itself. There have been several bitmap standards used internally in Windows applications over the years, and Windows still supports them all. In practice, you probably wouldn't want to touch the older ones with a ten-foot polecat, as they're very messy to work with.

Unfortunately, the Windows function reference doesn't use little polecat icons or other signals to indicate which functions and corresponding bitmap structures are obsolete. It's not always apparent exactly how you should deal with them.

It will probably be obvious from the foregoing discussion of bitmaps that their internal structure will vary considerably, depending on their color depth. As you might expect, the internal organization of a display card's screen memory will also vary, depending on its color depth, screen dimensions, and such. In this case, a display card is called a *device* by Windows. A bitmap that can be displayed on a particular device is called a *device-dependent* bitmap.

A device has a somewhat amorphous set of characteristics under Windows, called a *device context*. When it's time to update a window, the Windows BeginPaint function will provide you with a handle to the device context that represents your screen, called an HDC.

This is a bit like taking an old E-type Jaguar and an E-type Jaguar shop manual to a mechanic who's never seen either before. You needn't even crack the cover of the shop manual yourself—simply hand the works to the mechanic and, hopefully, your car will be fixed. In fact, this isn't all that good of an analogy. Windows functions that deal with your screen can always make sense of an HDC object. Relatively few mechanics can fix a Jag.

A device-dependent bitmap suitable for display on a 16-color device will not display correctly on a 256-color device. As such, this isn't the way bitmaps are usually stored under Windows. A generic image is called a *device-independent* bitmap. In displaying a device-independent bitmap, you must always make a device-dependent copy of it.

The structure of a device-independent bitmap is constant. It consists of three elements:

- A BITMAPINFOHEADER object to define the size and color depth of the bitmap, among other things.
- A list of RGBQUAD objects to define the palette colors.
- The bitmap data itself.

For the sake of this discussion, we'll allow that this is how all device-independent bitmaps are structured. In fact, it's not—there's a rather cavernous exception to it, which we'll deal with presently.

A BITMAPINFOHEADER object tells a function that wants to do something with a bitmap how the bitmap is ordered. This is the object itself:

```
typedef struct {
    DWORD biSize;
    DWORD biWidth;
    DWORD biHeight;
    WORD biPlanes;
    WORD biBitCount;
    DWORD biCompression;
    DWORD biSizeImage;
    DWORD biXPelsPerMeter;
    DWORD biYPelsPerMeter;
    DWORD biClrUsed;
    DWORD biClrImportant;
    } BITMAPINFOHEADER;
```

The biSize field of a BITMAPINFOHEADER defines the number of bytes used by the header—it's always (DWORD)sizeof(BITMAPINFOHEADER). This will turn out to be very important in a moment. The biWidth and biHeight fields define the dimensions of the bitmap in pixels. It's hard to say why these are DWORDS, or long integers, as the likelihood of bitmaps with dimensions greater than 65,535 pixels seems decidedly remote. The biPlanes field will always be one. The biBitCount field will be 1, 4, 8, or 24, representing the number of bits of color information in the bitmap in question. You can ignore the remaining fields for the moment—typically they'll all be set to zero.

Following a BITMAPINFOHEADER object, you'll find two or more RGBQUAD objects unless the file contains a 24-bit image, as 24-bit pictures don't have palettes. The number of RGBQUAD objects can be calculated as $2^{biBitCount}$. Each RGBQUAD defines one color in the palette for the image. An RGBQUAD looks like this:

```
typedef struct {
    BYTE rgbBlue;
```

```
    BYTE rgbGreen;
    BYTE rgbRed;
    BYTE rgbReserved;
    } RGBQUAD;
```

The rgbBlue, rgbGreen, and rgbRed fields of an RGBQUAD object specify the percentage of blue, green, and red light involved in the color being defined. The rgbReserved field should be set to zero, and isn't used. Following the RGBQUAD objects will be all the bitmap data itself, structured as has been discussed earlier in this chapter.

If you've meddled with Windows at all, you'll no doubt have encountered BMP files. The BMP format is Windows' proprietary structure for bitmapped images saved as disk files. They're used as wallpaper, as the native format of Windows Paintbrush, and for a number of more exotic functions when you write Windows applications, as you'll see.

A BMP file is really just all this data preceded by one more object, a BITMAPFILEHEADER. This is what one looks like:

```
    typedef struct {
    WORD bfType;
    DWORD bfSize;
    WORD bfReserved1;
    WORD bfReserved2;
    DWORD bfOffBits;
    } BITMAPFILEHEADER;
```

The bfType type field of a BITMAPFILEHEADER object will always contain the constant BM—for *bitmap*. The bfSize field specifies the size of the file in bytes. The bfOffBits field specifies the offset to the actual bitmap of the file.

The cavernous exception to all this, as mentioned earlier, is that there's a second sort of BMP file that occasionally turns up in Windows. In fact, it doesn't belong there—it's the bitmap structure for OS/2. The file extension for OS/2 bitmap files is also BMP, and because Windows and OS/2 sprang from the same primordial swamp, the internal structure of Windows and OS/2 BMP files is similar. The internal display functions of Windows will, in fact, display either type of bitmap.

In an OS/2 bitmap, however, the BITMAPINFOHEADER object and the list of RGBQUAD objects is replaced by a BITMAPCOREHEADER object and a list of RGBTRIPLE objects. Here's a BITMAPCOREHEADER:

```
    typedef struct {
    DWORD bcSize;
    WORD bcWidth;
    WORD bcHeight;
    WORD bcPlanes;
    WORD bcBitCount;
    } BITMAPCOREHEADER;
```

The bcSize element of a BITMAPCOREHEADER defines the size of the BITMAPCOREHEADER object, and will always be 12. In fact, this is extremely useful. If you open a BMP file to read it, you can determine whether you have a Windows BMP file or an OS/2 BMP file by reading in the BITMAPFILEHEADER at the start of the file and then reading one long integer. This will be the bcSize element of a BITMAPCOREHEADER object or the biSize element of a BITMAPINFOHEADER object. If the value of the long integer turns out to be 12—or sizeof(BITMAPCOREHEADDER), if you like—the file is an OS/2 bitmap. If it doesn't, the file is a Windows bitmap. An RGBTRIPLE object looks like this:

```
typedef struct {
    BYTE rgbtBlue;
    BYTE rgbtGreen;
    BYTE rgbtRed;
    } RGBTRIPLE;
```

As you'll see in a moment, it's possible to use either type of bitmap in simple display applications under Windows. There are instances in which an OS/2 bitmap will offend Windows, however, and you can avoid the possibility of encountering one by using conventional Windows-style bitmaps when you actually work graphics into an application.

Graphic Workshop for Windows will convert graphics in other formats into BMP files. By default, it writes Windows-style BMP files. If you convert BMP files of unknown origins from BMP to BMP with Graphic Workshop, they'll be written as Windows BMP files. You can use the Get Info function of Graphic Workshop to quickly determine whether a BMP file hails from Windows or OS/2, as shown in FIG. 4-8. The bottom field in the Get Info box will specify where a BMP file originated.

Displaying bitmaps

There are two broad classes of bitmap display functions that you're likely to want to use under Windows. The simplest—and the quickest—is BitBlt,

File Information

Name:	APR89.BMP
Dimensions:	640 × 480
Colours:	256
Packed size:	308278 bytes
Unpacked size:	307200 bytes
Comments:	Windows bitmap
File type:	[BMP] Windows

File Information

Name:	APR89.BMP
Dimensions:	640 × 480
Colours:	256
Packed size:	307994 bytes
Unpacked size:	307200 bytes
Comments:	OS/2 bitmap
File type:	[BMP] Windows

4-8   The Graphic Workshop for Windows Get Info box confronted with Windows (left) and OS/2 (right) BMP files.

or *bitmap block transfer*. The second is SetDIBitsToDevice. It's not as fast as BitBlt, but it uses memory less voraciously, and as such is capable of displaying larger bitmaps.

A simple example of BitBlt in action turned up as the wait-screen function of the compact disc audio player in the previous chapter. Here's the relevant bit of code:

```
HBITMAP hOldBitmap;
HDC hMemoryDC;
BITMAP bitmap;

if((hMemoryDC=CreateCompatibleDC(hdc)) != NULL) {
    hOldBitmap=SelectObject(hMemoryDC,hBitmap);
        if(hOldBitmap) {
            GetObject(hBitmap,sizeof(BITMAP),
                (LPSTR)&bitmap);
            BitBlt(hdc,
                0,
                0,
                bitmap.bmWidth,
                bitmap.bmHeight,
                hMemoryDC,
                0,
                0,
                SRCCOPY);
            SelectObject(hMemoryDC,hOldBitmap);
        }
        DeleteDC(hMemoryDC);
    }
}
```

In this example, hBitmap is a handle to a bitmap—the combination of structures dealt with in the previous section of this chapter, without a BITMAPFILEHEADER at the beginning. The hdc object is a device-context handle provided by BeginPaint in the WM_PAINT case of the message handler for the window in which this bitmap will be displayed.

The CreateCompatibleDC function generates a device context for a block of memory that's structured the same way as the screen memory of the HDC handle passed to it. In this application, the device context is used as a work space in which to assemble a device-dependent version of the device-independent bitmap to be displayed.

The SelectObject function selects the bitmap to be displayed into the new device context, that is, it causes a device-dependent copy of the bitmap to be created.

The GetObject call is a simple way to fetch the dimensions of a bitmap referenced by a handle. It temporarily locks the bitmap, copies the beginning of it into a BITMAP object, and then unlocks it again.

Finally, BitBlt displays the bitmap. Its true function is to copy rectangular blocks of bits from one device context to another, which is why the original bitmap was converted to a memory-based device context. In this application, the first argument to BitBlt is the device context of the device on which the bitmap is to be displayed. The second and third arguments are the location in pixels of the upper left corner of the bitmap relative to the upper left corner of the window. In this case, the bitmap will be displayed starting at point (0,0) of the window.

The fourth argument to BitBlt is the device context of the bitmap to be displayed. The fifth and sixth arguments are the location of the upper left corner in the source bitmap where the copy should begin. In this case, the whole bitmap is to be copied, and this point is also (0,0).

The final argument is a constant to specify how the source pixels are to relate to the pixels currently existing in the destination bitmap. The SRCCOPY constant tells BitBlt to copy the source pixels over the destination pixels. Other candidates for this post include:

SRCAND AND the source and destination bitmaps together.

SRCERASE Invert the destination bitmap and AND it with the source bitmap.

SRCINVERT Exclusive-OR the source and destination bitmaps together.

SRCPAINT OR the source and destination bitmaps together.

You might want to experiment with these operators if you're curious about what they do. While it's not difficult to understand what ORing monochrome bitmaps together will result in, for example, doing the same thing with color bitmaps often creates some unexpected results.

If your application for displaying bitmaps involves relatively small images, the BitBlt function illustrated here is a good way to handle them. If you anticipate working with larger graphics, you'll find yourself less likely to run out of memory—and hence have nothing at all displayed—if you use the approach to be dealt with next.

The SetDIBitsToDevice function will copy a bitmap to a device context. It's considerably more flexible than BitBlt—for example, it allows you to copy sections of a bitmap. It's rather more involved to implement, however.

In this example, hdc is a handle to the device context to be updated and picture is a handle to a bitmap. The width and depth values represent the dimensions of the bitmap. The bits value is the number of bits of color it supports.

```
LPBITMAPINFO bmp
RGBQUAD far *palette;
HANDLE hPal=NULL;
LPSTR image;
LOGPALETTE *pLogPal;
int i,j,n;
```

```
if((bmp=(LPBITMAPINFO)GlobalLock(picture)) != NULL) {
    n=1<<bits;
    j=min(n,256);

    palette=(RGBQUAD far *)((LPSTR)bmp+
        (unsigned int)bmp->bmiHeader.biSize);
    image=(LPSTR)bmp+(unsigned int)bmp->bmiHeader.biSize+
        (j*sizeof(RGBQUAD));

    if((pLogPal=(LOGPALETTE *)malloc(sizeof(LOGPALETTE)+
        (j*sizeof(PALETTEENTRY)))) != NULL) {
            pLogPal->palVersion=0x0300;
            pLogPal->palNumEntries=j;

            for(i=0;i<j;i++) {
                pLogPal->palPalEntry[i].peRed=
                    palette[i].rgbRed;
                pLogPal->palPalEntry[i].peGreen=
                    palette[i].rgbGreen;
                pLogPal->palPalEntry[i].peBlue=
                    palette[i].rgbBlue;
                pLogPal->palPalEntry[i].peFlags=0;
            }
            hPal=CreatePalette(pLogPal);
            free(pLogPal);

            SelectPalette(hdc,hPal,0);
            RealizePalette(hdc);
    }

    SetDIBitsToDevice(hdc,0,0,width,depth,
        0,0,0,depth,image,bmp,DIB_RGB_COLORS);

    if(hPal != NULL) DeleteObject(hPal);
    GlobalUnlock(picture);
}
```

Much of the foregoing code has to do with making the palette of the bitmap to be displayed compatible with the existing palette of the device context to receive it. This is called *realizing* a palette. The call to malloc creates a temporary buffer in which to store a LOGPALETTE—a logical palette. The palette is then created from the RGBQUAD array in the bitmap and selected into the device context.

The call to SetDIBitsToDevice actually copies the bitmap information to the window in which it's to be displayed. The first argument to SetDIBitsToDevice is a handle to the device context to receive the bitmap. The second and third arguments specify the window coordinates in which your bitmap will appear—where the upper left corner of the image should be placed. The fourth and fifth arguments specify the dimensions of the source bitmap in pixels. The sixth and seventh arguments specify the upper left corner of the rectangle that defines the area of the source bitmap to be copied to the destination window. The eighth argument is the number of the first scan line in the bitmap.

The ninth argument is a pointer to the bitmap data to be copied. The tenth argument is a pointer to a BITMAPINFO structure, which is in effect a BITMAPINFOHEADER followed by its attendant array of RGBQUADs, or a BITMAPCOREHEADER followed by some RGBTRIPLEs.

The final argument should be a constant, either DIB_RGB_COLORS or DIB_PAL_COLORS. This allows you to access a very useful secondary function of SetDIBitsToDevice. If the value passed is DIB_RGB_COLORS, SetDIBitsToDevice will assume that the color values in the BITMAPINFO object passed to it will be a normal array of RGBQUADs or RGBTRIPLEs. However, if it's DIB_PAL_COLORS, it will treat this data as an array of 16-bit words that represent indices into a previously realized palette. This allows it to paint multiple bitmaps with a common palette onto a single device context, a facility that will be dealt with later in this chapter.

A BMP file viewer

Perhaps the simplest application of bitmaps under Windows is a program to look at them, that is, to load a BMP file from disk and display its contents in a window. If you've followed the discussion of BMP files and bitmaps thus far, you'll probably imagine such an application as doing nothing more than reading a BMP file into memory and passing the whole ugly mess to the SetDIBitsToDevice code in the foregoing section.

This is actually just about all that needs be done. In practice, you must seek past the BITMAPFILEHEADER so it isn't read into memory as well, and some provision should be made to handle OS/2 bitmaps.

Figure 4-9 illustrates the main window of VIEWBMP, a simple bitmap viewer. If you select an entry from the main list box of VIEWBMP and click on View—or just double-click on an entry—the BMP file will be loaded into memory and displayed in a full-screen window. Double-click on the system menu of the display window to close it.

Figure 4-10 is the C language source code for VIEWBMP. Figure 4-11 is the resource file for VIEWBMP. It doesn't do anything that hasn't turned up in the earlier programs in this book. Finally, you'll need a DEF file, as follows:

```
NAME          BMPVIEW
DESCRIPTION   'Bitmap Viewer'
EXETYPE       WINDOWS
CODE          PRELOAD MOVEABLE
DATA          PRELOAD MOVEABLE MULTIPLE
SEGMENTS      WM_TEXT LOADONCALL
HEAPSIZE      8192
STACKSIZE     8192
```

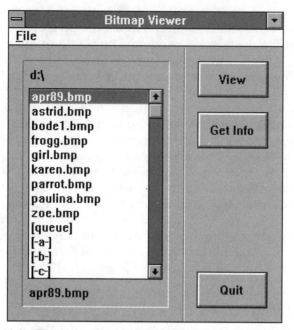

4-9 The main window of the bitmap viewer.

and a project file for VIEWBMP, as shown in FIG. 4-12. If you're using something other than the Borland C++ for Windows integrated development environment, you should create an appropriate MAKE file rather than a project. Unlike the other programs in this book, the ones in this chapter need not have MMSYSTEM.LIB in their project lists, as they make no calls to the Windows multimedia extensions.

The structure of VIEWBMP is very much like that of the other programs that have appeared in this book. Much of its principal SelectProc function is just an elaborate filename selector. It actually dispatches only two functions of note, these being the combination of GetInfo and ShowInfo to display the dimensions and color depth of a bitmap and ViewFile to display the picture itself.

The GetInfo function will fill a FILEINFO structure, as defined at the top of VIEWBMP.CPP, with information about a specific BMP file. Knowing the structure of a BMP file, it's fairly easy to see what GetInfo is up to. It opens the file in question and reads its BITMAPFILEHEADER into the object bmf. Assuming that the file does turn out to be a valid bitmap—that is, if the bfType field contains the constant BM—it reads the next four bytes of the file into a long integer to see if the following structure is a Windows BITMAPINFOHEADER or an OS/2 BITMAPCOREHEADER. It then reads the appropriate object and works out the image dimensions and color depth accordingly. The FILEINFO structure includes a flag, os2type, which will tell other functions in the application what type of BMP file is being handled.

4-10 The C language source listing for the bitmap viewer, VIEWBMP.CPP.

```c
/*
    Bitmap Viewer
    Copyright (c) 1993 Alchemy Mindworks Inc.
*/

#include <windows.h>
#include <stdio.h>
#include <stdlib.h>
#include <dir.h>
#include <ctype.h>
#include <alloc.h>
#include <string.h>
#include <io.h>
#include <bwcc.h>
#include <dos.h>
#include <errno.h>
#include <math.h>

#define say(s)         MessageBox(NULL,s,"Yo...",MB_OK | MB_ICONSTOP);
#define saynumber(f,s)    {char b[128]; sprintf((LPSTR)b,(LPSTR)f,s); \
                  MessageBox(NULL,b,"Debug Message",MB_OK | MB_ICONSTOP); }

#define ItemName(item,string)    { dlgH=GetDlgItem(hwnd,item); \
                                SetWindowText(dlgH,(LPSTR)string); }
#define ItemOn(item)     { dlgH=GetDlgItem(hwnd,item); EnableWindow(dlgH,TRUE); }
#define ItemOff(item)     { dlgH=GetDlgItem(hwnd,item); EnableWindow(dlgH,FALSE); }
#define pixels2bytes(n)     ((n+7)/8)

#define STRINGSIZE          129       /* how big is a string? */

#define MAIN_LIST           201       /* objects in the main window */

#define MAIN_TITLE          301
#define MAIN_PATH           302

#define MAIN_VIEW           102
#define MAIN_GETINFO        103
#define MAIN_ABOUT          105
#define MAIN_EXIT           107

#define MESSAGE_STRING      101       /* message box objects */

#define INFO_FILE           101       /* get info box objects */
#define INFO_COLOURS        102
```

```
#define INFO_DIMENSIONS      103
#define INFO_MEMORY          104


#define RGB_RED              0
#define RGB_GREEN            1
#define RGB_BLUE             2
#define RGB_SIZE             3

#ifndef max
#define max(a,b)            (((a)>(b))?(a):(b))
#endif
#ifndef min
#define min(a,b)            (((a)<(b))?(a):(b))
#endif

typedef struct {
    GLOBALHANDLE picture;
    char filename[16];
    unsigned int width;
    unsigned int depth;
    unsigned int bits;
    unsigned int os2type;
    unsigned long memory;
    } FILEINFO;

/* prototypes */
DWORD FAR PASCAL SelectProc(HWND hwnd,WORD message,WORD wParam,LONG lParam);
DWORD FAR PASCAL AboutDlgProc(HWND hwnd,WORD message,WORD wParam,LONG lParam);
DWORD FAR PASCAL MessageDlgProc(HWND hwnd,WORD message,WORD wParam,LONG lParam);
DWORD FAR PASCAL InfoDlgProc(HWND hwnd,WORD message,WORD wParam,LONG lParam);

long FAR PASCAL PictureProc(HWND hwnd,unsigned int message,
                unsigned int wParam,LONG lParam);

void ShowInfo(HWND hwnd,FILEINFO *fi);
void DoMessage(HWND hwnd,LPSTR message);
void ResetSelectorList(HWND hwnd);

int testdisk(int n);
int GetInfo(FILEINFO *fi,LPSTR path);
int ViewFile(HWND hwnd,LPSTR path);

/* globals */
LPSTR messagehook;
char szAppName[]="BmpViewer";
```

```
HANDLE hInst;

char orthopalette[] = {
    0x00,0x00,0x00,0x00,0x00,0x55,0x00,0x00,
    0xaa,0x00,0x00,0xff,0x00,0x24,0x00,0x00,
    0x24,0x55,0x00,0x24,0xaa,0x00,0x24,0xff,
    0x00,0x49,0x00,0x00,0x49,0x55,0x00,0x49,
    0xaa,0x00,0x49,0xff,0x00,0x6d,0x00,0x00,
    0x6d,0x55,0x00,0x6d,0xaa,0x00,0x6d,0xff,
    0x00,0x92,0x00,0x00,0x92,0x55,0x00,0x92,
    0xaa,0x00,0x92,0xff,0x00,0xb6,0x00,0x00,
    0xb6,0x55,0x00,0xb6,0xaa,0x00,0xb6,0xff,
    0x00,0xdb,0x00,0x00,0xdb,0x55,0x00,0xdb,
    0xaa,0x00,0xdb,0xff,0x00,0xff,0x00,0x00,
    0xff,0x55,0x00,0xff,0xaa,0x00,0xff,0xff,
    0x24,0x00,0x00,0x24,0x00,0x55,0x24,0x00,
    0xaa,0x24,0x00,0xff,0x24,0x24,0x00,0x24,
    0x24,0x55,0x24,0x24,0xaa,0x24,0x24,0xff,
    0x24,0x49,0x00,0x24,0x49,0x55,0x24,0x49,
    0xaa,0x24,0x49,0xff,0x24,0x6d,0x00,0x24,
    0x6d,0x55,0x24,0x6d,0xaa,0x24,0x6d,0xff,
    0x24,0x92,0x00,0x24,0x92,0x55,0x24,0x92,
    0xaa,0x24,0x92,0xff,0x24,0xb6,0x00,0x24,
    0xb6,0x55,0x24,0xb6,0xaa,0x24,0xb6,0xff,
    0x24,0xdb,0x00,0x24,0xdb,0x55,0x24,0xdb,
    0xaa,0x24,0xdb,0xff,0x24,0xff,0x00,0x24,
    0xff,0x55,0x24,0xff,0xaa,0x24,0xff,0xff,
    0x49,0x00,0x00,0x49,0x00,0x55,0x49,0x00,
    0xaa,0x49,0x00,0xff,0x49,0x24,0x00,0x49,
    0x24,0x55,0x49,0x24,0xaa,0x49,0x24,0xff,
    0x49,0x49,0x00,0x49,0x49,0x55,0x49,0x49,
    0xaa,0x49,0x49,0xff,0x49,0x6d,0x00,0x49,
    0x6d,0x55,0x49,0x6d,0xaa,0x49,0x6d,0xff,
    0x49,0x92,0x00,0x49,0x92,0x55,0x49,0x92,
    0xaa,0x49,0x92,0xff,0x49,0xb6,0x00,0x49,
    0xb6,0x55,0x49,0xb6,0xaa,0x49,0xb6,0xff,
    0x49,0xdb,0x00,0x49,0xdb,0x55,0x49,0xdb,
    0xaa,0x49,0xdb,0xff,0x49,0xff,0x00,0x49,
    0xff,0x55,0x49,0xff,0xaa,0x49,0xff,0xff,
    0x6d,0x00,0x00,0x6d,0x00,0x55,0x6d,0x00,
    0xaa,0x6d,0x00,0xff,0x6d,0x24,0x00,0x6d,
    0x24,0x55,0x6d,0x24,0xaa,0x6d,0x24,0xff,
    0x6d,0x49,0x00,0x6d,0x49,0x55,0x6d,0x49,
    0xaa,0x6d,0x49,0xff,0x6d,0x6d,0x00,0x6d,
    0x6d,0x55,0x6d,0x6d,0xaa,0x6d,0x6d,0xff,
    0x6d,0x92,0x00,0x6d,0x92,0x55,0x6d,0x92,
```

4-10 Continued.

```
0xaa,0x6d,0x92,0xff,0x6d,0xb6,0x00,0x6d,
0xb6,0x55,0x6d,0xb6,0xaa,0x6d,0xb6,0xff,
0x6d,0xdb,0x00,0x6d,0xdb,0x55,0x6d,0xdb,
0xaa,0x6d,0xdb,0xff,0x6d,0xff,0x00,0x6d,
0xff,0x55,0x6d,0xff,0xaa,0x6d,0xff,0xff,
0x92,0x00,0x00,0x92,0x00,0x55,0x92,0x00,
0xaa,0x92,0x00,0xff,0x92,0x24,0x00,0x92,
0x24,0x55,0x92,0x24,0xaa,0x92,0x24,0xff,
0x92,0x49,0x00,0x92,0x49,0x55,0x92,0x49,
0xaa,0x92,0x49,0xff,0x92,0x6d,0x00,0x92,
0x6d,0x55,0x92,0x6d,0xaa,0x92,0x6d,0xff,
0x92,0x92,0x00,0x92,0x92,0x55,0x92,0x92,
0xaa,0x92,0x92,0xff,0x92,0xb6,0x00,0x92,
0xb6,0x55,0x92,0xb6,0xaa,0x92,0xb6,0xff,
0x92,0xdb,0x00,0x92,0xdb,0x55,0x92,0xdb,
0xaa,0x92,0xdb,0xff,0x92,0xff,0x00,0x92,
0xff,0x55,0x92,0xff,0xaa,0x92,0xff,0xff,
0xb6,0x00,0x00,0xb6,0x00,0x55,0xb6,0x00,
0xaa,0xb6,0x00,0xff,0xb6,0x24,0x00,0xb6,
0x24,0x55,0xb6,0x24,0xaa,0xb6,0x24,0xff,
0xb6,0x49,0x00,0xb6,0x49,0x55,0xb6,0x49,
0xaa,0xb6,0x49,0xff,0xb6,0x6d,0x00,0xb6,
0x6d,0x55,0xb6,0x6d,0xaa,0xb6,0x6d,0xff,
0xb6,0x92,0x00,0xb6,0x92,0x55,0xb6,0x92,
0xaa,0xb6,0x92,0xff,0xb6,0xb6,0x00,0xb6,
0xb6,0x55,0xb6,0xb6,0xaa,0xb6,0xb6,0xff,
0xb6,0xdb,0x00,0xb6,0xdb,0x55,0xb6,0xdb,
0xaa,0xb6,0xdb,0xff,0xb6,0xff,0x00,0xb6,
0xff,0x55,0xb6,0xff,0xaa,0xb6,0xff,0xff,
0xdb,0x00,0x00,0xdb,0x00,0x55,0xdb,0x00,
0xaa,0xdb,0x00,0xff,0xdb,0x24,0x00,0xdb,
0x24,0x55,0xdb,0x24,0xaa,0xdb,0x24,0xff,
0xdb,0x49,0x00,0xdb,0x49,0x55,0xdb,0x49,
0xaa,0xdb,0x49,0xff,0xdb,0x6d,0x00,0xdb,
0x6d,0x55,0xdb,0x6d,0xaa,0xdb,0x6d,0xff,
0xdb,0x92,0x00,0xdb,0x92,0x55,0xdb,0x92,
0xaa,0xdb,0x92,0xff,0xdb,0xb6,0x00,0xdb,
0xb6,0x55,0xdb,0xb6,0xaa,0xdb,0xb6,0xff,
0xdb,0xdb,0x00,0xdb,0xdb,0x55,0xdb,0xdb,
0xaa,0xdb,0xdb,0xff,0xdb,0xff,0x00,0xdb,
0xff,0x55,0xdb,0xff,0xaa,0xdb,0xff,0xff,
0xff,0x00,0x00,0xff,0x00,0x55,0xff,0x00,
0xaa,0xff,0x00,0xff,0xff,0x24,0x00,0xff,
0x24,0x55,0xff,0x24,0xaa,0xff,0x24,0xff,
0xff,0x49,0x00,0xff,0x49,0x55,0xff,0x49,
```

```
        0xaa,0xff,0x49,0xff,0xff,0x6d,0x00,0xff,
        0x6d,0x55,0xff,0x6d,0xaa,0xff,0x6d,0xff,
        0xff,0x92,0x00,0xff,0x92,0x55,0xff,0x92,
        0xaa,0xff,0x92,0xff,0xff,0xb6,0x00,0xff,
        0xb6,0x55,0xff,0xb6,0xaa,0xff,0xb6,0xff,
        0xff,0xdb,0x00,0xff,0xdb,0x55,0xff,0xdb,
        0xaa,0xff,0xdb,0xff,0xff,0xff,0x00,0xff,
        0xff,0x55,0xff,0xff,0xaa,0xff,0xff,0xff
        };

#pragma warn -par
int PASCAL WinMain(HANDLE hInstance,HANDLE hPrevInstance,
                   LPSTR lpszCmdParam,int nCmdShow)
{
    FARPROC dlgProc;
    unsigned short r;

    BWCCGetVersion();

    hInst=hInstance;

    dlgProc=MakeProcInstance((FARPROC)SelectProc,hInst);
    r=DialogBox(hInst,"MainScreen",NULL,dlgProc);

    FreeProcInstance(dlgProc);

    return(r);
}

DWORD FAR PASCAL SelectProc(HWND hwnd,WORD message,WORD wParam,LONG lParam)
{
    FILEINFO fi;
    PAINTSTRUCT ps;
    static HICON hIcon;
    HWND dlgH;
    HMENU hmenu;
    FARPROC lpfnDlgProc;
    POINT point;
    char b[STRINGSIZE+1];
    long l;
    int i;

    switch(message) {
        case WM_CTLCOLOR:
            if(HIWORD(lParam)==CTLCOLOR_STATIC ||
                HIWORD(lParam)==CTLCOLOR_DLG) {
```

```
            SetBkColor(wParam,RGB(192,192,192));
            SetTextColor(wParam,RGB(0,0,0));

            ClientToScreen(hwnd,&point);
            UnrealizeObject(GetStockObject(LTGRAY_BRUSH));
            SetBrushOrg(wParam,point.x,point.y);

            return((DWORD)GetStockObject(LTGRAY_BRUSH));

        }
        if(HIWORD(lParam)==CTLCOLOR_BTN) {
            SetBkColor(wParam,RGB(192,192,192));
            SetTextColor(wParam,RGB(0,0,0));

            ClientToScreen(hwnd,&point);
            UnrealizeObject(GetStockObject(BLACK_BRUSH));
            SetBrushOrg(wParam,point.x,point.y);

            return((DWORD)GetStockObject(BLACK_BRUSH));
        }
        break;
    case WM_SYSCOMMAND:
        switch(wParam & 0xfff0) {
            case SC_CLOSE:
                SendMessage(hwnd,WM_COMMAND,MAIN_EXIT,0L);
                break;
        }
        break;
    case WM_INITDIALOG:
        hIcon=LoadIcon(hInst,szAppName);
        SetClassWord(hwnd,GCW_HICON,(WORD)hIcon);
        ResetSelectorList(hwnd);

        if((l=SendDlgItemMessage(hwnd,MAIN_LIST,LB_GETCURSEL,0,0L)) != LB_ERR) {
            SendDlgItemMessage(hwnd,MAIN_LIST,LB_GETTEXT,
                (unsigned int)l,(long)b);
            if(b[0]=='[') {
                ItemName(MAIN_TITLE," ");
            }
            else {
                ItemName(MAIN_TITLE,b);
            }

            hmenu=GetMenu(hwnd);
            if(b[0]=='[') {
```

```
                ItemOff(MAIN_VIEW);
                ItemOff(MAIN_GETINFO);
                EnableMenuItem(hmenu,MAIN_VIEW,MF_GRAYED);
                EnableMenuItem(hmenu,MAIN_GETINFO,MF_GRAYED);
            }
            else {
                ItemOn(MAIN_VIEW);
                ItemOn(MAIN_GETINFO);
                EnableMenuItem(hmenu,MAIN_VIEW,MF_ENABLED);
                EnableMenuItem(hmenu,MAIN_GETINFO,MF_ENABLED);
            }
        }
        break;
    case WM_PAINT:
        BeginPaint(hwnd,&ps);
        EndPaint(hwnd,&ps);
        break;
    case WM_COMMAND:
        switch(wParam) {
            case MAIN_LIST:
                switch(HIWORD(lParam)) {
                    case LBN_DBLCLK:
                        if(DlgDirSelect(hwnd,b,MAIN_LIST)) {
                            i=lstrlen(b);
                            if(b[i-1]=='\\') {
                                b[i-1]=0;
                                chdir(b);
                            }
                            else {
                                if(!testdisk(b[0]-'A'))
                                    setdisk(toupper(b[0])-'A');
                                else DoMessage(hwnd,"That drive is off line. "
                                "Please check to see that "
                                "there's a disk in it.");
                            }
                            ResetSelectorList(hwnd);
                        }
                        else PostMessage(hwnd,WM_COMMAND,MAIN_VIEW,0L);
                    }
                    if((l=SendDlgItemMessage(hwnd,MAIN_LIST,
                      LB_GETCURSEL,0,0L)) != LB_ERR) {
                        SendDlgItemMessage(hwnd,MAIN_LIST,LB_GETTEXT,
                          (unsigned int)l,(long)b);
                        if(b[0]=='[') {
                            ItemName(MAIN_TITLE," ");
```

```
                        }
                        else {
                            ItemName(MAIN_TITLE,b);
                        }

                        hmenu=GetMenu(hwnd);
                        if(b[0]=='[') {
                            ItemOff(MAIN_VIEW);
                            ItemOff(MAIN_GETINFO);
                            EnableMenuItem(hmenu,MAIN_VIEW,MF_GRAYED);
                            EnableMenuItem(hmenu,MAIN_GETINFO,MF_GRAYED);
                        }
                        else {
                            ItemOn(MAIN_VIEW);
                            ItemOn(MAIN_GETINFO);
                            EnableMenuItem(hmenu,MAIN_VIEW,MF_ENABLED);
                            EnableMenuItem(hmenu,MAIN_GETINFO,MF_ENABLED);
                        }
                    }
                    break;
                case MAIN_GETINFO:
                    if((l=SendDlgItemMessage(hwnd,MAIN_LIST,
                      LB_GETCURSEL,0,0L)) != LB_ERR) {
                        SendDlgItemMessage(hwnd,MAIN_LIST,LB_GETTEXT,
                          (unsigned int)l,(DWORD)b);
                        if(GetInfo(&fi,b)) {
                            ShowInfo(hwnd,&fi);
                        } else DoMessage(hwnd,"Error getting information");
                    }
                    break;
                case MAIN_VIEW:
                    if((l=SendDlgItemMessage(hwnd,MAIN_LIST,
                      LB_GETCURSEL,0,0L)) != LB_ERR) {
                        SendDlgItemMessage(hwnd,MAIN_LIST,
                          LB_GETTEXT,(unsigned int)l,(DWORD)b);
                        ViewFile(hwnd,b);
                    }
                    break;
                case MAIN_ABOUT:
                    if((lpfnDlgProc=MakeProcInstance((FARPROC)
                      AboutDlgProc,hInst)) != NULL) {
                        DialogBox(hInst,"AboutBox",hwnd,lpfnDlgProc);
                        FreeProcInstance(lpfnDlgProc);
                    }
                    break;
```

```
                case MAIN_EXIT:
                    FreeResource(hIcon);
                    PostQuitMessage(0);
                    break;
            }
            break;

    }

    return(FALSE);
}

DWORD FAR PASCAL AboutDlgProc(HWND hwnd,WORD message,WORD wParam,LONG lParam)
{
    POINT point;

    switch(message) {
        case WM_INITDIALOG:
            return(TRUE);
        case WM_CTLCOLOR:
            if(HIWORD(lParam)==CTLCOLOR_STATIC ||
               HIWORD(lParam)==CTLCOLOR_DLG) {
                SetBkColor(wParam,RGB(192,192,192));
                SetTextColor(wParam,RGB(0,0,0));

                ClientToScreen(hwnd,&point);
                UnrealizeObject(GetStockObject(LTGRAY_BRUSH));
                SetBrushOrg(wParam,point.x,point.y);

                return((DWORD)GetStockObject(LTGRAY_BRUSH));

            }
            if(HIWORD(lParam)==CTLCOLOR_BTN) {
                SetBkColor(wParam,RGB(192,192,192));
                SetTextColor(wParam,RGB(0,0,0));

                ClientToScreen(hwnd,&point);
                UnrealizeObject(GetStockObject(BLACK_BRUSH));
                SetBrushOrg(wParam,point.x,point.y);

                return((DWORD)GetStockObject(BLACK_BRUSH));
            }
            break;
        case WM_COMMAND:
            switch(wParam) {
                case IDOK:
```

```
                        EndDialog(hwnd,wParam);
                        return(TRUE);
                }
                break;
        }

    return(FALSE);
}

void DoMessage(HWND hwnd,LPSTR message)
{
    FARPROC lpfnDlgProc;

    messagehook=message;

    if((lpfnDlgProc=MakeProcInstance((FARPROC)MessageDlgProc,hInst)) != NULL) {
        DialogBox(hInst,"MessageBox",hwnd,lpfnDlgProc);
        FreeProcInstance(lpfnDlgProc);
    }
}

DWORD FAR PASCAL MessageDlgProc(HWND hwnd,WORD message,WORD wParam,LONG lParam)
{
    POINT point;
    HWND dlgH;

    switch(message) {
        case WM_INITDIALOG:
            dlgH=GetDlgItem(hwnd,MESSAGE_STRING);
            SetWindowText(dlgH,messagehook);
            return(TRUE);
        case WM_CTLCOLOR:
            if(HIWORD(lParam)==CTLCOLOR_STATIC ||
               HIWORD(lParam)==CTLCOLOR_DLG) {
                SetBkColor(wParam,RGB(192,192,192));
                SetTextColor(wParam,RGB(0,0,0));

                ClientToScreen(hwnd,&point);
                UnrealizeObject(GetStockObject(LTGRAY_BRUSH));
                SetBrushOrg(wParam,point.x,point.y);

                return((DWORD)GetStockObject(LTGRAY_BRUSH));

            }
            if(HIWORD(lParam)==CTLCOLOR_BTN) {
```

```
                    SetBkColor(wParam,RGB(192,192,192));
                    SetTextColor(wParam,RGB(0,0,0));

                    ClientToScreen(hwnd,&point);
                    UnrealizeObject(GetStockObject(BLACK_BRUSH));
                    SetBrushOrg(wParam,point.x,point.y);

                    return((DWORD)GetStockObject(BLACK_BRUSH));
                }
                break;
            case WM_COMMAND:
                switch(wParam) {
                    case IDCANCEL:
                    case IDOK:
                    case IDYES:
                    case IDNO:
                        EndDialog(hwnd,wParam);
                        return(TRUE);
                }
                break;
        }

    return(FALSE);
}


void ResetSelectorList(HWND hwnd)
{
    HWND dlgH;
    HCURSOR hSaveCursor,hHourGlass;
    char b[STRINGSIZE+1];

    hHourGlass=LoadCursor(NULL,IDC_WAIT);
    hSaveCursor=SetCursor(hHourGlass);

    dlgH=GetDlgItem(hwnd,MAIN_LIST);
    SendDlgItemMessage(hwnd,MAIN_LIST,LB_RESETCONTENT,0,0L);
    SendMessage(dlgH,WM_SETREDRAW,FALSE,0L);

    SendDlgItemMessage(hwnd,MAIN_LIST,LB_DIR,0x0000,(long )"*.BMP");

    SendDlgItemMessage(hwnd,MAIN_LIST,LB_DIR,0xc010,(long )"*.*");

    SendDlgItemMessage(hwnd,MAIN_LIST,LB_SETCURSEL,0,0L);
    SendDlgItemMessage(hwnd,MAIN_LIST,LB_GETTEXT,0,(long)b);

    SendMessage(dlgH,WM_SETREDRAW,TRUE,0L);
```

```
    ItemName(MAIN_TITLE,b);

    getcwd(b,STRINGSIZE);
    strlwr(b);
    ItemName(MAIN_PATH,b);

    SetCursor(hSaveCursor);
}

int testdisk(int n)
{
    FILE *fp;
    char b[32];
    int r;

    SetErrorMode(1);
    sprintf(b,"%c:\\TEMP.DAT",n+'A');
    if((fp=fopen(b,"r")) != NULL) fclose(fp);

    if(_doserrno==ENOPATH) r=1;
    else r=0;

    SetErrorMode(0);
    return(r);
}

int GetInfo(FILEINFO *fi,LPSTR path)
{
    BITMAPFILEHEADER bmf;
    BITMAPCOREHEADER bci;
    BITMAPINFOHEADER bmi;
    unsigned long l;
    int fh;

    lstrcpy(fi->filename,path);
    strupr(fi->filename);

    if((fh=_lopen(path,OF_READ))==-1) return(0);

    if(_lread(fh,(char *)&bmf,sizeof(BITMAPFILEHEADER))==sizeof(BITMAPFILEHEADER)) {
        if(!memcmp((char *)&bmf.bfType,"BM",2)) {
            _lread(fh,(LPSTR)&l,sizeof(unsigned long));
            _llseek(fh,-4L,SEEK_CUR);

            if(l==12L) {
```

```
                if(_lread(fh,(char *)&bci,sizeof(BITMAPCOREHEADER)) !=
                    sizeof(BITMAPCOREHEADER)) {
                    _lclose(fh);
                    return(0);
                }

                fi->width=bci.bcWidth;
                fi->depth=bci.bcHeight;
                fi->bits=bci.bcBitCount;
                fi->os2type=TRUE;
            }
            else {
                if(_lread(fh,(char *)&bmi,sizeof(BITMAPINFOHEADER)) !=
                    sizeof(BITMAPINFOHEADER)) {
                    _lclose(fh);
                    return(0);
                }

                fi->width=(int)bmi.biWidth;
                fi->depth=(int)bmi.biHeight;
                fi->bits=bmi.biBitCount;
                fi->os2type=FALSE;
            }

            fi->memory=(long)pixels2bytes(fi->width)*(long)fi->bits*(long)fi->depth;

            _lclose(fh);
            return(1);
        }
        else {
            _lclose(fh);
            return(0);
        }
    }
    else {
        _lclose(fh);
        return(0);
    }
}


void ShowInfo(HWND hwnd,FILEINFO *fi)
{
    FARPROC lpfnDlgProc;

    messagehook=(LPSTR)fi;
```

```
    if((lpfnDlgProc=MakeProcInstance((FARPROC)InfoDlgProc,hInst)) != NULL) {
        DialogBox(hInst,"InfoBox",hwnd,lpfnDlgProc);
        FreeProcInstance(lpfnDlgProc);
    }
}

DWORD FAR PASCAL InfoDlgProc(HWND hwnd,WORD message,WORD wParam,LONG lParam)
{
    static FILEINFO *fi;
    HWND dlgH;
    POINT point;
    PAINTSTRUCT ps;
    char b[STRINGSIZE+1];

    switch(message) {
        case WM_INITDIALOG:
            fi=(FILEINFO *)messagehook;
            ItemName(INFO_FILE,fi->filename);

            switch(fi->bits) {
                case 1:
                    ItemName(INFO_COLOURS,"Monochrome");
                    break;
                case 4:
                    ItemName(INFO_COLOURS,"16 colours");
                    break;
                case 8:
                    ItemName(INFO_COLOURS,"256 colours");
                    break;
                case 24:
                    ItemName(INFO_COLOURS,"16,777,216 colours");
                    break;
            }

            wsprintf(b,"%u x %u",fi->width,fi->depth);
            ItemName(INFO_DIMENSIONS,(LPSTR)b)

            wsprintf(b,"%lu bytes",(unsigned long)fi->memory);
            ItemName(INFO_MEMORY,(LPSTR)b)

            return(TRUE);
        case WM_CTLCOLOR:
            if(HIWORD(lParam)==CTLCOLOR_STATIC ||
               HIWORD(lParam)==CTLCOLOR_DLG) {
                SetBkColor(wParam,RGB(192,192,192));
```

```
                SetTextColor(wParam,RGB(0,0,0));

                ClientToScreen(hwnd,&point);
                UnrealizeObject(GetStockObject(LTGRAY_BRUSH));
                SetBrushOrg(wParam,point.x,point.y);

                return((DWORD)GetStockObject(LTGRAY_BRUSH));

            }
            if(HIWORD(lParam)==CTLCOLOR_BTN) {
                SetBkColor(wParam,RGB(192,192,192));
                SetTextColor(wParam,RGB(0,0,0));

                ClientToScreen(hwnd,&point);
                UnrealizeObject(GetStockObject(BLACK_BRUSH));
                SetBrushOrg(wParam,point.x,point.y);

                return((DWORD)GetStockObject(BLACK_BRUSH));
            }
            break;
        case WM_PAINT:
            BeginPaint(hwnd,&ps);
            EndPaint(hwnd,&ps);
            break;
        case WM_COMMAND:
            switch(wParam) {
                case IDOK:
                    EndDialog(hwnd,wParam);
                    return(TRUE);
            }
            break;
    }

    return(FALSE);
}


int ViewFile(HWND hwnd,LPSTR path)
{
    BITMAPFILEHEADER bmf;
    FILEINFO fi;
    HCURSOR hSaveCursor,hHourGlass;
    HWND childhwnd;
    MSG msg;
    WNDCLASS wndclass;
    char huge *p;
    unsigned long size;
```

4-10 Continued.

```
    int fh;

    hHourGlass=LoadCursor(NULL,IDC_WAIT);
    hSaveCursor=SetCursor(hHourGlass);

    if(!GetInfo(&fi,path)) {
        SetCursor(hSaveCursor);
        DoMessage(hwnd,"Error getting information");
        return(0);
    }

    if((fh=_lopen(path,OF_READ))==-1) {
        SetCursor(hSaveCursor);
        return(0);
    }

    if(_lread(fh,(char *)&bmf,sizeof(BITMAPFILEHEADER))!=sizeof(BITMAPFILEHEADER)) {
        SetCursor(hSaveCursor);
        _lclose(fh);
        DoMessage(hwnd,"Error reading file header");
        return(0);
    }

    size=bmf.bfSize-(long)sizeof(BITMAPFILEHEADER);

    if((fi.picture=GlobalAlloc(GMEM_MOVEABLE,size))==NULL) {
        SetCursor(hSaveCursor);
        _lclose(fh);
        DoMessage(hwnd,"Error allocating memory");
        return(0);
    }

    if((p=(char huge *)GlobalLock(fi.picture))==NULL) {
        GlobalFree(fi.picture);
        SetCursor(hSaveCursor);
        _lclose(fh);
        DoMessage(hwnd,"Error locking memory");
        return(0);
    }

    if(_hread(fh,p,size) != size) {
        GlobalUnlock(fi.picture);
        GlobalFree(fi.picture);
        SetCursor(hSaveCursor);
        _lclose(fh);
```

```
            DoMessage(hwnd,"Error reading the file");
            return(0);
    }

    _lclose(fh);


    GlobalUnlock(fi.picture);

    SetCursor(hSaveCursor);

    messagehook=(LPSTR)&fi;
    wndclass.style=CS_HREDRAW | CS_VREDRAW;
    wndclass.lpfnWndProc=PictureProc;
    wndclass.cbClsExtra=0;
    wndclass.cbWndExtra=0;
    wndclass.hInstance=hInst;
    wndclass.hIcon=LoadIcon(NULL,IDI_APPLICATION);
    wndclass.hCursor=LoadCursor(NULL,IDC_ARROW);
    wndclass.hbrBackground=GetStockObject(BLACK_BRUSH);
    wndclass.lpszMenuName=NULL;
    wndclass.lpszClassName=szAppName;

    RegisterClass(&wndclass);

    childhwnd = CreateWindow(szAppName,path,
        WS_POPUP | WS_CAPTION | WS_SYSMENU | WS_VSCROLL | WS_HSCROLL,
        CW_USEDEFAULT,CW_USEDEFAULT,CW_USEDEFAULT,CW_USEDEFAULT,
        hwnd,NULL,hInst,NULL);

    ShowWindow(childhwnd,SW_SHOWMAXIMIZED);
    UpdateWindow(childhwnd);

    while(GetMessage(&msg,NULL,0,0)) {
        TranslateMessage(&msg);
        DispatchMessage(&msg);
    }

    UnregisterClass(szAppName,hInst);

    GlobalUnlock(fi.picture);
    GlobalFree(fi.picture);
    return(1);
}

long FAR PASCAL PictureProc(HWND hwnd,unsigned int message,
```

```
                              unsigned int wParam,LONG lParam)
{
    static FILEINFO far *fi;
    LPBITMAPINFO bmp;
    LOGPALETTE *pLogPal;
    HANDLE hPal=NULL;
    LPSTR image;
    RGBQUAD far *palette;
    RGBTRIPLE far *corepalette;
    HDC hdc;
    PAINTSTRUCT ps;
    RECT rect;
    static int vpos,hpos;
    int vsize,hsize,vjump,hjump;
    int i,j,n;

    switch (message) {
        case WM_VSCROLL:
            GetClientRect(hwnd,&rect);
            vsize=rect.bottom-rect.top;
            vjump=vsize/4;
            switch(wParam) {
                case SB_LINEUP:
                    vpos-=1;
                    break;
                case SB_LINEDOWN:
                    vpos+=1;
                    break;
                case SB_PAGEUP:
                    vpos-=vjump;
                    break;
                case SB_PAGEDOWN:
                    vpos+=vjump;
                    break;
                case SB_THUMBPOSITION:
                    vpos=LOWORD(lParam);
                    break;
            }

            if(vpos < 0 || fi->depth < vsize) vpos=0;
            else if(vpos > (fi->depth-vsize)) vpos=fi->depth-vsize;

            if(vpos != GetScrollPos(hwnd,SB_VERT)) {
                SetScrollPos(hwnd,SB_VERT,vpos,TRUE);
                InvalidateRect(hwnd,NULL,FALSE);
```

```
        }
        return(0);
case WM_HSCROLL:
        GetClientRect(hwnd,&rect);
        hsize=rect.right-rect.left;
        hjump=hsize/4;
        switch(wParam) {
            case SB_LINEUP:
                hpos-=1;
                break;
            case SB_LINEDOWN:
                hpos+=1;
                break;
            case SB_PAGEUP:
                hpos-=hjump;
                break;
            case SB_PAGEDOWN:
                hpos+=hjump;
                break;
            case SB_THUMBPOSITION:
                hpos=LOWORD(lParam);
                break;
        }

        if(hpos < 0 || fi->width < hsize) hpos=0;
        else if(hpos > (fi->width-hsize)) hpos=fi->width-hsize;

        if(hpos != GetScrollPos(hwnd,SB_HORZ)) {
            SetScrollPos(hwnd,SB_HORZ,hpos,TRUE);
            InvalidateRect(hwnd,NULL,FALSE);
        }
        return(0);
case WM_CREATE:
        fi=(FILEINFO far *)messagehook;
        vpos=hpos=0;

case WM_SIZE:
        GetClientRect(hwnd,&rect);
        vsize=rect.bottom-rect.top;
        if(fi->depth > vsize)
            SetScrollRange(hwnd,SB_VERT,0,fi->depth-vsize,TRUE);
        else
            SetScrollRange(hwnd,SB_VERT,0,1,TRUE);
        hsize=rect.right-rect.left;
        if(fi->width > hsize)
            SetScrollRange(hwnd,SB_HORZ,0,fi->width-hsize,TRUE);
```

4-10 Continued.

```
          else
              SetScrollRange(hwnd,SB_HORZ,0,1,TRUE);
          return(0);
      case WM_PAINT:
          hdc=BeginPaint(hwnd,&ps);

          if((bmp=(LPBITMAPINFO)GlobalLock(fi->picture)) != NULL) {

              n=1<<fi->bits;
              j=min(n,256);

              if(fi->os2type) {
                  corepalette=(RGBTRIPLE far *)
                      ((LPSTR)bmp+(unsigned int)bmp->bmiHeader.biSize);
                  image=(LPSTR)bmp+(unsigned int)bmp->bmiHeader.biSize+
                      (j*sizeof(RGBTRIPLE));
              }
              else {
                  palette=(RGBQUAD far *)((LPSTR)bmp+
                      (unsigned int)bmp->bmiHeader.biSize);
                  image=(LPSTR)bmp+(unsigned int)bmp->bmiHeader.biSize+
                      (j*sizeof(RGBQUAD));
              }

              if((pLogPal=(LOGPALETTE *)malloc(sizeof(LOGPALETTE)+
                (j*sizeof(PALETTEENTRY)))) != NULL) {
                  pLogPal->palVersion=0x0300;
                  pLogPal->palNumEntries=j;

                  if(fi->bits==24) {
                      for(i=0;i<j;i++) {
                          pLogPal->palPalEntry[i].peRed=
                              orthopalette[i*RGB_SIZE+RGB_RED];
                          pLogPal->palPalEntry[i].peGreen=
                              orthopalette[i*RGB_SIZE+RGB_GREEN];
                          pLogPal->palPalEntry[i].peBlue=
                              orthopalette[i*RGB_SIZE+RGB_BLUE];
                          pLogPal->palPalEntry[i].peFlags=0;
                      }

                  }
                  else {
                      if(fi->os2type) {
                          for(i=0;i<j;i++) {
                              pLogPal->palPalEntry[i].peRed=
```

```
                                corepalette[i].rgbtRed;
                        pLogPal->palPalEntry[i].peGreen=
                                corepalette[i].rgbtGreen;
                        pLogPal->palPalEntry[i].peBlue=
                                corepalette[i].rgbtBlue;
                        pLogPal->palPalEntry[i].peFlags=0;
                    }
                }
                else {
                    for(i=0;i<j;i++) {
                        pLogPal->palPalEntry[i].peRed=
                                palette[i].rgbRed;
                        pLogPal->palPalEntry[i].peGreen=
                                palette[i].rgbGreen;
                        pLogPal->palPalEntry[i].peBlue=
                                palette[i].rgbBlue;
                        pLogPal->palPalEntry[i].peFlags=0;
                    }
                }
            }

            hPal=CreatePalette(pLogPal);
            free(pLogPal);

            SelectPalette(hdc,hPal,0);
            RealizePalette(hdc);
        }

        SetDIBitsToDevice(hdc,0,0,fi->width,fi->depth,
            hpos,-vpos,0,fi->depth,image,bmp,DIB_RGB_COLORS);

        if(hPal != NULL) DeleteObject(hPal);
        GlobalUnlock(fi->picture);

    } else MessageBeep(0);

    EndPaint(hwnd,&ps);
    return(0);
case WM_DESTROY:
    PostQuitMessage(0);
    break;
case WM_SYSCOMMAND:
    switch(wParam & 0xfff0) {
        case SC_CLOSE:
            SendMessage(hwnd,WM_DESTROY,0,0L);
            break;
```

4-10   Continued.

```
            }
            break;

    }

    return(DefWindowProc(hwnd,message,wParam,lParam));
}
```

4-11   The resource script for the bitmap viewer, VIEWBMP.RC.

```
MainScreen DIALOG 117, 55, 156, 152
STYLE WS_POPUP | WS_CAPTION | WS_SYSMENU | WS_MINIMIZEBOX
CAPTION "Bitmap Viewer"
MENU MainMenu
BEGIN
  CONTROL "", 201, "LISTBOX", LBS_STANDARD | WS_CHILD | WS_VISIBLE,
     12, 24, 76, 108
  LTEXT "", 301, 12, 132, 76, 8, WS_CHILD | WS_VISIBLE | WS_GROUP
  CONTROL "", -1, "BorShade", BSS_GROUP | WS_CHILD | WS_VISIBLE, 8, 8, 84, 136
  DEFPUSHBUTTON "View", 102, 108, 8, 40, 20, WS_CHILD | WS_VISIBLE | WS_TABSTOP
  PUSHBUTTON "Get Info", 103, 108, 36, 40, 20, WS_CHILD | WS_VISIBLE | WS_TABSTOP
  PUSHBUTTON "Quit", 107, 108, 124, 40, 20, WS_CHILD | WS_VISIBLE | WS_TABSTOP
  CONTROL "", -1, "BorShade", BSS_VDIP | WS_CHILD | WS_VISIBLE, 100, 0, 1, 152
  LTEXT "", 302, 12, 12, 76, 8, WS_CHILD | WS_VISIBLE | WS_GROUP
END


MainMenu MENU
BEGIN
    POPUP "&File"
    BEGIN
        MENUITEM "&View", 102
        MENUITEM "&Get Info", 103
        MENUITEM "&About", 105
        MENUITEM SEPARATOR
        MENUITEM "E&xit", 107
    END

END


AboutBox DIALOG 18, 18, 156, 104
STYLE WS_POPUP | WS_CAPTION
CAPTION "About Bitmap Viewer..."
BEGIN
  CONTROL "", 102, "BorShade", BSS_GROUP | WS_CHILD | WS_VISIBLE | WS_TABSTOP,
     8, 8, 140, 68
```

```
        LTEXT "Bitmap Viewer 1.0\nCopyright (c) 1993\nAlchemy Mindworks Inc.\n"
          "This program is part of the book Multimedia Programming for Windows "
          "by Steven William Rimmer, published by Windcrest (Book 4484).",
          -1, 12, 12, 128, 60, WS_CHILD | WS_VISIBLE | WS_GROUP
        DEFPUSHBUTTON "Ok", IDOK, 116, 80, 32, 20, WS_CHILD | WS_VISIBLE | WS_TABSTOP
END


MessageBox DIALOG 72, 72, 144, 80
STYLE DS_MODALFRAME | WS_POPUP | WS_CAPTION
CAPTION "Message"
BEGIN
        CONTROL "", 102, "BorShade", BSS_GROUP | WS_CHILD | WS_VISIBLE, 4, 8, 136, 44
        CTEXT "", 101, 8, 12, 128, 36, WS_CHILD | WS_VISIBLE | WS_GROUP
        DEFPUSHBUTTON "Ok", IDOK, 108, 56, 32, 20, WS_CHILD | WS_VISIBLE | WS_TABSTOP
END


InfoBox DIALOG 6, -11, 180, 92
STYLE DS_MODALFRAME | WS_POPUP | WS_CAPTION
CAPTION "Get Info"
BEGIN
        DEFPUSHBUTTON "Ok", IDOK, 140, 64, 32, 20, WS_CHILD | WS_VISIBLE | WS_TABSTOP
        RTEXT "File:", -1, 8, 12, 44, 8, SS_RIGHT | WS_CHILD | WS_VISIBLE | WS_GROUP
        RTEXT "Colours:", -1, 8, 24, 44, 8, SS_RIGHT | WS_CHILD | WS_VISIBLE | WS_GROUP
        RTEXT "Dimensions:", -1, 8, 36, 44, 8, SS_RIGHT | WS_CHILD | WS_VISIBLE | WS_GROUP
        RTEXT "Memory:", -1, 8, 48, 44, 8, SS_RIGHT | WS_CHILD | WS_VISIBLE | WS_GROUP
        LTEXT "", 101, 60, 12, 60, 8, WS_CHILD | WS_VISIBLE | WS_GROUP
        LTEXT "", 102, 60, 24, 60, 8, WS_CHILD | WS_VISIBLE | WS_GROUP
        LTEXT "", 103, 60, 36, 60, 8, WS_CHILD | WS_VISIBLE | WS_GROUP
        LTEXT "", 104, 60, 48, 60, 8, WS_CHILD | WS_VISIBLE | WS_GROUP
END


BmpView ICON LOADONCALL MOVEABLE DISCARDABLE
BEGIN
        '00 00 01 00 02 00 20 20 02 00 00 00 00 00 30 01'
        '00 00 26 00 00 00 20 20 10 00 00 00 00 00 E8 02'
        '00 00 56 01 00 00 28 00 00 00 20 00 00 00 40 00'
        '00 00 01 00 01 00 00 00 00 00 01 00 00 00 00 00'
        '00 00 00 00 00 00 00 00 00 00 00 00 00 00 00 00'
        '00 00 FF FF FF 00 00 00 00 00 00 FF C0 00 03 FF'
        'E0 00 03 FF D0 00 03 FF E0 00 03 FF D0 00 03 FF'
        'E0 00 03 FF D0 00 03 FF E0 00 03 00 10 00 00 FF'
        'C0 00 03 00 30 00 04 E5 88 00 03 E4 D0 00 03 D5'
        '60 00 03 D5 B8 00 07 C4 14 7C 07 84 0F 86 07 84'
        '04 82 01 80 04 42 0E 04 06 26 1F 04 09 1C 1F 04'
        '08 80 23 00 08 40 1D 0E 08 40 22 0E 0C C0 0A 04'
        '07 80 00 00 00 00 00 00 00 00 00 00 00 00 00 00'
```

```
'00 00 00 00 00 00 FF 00 3F FF FC 00 0F FF F8 00'
'07 FF F8 00 07 FF F8 00 07 FF F8 00 07 FF F8 00'
'07 FF F8 00 07 FF F8 00 07 FF F8 00 07 FF F8 00'
'07 FF F0 00 03 FF F0 00 03 FF F0 00 03 FF F8 00'
'07 FF F8 00 01 83 F0 00 00 01 F0 31 E0 00 F0 31'
'F0 38 E0 31 F1 18 E0 71 F0 80 C0 71 E0 41 C0 71'
'E2 23 80 71 E3 1F 80 60 E3 1F 80 60 E0 1F C0 60'
'F0 3F E0 E1 F8 7F FF E1 FF FF FF E3 FF FF FF E7'
'FF FF FF DF FF FF 28 00 00 00 20 00 00 00 40 00'
'00 00 01 00 04 00 00 00 00 00 80 02 00 00 00 00'
'00 00 00 00 00 00 00 00 00 00 00 00 00 00 00 00'
'00 00 00 00 80 00 00 80 00 00 00 80 80 00 80 00'
'00 00 80 00 80 00 80 80 00 00 80 80 80 00 C0 C0'
'C0 00 00 00 FF 00 00 FF 00 00 00 FF FF 00 FF 00'
'00 00 FF 00 FF 00 FF FF 00 00 FF FF FF 00 00 00'
'00 00 00 00 00 00 00 00 00 00 00 00 00 00 00 00'
'00 00 88 88 88 88 86 00 00 00 00 00 00 00 00 00'
'00 68 EE EE EE EE E8 66 00 00 00 00 00 00 00 00'
'00 68 E8 FE EE EE E8 66 00 00 00 00 00 00 00 00'
'00 68 EF FE EE EE E8 66 00 00 00 00 00 00 00 00'
'00 68 EF EE EE EE E8 66 00 00 00 00 00 00 00 00'
'00 68 EF EE EE EE E8 66 00 00 00 00 00 00 00 00'
'00 68 EE EE EE EE 66 66 00 00 00 00 00 00 00 00'
'00 66 66 66 66 66 66 00 00 00 00 00 00 00 00 00'
'00 66 00 00 00 00 00 66 00 00 00 00 00 00 00 00'
'00 00 EF EF EF EF EF 00 00 00 00 00 00 00 00 00'
'00 FE 00 00 00 00 00 E6 00 00 00 00 00 00 00 00'
'06 00 33 30 09 08 80 00 60 00 00 00 00 00 00 00'
'00 3B 83 30 09 00 88 07 00 00 00 00 00 00 00 00'
'00 B8 83 06 09 06 08 80 00 00 00 00 00 00 00 00'
'00 B8 33 0E 09 0E 60 88 80 00 00 00 00 00 00 00'
'03 B8 33 00 09 00 00 08 08 00 07 88 87 00 00 00'
'0B 88 30 00 09 00 00 00 88 88 80 00 08 70 00 00'
'0B 83 30 00 09 00 00 00 08 00 80 00 00 80 00 00'
'00 03 30 00 00 00 00 00 08 00 08 00 00 80 00 00'
'BB 80 00 00 0F 00 00 00 08 80 00 80 08 70 00 03'
'B8 83 00 00 08 00 00 00 70 08 00 08 87 00 00 0B'
'B8 33 00 00 07 00 00 00 80 00 80 00 00 00 00 30'
'00 33 00 00 00 00 00 00 80 00 08 00 00 00 00 0B'
'33 03 00 00 87 70 00 00 80 00 08 00 00 00 00 B0'
'00 30 00 00 88 70 00 00 78 00 87 00 00 00 00 00'
'B0 30 00 00 CF C0 00 00 07 88 70 00 00 00 00 00'
'00 00 00 00 CC 00 00 00 00 00 00 00 00 00 00 00'
'00 00 00 00 CC 00 00 00 00 00 00 00 00 00 00 00'
'00 00 00 00 C0 00 00 00 00 00 00 00 00 00 00 00'
```

```
'00 00 00 00 00 00 00 00 00 00 00 00 00 00 00 00'
'00 00 00 00 00 00 00 00 00 00 00 00 00 00 FF 00'
'3F FF FC 00 0F FF F8 00 07 FF F8 00 07 FF F8 00'
'07 FF F8 00 07 FF F8 00 07 FF F8 00 07 FF F8 00'
'07 FF F8 00 07 FF F8 00 07 FF F0 00 03 FF F0 00'
'03 FF F0 00 03 FF F8 00 07 FF F8 00 01 83 F0 00'
'00 01 F0 31 E0 00 F0 31 F0 38 E0 31 F1 18 E0 71'
'F0 80 C0 71 E0 41 C0 71 E2 23 80 71 E3 1F 80 60'
'E3 1F 80 60 E0 1F C0 60 F0 3F E0 E1 F8 7F FF E1'
'FF FF FF E3 FF FF FF E7 FF FF FF DF FF FF'
END
```

4-12 The project file for the bitmap viewer, VIEWBMP.PRJ.

The ShowInfo function formats the data in a FILEINFO filled in by GetInfo and displays it in a dialog, as shown in FIG. 4-13.

The ViewFile function uses a lot of code, but very little of it should prove particularly inscrutable. It begins by calling GetInfo to ascertain the dimensions of the bitmap to be read. It then opens the source file, reads past its BITMAPFILEHEADER, and then just inhales the whole works into memory with a call to _hread.

The latter half of ViewFile opens a new window with CreateWindow. Its message handler is PictureProc.

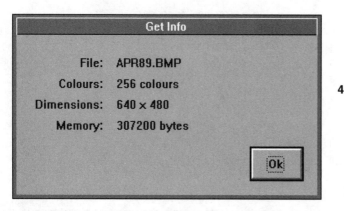

4-13 The Get Info dialog of the bitmap viewer.

The PictureProc function handles displaying the bitmap in question in its WM_PAINT function, using a call to SetDIBitsToDevice like the one in the previous section. One important difference between this real-world application and the theoretical one you looked at earlier is that this one allows for sections of the bitmap in question to be displayed if the whole bitmap won't fit in the display window at once. The sections are defined by the position of the window's scroll bars.

Note also that the code in the WM_PAINT case allows for OS/2 bitmaps, based on the setting of the os2type flag in the FILEINFO object for the bitmap being displayed.

The large object at the top of the VIEWBMP.CPP listing called orthopalette is a table of color values for the orthogonal palette discussed earlier in this chapter. If you attempt to have VIEWBMP display a 24-bit BMP file on a system that supports 256 colors, the image will be remapped to a palette by Windows. Specifying a palette with a good dispersal of colors, such as this one, will produce the least unattractive results if this happens. Mind you, the least unattractive results are still pretty ugly.

While there are unquestionably uses for handling bitmaps as BMP files, in most Windows applications you probably won't want your graphics stored on disk in quite this way. As was done in the wait screen of the compact disc audio player, it's also possible to store them as resources for your application. An example of this will appear next.

Displaying multiple bitmaps in one window

The graphic in FIG. 4-14 has a number of salient characteristics. While it's reproduced as a gray-scale image here, it was generated in full color. You can see the color version if you run the MANYBMP.EXE program from the \APPS directory of the companion CD-ROM for this book. It will display twelve 256-color images in a window on a system with a 256-color screen driver. It has been designed to run on a system with a 800×600-pixel resolution—if you have a 640×480-pixel driver in your system, some of the images will be cropped.

The 12 images in MANYBMP.EXE were drawn from a number of disparate public-domain GIF files and converted and cropped with Graphic Workshop for Windows. As you might expect, each of the images had a different palette, and as such what appears in FIG. 4-14 should be impossible on a system with 256-color screen driver. In effect, it would involve displaying as many as 3072 different colors on a system that can handle only a maximum of 256.

If you run MANYBMP.EXE, you'll find that it does work, and that all the graphics will appear with appropriate colors. Clearly, there's something tricky at work here.

Being able to display multiple photorealistic images in a single window can be very useful for multimedia applications that manipulate a lot of graphics. In a sense, doing so requires a way to eliminate the unique palettes of the individual graphics involved and have a common palette for all of them, as well as for whatever else you might want to draw in your application window. Something like this turned up earlier in this chapter—the orthographic palette option of Graphic Workshop for Windows' Effects box will reduce 24-bit images to 256-color images with a common fixed palette.

4-14 The main window of MANYBMP, an application that displays several color images in one window.

In fact, you can do this with any image having more than two colors. When you use the Effects box of Graphic Workshop, it temporarily converts whatever images it reads into internal 24-bit bitmaps. If you reduce a 256-color graphic to 256 colors this way, it will be turned into a 24-bit graphic and then redithered back down to 256 colors, but the 256 colors will be those of the orthogonal palette, rather than the palette the image initially used.

This can introduce a slight color shift in some graphics, but you'd pretty well have to look at the source and destination images side by side to notice it. It can also introduce dithering aberrations, at least in theory, as dithering an image that has previously been dithered can create interference patterns. Again, this is rarely noticeable. In real-world applications, you can avoid this latter situation very easily be working from 24-bit source graphics rather than 8-bit GIF files—the 24-bit graphics will not have been dithered.

In the previous example of displaying a bitmap with SetDIBitsToDevice, the palette of the bitmap was realized and SetDIBitsToDevice treated its colors as colors. As was mentioned in the foregoing section, however, you can also realize a palette and have SetDIBitsToDevice regard its color table as a list of indices into the palette. Aside from allowing you to have multiple bitmaps in a window at once—as long as they all have a common palette— this works somewhat faster.

Figure 4-15 is the C language source listing for the MANYBMP application, the program that created the graphic in FIG. 4-14. It's pretty simple as Windows applications go. Figure 4-16 is the resource script for MANYBMP. It's pretty simple too. You'll note the lines at the end of the listing that deal with the bitmap image files. This is the syntax for including BMP files as resource data in a Windows resource script.

4-15 The C language source listing for the multiple bitmap viewer, MANYBMP.CPP.

```
/*

    Multiple Bitmap Demo
    Copyright (c) 1993 Alchemy Mindworks Inc.
*/

#include <windows.h>
#include <stdio.h>
#include <stdlib.h>
#include <dir.h>
#include <ctype.h>
#include <alloc.h>
#include <string.h>
#include <io.h>
#include <bwcc.h>
#include <dos.h>
```

```
#include <errno.h>
#include <math.h>

#define say(s)        MessageBox(NULL,s,"Yo...",MB_OK | MB_ICONSTOP);
#define saynumber(f,s)   {char b[128]; sprintf((LPSTR)b,(LPSTR)f,s); \
                   MessageBox(NULL,b,"Debug Message",MB_OK | MB_ICONSTOP); }

#define ItemName(item,string)    { dlgH=GetDlgItem(hwnd,item); \
                          SetWindowText(dlgH,(LPSTR)string); }
#define ItemOn(item)        { dlgH=GetDlgItem(hwnd,item); EnableWindow(dlgH,TRUE); }
#define ItemOff(item)       { dlgH=GetDlgItem(hwnd,item); EnableWindow(dlgH,FALSE); }
#define pixels2bytes(n)   ((n+7)/8)

#define STRINGSIZE          129        /* how big is a string? */

#define MAIN_ABOUT          105
#define MAIN_EXIT           107

#define RGB_RED             0
#define RGB_GREEN           1
#define RGB_BLUE            2
#define RGB_SIZE            3

#define MAXIMAGE            12

#define IMAGE_WIDE          192
#define IMAGE_DEEP          192
#define IMAGE_COLOURS       256

#define PALETTE_COLOURS     256

#define MARGIN              1

#ifndef max
#define max(a,b)          (((a)>(b))?(a):(b))
#endif
#ifndef min
#define min(a,b)          (((a)<(b))?(a):(b))
#endif

/* prototypes */
DWORD FAR PASCAL SelectProc(HWND hwnd,WORD message,WORD wParam,LONG lParam);
DWORD FAR PASCAL AboutDlgProc(HWND hwnd,WORD message,WORD wParam,LONG lParam);
void DrawImage(HDC hdc,int x,int y,HBITMAP image);

/* globals */
```

4-15 Continued.
```
LPSTR messagehook;
char szAppName[]="ManyBmp";

HANDLE hInst;

char orthopalette[] = {
    0x00,0x00,0x00,0x00,0x00,0x55,0x00,0x00,
    0xaa,0x00,0x00,0xff,0x00,0x24,0x00,0x00,
    0x24,0x55,0x00,0x24,0xaa,0x00,0x24,0xff,
    0x00,0x49,0x00,0x00,0x49,0x55,0x00,0x49,
    0xaa,0x00,0x49,0xff,0x00,0x6d,0x00,0x00,
    0x6d,0x55,0x00,0x6d,0xaa,0x00,0x6d,0xff,
    0x00,0x92,0x00,0x00,0x92,0x55,0x00,0x92,
    0xaa,0x00,0x92,0xff,0x00,0xb6,0x00,0x00,
    0xb6,0x55,0x00,0xb6,0xaa,0x00,0xb6,0xff,
    0x00,0xdb,0x00,0x00,0xdb,0x55,0x00,0xdb,
    0xaa,0x00,0xdb,0xff,0x00,0xff,0x00,0x00,
    0xff,0x55,0x00,0xff,0xaa,0x00,0xff,0xff,
    0x24,0x00,0x00,0x24,0x00,0x55,0x24,0x00,
    0xaa,0x24,0x00,0xff,0x24,0x24,0x00,0x24,
    0x24,0x55,0x24,0x24,0xaa,0x24,0x24,0xff,
    0x24,0x49,0x00,0x24,0x49,0x55,0x24,0x49,
    0xaa,0x24,0x49,0xff,0x24,0x6d,0x00,0x24,
    0x6d,0x55,0x24,0x6d,0xaa,0x24,0x6d,0xff,
    0x24,0x92,0x00,0x24,0x92,0x55,0x24,0x92,
    0xaa,0x24,0x92,0xff,0x24,0xb6,0x00,0x24,
    0xb6,0x55,0x24,0xb6,0xaa,0x24,0xb6,0xff,
    0x24,0xdb,0x00,0x24,0xdb,0x55,0x24,0xdb,
    0xaa,0x24,0xdb,0xff,0x24,0xff,0x00,0x24,
    0xff,0x55,0x24,0xff,0xaa,0x24,0xff,0xff,
    0x49,0x00,0x00,0x49,0x00,0x55,0x49,0x00,
    0xaa,0x49,0x00,0xff,0x49,0x24,0x00,0x49,
    0x24,0x55,0x49,0x24,0xaa,0x49,0x24,0xff,
    0x49,0x49,0x00,0x49,0x49,0x55,0x49,0x49,
    0xaa,0x49,0x49,0xff,0x49,0x6d,0x00,0x49,
    0x6d,0x55,0x49,0x6d,0xaa,0x49,0x6d,0xff,
    0x49,0x92,0x00,0x49,0x92,0x55,0x49,0x92,
    0xaa,0x49,0x92,0xff,0x49,0xb6,0x00,0x49,
    0xb6,0x55,0x49,0xb6,0xaa,0x49,0xb6,0xff,
    0x49,0xdb,0x00,0x49,0xdb,0x55,0x49,0xdb,
    0xaa,0x49,0xdb,0xff,0x49,0xff,0x00,0x49,
    0xff,0x55,0x49,0xff,0xaa,0x49,0xff,0xff,
    0x6d,0x00,0x00,0x6d,0x00,0x55,0x6d,0x00,
    0xaa,0x6d,0x00,0xff,0x6d,0x24,0x00,0x6d,
    0x24,0x55,0x6d,0x24,0xaa,0x6d,0x24,0xff,
```

```
0x6d,0x49,0x00,0x6d,0x49,0x55,0x6d,0x49,
0xaa,0x6d,0x49,0xff,0x6d,0x6d,0x00,0x6d,
0x6d,0x55,0x6d,0x6d,0xaa,0x6d,0x6d,0xff,
0x6d,0x92,0x00,0x6d,0x92,0x55,0x6d,0x92,
0xaa,0x6d,0x92,0xff,0x6d,0xb6,0x00,0x6d,
0xb6,0x55,0x6d,0xb6,0xaa,0x6d,0xb6,0xff,
0x6d,0xdb,0x00,0x6d,0xdb,0x55,0x6d,0xdb,
0xaa,0x6d,0xdb,0xff,0x6d,0xff,0x00,0x6d,
0xff,0x55,0x6d,0xff,0xaa,0x6d,0xff,0xff,
0x92,0x00,0x00,0x92,0x00,0x55,0x92,0x00,
0xaa,0x92,0x00,0xff,0x92,0x24,0x00,0x92,
0x24,0x55,0x92,0x24,0xaa,0x92,0x24,0xff,
0x92,0x49,0x00,0x92,0x49,0x55,0x92,0x49,
0xaa,0x92,0x49,0xff,0x92,0x6d,0x00,0x92,
0x6d,0x55,0x92,0x6d,0xaa,0x92,0x6d,0xff,
0x92,0x92,0x00,0x92,0x92,0x55,0x92,0x92,
0xaa,0x92,0x92,0xff,0x92,0xb6,0x00,0x92,
0xb6,0x55,0x92,0xb6,0xaa,0x92,0xb6,0xff,
0x92,0xdb,0x00,0x92,0xdb,0x55,0x92,0xdb,
0xaa,0x92,0xdb,0xff,0x92,0xff,0x00,0x92,
0xff,0x55,0x92,0xff,0xaa,0x92,0xff,0xff,
0xb6,0x00,0x00,0xb6,0x00,0x55,0xb6,0x00,
0xaa,0xb6,0x00,0xff,0xb6,0x24,0x00,0xb6,
0x24,0x55,0xb6,0x24,0xaa,0xb6,0x24,0xff,
0xb6,0x49,0x00,0xb6,0x49,0x55,0xb6,0x49,
0xaa,0xb6,0x49,0xff,0xb6,0x6d,0x00,0xb6,
0x6d,0x55,0xb6,0x6d,0xaa,0xb6,0x6d,0xff,
0xb6,0x92,0x00,0xb6,0x92,0x55,0xb6,0x92,
0xaa,0xb6,0x92,0xff,0xb6,0xb6,0x00,0xb6,
0xb6,0x55,0xb6,0xb6,0xaa,0xb6,0xb6,0xff,
0xb6,0xdb,0x00,0xb6,0xdb,0x55,0xb6,0xdb,
0xaa,0xb6,0xdb,0xff,0xb6,0xff,0x00,0xb6,
0xff,0x55,0xb6,0xff,0xaa,0xb6,0xff,0xff,
0xdb,0x00,0x00,0xdb,0x00,0x55,0xdb,0x00,
0xaa,0xdb,0x00,0xff,0xdb,0x24,0x00,0xdb,
0x24,0x55,0xdb,0x24,0xaa,0xdb,0x24,0xff,
0xdb,0x49,0x00,0xdb,0x49,0x55,0xdb,0x49,
0xaa,0xdb,0x49,0xff,0xdb,0x6d,0x00,0xdb,
0x6d,0x55,0xdb,0x6d,0xaa,0xdb,0x6d,0xff,
0xdb,0x92,0x00,0xdb,0x92,0x55,0xdb,0x92,
0xaa,0xdb,0x92,0xff,0xdb,0xb6,0x00,0xdb,
0xb6,0x55,0xdb,0xb6,0xaa,0xdb,0xb6,0xff,
0xdb,0xdb,0x00,0xdb,0xdb,0x55,0xdb,0xdb,
0xaa,0xdb,0xdb,0xff,0xdb,0xff,0x00,0xdb,
0xff,0x55,0xdb,0xff,0xaa,0xdb,0xff,0xff,
0xff,0x00,0x00,0xff,0x00,0x55,0xff,0x00,
```

```
    0xaa,0xff,0x00,0xff,0xff,0x24,0x00,0xff,
    0x24,0x55,0xff,0x24,0xaa,0xff,0x24,0xff,
    0xff,0x49,0x00,0xff,0x49,0x55,0xff,0x49,
    0xaa,0xff,0x49,0xff,0xff,0x6d,0x00,0xff,
    0x6d,0x55,0xff,0x6d,0xaa,0xff,0x6d,0xff,
    0xff,0x92,0x00,0xff,0x92,0x55,0xff,0x92,
    0xaa,0xff,0x92,0xff,0xff,0xb6,0x00,0xff,
    0xb6,0x55,0xff,0xb6,0xaa,0xff,0xb6,0xff,
    0xff,0xdb,0x00,0xff,0xdb,0x55,0xff,0xdb,
    0xaa,0xff,0xdb,0xff,0xff,0xff,0x00,0xff,
    0xff,0x55,0xff,0xff,0xaa,0xff,0xff,0xff
    };


#pragma warn -par
int PASCAL WinMain(HANDLE hInstance,HANDLE hPrevInstance,
                  LPSTR lpszCmdParam,int nCmdShow)
{
    FARPROC dlgProc;
    unsigned short r;

    BWCCGetVersion();

    hInst=hInstance;

    dlgProc=MakeProcInstance((FARPROC)SelectProc,hInst);
    r=DialogBox(hInst,"MainScreen",NULL,dlgProc);

    FreeProcInstance(dlgProc);

    return(r);
}


DWORD FAR PASCAL SelectProc(HWND hwnd,WORD message,WORD wParam,LONG lParam)
{
    static HBITMAP image[MAXIMAGE];
    LPBITMAPINFO pDibInfo;
    LOGPALETTE *pLogPal;
    HANDLE hPal=NULL;
    PAINTSTRUCT ps;
    HMENU hmenu;
    static HICON hIcon;
    FARPROC lpfnDlgProc;
    POINT point;
    HDC hdc;
    LPSTR p;
```

```
char b[STRINGSIZE+1];
int i,j,x,y,far *ip;

switch(message) {
    case WM_CTLCOLOR:
        if(HIWORD(lParam)==CTLCOLOR_STATIC ||
            HIWORD(lParam)==CTLCOLOR_DLG) {
            SetBkColor(wParam,RGB(192,192,192));
            SetTextColor(wParam,RGB(0,0,0));

            ClientToScreen(hwnd,&point);
            UnrealizeObject(GetStockObject(BLACK_BRUSH));
            SetBrushOrg(wParam,point.x,point.y);

            return((DWORD)GetStockObject(BLACK_BRUSH));

        }
        if(HIWORD(lParam)==CTLCOLOR_BTN) {
            SetBkColor(wParam,RGB(192,192,192));
            SetTextColor(wParam,RGB(0,0,0));

            ClientToScreen(hwnd,&point);
            UnrealizeObject(GetStockObject(BLACK_BRUSH));
            SetBrushOrg(wParam,point.x,point.y);

            return((DWORD)GetStockObject(BLACK_BRUSH));
        }
        break;
    case WM_SYSCOMMAND:
        switch(wParam & 0xfff0) {
            case SC_CLOSE:
                SendMessage(hwnd,WM_COMMAND,MAIN_EXIT,0L);
                break;
        }
        switch(wParam) {
            case MAIN_ABOUT:
                SendMessage(hwnd,WM_COMMAND,MAIN_ABOUT,0L);
                break;
        }
        break;
    case WM_INITDIALOG:
        hIcon=LoadIcon(hInst,szAppName);
        SetClassWord(hwnd,GCW_HICON,(WORD)hIcon);

        for(i=0;i<MAXIMAGE;++i) {
            wsprintf(b,"IMAGE%03.3u",i);
```

```
            image[i]=LoadResource(hInst,FindResource(hInst,b,RT_BITMAP));

            if((p=LockResource(image[i])) != NULL) {
                pDibInfo=(LPBITMAPINFO)p;
                ip=(int far *)&pDibInfo->bmiColors[0];
                for(j=0;j<IMAGE_COLOURS;++j) *ip++=j;
                UnlockResource(image[i]);
            }
        }
    }

    hmenu=GetSystemMenu(hwnd,FALSE);
    AppendMenu(hmenu,MF_SEPARATOR,0,NULL);
    AppendMenu(hmenu,MF_STRING,MAIN_ABOUT,(LPSTR)"&About...");

    SendMessage(hwnd,WM_SYSCOMMAND,SC_MAXIMIZE,0L);

    break;
  case WM_PAINT:
    hdc=BeginPaint(hwnd,&ps);

    if((pLogPal=(LOGPALETTE *)LocalAlloc(LMEM_FIXED,sizeof(LOGPALETTE)+
        256*sizeof(PALETTEENTRY))) != NULL) {
        pLogPal->palVersion=0x0300;
        pLogPal->palNumEntries=PALETTE_COLOURS;

        p=orthopalette;
        for(i=0;i<PALETTE_COLOURS;i++) {
            pLogPal->palPalEntry[i].peRed=*p++;
            pLogPal->palPalEntry[i].peGreen=*p++;
            pLogPal->palPalEntry[i].peBlue=*p++;
            pLogPal->palPalEntry[i].peFlags=0;
        }

        hPal=CreatePalette(pLogPal);
        LocalFree((HANDLE)pLogPal);

        SelectPalette(hdc,hPal,0);
        RealizePalette(hdc);
    }

    for(i=0;i<MAXIMAGE;++i) {
        x=(i%4)*(IMAGE_WIDE+MARGIN)+14;
        y=(i/4)*(IMAGE_DEEP+MARGIN)+MARGIN;
        DrawImage(hdc,x,y,image[i]);
    }
```

```
                EndPaint(hwnd,&ps);
                break;
        case WM_COMMAND:
            switch(wParam) {
                case MAIN_ABOUT:
                    if((lpfnDlgProc=MakeProcInstance((FARPROC)
                      AboutDlgProc,hInst)) != NULL) {
                        DialogBox(hInst,"AboutBox",hwnd,lpfnDlgProc);
                        FreeProcInstance(lpfnDlgProc);
                    }
                    break;

                case MAIN_EXIT:
                    FreeResource(hIcon);
                    for(i=0;i<MAXIMAGE;++i) {
                        if(image[i] != NULL) FreeResource(image[i]);
                    }

                    PostQuitMessage(0);
                    break;
            }
            break;

    }

    return(FALSE);
}

DWORD FAR PASCAL AboutDlgProc(HWND hwnd,WORD message,WORD wParam,LONG lParam)
{
    POINT point;

    switch(message) {
        case WM_INITDIALOG:
            return(TRUE);
        case WM_CTLCOLOR:
            if(HIWORD(lParam)==CTLCOLOR_STATIC ||
               HIWORD(lParam)==CTLCOLOR_DLG) {
                SetBkColor(wParam,RGB(192,192,192));
                SetTextColor(wParam,RGB(0,0,0));

                ClientToScreen(hwnd,&point);
                UnrealizeObject(GetStockObject(LTGRAY_BRUSH));
                SetBrushOrg(wParam,point.x,point.y);

                return((DWORD)GetStockObject(LTGRAY_BRUSH));
```

```
                }
            if(HIWORD(lParam)==CTLCOLOR_BTN) {
                SetBkColor(wParam,RGB(192,192,192));
                SetTextColor(wParam,RGB(0,0,0));

                ClientToScreen(hwnd,&point);
                UnrealizeObject(GetStockObject(BLACK_BRUSH));
                SetBrushOrg(wParam,point.x,point.y);

                return((DWORD)GetStockObject(BLACK_BRUSH));
            }
            break;
        case WM_COMMAND:
            switch(wParam) {
                case IDOK:
                    EndDialog(hwnd,wParam);
                    return(TRUE);
            }
            break;
    }

    return(FALSE);
}


void DrawImage(HDC hdc,int x,int y,HBITMAP image)
{
    LPSTR p,pi;
    HDC hMemoryDC;
    HBITMAP hBitmap,hOldBitmap;

    if(image==NULL) return;

    if((p=LockResource(image))==NULL) return;

    pi=p+sizeof(BITMAPINFOHEADER)+IMAGE_COLOURS*sizeof(RGBQUAD);

    if((hBitmap=CreateDIBitmap(hdc,(LPBITMAPINFOHEADER)p,CBM_INIT,pi,
        (LPBITMAPINFO)p,DIB_PAL_COLORS)) != NULL) {
        if((hMemoryDC=CreateCompatibleDC(hdc)) != NULL) {
            hOldBitmap=SelectObject(hMemoryDC,hBitmap);
            if(hOldBitmap) {
                BitBlt(hdc,x,y,IMAGE_WIDE,IMAGE_DEEP,hMemoryDC,0,0,SRCCOPY);
                SelectObject(hMemoryDC,hOldBitmap);
            }
            DeleteDC(hMemoryDC);
```

```
            }
            DeleteObject(hBitmap);
        }

        UnlockResource(image);
}
```

4-16 The resource script for the multiple bitmap viewer, MANYBMP.RC.

```
MainScreen DIALOG 17, 26, 192, 192
STYLE WS_POPUP ¦ WS_CAPTION ¦ WS_SYSMENU ¦ WS_THICKFRAME ¦
    WS_MINIMIZEBOX ¦ WS_MAXIMIZEBOX
CAPTION "Multiple Bitmap Demo"
BEGIN
END


AboutBox DIALOG 18, 18, 156, 104
STYLE WS_POPUP ¦ WS_CAPTION
CAPTION "About Multiple Bitmap Demo..."
BEGIN
    CONTROL "", 102, "BorShade", BSS_GROUP ¦ WS_CHILD ¦ WS_VISIBLE ¦ WS_TABSTOP,
        8, 8, 140, 68
    LTEXT "Multiple Bitmap Demo 1.0\nCopyright (c) 1993\nAlchemy Mindworks Inc.\n"
        "This program is part of the book Multimedia Programming for Windows by "
        "Steven William Rimmer, published by Windcrest (Book 4484).",
        -1, 12, 12, 128, 60, WS_CHILD ¦ WS_VISIBLE ¦ WS_GROUP
    DEFPUSHBUTTON "Ok", IDOK, 116, 80, 32, 20, WS_CHILD ¦ WS_VISIBLE ¦ WS_TABSTOP
END


IMAGE000 BITMAP IMAGE000.BMP

IMAGE001 BITMAP IMAGE001.BMP

IMAGE002 BITMAP IMAGE002.BMP

IMAGE003 BITMAP IMAGE003.BMP

IMAGE004 BITMAP IMAGE004.BMP

IMAGE005 BITMAP IMAGE005.BMP

IMAGE006 BITMAP IMAGE006.BMP

IMAGE007 BITMAP IMAGE007.BMP

IMAGE008 BITMAP IMAGE008.BMP
```

4-16 Continued.

IMAGE009 BITMAP IMAGE009.BMP

IMAGE010 BITMAP IMAGE010.BMP

IMAGE011 BITMAP IMAGE011.BMP

ManyBmp ICON LOADONCALL MOVEABLE DISCARDABLE
BEGIN
```
'00 00 01 00 02 00 20 20 02 00 00 00 00 00 30 01'
'00 00 26 00 00 00 20 20 10 00 00 00 00 00 E8 02'
'00 00 56 01 00 00 28 00 00 00 20 00 00 00 40 00'
'00 00 01 00 01 00 00 00 00 00 00 01 00 00 00 00'
'00 00 00 00 00 00 00 00 00 00 00 00 00 00 00 00'
'00 00 FF FF FF 00 FF FF FF FF E0 00 00 07 E0 00'
'00 03 80 00 00 61 BF FF FE F0 BF 55 5D F8 BA AA'
'AD F4 B5 55 56 EA BF FF FE 56 80 00 00 2D F0 00'
'00 DB EF FF F8 E5 E8 00 08 FE EA AA A8 FE E9 04'
'48 FE EA AA A8 BD E9 50 48 E3 EA AA A8 FF 80 04'
'48 FF EE EA A8 FF 00 05 48 FF EE E0 09 FF 66 6F'
'FB FF 22 20 07 FF 22 2F FF FF 22 2F FF FF 66 6F'
'FF FF EE EF FF FF 00 0F FF FF 55 5F FF FF 13 1F'
'FF FF BB BF FF FF FF FF FF FF E0 00 00 07 E0 00'
'00 03 80 00 00 01 80 00 00 00 80 00 00 00 80 00'
'00 00 80 00 00 00 80 00 00 00 80 00 00 01 F0 00'
'00 C3 E0 00 00 E5 E0 00 00 FE E0 00 00 FE E0 00'
'00 FE E0 00 00 BD E0 00 00 E3 E0 00 00 FF 80 00'
'00 FF 00 00 00 FF 00 00 00 FF 00 00 01 FF 00 00'
'03 FF 00 00 07 FF 00 0F FF FF 00 0F FF FF 00 0F'
'FF FF 00 0F FF FF 00 0F FF FF 11 1F FF FF 13 1F'
'FF FF BB BF FF FF 28 00 00 00 20 00 00 00 40 00'
'00 00 01 00 04 00 00 00 00 80 02 00 00 00 00'
'00 00 00 00 00 00 00 00 00 00 00 00 00 00 00 00'
'00 00 00 00 BF 00 00 BF 00 00 00 BF BF 00 BF 00'
'00 00 BF 00 BF 00 BF BF 00 00 C0 C0 C0 00 80 80'
'80 00 00 00 FF 00 00 FF 00 00 00 FF FF 00 FF 00'
'00 00 FF 00 FF 00 FF FF 00 00 FF FF FF 00 00 00'
'00 00 00 00 00 00 00 00 00 00 00 00 00 00 00 08'
'88 88 88 88 88 88 88 88 88 88 88 80 00 00 08'
'88 88 88 88 88 88 88 88 88 88 80 00 88 00 00 00'
'00 00 00 00 00 00 00 00 00 00 0F F0 08 80 00 77'
'77 77 77 77 77 77 77 77 77 70 FF FF 00 88 00 77'
'77 77 07 07 07 07 07 07 77 0F FF FF F0 08 00 77'
'70 70 70 70 70 70 70 70 77 0F FF FF 8F 00 00 77'
'07 07 07 07 07 07 07 07 07 70 FF F0 F8 F0 00 77'
'77 77 77 77 77 77 77 77 77 70 0F 0F 0F F0 00 00'
```

```
'00 00 00 00 00 00 00 00 00 00 80 F0 FF 00 00 00'
'00 00 00 00 00 00 00 00 08 88 00 0F F0 00 00 00'
'77 77 77 77 77 77 77 77 70 88 00 00 00 00 00 00'
'70 00 00 00 00 00 00 00 70 88 00 00 00 00 00 00'
'70 8E EE 84 44 82 22 80 70 88 00 00 00 00 00 00'
'70 8E EE 84 44 82 22 80 70 80 00 00 00 00 00 00'
'70 8E EE 84 44 82 22 80 70 88 00 00 00 00 00 00'
'70 88 88 88 88 88 88 80 70 88 00 00 00 00 00 00'
'70 8C CC 8A AA 8B BB 80 70 88 00 00 00 00 08 88'
'88 88 88 88 AA 8B BB 80 70 88 00 00 00 00 99 98'
'AA A8 CC C8 AA 8B BB 80 70 88 00 00 00 00 00 08'
'00 08 00 08 88 88 88 80 70 88 00 00 00 00 99 98'
'AA A8 CC C8 00 00 00 00 70 80 00 00 00 00 09 98'
'0A A8 0C C8 77 77 77 77 70 00 00 00 00 00 00 98'
'00 A8 00 C8 00 00 00 00 00 00 00 00 00 00 00 98'
'00 A8 00 C8 00 00 00 00 00 00 00 00 00 00 00 98'
'00 A8 00 C8 00 00 00 00 00 00 00 00 00 00 09 98'
'0A A8 0C C8 00 00 00 00 00 00 00 00 00 00 99 98'
'AA A8 CC C8 00 00 00 00 00 00 00 00 00 00 00 08'
'00 08 00 08 00 00 00 00 00 00 00 00 00 00 19 90'
'2A A0 4C C0 00 00 00 00 00 00 00 00 00 00 71 70'
'72 00 74 70 00 00 00 00 00 00 00 00 00 00 01 00'
'02 00 04 00 00 00 00 00 00 00 00 00 00 00 FF FF'
'FF FF E0 00 00 07 E0 00 00 03 80 00 00 01 80 00'
'00 00 80 00 00 00 80 00 00 00 80 00 00 00 80 00'
'00 00 80 00 00 01 F0 00 00 C3 E0 00 00 E5 E0 00'
'00 FE E0 00 00 FE E0 00 00 FE E0 00 00 BD E0 00'
'00 E3 E0 00 00 FF 80 00 00 FF 00 00 00 FF 00 00'
'00 FF 00 00 01 FF 00 00 03 FF 00 00 07 FF 00 0F'
'FF FF 00 0F FF FF 00 0F FF FF 00 0F FF FF 00 0F'
'FF FF 11 1F FF FF 13 1F FF FF BB BF FF FF'
END
```

As with the bitmap viewer in the previous section, you'll need a DEF file, as follows:

```
NAME          MANYBMP
DESCRIPTION   'Multiple Bitmap Demo'
EXETYPE       WINDOWS
CODE          PRELOAD MOVEABLE
DATA          PRELOAD MOVEABLE MULTIPLE
SEGMENTS      WM_TEXT LOADONCALL
HEAPSIZE      8192
STACKSIZE     8192
```

and a project file for MANYBMP, as shown in FIG. 4-17. If you're using something other than the Borland C++ for Windows integrated development environment, you should create an appropriate MAKE file rather than a project.

To keep the MANYBMP application simple, the 12 bitmapped images it displays have common dimensions as well as a common palette—they're all 192×192 pixels. I used the Crop function of Graphic Workshop to arrive at this. In a more elaborate application of this sort, you'd probably want to have the software determine the size of each graphic, as was done in the VIEWBMP program.

There are a number of fairly sneaky things happening in MANYBMP. The first one takes place in the WM_INITDIALOG case of SelectProc. The for loop loads the 12 graphics from the resource file of the application and stores handles to them in an array of HBITMAP objects. Note that this array is declared static, as it must stick around throughout the life of the application.

The FindResource and LoadResource functions will fetch a resource from the resource file of your application—essentially the resource area of its EXE file—and load the resource into memory. In theory, this is analogous to what VIEWBMP did when it allocated a buffer and loaded a BMP file into it. In fact, this comparison is a bit dangerous, as the resulting handle must be dealt with using resource functions rather than allocation

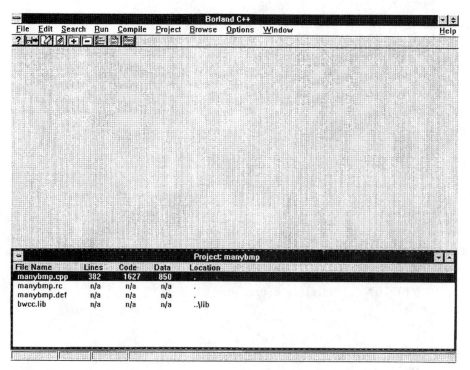

4-17 The project file for the multiple bitmap viewer, MANYBMP.PRJ.

functions. Specifically, you must lock and unlock it with LockResource and UnlockResource, rather than with GlobalLock and GlobalUnlock.

The palette of each of the bitmapped graphics is known, as they've all been remapped to the orthogonal palette of Graphic Workshop for Windows. That's the same palette as is found in the orthopalette object at the top of the MANYBMP.CPP listing. Since the color tables of the individual images aren't used, they can be overwritten with a list of 16-bit indices into the current palette, as is required by SetDIBitsToDevice if it's to use its DIB_PAL_COLORS mode, as was discussed earlier. You can see this being done in the for loop in the WM_INITDIALOG case.

The WM_INITDIALOG case also handles two other bits of house-keeping. Because the MANYBMP application doesn't have a menu bar—in turn, because there wasn't room for one if all the graphics were to fit in the window—its About item appears in its System menu. The code after the for loop illustrates how to append an item to the System menu.

Finally, the call to SendMessage will tell the window to maximize itself on startup, so all the images can be seen.

The other batch of sneaky elements in MANYBMP appears in the WM_PAINT case of SelectProc. This might look a bit like the code in VIEWBMP that handled realizing a palette. It is, in a sense, except that it realizes one palette and then displays 12 images with it. The DrawImage function illustrates how to use SetDIBitsToDevice in this way.

Some Windows animation: Murphy hears a cheese wrapper

Labrador retrievers are an interesting study in evolutionary dynamics. Too brain dead to actually survive by animal cunning were they left to their own devices, they've been bred through successive generations to look endearing as puppies so they can find comfortable homes before anyone realizes what they've gotten themselves into.

A typical Labrador retriever will grow to anywhere from 100 to 150 pounds if you feed it enough—which you will do, if you value your furniture. Their breed notwithstanding, Labrador retrievers don't like to retrieve things. They live to eat.

Murphy, upon whom the program in this section is based, tips the scale at the heavy end of the spectrum for Labrador retrievers. Aside from the two-ounce organ in his head that he uses to think with, all of this is muscle and stomach. The only way to keep Murphy in one place is to wind a large bolt into the ground and have someone in China wind a nut on the other end of it. He can snap anything up to four-inch bridge cable if he thinks he hears the distant sound of a can opener, the top of a beer can being removed, or the rustle of a cheese wrapper.

Figure 4-18 illustrates the screen of a Windows application that simulates the effect of a cheese wrapper on Murphy. This is a program called

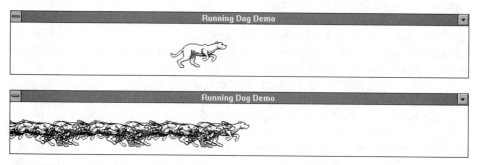

4-18 The running dog application.

RUNDOG, an animated view of a Labrador retriever in a window. If you run the RUNDOG.EXE program from the \APPS directory of the companion CD-ROM for this book, you can see it in action. The upper window in FIG. 4-18 shows RUNDOG as it really looks. The lower one has been cooked a bit, and illustrates all the cells involved in making this rather smaller and less voracious Labrador retriever lunge across your monitor.

The RUNDOG program is a fairly simple example of animation under Windows. There's very little in it that's genuinely new, and with the graphic facilities discussed earlier in this chapter you can manage animation like this without a lot of additional code. Computer animation with bitmapped images works just like traditional Disney animation with acetate cells. The illusion of motion can be created by displaying successive frames rapidly enough that the individual graphics aren't perceptible as such. In this case, the cells are updated at a rate of one cell every 90 milliseconds, or about eleven frames a second. This isn't quite up to Fantasia, but it's about as good as things get on a computer monitor.

Figure 4-19 illustrates the C language source code for RUNDOG. Commensurate with a program having virtually no practical uses, it's very short. In addition to RUNDOG.CPP, you'll need the resource script for RUNDOG. It's even simpler than the C language part of the program, as shown in FIG. 4-20.

4-19 The C language source listing for the running dog application, RUNDOG.CPP.

```
/*

    Running Dog Demo
    Copyright (c) 1993 Alchemy Mindworks Inc.

    This is a simple animation of Murphy the 150-pound Labrador retriever
    running across the room. Murphy can hear a cheese wrapper at a thousand
    yards. Mind, he hasn't entirely mastered stopping on a tile floor as yet...

*/
```

```c
#include <windows.h>
#include <stdio.h>

#define say(s)      MessageBox(NULL,s,"Yo...",MB_OK | MB_ICONSTOP);
#define saynumber(f,s)    {char b[128]; sprintf((LPSTR)b,(LPSTR)f,s); \
                MessageBox(NULL,b,"Debug Message",MB_OK | MB_ICONSTOP); }


#define ItemName(item,string)    { dlgH=GetDlgItem(hwnd,item); \
                                SetWindowText(dlgH,(LPSTR)string); }
#define ItemOn(item)     { dlgH=GetDlgItem(hwnd,item); EnableWindow(dlgH,TRUE); }
#define ItemOff(item)     { dlgH=GetDlgItem(hwnd,item); EnableWindow(dlgH,FALSE); }


#define STRINGSIZE              129         /* how big is a string? */


#define MAIN_ABOUT              105
#define MAIN_EXIT               107


#define MAXIMAGE                6


#define FOOTSTEP                10
#define DOGSIZE                 65
#define DOGSTART                -100


#define IMAGE_COLOURS           2


#ifndef max
#define max(a,b)        (((a)>(b))?(a):(b))
#endif
#ifndef min
#define min(a,b)        (((a)<(b))?(a):(b))
#endif

/* prototypes */
DWORD FAR PASCAL SelectProc(HWND hwnd,WORD message,WORD wParam,LONG lParam);
DWORD FAR PASCAL AboutDlgProc(HWND hwnd,WORD message,WORD wParam,LONG lParam);
void DrawImage(HDC hdc,int x,int y,HBITMAP image);

/* globals */
char szAppName[]="RunDog";

HANDLE hInst;

#pragma warn -par
int PASCAL WinMain(HANDLE hInstance,HANDLE hPrevInstance,
                LPSTR lpszCmdParam,int nCmdShow)
```

```
{
    FARPROC dlgProc;
    unsigned short r;

    hInst=hInstance;

    dlgProc=MakeProcInstance((FARPROC)SelectProc,hInst);
    r=DialogBox(hInst,"MainScreen",NULL,dlgProc);

    FreeProcInstance(dlgProc);

    return(r);
}

DWORD FAR PASCAL SelectProc(HWND hwnd,WORD message,WORD wParam,LONG lParam)
{
    RECT rect;
    static HBITMAP image[MAXIMAGE];
    PAINTSTRUCT ps;
    HMENU hmenu;
    static HICON hIcon;
    FARPROC lpfnDlgProc;
    HDC hdc;
    char b[STRINGSIZE+1];
    static int thiscell;
    static int cellpos;
    int i,y;

    switch(message) {
        case WM_SYSCOMMAND:
            switch(wParam & 0xfff0) {
                case SC_CLOSE:
                    SendMessage(hwnd,WM_COMMAND,MAIN_EXIT,0L);
                    break;
            }
            switch(wParam) {
                case MAIN_ABOUT:
                    SendMessage(hwnd,WM_COMMAND,MAIN_ABOUT,0L);
                    break;
            }
            break;
        case WM_INITDIALOG:
            hIcon=LoadIcon(hInst,szAppName);
            SetClassWord(hwnd,GCW_HICON,(WORD)hIcon);
```

```
for(i=0;i<MAXIMAGE;++i) {
    wsprintf(b,"IMAGE%03.3u",i);
    image[i]=LoadResource(hInst,FindResource(hInst,b,RT_BITMAP));
}

hmenu=GetSystemMenu(hwnd,FALSE);
AppendMenu(hmenu,MF_SEPARATOR,0,NULL);
AppendMenu(hmenu,MF_STRING,MAIN_ABOUT,(LPSTR)"&About...");

thiscell=0;
cellpos=DOGSTART;

SetTimer(hwnd,1,90,NULL);

y=GetSystemMetrics(SM_CXSCREEN);
GetWindowRect(hwnd,&rect);

SetWindowPos(hwnd,NULL,4,rect.top,y-8,
    rect.bottom-rect.top,SWP_NOZORDER);


    break;
case WM_TIMER:
    InvalidateRect(hwnd,NULL,FALSE);
    break;
case WM_PAINT:
    hdc=BeginPaint(hwnd,&ps);
    GetClientRect(hwnd,&rect);
    DrawImage(hdc,cellpos,10,image[thiscell]);

    ++thiscell;
    if(thiscell >= MAXIMAGE) {
        thiscell=0;
        cellpos+=DOGSIZE;
    }

    cellpos+=FOOTSTEP;
    if(cellpos >= (rect.right-rect.left)) cellpos=DOGSTART;

    EndPaint(hwnd,&ps);
    break;
case WM_COMMAND:
    switch(wParam) {
        case MAIN_ABOUT:
            if((lpfnDlgProc=MakeProcInstance((FARPROC)
                AboutDlgProc,hInst)) != NULL) {
```

Some Windows animation: Murphy hears a cheese wrapper   **233**

```
                        DialogBox(hInst,"AboutBox",hwnd,lpfnDlgProc);
                        FreeProcInstance(lpfnDlgProc);
                    }
                    break;

                case MAIN_EXIT:
                    KillTimer(hwnd,1);
                    FreeResource(hIcon);
                    for(i=0;i<MAXIMAGE;++i) {
                        if(image[i] != NULL) FreeResource(image[i]);
                    }

                    PostQuitMessage(0);
                    break;
            }
            break;

    }

    return(FALSE);
}

DWORD FAR PASCAL AboutDlgProc(HWND hwnd,WORD message,WORD wParam,LONG lParam)
{
    POINT point;

    switch(message) {
        case WM_INITDIALOG:
            return(TRUE);
        case WM_CTLCOLOR:
            if(HIWORD(lParam)==CTLCOLOR_STATIC ||
               HIWORD(lParam)==CTLCOLOR_DLG) {
                SetBkColor(wParam,RGB(192,192,192));
                SetTextColor(wParam,RGB(0,0,0));

                ClientToScreen(hwnd,&point);
                UnrealizeObject(GetStockObject(LTGRAY_BRUSH));
                SetBrushOrg(wParam,point.x,point.y);

                return((DWORD)GetStockObject(LTGRAY_BRUSH));

            }
            if(HIWORD(lParam)==CTLCOLOR_BTN) {
                SetBkColor(wParam,RGB(192,192,192));
                SetTextColor(wParam,RGB(0,0,0));
```

```
                ClientToScreen(hwnd,&point);
                UnrealizeObject(GetStockObject(BLACK_BRUSH));
                SetBrushOrg(wParam,point.x,point.y);

                return((DWORD)GetStockObject(BLACK_BRUSH));
            }
            break;
        case WM_COMMAND:
            switch(wParam) {
                case IDOK:
                    EndDialog(hwnd,wParam);
                    return(TRUE);
            }
            break;
    }

    return(FALSE);
}

void DrawImage(HDC hdc,int x,int y,HBITMAP image)
{
    LPSTR p,pi;
    HDC hMemoryDC;
    BITMAP bitmap;
    HBITMAP hBitmap,hOldBitmap;

    if(image==NULL) return;

    if((p=LockResource(image))==NULL) return;

    pi=p+sizeof(BITMAPINFOHEADER)+IMAGE_COLOURS*sizeof(RGBQUAD);

    GetObject(image,sizeof(BITMAP),(LPSTR)&bitmap);

    if((hBitmap=CreateDIBitmap(hdc,(LPBITMAPINFOHEADER)p,CBM_INIT,pi,
        (LPBITMAPINFO)p,DIB_RGB_COLORS)) != NULL) {
        if((hMemoryDC=CreateCompatibleDC(hdc)) != NULL) {
            hOldBitmap=SelectObject(hMemoryDC,hBitmap);
            if(hOldBitmap) {
                BitBlt(hdc,
                    x,
                    y,
                    bitmap.bmWidth,
                    bitmap.bmHeight,
                    hMemoryDC,
                    0,
```

4-19 Continued.

```
                    0,
                    SRCCOPY);
                SelectObject(hMemoryDC,hOldBitmap);
            }
            DeleteDC(hMemoryDC);
        }
        DeleteObject(hBitmap);
    }

    UnlockResource(image);
}
```

4-20 The resource script for the running dog application, RUNDOG.RC.

```
MainScreen DIALOG 7, 138, 355, 43
STYLE WS_POPUP | WS_CAPTION | WS_SYSMENU | WS_MINIMIZEBOX
CAPTION "Running Dog Demo"
BEGIN
END


AboutBox DIALOG 18, 18, 156, 104
STYLE WS_POPUP | WS_CAPTION
CAPTION "About Running Dog Demo..."
BEGIN
  CONTROL "", 102, "BorShade", BSS_GROUP | WS_CHILD | WS_VISIBLE | WS_TABSTOP,
      8, 8, 140, 68
  LTEXT "Running Dog Demo 1.0\nCopyright (c) 1993\nAlchemy Mindworks Inc.\n"
    "This program is part of the book Multimedia Programming for Windows by "
    "Steven William Rimmer, published by Windcrest (Book 4484).",
    -1, 12, 12, 128, 60, WS_CHILD | WS_VISIBLE | WS_GROUP
  DEFPUSHBUTTON "Ok", IDOK, 116, 80, 32, 20, WS_CHILD | WS_VISIBLE | WS_TABSTOP
END


IMAGE000 BITMAP CELL000.BMP


IMAGE001 BITMAP CELL001.BMP


IMAGE002 BITMAP CELL002.BMP


IMAGE003 BITMAP CELL003.BMP


IMAGE004 BITMAP CELL004.BMP


IMAGE005 BITMAP CELL005.BMP
```

```
RunDog ICON
BEGIN
        '00 00 01 00 02 00 20 20 02 00 00 00 00 00 30 01'
        '00 00 26 00 00 00 20 20 10 00 00 00 00 00 E8 02'
        '00 00 56 01 00 00 28 00 00 00 20 00 00 00 40 00'
        '00 00 01 00 01 00 00 00 00 00 00 01 00 00 00 00'
        '00 00 00 00 00 00 00 00 00 00 00 00 00 00 00 00'
        '00 00 FF FF FF 00 FF FF FF FF E0 00 00 07 E0 00'
        '00 03 80 00 00 61 BF FF FE F0 BF 55 5D F8 BA AA'
        'AD F4 B5 55 56 EA BF FF FE 56 80 00 00 2D F0 00'
        '00 DB EF FF F8 E5 E8 00 08 FE EA AA A8 FE E9 04'
        '48 FE EA AA A8 BD E9 50 48 E3 EA AA A8 FF 80 04'
        '48 FF EE EA A8 FF 00 05 48 FF EE E0 09 FF 66 6F'
        'FB FF 22 20 07 FF 22 2F FF FF 22 2F FF FF 66 6F'
        'FF FF EE EF FF FF 00 0F FF FF 55 5F FF FF 13 1F'
        'FF FF BB BF FF FF FF FF FF FF E0 00 00 07 E0 00'
        '00 03 80 00 00 01 80 00 00 00 80 00 00 00 80 00'
        '00 00 80 00 00 00 80 00 00 00 80 00 00 01 F0 00'
        '00 C3 E0 00 00 E5 E0 00 00 FE E0 00 00 FE E0 00'
        '00 FE E0 00 00 BD E0 00 00 E3 E0 00 00 FF 80 00'
        '00 FF 00 00 00 FF 00 00 00 FF 00 00 01 FF 00 00'
        '03 FF 00 00 07 FF 00 0F FF FF 00 0F FF FF 00 0F'
        'FF FF 00 0F FF FF 00 0F FF FF 11 1F FF FF 13 1F'
        'FF FF BB BF FF FF 28 00 00 00 20 00 00 00 40 00'
        '00 00 01 00 04 00 00 00 00 00 80 02 00 00 00 00'
        '00 00 00 00 00 00 00 00 00 00 00 00 00 00 00 00'
        '00 00 00 00 BF 00 00 BF 00 00 00 BF BF 00 BF 00'
        '00 00 BF 00 BF 00 BF BF 00 00 C0 C0 C0 00 80 80'
        '80 00 00 00 FF 00 00 FF 00 00 00 FF FF 00 FF 00'
        '00 00 FF 00 FF 00 FF FF 00 00 FF FF FF 00 00 00'
        '00 00 00 00 00 00 00 00 00 00 00 00 00 00 00 00'
        '00 00 00 00 00 00 00 00 00 00 00 00 00 00 00 00'
        '00 00 00 00 00 00 00 00 00 00 00 00 00 00 00 00'
        '00 00 00 00 00 00 00 00 00 00 00 00 00 00 00 00'
        '00 00 00 00 00 00 00 00 00 00 00 00 00 00 00 00'
        '00 00 00 00 00 00 00 00 00 00 00 00 00 00 00 00'
        '00 00 00 00 00 00 00 00 00 00 00 00 00 00 00 00'
        '00 00 00 00 00 00 00 00 00 00 00 00 00 00 00 00'
        '00 00 00 00 00 00 00 00 00 00 00 00 00 00 00 00'
        '00 00 00 00 00 00 00 00 00 00 00 00 00 00 00 00'
        '00 00 00 00 00 00 00 00 00 00 00 00 00 00 00 00'
        '00 00 00 00 00 00 00 00 00 00 00 00 00 00 F0 00'
        '00 00 00 00 00 00 00 00 00 00 00 00 00 00 F0 FF'
        '00 00 00 00 00 00 00 00 00 00 00 00 00 00 FF 0F'
        'FF 00 00 00 00 00 00 00 00 00 00 00 00 00 F0 FF'
        'FF FF FF 00 00 00 00 00 00 00 00 00 00 00 FF 0F'
```

```
'FF 0F FF 0F 0F 0F FF FF 00 00 00 00 00 00 FF FF'
'FF FF F0 F0 F0 FF FF FF FF 00 00 00 00 00 FF FF'
'FF FF F0 FF FF FF FF FF FF F0 00 00 00 00 FF FF'
'FF FF 0F FF FF FF FF FF FF F0 00 00 00 00 FF FF'
'FF FF FF FF FF FF FF FF FF 00 00 00 00 00 FF FF'
'FF FF 0F FF FF F0 0F FF 00 00 00 00 00 00 FF FF'
'FF F0 00 00 0F F0 0F 00 00 00 00 00 00 00 00 0F'
'FF 00 FF 00 FF FF FF 00 00 00 00 00 00 00 00 00'
'F0 0F F0 0F FF FF F0 00 00 00 00 00 00 00 00 00'
'00 00 00 F0 FF F0 00 00 00 00 00 00 00 00 00 00'
'00 FF FF F0 00 00 00 00 00 00 00 00 00 00 00 00'
'00 00 00 00 00 00 00 00 00 00 00 00 00 00 00 00'
'00 00 00 00 00 00 00 00 00 00 00 00 00 00 00 00'
'00 00 00 00 00 00 00 00 00 00 00 00 00 00 00 00'
'00 00 00 00 00 00 00 00 00 00 00 00 00 00 00 00'
'00 00 00 00 00 00 00 00 00 00 00 00 00 00 FF FF'
'FF FF FF FF FF FF FF FF FF FF FF FF FF FF FF FF'
'FF FF FF FF FF FF FF FF FF FF FF FF FF FF FF FF'
'FF FF FF FF FF FF FF FF FF FF 3F FF FF FF 0F FF'
'FF FF 03 FF FF FF 00 3F FF FF 00 00 0F FF 00 00'
'03 FF 00 00 01 FF 00 00 00 FF 00 00 00 FF 00 00'
'00 FF 00 00 01 FF 00 00 0F FF 00 00 1F FF E0 00'
'3F FF F0 00 7F FF F8 01 FF FF FC 1F FF FF FF FF'
'FF FF FF FF FF FF FF FF FF FF FF FF FF FF'
END
```

You'll also need a DEF file and a project file for RUNDOG; the project file is shown in FIG. 4-21, and the DEF file is as follows:

```
NAME            RUNDOG
DESCRIPTION     'Running Dog Demo'
EXETYPE         WINDOWS
CODE            PRELOAD MOVEABLE
DATA            PRELOAD MOVEABLE MULTIPLE
SEGMENTS        WM_TEXT LOADONCALL
HEAPSIZE        8192
STACKSIZE       8192
```

If you're using something other than the Borland C++ for Windows integrated development environment, you should create an appropriate MAKE file rather than a project. The RUNDOG application doesn't use any Borland custom controls—you need not include BWCC.LIB in your project.

As with the MANYBMP application in the previous section, the RUNDOG program loads its images from its resource file. There are six cells in the running dog, and to keep the code simple, they have constant dimen-

```
 ═                        Borland C++                          ▼ ▲
 File  Edit  Search  Run  Compile  Project  Browse  Options  Window                    Help
 ? ┃→ ▨ ▨ ┿ ┿ ┿ ┋ ┋ ┋




 ═                        Project: rundog                       ▼ ▲
 File Name      Lines    Code    Data    Location
 rundog.cpp      244     1245     69      .
 rundog.def      n/a     n/a     n/a      .
 rundog.rc       n/a     n/a     n/a      .
 bwcc.lib        n/a     n/a     n/a      ..\lib
```

4-21 The project file for the running dog application, RUNDOG.PRJ.

sions. They're black and white, and as such won't encounter any palette problems.

One of the important tenets of computer animation is that small things can be animated a lot more readily than big things. Likewise, images with fewer colors are less likely to prove troublesome. The RUNDOG application works by having a Windows timer send a WM_TIMER message to the SelectProc message handler for its main window once every 90 milliseconds. When a WM_TIMER message is received, the window is updated with the next cell in the sequence. Clearly, all the updating must take place in less than 90 milliseconds—that is, before the next WM_TIMER message appears—or unspeakable things will happen.

The timer is initiated in the WM_INITDIALOG case, which is also responsible for loading the image cells. It adjusts the width of the application window so it will fit on your screen.

The WM_PAINT case of SelectProc handles updating the cells, calling DrawImage. The DrawImage function uses BitBlt, rather than SetDIBitsToDevice, as the former is a bit quicker and the animation cells are pretty small graphics.

A program that supports animation is typically confronted with the problem of divots—that is, with replacing the area behind a cell before a new cell can be drawn. The RUNDOG application deals with this in a very simple way—it ignores it. Because the background of each cell is white and the background of the window is also white, it's easy to make the cells wide enough so each one overwrites the previous one, even allowing for the displacement between successive cells.

If you must have a complex background in your application window, such that this approach won't work, you'll have to copy the area where each cell will be drawn to a temporary bitmap, draw the cell, and then replace the area behind it when it comes time to erase it. Aside from being more complex to initiate, this approach requires a lot more time to handle, further restricting the size of the objects you can safely animate.

Bigger graphics

This chapter deals with the most elemental issues of bitmapped graphics in Windows applications. While there are all sorts of other graphic facilities offered by Windows that you might want to explore, most of what's likely to turn up in a multimedia application is discussed here.

There are all sorts of specialized applications for bitmapped graphics under Windows. The next chapter deals with one of the more leading-edge ones, the Kodak Photo-CD standard. However, despite its being very trendy and sophisticated, you'll find a lot of the code from this chapter turning up there. There are a finite number of ways to handle a bitmap, and even Photo-CD images are ultimately just bitmaps.

5
Viewing Kodak Photo-CD images

"An idea isn't responsible for the people who believe in it."

Photography is a technology even older than that of recorded sound. It combines optics from the latter Middle Ages, some chemistry from the eighteenth century, and a lot of marketing around the turn of the century. The "black arts" of photographic materials have been one of the richest areas for tinkering of the last hundred years.

Much of our notion of image resolution—the amount of detail graphics should be able to reproduce—is based indirectly on the quality of photographic images. In a real sense, a photograph is a matrix of pixels just like a bitmapped graphic file is, although the pixels are smaller and the matrix is somewhat less regular. In the case of a photograph, the matrix is of silver salt crystals, rather than phosphor dots.

Unfortunately, digitizing a photograph at anything approaching the resolution of its internal matrix of dots would require several gigabytes of memory. The result would an unworkably large file, usable by virtually no contemporary software and certainly not reproducible on any PC hardcopy devices on the planet.

In most practical applications of commercial photography, the final medium isn't actually a photograph at all. While images typically start out as chemical photographs, they wind up being commercially printed or displayed on television set, for example. These are media with vastly less resolution than that of a 35-millimeter slide.

When you scan a photograph into an image file, most of the detail of the image is lost in the scanner. However, because computer monitors and printers are effectively very low-resolution devices in comparison to a photograph, the detail that remains is sufficient to reproduce the image to the limits of your hardware. Photographers will see this as a criminal waste of the reproduction quality of the photographic medium. Graphic artists who work with computers might well rebut this by noting that there's far more detail in a photograph than is really required, inasmuch as you can scan one, display it on a monitor, and have the display look indistinguishable from the original photograph.

The problem with this argument is that photographers have been at it longer—leathery old curmudgeons with cameras battering together about their necks are not the sort of characters to get into a war of words with.

It's probably worth noting that there are a number of digital cameras, such as the Canon Xapshot and the Dycam, also sold as the Logitech Photoman. These are interesting devices, in that they digitize images in the camera, leaving you with an image file, rather than a photograph. The drawback to them is that at present they still have fairly limited resolutions. Figure 5-1 illustrates a photograph taken with a conventional camera—and subsequently digitized through a Kodak Photo-CD—and the same image photographed through a Dycam digital camera.

There are a lot of applications for these electronic cameras in situations where high-resolution photography isn't really needed. They're used, for example, to create the photographs of houses in real estate agents' multiple listing books. You might not want to have your wedding pictures done this way, however.

I should note that the photographs included in the \PHOTO_CD\ IMAGES directory of the companion CD-ROM for this book were all created using a Canon EOS 35 millimeter camera—one of those cranky mechanical things that requires film. In fact, I hauled the camera over three thousand miles to the hills of Wales for some of them. I mention this because it points up another limitation of digital cameras. It was relatively easy to take the EOS and numerous rolls of film up among the slate and the sheep. A Dycam digital camera, on the other hand, has a finite capacity for images, after which they must be downloaded to a PC. Had I knocked on the door of the nearest farmhouse and asked to use their computer to download my camera, I would no doubt have received some fairly odd looks.

Old-style photography, with all its chemical reactions and environmentally unfriendly substances, still has its place. That's what this chapter is about, to a large extent. It will deal with a technology to make the interface between cameras and computers a bit more useful than it has been in the past. This interface is the Kodak Photo-CD standard.

5-1 The now somewhat rare Pontiac Fiero SE 2M6, as seen through a photo-CD (top) and a Dycam digital camera (bottom).

Understanding Photo-CDs

It's very often intriguing to regard a new bit of technology and wonder what was in the mind of the person who first conceived it. This applies to things other than computers, of course. The car back in FIG. 5-1, a Pontiac Fiero, has often struck me as a vehicle that no one but me could love. It has only two seats, requires considerable athletic prowess to get into and out of, and offers a trunk so small as to be more of a file drawer on wheels. Most of them, FIG. 5-1 excepted, came with diminutive four-cylinder engines. Somebody must have thought it had a future, however.

It didn't, of course—Fieros were made for only about four years. Hopefully, Photo-CDs will stick around for somewhat longer. I suspect that, like the Fiero, Photo-CDs will turn out to have applications rather different from those their designers intended. However, they're truly superb for the things this chapter will get into.

A Photo-CD is, in its simplest sense, a custom-made CD-ROM with digitized pictures on it. It allows anyone with a camera to have their photographs made into machine-readable files. In fact, there's a lot more to Photo-CD imaging than this.

The ostensible purpose for Photo-CDs is a bit peculiar, and perhaps more than a little over-optimistic. Kodak offers a dedicated CD-ROM reader to handle them, which drives a conventional broadcast television set. If you've caught one of the commercials for these things, the idea is to have your family photographs potted on a Photo-CD and then take turns sitting around the tube giggling and playing with the remote control. However, Photo-CD players aren't cheap, Photo-CD images don't display particularly quickly, and somehow the whole concept of seeing photographs this way lacks the warmth and amusement value of traditional paper pictures.

In addition, Photo-CDs can't be erased. If you store something embarrassing on one, it's there for good.

The truly superb application for Photo-CD images is in putting a Photo-CD is a conventional CD-ROM drive and reading the files with a personal computer. The disk structure of a Photo-CD looks like any other DOS volume, and the image files themselves, while rather exotic, can be dealt with much as the dedicated PC image file formats discussed in the previous chapter were. All it takes is the right CD-ROM drive and the Kodak Photo-CD software development toolkit. It's shown in FIG. 5-2.

The quality of a picture scanned as a Photo-CD image is typically far better than anything that can be arrived at with a conventional flatbed scanner.

The Kodak Photo-CD software development toolkit allows you to treat Photo-CDs as dark, mysterious objects with ineffable qualities about them and never learn their deeper secrets. With the Kodak library on hand, you can request an image, have it provided to your application in a useful format, and not bother yourself with how it got there. The extensive data manipulation that typically accompanies dealing with any proprietary data format—and image file formats in particular—never turns up in working with Photo-CDs. It's a good thing, too, as the internal format of a Photo-CD image file is truly weird. I'll touch on it later in this chapter, but for practical purposes you'll never have to get involved with it.

The modular nature of the Kodak Photo-CD libraries also means that, as the Photo-CD format evolves and matures, applications that support it will have little difficulty in keeping up. Just update the libraries, recompile your application if need be, and get back to trying to figure out how to load the film in your camera. In fact, since most of the smarts of the Photo-CD software are contained in a Windows dynamic link library, a DLL file, you can usually keep up with changes and bug fixes by just copying the latest

KODAK

Photo CD Access

Developer   Toolkit

5-2   The Kodak Photo-CD software development toolkit.

DLL file into your \WINDOWS\SYSTEM directory. I'll get into this in more detail in a moment too.

There *is* a catch to all this, and it's a moderately substantial one. As of this writing, Kodak offers its Photo-CD software development toolkit package for Windows and Macintosh platforms. As this sort of thing goes, the software in the Windows implementation is superb, and creating applications with it will prove to be pretty simple. However, all this seamless integration is not without its price. The price, as of this writing, is $768.00. This might seem like rather a lot for a floppy disk, a CD-ROM, and a small, spiral-bound manual. Well it is. However, it's also the only way to integrate Photo-CD images into your own software and, as a medium for high-quality scanned photographs, Photo-CDs are without equal.

It's also worth noting that, as is often the case, Kodak's documentation for the Photo-CD software development toolkit was written by people who understand the whole circus, very possibly under the assumption that everyone who reads it will too. It has a nice description of what a Photo-YCC-format image is, for example—something you'll never need to know—but if you crack the book with the intent of just putting together a Photo-CD image reader for your application and then climbing into a Fiero and driving off, your car will probably get pretty dusty in the interval. Save for one inscrutable—and rather badly formatted—C language program, the toolkit comes with no meaningful example code.

This is why this chapter runs for quite a few pages, rather than simply beginning with the title and a quote, followed by a sentence that says "Read the Kodak manual and have a nice day."

Figure 5-3 illustrates the Graphic Workshop for Windows package, displaying a directory of Photo-CD image thumbnails, small preview versions of the pictures in Photo-CD image files. You'll find Graphic Workshop for Windows on the companion CD-ROM for this book, in the directory \GWSWIN. You'll also find some Photo-CD images to try it out on in the \PHOTO_CD\IMAGES directory. As I'll get to, this is where they'd be on a real Photo-CD. The thumbnails in FIG. 5-3 are actually from the example Photo-CD that comes with the Kodak software development toolkit.

As a final preliminary note about the Photo-CD software development toolkit, this chapter will provide you with a painless way to get into using it. While for most applications it will tell you everything you need to know about its functions, it's by no means exhaustive. There are all sorts of calls and nuances I won't even mention, as doing so could easily double the size of this book and make its discussion of Photo-CDs truly impenetrable. If you want to do something really unusual with the Photo-CD library, you'll probably have to resort to its manual.

Photo-CD contents

Despite their being a bit exotic, Photo-CDs are pretty easy to have made. Any photofinisher who will send your pictures off to Kodak for processing can also arrange to have a Photo-CD created. I discovered that the drug store in the next village over could arrange to get one done, although they'd never been asked to do so.

Typically, you'd show up with negatives of the images you wanted ensconced on a disc, much as you would to get photographic reprints made. There's a cost for the disc itself, about $15, and then a cost of about $1.50 for each image you want to have added to it.

Photo-CDs look and work like conventional CD-ROMs, but they're structured differently. Rather than having their data stored as pits in an aluminum surface, they use a layer of dye. The dye modulates a laser just like pitted aluminum does, and a CD-ROM reader won't be able to tell the difference between a CD-ROM and a Photo-CD. However, because Photo-CDs are based on a chemical process rather than a mechanical one, you can write to a Photo-CD in multiple sessions.

A Photo-CD is a write-once device, in that once an image is stored on one it can't be erased or modified. However, you can have a batch of pictures written to a Photo-CD today and then have another batch added to it next week, repeating the process as often as you like until the disc is full. A Photo-CD can hold about 100 images.

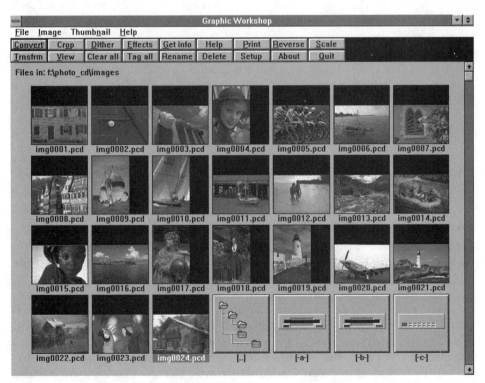

5-3 Graphic Workshop for Windows displaying the thumbnails for a Photo-CD.

As of this writing, the hardware that creates Photo-CD images, what the technical people like to call an *authoring station*, is available to handle only 35-millimeter film. Authoring stations for larger negative formats are expected shortly.

The multisession nature of Photo-CDs requires that you consider what kind of CD-ROM drive you'll be using to read them. As described in chapter 3, early first-generation CD-ROM drives won't read Photo-CDs at all. Somewhat newer drives can read only the first session of a Photo-CD with multiple sessions written to it. You'll need a fairly state-of-the-art drive to read Photo-CDs correctly.

All Photo-CDs have the same directory structure, as illustrated in FIG. 5-4. All the files you'll need to read Photo-CD images have the extension PCD. You'll find a file called OVERVIEW.PCD in the \PHOTO__CD directory. This file provides access to the thumbnails and statistics of the Photo-CD images on the disc. The images themselves live in the directory \PHOTO__CD\IMAGES. They're stored in files named IMG0001.PCD, IMG0002.PCD, IMG0003.PCD, and so on, for as many images as are on the disk. If a Photo-CD contains multiple sessions, the latter images will be appended to this sequence, and the fact that they were added after the disc was made won't be apparent to a Photo-CD reader.

A typical PCD image file will occupy between 3 and 5 megabytes. Each file contains multiple versions of the same image, scanned at different resolutions. This is called *pyramid encoding*—imagine a stack of images, with the large ones at the bottom and the smaller ones at the top. For a normal PCD file made from a 35-millimeter original, there will be five available images, as follows:

Image	Resolution
PCD__BASE__OVER__16	128×192 pixels
PCD__BASE__OVER__4	256×384 pixels
PCD__BASE	512×768 pixels
PCD__4BASE	1024×1536 pixels
PCD__16BASE	2048×3072 pixels

The constants used to name the various image resolutions in a PCD file are defined by the Photo-CD software development toolkit. They'll turn up later when we look at how to actually tell the Photo-CD library to provide you with an image from a Photo-CD disc.

It's worth noting that these dimensions apply no matter how an image is oriented. They presuppose landscape-oriented originals. If you attempt to have an image scanned from a negative in portrait orientation, it will be inset into a landscape-orientation frame. As a result, the useful area of such a picture would effectively be scanned at a lower resolution than would have been the case if it had been a landscape-oriented picture.

The image data in a Photo-CD is stored in a format similar to the color format of a C-41 photographic negative, referred to as PhotoYCC. Each pixel is encoded with one byte of brightness information and two color vectors. If the RGB color model discussed in the previous chapter made sense to you, you might find yourself grappling with the Photo-YCC model. It's derived from inorganic chemistry, rather than data. The best thing you can say about it is that you'll never have to deal with it to write software that reads Photo-CD images, as the Photo-CD library can be instructed to translate images to RGB files as it hands them to you.

For practical purposes, then, each PCD file can be said to contain five true-color images at the resolutions listed earlier. If you have a calculator handy, you can observe one of the immediate problems this poses for a Windows application that seeks to read Photo-CD images. A true-color pixel requires three bytes. The highest-resolution image available in a PCD file, 2048×3072 pixels, would contain 6,291,456 pixels or 18,874,368 bytes. Windows can address only a maximum of 16 megabytes of memory and, with Windows itself and your application loaded, you'll have somewhat less than this on hand. A Windows application that reads Photo-CD images by reading the whole image into memory would be unable to do so for the PCD__16BASE resolution.

If you require access to PCD__16BASE images, you can handle them in sections, something else I'll deal with later in this chapter. The various parties concerned with trying to sell new operating systems at Microsoft and IBM will occasionally cite this sort of thing as justification for Windows NT and OS/2 respectively, as both overcome the 16Mb

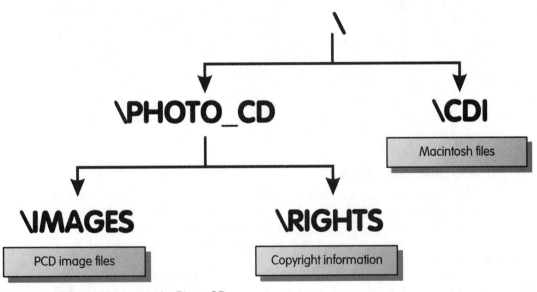

5-4 The directory structure of a Photo-CD.

memory barrier of conventional Windows. It's a fair bet, however, that few if any of these people have ever tried to write software to access Photo-CDs.

In addition to the images in a PCD file, there are thumbnails associated with it. These are defined by the following constants:

Image	Resolution
PCD__BASE__OVER__64	64 by 96 pixels
PCD__BASE__OVER__16	128 by 192 pixels

Because the filenames of Photo-CD images don't offer even the tersest of descriptions of what the files in question contain, the only really meaningful way to select among Photo-CD images to view or convert is by looking at a list of thumbnails, as Graphic Workshop for Windows provides. Graphic Workshop uses the 64×96-pixel thumbnails.

The thumbnail images of all the PCD files on a Photo-CD are stored in the OVERVIEW.PCD file for the disc. This allows a Photo-CD reader to quickly obtain thumbnails for all or part of the contents of a Photo-CD without having to open each PCD image file explicitly. Opening and closing files on a Photo-CD obeys the law of all file access for CD-ROMs—it's slow.

True-color images are inherently awkward to display. Unless you have a high-end true-color display card in your system, a Photo-CD viewing application will be confronted with displaying a picture with 16 million possible colors on a device that can handle only 256 colors at a time. Worse still would be trying to do the same thing with the default Windows 16-color screen driver.

The Photo-CD library offers a solution for this, one you'll probably find to be extremely effective. You can ask it for an image either in the true-color RGB format or as a 256-color dithered picture. The latter format will provide you with the best possible 256-color representation of a true-color original. Such an image can be displayed directly by a 256-color Windows screen driver.

You can also ask the Photo-CD library for a gray-scale image when you read a PCD file. Gray-scale images are, in effect, 256-color images in which all the colors are levels of gray.

A digression about dithering

It's worth understanding a bit about what the Photo-CD library does when you ask for a 256-color dithered image, what it calls a PCD__PALETTE image. The process is a bit technical, but knowing what it's really up to will help you to better choose which of the image formats is applicable to your requirements.

A true-color image has about 16 million possible colors, and in dealing with one you must assume that all these colors could be present in the image. They won't be—for one thing, even a PCD__16BASE image doesn't have 16 million discrete pixels. However, there's no practical way to know how many distinct colors have been used in a particular image.

Creating a 256-color image from a 16-million-color image involves throwing away some of the color information in the original image, hopefully in a way that will preserve as much of the source image as possible. The simplest way to do this is to "remap" the colors. Allowing that you have a list of 256 suitable colors in a destination palette, you can replace each color in the source image with its closest match from the new 256-color palette. The result will be an image with no more than 256 distinct colors.

The result will also probably look pretty ghastly. You can't remap a photographic image to 256 colors without having it turn into something resembling an Andy Wharhol poster.

The way around this is to dither the original. In its simplest sense, *dithering* is a process that generates colors that don't exist in a fixed palette from those that do. As a basic example of dithering, consider trying to paint an area of your monitor with orange when there's no orange available. You could come up with a pretty reasonable approximation of orange by painting all the even numbered pixels yellow and all the odd numbered pixels red. Windows does this sort of thing all the time.

Dithering an image is a bit more involved, and for the sake of this discussion it's not necessary to get into the grotty details of how it works. There's a whole chapter about it in my book *Supercharged Bitmapped Graphics*, also published by Windcrest/McGraw-Hill, should you want to know more about it. The result of a dithered image, however, will be a picture that approximates the colors of its original true-color parent by alternating colored pixels. The result of doing this is often a 256-color picture that's all but indistinguishable from the true-color image it was dithered from.

True-color images are monumentally large, as you've seen. A 256-color representation of a true-color image will be a third the size of its parent. Beyond this, however, true-color images don't compress very effectively, while 256-color ones often do. As such, a 256-color image file, such as a GIF file, will usually take up a fraction of the space required by its true-color source image.

You can use the Graphic Workshop for Windows application to convert Photo-CD images to GIF files. The Photo-CD library also offers a limited range of export options for popular image file formats.

There's a very important catch to working with dithered images. You can view and store them much more readily than you can true-color pictures, but you can't manipulate them nearly as well. If you attempt to scale a dithered image, the carefully worked-out patterns of alternating pixels will be disrupted, usually resulting in visible aberrations in your picture, areas with pronounced color shifts, and so on. If you were to load a dithered image into a photographic retouching package, such as Aldus PhotoStyler, you'd find that even after it's converted back to a true-color image, many of the image-manipulation tools and filters that work well on real true-color pictures won't behave themselves when they're applied to your image.

Finally, if you intend to use Photo-CDs as a source of high-quality scans, you should keep in mind that dithering is a very clever way to reduce the color information in a picture, but it does destroy a significant amount of the image detail you'll have gone to all this trouble to obtain. If the ultimate destination of your Photo-CD images is something like commercial four-color printing, you should work with true-color pictures, rather than dithered ones.

One of the things that distinguishes dithering procedures is the process used to select the destination 256-color palette for the final image. The best way, although often not the most effective one, is to *quantize* the source image. This involves analyzing all the source pixels and deriving a list of 256 colors that best reflects the dispersal of colors in the source. The algorithm to do this is very sneaky—again, if you'd like to see it at work you can find it under glass in *Supercharged Bitmapped Graphics*.

The drawback to this approach of finding a suitable palette is that some images trick the algorithm into choosing a less-than-optimum palette. Consider the blue parrots that turned up as the wait box for the CDPLAY application. They're a 16-color bitmap there, but they started life as a scanned true-color original. Almost the entire image is blue and green. Quantizing such a picture would produce a palette that contained mostly blue and green entries. The parrots' eyes are orange, and this quantized palette would have a dearth of orange entries. While the quantization algorithm doesn't regard the colors in the parrots' eyes to be particularly important, as they're used in relatively few pixels, they're unquestionably important to the picture—not to mention to the parrots.

Because many pictures have small details with colors that differ from the rest of the image, a safer approach to deriving a suitable 256-color palette to dither to is to use a fixed palette with an even dispersal of colors. While this would seem as if it should introduce more radical color shifts in the final dithered image—as, in fact, it often does—it usually produces more attractive results. It eliminates "bald spots"—areas of a dithered image in which details have vanished because there were too few suitable colors to represent them.

The Photo-CD library uses a fixed palette called a 3:3:2, or an *orthogonal palette*. It's extremely simple to understand. If you wanted to create a 16-million-color palette with every entry different, you would do this:

```
static char palette[50331648]; /* don't try this at home */
long index;
int x,y,z;

for(z=0;z<256;++z) {
```

```
for(y=0;y<256;++y) {
    for(x=0;x<256;++x) {
        index=(long)x*(long)y*(long)z*(long)RGB_SIZE;
        palette[index+RGB_RED]=x;
        palette[index+RGB_GREEN]=y;
        palette[index+RGB_BLUE]=z;
    }
  }
}
```

In fact, this is impossible to do in the real world—that static allocation of 50 megabytes of storage will fox most C compilers. Consider what would happen if you replaced the three assignments of the inner for loop with these lines:

```
palette[index+RGB_RED]=x & 0xe0;
palette[index+RGB_GREEN]=y & 0xe0 ;
palette[index+RGB_BLUE]=z & 0xc0;
```

There would still be 16 million entries in the palette buffer, but most of them would be the same. The masks used here would have eliminated most of the minor variations in color, leaving you with only 8 bits worth of real color information. This amounts to 256 distinct colors. You could rewrite the foregoing bit of code so it would work in real world applications, as follows:

```
static char palette[768];
int index=0;
int x,y,z;

for(z=0;z<4;++z) {
    for(y=0;y<8;++y) {
        for(x=0;x<8;++x) {
            palette[index+RGB_RED]=x*32;
            palette[index+RGB_GREEN]=y*32;
            palette[index+RGB_BLUE]=z*64;
            index+=RGB_SIZE;
        }
    }
}
```

This will produce a palette with an evenly dispersed range of colors from pure black, the RGB value (0,0,0), through pure white, (255,255,255).

There's another advantage to this palette. In the earlier discussion of dithering and remapping, you might have noted that an algorithm to perform either must locate the closest match for source colors in the destination palette. There's a way to do this, actually—it involves calculating the offset between two colors in color space. This is both awkward to envision and reasonably slow to do, especially when you're confronted with doing it once for every pixel in an image. You can cheat, however, with a fixed palette like the one here.

Because this fixed palette is really a 16-million-color palette with most of the similar colors removed, you can locate entries in it that are closest to real true-color pixels by doing to the true-color pixels what you did to the palette entries. Specifically, if (r,g,b) is a true-color pixel you'd like to find a match for, this would be the index of the matching color in the fixed palette:

```
((b >> 6) | ((g >> 3) & 0x1c) | (r & 0xe0))
```

Rather than doing a lot of searching for a palette index, you can derive it with some fairly rapid bit shifting.

You won't have to deal with any of this in reading Photo-CD images, as the Photo-CD library will do it for you if you specify a 256-color image. However, it's important to note that all 256-color Photo-CD images created this way will have the same palette, and you can locate indices in it this way.

PCD file naming and thumbnails

In creating a large application to work with Photo-CD images, it's worth knowing how the relationship of the filenames, the numbers embedded in them, and the thumbnails relate to each other. In fact, they're very consistent and, according to Kodak, they're constrained to stay that way.

The sequence of numbers embedded in PCD filenames always starts at 1 and runs in an unbroken list for as many images as exist on a Photo-CD. Because you can't delete files from a Photo-CD, there's no possibility for the sequence to change. If you read the filenames from the \PHOTO__ CD\IMAGE directory of a Photo-CD into a buffer—or a Windows list box—the index of an entry in the buffer will always be one less than the number embedded in its filename, as C language arrays start with element zero, while Photo-CD image file-names start with 1.

As I'll get to presently, you can request specific thumbnails from OVERVIEW.PCD by index. Once again, the indices start with 1, rather than zero. However, they're constrained to correspond to the numbers embedded in the PCD filenames and, indirectly, to the order of the files in the \PHOTO__CD\IMAGE directory of a Photo-CD.

You'll be able to see this relationship in use when you look at PCD-VIEW, an application to display Photo-CD images, later in this chapter. You can juggle it differently, depending on whether your use of Photo-CD images requires that they be selected visually by thumbnails, numerically by their position in a list, or just by their filenames.

Using the Photo-CD software development toolkit

The Kodak libraries are unusually well written, and integrate easily with the sorts of C language programs that have appeared thus far in this book. There are three elements you'll need to write an application to view or otherwise read Photo-CD PCD images. Specifically, you'll want:

PCDLIB.LIB   Links to your C program

PCDLIB.DLL   Loaded by Windows

PCDLIB.H   Included in your C program

The PCDLIB.DLL file should reside either in your \WINDOWS\SYSTEM directory or in the same directory as the application you're creating. It's located by Windows the first time your application makes a call to the Photo-CD library. In a properly constructed Windows application, this will be pretty well as soon as your application boots up.

The PCDLIB.LIB file provides the callable hooks into PCDLIB.DLL, while PCDLIB.H provides the prototypes, data structures, and constants required to correctly call the functions in PCDLIB.LIB.

There are a number of basic functions the Photo-CD library provides for an application that interfaces to it. Here are the basic functions it will perform:

- Provide image information
- Provide thumbnail images
- Set the read format for Photo-CD images
- Read Photo-CD bitmaps
- Do some basic image transformations
- Do some internal housekeeping

In fact, there's rather more to using the library than this might suggest. It offers a number of facilities you probably won't need, and pretty well anything you do with it will require several calls to it. Some operations, such as dealing with the really huge bitmaps that Photo-CDs can contain, will also require a degree of stealth.

One of the convenient things about the Photo-CD library is that it deals with its internal functions in a way that will be familiar to Windows programmers. For example, when you ask it to hand you a bitmap of a Photo-CD image, the object you receive will actually be a handle to a conventional Windows bitmap. You won't have to perform any complex Photo-CD-to-Windows conversion, for example. You'll also find that most of the file management that goes on in the Photo-CD library works pretty much like conventional file management using the Windows block-based file functions. All the function names are different, of course.

All the function names used by the Photo-CD library begin with PCD. They return error codes whose constants are defined in PCDLIB.H. The constant for a successful call is pcdSuccess. Here's a simple example of how you'd call the library to retrieve a Photo-CD image. Some of these calls will require a bit more explaining.

```
PCDphotoHdl PCDhandle;
PCDbitmapHdl PCDbitmap;
char b[STRINGSIZE+1];

if(PCDopen("IMG0001.PCD",&PCDhandle) != pcdSuccess) {
    DoMessage(hwnd,"Error opening the image");
        return(0);
}

PCDsetFormat(PCDhandle,PCD__PALETTE);
PCDsetResolution(PCDhandle,PCD__BASE);

if(PCDloadImage(PCDhandle,NULL,&PCDbitmap) != pcdSuccess) {
    PCDclose(PCDhandle);
    DoMessage(hwnd,"Error loading the image");
        return(0);
}

/* do something with the image */

PCDfreeBitmap(PCDbitmap);
PCDclose(PCDhandle);

return(1);
```

This code is part of a function that would load and process the first image in the \PHOTO__CD\IMAGE directory of a Photo-CD—the process might be a function to display the file, for example. It assumes that the current directory has been set to \PHOTO__CD\IMAGE.

The first call to the Photo-CD library is PCDopen, which is analogous to the more conventional __lopen or fopen functions used for general file access under Windows. However, note that it does not return a file handle per se. Rather, it returns an error code and stores a file handle in the PCD-photoHdl object it has passed a pointer to. It's important to keep track of which of the Photo-CD functions expect to have objects passed to them, and which expect pointers to objects.

The return value of PCDopen should be pcdSuccess, in which case all is well. The error constants it could return include:

ENOMEM   Not enough memory.

ENOENT   File not found.

EIO   A general I/O error.

EPERM   Permission denied.

EMFILE   No more file handles are available.

pcdBadFmt   The PCD file has been corrupted.

pcdReentry   Can't execute this function because another protected function is currently executing.

The PCDsetFormat function tells the Photo-CD library how to present your image when it's ultimately read. There are four options:

PCD_YCC   Create a bitmap in the PhotoYCC format.

PCD_RGB   Create a 24-bit true-color bitmap.

PCD_SINGLE   Create a 256-level gray-scale bitmap.

PCD_PALETTE   Create a 256-color dithered bitmap.

The first argument to PCDsetFormat should be the PCDphotoHdl object filled in by PCDopen. The second argument should be one of the foregoing constants.

The PCDsetResolution function tells the Photo-CD library which of the five resolutions available in a Photo-CD PCD file should be retrieved. Its first argument is the PCDphotoHdl object for the file in question. Its second should be one of the PCD_BASE constants listed earlier in this chapter. In this example, the Photo-CD library has been set up to return a 512×768-pixel, 256-color dithered image.

There are a number of other parameters you might set before you call for an image—the Photo-CD library sets them to intelligent defaults, and in most cases you can leave them alone. We'll have a look at some of them later in this chapter.

The PCDloadImage function does a considerable amount of work for you in one step. When you call it, it allocates memory for your bitmap, fetches the appropriate image from your Photo-CD, converts and dithers it if necessary, and then provides you with a handle to a standard Windows device-independent bitmap. It will also excise chunks of a larger image for you if you like, something I'll touch on in a moment.

The first argument to PCDloadImage is the PCDphotoHdl for the PCD file being read. The second is a pointer to a RECT object, which defines the area in the complete image to be read. If this pointer is NULL, as it is here, the whole image will be read. The third argument is a pointer to a PCD-bitmapHdl object, which will be filled in with a valid bitmap handle when PCDloadImage is done. It's worth noting that a PCDbitmapHdl is equivalent to a conventional Windows HBITMAP handle.

The convolution of pointers and addresses under C is often among its most befuddling aspects for new programmers. You might want to consider that if a handle is generically a pointer to a pointer, the third argument to PCDloadImage is a pointer to a pointer to a pointer—indirection at its extreme. In fact, Windows gurus will note that, under Windows, handles are usually indices into a table of pointers, or they're "magic cookie" handles, which address nothing directly, possibly mitigating this to some extent.

Once PCDloadImage is complete, you can work with the bitmap it has generated any way you would a normal Windows device-independent bitmap, as discussed in detail in the previous chapter. When you're done with it, you should execute two more calls to the Photo-CD library—PCDfreeBitmap to free the bitmap and PCDclose to close the PCD file.

The hitherto unused second argument to PCDloadImage offers ways to deal with several rather troublesome aspects of Photo-CD images. By far the nastiest of these is the problem of handling bitmaps that require more memory than Windows has on tap. In the example just presented, the whole bitmap was read into memory at once. However, to work with very large bitmaps you might want to read one horizontal strip at a time, process it, and then read another strip. If the strips are fairly narrow, this will reduce the memory requirements considerably. For example, if you have PCDloadImage load a 64-line strip of a 2048×3072-pixel, true-color image, the allocated memory required to work with the file will drop from 18Mb to 384K.

Handling pictures one strip at a time is usually workable if your application is printing, converting or manipulating them. It's probably not as much use if you want to view them, as panning over a large picture will typically require that the relevant strips be read from the source PCD file over and over again. Photo-CDs are not not very fast to access. However, you'll probably find that there's very little call to view an image of these dimensions and color depth on your monitor. One of the things that makes PCD files such an attractive medium is the availability of small scans to look at and big scans to print. Here's how you'd handle a Photo-CD image one strip at a time:

```
#define PCDBANDSIZE 64

PCDphotoHdl PCDhandle;
PCDbitmapHdl PCDbitmap;
RECT size,band;
char b[STRINGSIZE+1];
unsigned int i,thisbandsize;

if(PCDopen("IMG0001.PCD",&PCDhandle) != pcdSuccess) {
    DoMessage(hwnd,"Error opening the image");
        return(0);
        }

PCDsetFormat(PCDhandle,PCD__PALETTE);
PCDsetResolution(PCDhandle,PCD__BASE);
PCDgetSize(PCDhandle,&size);

for(i=0;i<size.bottom;i+=PCDBANDSIZE) {
```

```
thisbandsize=min(PCDBANDSIZE,size.bottom-i);

band.top=i;
band.bottom=i+thisbandsize;
band.left=size.left;
band.right=size.right;

PCDloadImage(PCDhandle,&band,&bitmap);

if(bitmap==NULL) {
    PCDclose(PCDhandle);
    DoMessage(hwnd,"Error loading the image");
    return(0);
}

/* do something with the band */

PCDfreeBitmap(bitmap);
}

PCDclose(PCDhandle);

return(1);
```

This bit of code works a lot like the earlier Photo-CD image reader that dealt with a whole image in one swallow. However, it uses a few additional calls to the Photo-CD library. The PCDgetSize function fills in a RECT object with the area represented by the PCDphotoHdl it's passed. The left and top elements of the RECT is always zero, and the right and bottom elements represent the horizontal and vertical dimensions of the picture, respectively.

Knowing the size of the complete image, it's possible to create rectangles that define narrow horizontal strips of it, moving the area covered by the strip down with each pass. As was noted earlier, the PCDloadImage function will read only a portion of an image if you ask it to.

The number of lines in one band is defined here as PCDBANDSIZE. There's a tradeoff in determining this value. If you make it small, your Photo-CD reader will require less memory to work with an image. However, it will suffer a meaningful speed penalty, as PCDloadImage will have to initiate more disc accesses, which are particularly time consuming for a CD-ROM.

One possible drawback to using PCDloadImage this way, depending on how your application is structured, is that the bitmap fragment it hands you with each pass will have to be locked before it can be used. This will make better use of Windows memory-management facilities, but it will take a bit longer to do, especially on a system with restricted memory. It also means that there's a possibility that PCDloadImage might not be able to allocate memory in which to store your bitmap.

The Photo-CD library offers an alternate function to perform almost the same task as PCDloadImage, called PCDgetBlock. The distinction between these two functions is that PCDgetBlock assumes you'll have allocated a buffer for it in which to load its strips. When you call it, you can pass it a pointer to a locked global buffer, rather than a handle.

To use PCDgetBlock rather than PCDloadImage in the previous example, you would do the following. To begin with, you'll need to know how many bytes one line of image data for the image in question requires. In fact, you can work this out for yourself without any heavy math, but the Photo-CD library offers a function to do it for you:

```
long stride;
PCDgetBytesPerRow(PCDhandle,size.right,&stride);
```

The PCDgetRowBytes expects to have a PCDphotoHdl handle as its first argument, the width of the bitmap in question as its second, and a pointer to a long integer as its third. It will fill in the long integer with the number of bytes in a row—which, in fact, will be the width value for the 256-color or gray-level formats, or three times this for the true-color formats.

Knowing the image width and the band depth, you can allocate a global buffer to contain one strip:

```
GLOBALHANDLE striphandle;
char huge *stripbuffer;
unsigned long stripsize;

stripsize=stride*(long)PCDBANDSIZE;
if((striphandle=GlobalAlloc(GMEM_MOVEABLE,stripsize)) == NULL) {
    DoMessage(hwnd,"Error allocating memory");
    return(0);
}

stripbuffer=GlobalLock(striphandle);
```

You can now fetch strips of an image into the buffer at stripbuffer like this:

```
for(i=0;i<size.bottom;i+=PCDBANDSIZE) {
    thisbandsize=min(PCDBANDSIZE,size.bottom-i);

    band.top=i;
    band.bottom=i+thisbandsize;
    band.left=size.left;
    band.right=size.right;

    PCDgetBlock(PCDhandle,&band,stripbuffer,stride);

    /* do something with the band */
}
```

You must make sure to explicitly unlock and free the striphandle memory handle when you're done with it. In a real-world application, you would also check the return value of PCDgetBlock to make sure it has returned pcdSuccess with each iteration.

In deciding whether you'll be using PCDloadImage or PCDgetBlock, you should keep the memory-management considerations discussed in the first chapter of this book in mind. For as long as the buffer referenced by striphandle in the foregoing example is allocated and locked—for practical purposes, for as long as the image is being read—Windows will be at something of a memory disadvantage. Now, the earlier example of this loop, which used PCDloadImage, wouldn't be all that much different, because immediately after a strip handle was returned it would probably be locked so you could work with it. If your Photo-CD reader function will spend relatively little absolute time in this loop, you can probably enjoy the slight performance improvement of PCDgetBlock without affecting Windows unduly.

Using Photo-CD thumbnails

The most obvious way to get thumbnail images of the contents of a Photo-CD would appear to be to load the PCD__BASE__OVER__16 image from each PCD file on this disk. This would work, but it's a relatively slow way to do it. The thumbnails also exist in the OVERVIEW.PCD file in the \PHOTO__CD directory of each Photo-CD. They can be retrieved from OVERVIEW.PCD by a set of dedicated calls to the Photo-CD library. These calls all begin with PCDO—the O stands for *overview*.

In a typical application for Photo-CD thumbnails, you'd probably want them dithered to 256 colors. Because the Photo-CD library dithers all images to a common palette by default, you can display any number of these thumbnails in a window at once, even if your display card can handle only 256 colors. If you realize a 256-color palette, those of its colors that best match the Windows reserved colors will be mapped to them, which in theory should produce a slight color shift. In fact, there are entries in the 3:3:2 palette used by the Photo-CD library that match the Windows reserved colors exactly, so no color shift will actually take place.

As an aside, it's unlikely that a perceptible color shift would be noticeable in any case. Windows is exceedingly clever about how it cheats when it's asked to display a full-color bitmap to a 256-color screen driver.

If you're writing an application to work with Photo-CD images on high-end display hardware, it's worth noting that you can ask the Photo-CD library for thumbnails stored as true-color bitmaps as well. This will unquestionably create a more accurate display of the thumbnail images on a Photo-CD, albeit while tying up about three times the memory for each thumbnail image in use. It could probably be argued that 256-color thumbnails are satisfactory to see what's stored in a PCD file.

As with Photo-CD images themselves, the Photo-CD library will retrieve thumbnails as standard Windows device-independent bitmaps. The procedure for doing so is similar, too, save that the thumbnail images will actually be coming from the OVERVIEW.PCD file in the \PHOTO__CD directory of the Photo-CD being read.

To begin with, you must open the OVERVIEW.PCD file on your Photo-CD. Here's how to do it:

```
PCDoviewHdl PCDOhandle;

if(PCDOopen((LPSTR)"\\PHOTO_CD\\OVERVIEW.PCD",&PCDOhandle) !=
    pcdSuccess)) {
    DoMessage(hwnd,"Error opening the overview file");
    return(0);
}
```

The first argument to PCDOopen is a path to the overview file to open. This will always be the same, allowing that your application is logged into your CD-ROM drive at the moment. The second argument is a pointer to a PCDoviewHdl handle, which will be filled in if the request to open the OVERVIEW.PCD file is successful.

Having opened an OVERVIEW.PCD file, you must tell the Photo-CD library which resolution and color model you'd like the thumbnail images retrieved as. Here are the calls to do this:

```
PCDOsetResolution(PCDOhandle,PCD_BASE_OVER_64);
PCDOsetFormat(PCDOhandle,PCD_PALETTE);
```

The call to PCDOsetResolution tells the Photo-CD library to supply 64×96-pixel images, which is what PCD_BASE_OVER_64 means. The other option would be PCD_BASE_OVER_16, which specifies 128×192-pixel images. As with the PCDsetFormat function discussed earlier in this chapter, the PCD_PALETTE argument to PCDOsetFormat specifies 256-color dithered thumbnails.

The next step in fetching a thumbnail is to tell the Photo-CD library which thumbnail image you'd like to have it retrieve. Here's the call to do this:

```
if(PCDOsetSelect(PCDOhandle,number) != pcdSuccess) {
    DoMessage(hwnd,"Error selecting a thumbnail");
    return(0);
}
```

Note that the numbers of Photo-CD thumbnails, as with Photo-CD images, begin with 1, rather than with zero. One of the more likely reasons for PCDOsetSelect not to return the pcdSuccess constant is attempting to pass it either zero or a value specifying a nonexistent thumbnail as its second argument.

You can find out how many thumbnail images are available in OVERVIEW.PCD with the PCDOgetCount function, like this:

```
int count;

if(PCDOgetCount(PCDOhandle,&count) != pcdSuccess) {
    DoMessage(hwnd,"Error getting the thumbnail count");
```

```
    return(0);
}
```

The value stored in count is the number of the last thumbnail image in OVERVIEW.PCD. The theoretical maximum number of thumbnails in an OVERVIEW.PCD file is 2045, although since every thumbnail must correspond to a Photo-CD image the real maximum value won't be much larger than 100. At this point, you're ready to fetch a thumbnail:

```
PCDbitmapHdl PCDthumbnail;

if(PCDOloadImage(PCDOhandle,&PCDthumbnail) != pcdSucess) {
    DoMessage(hwnd,"Error getting the thumbnail");
    return(0);
}
```

The value filled in as PCDthumbnail should be a handle to a Windows device-independent bitmap having the dimensions and the color format you've specified. When you're done with it, make sure you free it with a call to PCDfreeBitmap and close OVERVIEW.PCD by calling PCDOclose.

The same code that was used in the previous chapter to display bitmaps from more conventional sources can be used to display Photo-CD thumbnails.

Getting information about Photo-CD images

In the previous chapter, the section dealing with Windows BMP image files explained that getting information about specific files involved learning their dimensions, color depth, and so on. These things don't apply to PCD files, of course, as they all have the same dimensions—or rather, sets of dimensions—as well as the same absolute color depth. However, there's a block of information available for each Photo-CD image on a disk. It will tell you things like when the image was scanned, the sort of film used to create it originally, and what copyright restrictions obtain for it.

Figure 5-5 illustrates the Get Info dialog of the Photo-CD viewer to be dealt with later in this chapter. It's worth noting that the items in this dialog don't represent all the information available for a Photo-CD image—if you set up something like this for your own application, you might choose to display other fields.

The function PCDreadImageInfo will fetch a block of information called a PCDpacInfoRec from a PCD file. Here's how you'd call it:

```
PCDpacInfoRec PCDinfo;

if(PCDreadImageInfo(PCDhandle,&PCDinfo) != pcdSuccess) {
    DoMessage(hwnd,"Error getting image information");
    return(0);
}
```

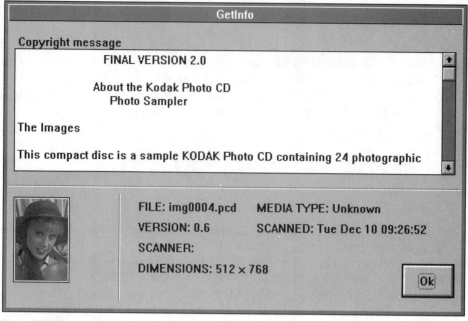

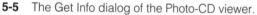

5-5 The Get Info dialog of the Photo-CD viewer.

The PCDhandle argument to PCDreadImageInfo should be a PCD file handle filled in by PCDopen, just as would be used to read an image from a PCD file. A PCDpacInfoRec structure is a fairly complex entity, stuffed full of things you probably never knew were worth knowing about a picture. Here's what it looks like:

```
typedef struct {
    unsigned short version;
    unsigned short piwVersion;
    unsigned short magnification;
    unsigned long scanTime;
    unsigned long modTime;
    char mediaId;
    char mediaType[20];
    char scannerVendor[20];
    char scannerProdID[16];
    char scannerFirmRev[4];
    char scannerFirmDate[8];
    char scannerSerial[20];
    unsigned char scannerSize[2];
    char piwEquipment[20];
    char nameCharSet;
    char nameEscapes[32];
```

```
char photofinisher[60];
char SBAdata[106];
char copyright;
char copyrightFile[30];
} PCDpacInfoRec;
```

Clearly, the major shortcoming of a PCDpacInfoRec data structure is that it offers no way to store the average number of hairs per square inch on the forearm of the photographer who originally took the picture in question. This is, however, pretty well the only item of information it doesn't contain.

In using the information in a PCDpacInfoRec object, you should keep in mind that you're free to ignore most of it if you like. Actually, you should also keep in mind that many Photo-CD images do this as well—not all the fields will be filled in for all images.

One of the things that's very civil indeed about the data in a PCDpac-InfoRec is that all its various fields are structured in a way to make them easily workable in a Windows environment, as you'll see.

I won't deal with all the elements in the PCDpacInfoRec data structure—some are sufficiently obscure as to be of virtually no practical use. Here are the genuinely helpful ones.

The version element of a PCDpacInfoRec object is the revision level of the Photo-CD specification that was used to create the image in question. The high-order byte is the major version number, and the low-order byte is the minor version number. As of this writing, the version number is 0.6.

In most applications, version numbers of less than 1 suggest that whatever is responsible for the version number in question is still in its beta cycle. It's unclear whether this is the case for Photo-CDs, or whether the designers of the Photo-CD specification simply couldn't see the point in wasting a lot of perfectly good numbers from zero through 1.

The mediaID element of a PCDpacInfoRec object contains a constant that specifies the type of photographic film used to create the image in question. Here's a list of the current values this field can contain:

```
#define PCD_COLOR_NEGATIVE       0
#define PCD_COLOR_REVERSAL       1
#define PCD_COLOR_HARDCOPY       2
#define PCD_THERMAL_HARDCOPY     3
#define PCD_BW_NEGATIVE          4
#define PCD_BW_REVERSAL          5
#define PCD_BW_HARDCOPY          6
#define PCD_INTERNEGATIVE        7
#define PCD_SYNTHETIC_IMAGE      8
```

The mediaType element should contain the actual name of the film that was used, stored as a conventional null-terminated C language string. In many cases this will be one of Kodak's four-digit film codes.

The scanTime and modTime fields of a PCDpacInfoRec object contain a time and date stamp for the scan time and modification time, respectively, of the image in question. In theory, these should be the same. These values are formatted up as normal PC time stamps, and as such if you use one as an argument to the Borland C++ ctime function you'll have the appropriate time and date formatted in English.

The multisession capabilities of Kodak Photo-CDs are so transparent that the scanTime fields of the images on a disc represent pretty well the only way to find out whether a particular image has been added to the disc when it was first created, or sometime after the fact. Images added in later sessions will have markedly later scan times.

The scannerVendor field is a C language string that defines who made the scanner used to reproduce the image in question. The scannerProdID field should contain the name or model number of the scanner. The scannerFirmRev field will contain the scanner's SCSI firmware revision number, if it's applicable, and the scannerSerial field will contain the scanner's serial number. The usefulness of these latter fields to most applications of Photo-CD imaging are right up there with the number of hairs per square inch on the photographer's forearm.

The photofinisher field of a PCDpacInfoRec object is a C language string that defines the name of the company that wrote the image in question to your disc. The copyright field of a PCDpacInfoRec object will be 1 if there are copyright restrictions on the image in question. If this is the case, the copyrightFile field will contain the name of an ASCII text file that defines the copyright restrictions. The file will be located in the \PHOTO-CD\RIGHTS directory of your Photo-CD.

The large list box in the upper half of FIG. 5-5 holds the copyright information for the Photo-CD that comes with the Kodak software development toolkit package.

Exporting Photo-CD images

Many of the really interesting applications of Photo-CD images involve reading them from a Photo-CD and writing them out to a conventional magnetic disk in a more commonly accepted format. The Photo-CD library includes a number of dynamic-link libraries that will handle this for you. They're accessed through the PCDexport function. The PCDexport function can export images to the following file formats:

- Windows (BMP)
- Tagged image file format (TIFF)
- Encapsulated PostScript (EPS)
- Windows multimedia (RIFF)
- PC Paintbrush (PCX)

In order for the PCDexport function to work, the appropriate export DLLs, provided with the Photo-CD toolkit, must be available either in the \WIN-DOWS\SYSTEM directory of your hard drive or in the directory in which your application resides. These are the DLL files in question:

- PCDXBMP.DLL
- PCDXTIF.DLL
- PCDXEPS.DLL
- PCDXRIF.DLL
- PCDXPCX.DLL

The destination file type supported by each DLL is indicated by the last three letters of each filename.

The export function of the Photo-CD library is unquestionably useful, and you will probably find it adequate for most simple applications that use Photo-CD files. It lacks a lot of the control that more sophisticated imaging software will probably require—you can't, for example, define its TIFF file structure, the level of PostScript used by its EPS files, and so on. Graphic Workshop for Windows, which offers similar facilities, uses its own internal export filters. If your requirements for exporting files exceeds the capabilities of the PCDexport function, you might want to have a look at my book *Windows Bitmapped Graphics*, published by Windcrest/McGraw-Hill, which includes code to export images in most of the popular bitmapped file formats. Here's an example of how you'd call PCDexport:

```
if(PCDexport(PCDhandle,NULL,"BMP","C:\\PICTURE.BMP") !=
    pcdSuccess) {
    DoMessage(hwnd,"Error exporting");
    return(0);
}
```

The PCDhandle argument is a Photo-CD image handle, as created by PC-Dopen. This is the same object you'd use to read a Photo-CD image from a PCD file. The second argument to PCDexport should be a pointer to a RECT object that defines the area of the image to be exported, or NULL if you want to export the whole image. The third argument should be a three-character string that defines the latter three characters of the DLL file-name you want to use to export the image—specifically, it must be BMP, TIF, EPS, RIF, or PCX. The last argument should be a path to the file to which you want your image exported. If your application will be logged into your CD-ROM drive at the time PCDexport is called, make sure that the path includes a drive letter, as your destination file certainly can't be written to a Photo-CD. The simplicity of this procedure belies the complexity of what it does.

Keep in mind that the exported file sizes aren't likely to be smaller than the uncompressed bitmaps stored in a Photo-CD file, and in most cases will probably be bigger. If you export an 18Mb Photo-CD image to the PCX format, for example, you'll probably wind up with an 18Mb PCX file on your hard drive. The PCX format actually attempts to compress images stored in it, but compression doesn't usually prove very effective with scanned or dithered images. You might find that writing a Photo-CD image to a PCX file actually leaves you with a file that takes up more disk space than the uncompressed image would have. Certainly for true-color images, the uncompressed BMP format is usually a better choice.

You can, of course, select one of the lower-resolution Photo-CD images to export, just as you can to read an image into memory. You can select a 256-color dithered image rather than a true-color file the same way.

A Photo-CD image written to, say, a PCX file, will lose none of its resolution or quality. The same image that returned in bitmap form by PCDloadImage will be available to a PCX reader.

The EPS format generated by PCDexport is intended for applications that import Photo-CD images into desktop-publishing documents. The EPS files it creates can be interpreted by a PostScript output device, but they won't be readable by Windows applications that purport to import EPS files, such as Corel Draw.

The PCDVIEW application

Figure 5-6 illustrates the main window of PCDVIEW, a simple Photo-CD viewer. In fact, it's arguably a bit too simple, in that it allows you to select Photo-CD images based on their somewhat meaningless filenames, rather than by their thumbnails. The lack of a thumbnail selection mode in PCDVIEW is a consideration of space—the PCDVIEW program is intended to illustrate how to make calls to the Photo-CD library, rather than be a serious commercial application. (There's a lot to be said for not including listings in books like this that are so long as to be virtually unintelligible.)

The PCDVIEW application will allow you to load and view Photo-CD images, and to fetch an information box like the one back in FIG. 5-5 for each image on a disc. In this implementation, PCDVIEW is hard-wired to fetch 256-color images with the dimensions 512×768 pixels. The information box also includes a thumbnail image.

Figure 5-7 is the complete C language source code for PCDVIEW. Note that it requires that PCDLIB.H be available—you'll want to modify the included directories in your compiler's project or make a file to allow PCDLIB.H to be found where it was placed by the Photo-CD software development toolkit installation procedure.

In addition to PCDVIEW.CPP, you'll also need PCDVIEW.RC, which defines the resource script for the PCDVIEW application. It doesn't do anything particularly exciting, and much of it will look pretty much like the earlier resource files that have turned up in this book. The icon in PCD-

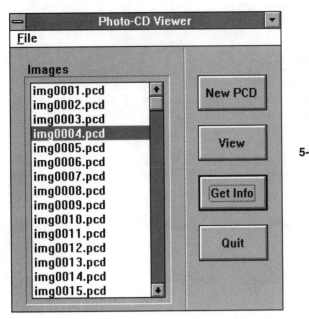

5-6 The main window of the Photo-CD viewer.

VIEW.RC is one that comes with the Photo-CD software development toolkit. The PCDVIEW.RC source code can be found in FIG. 5-8. Finally, you'll need a DEF file for PCDVIEW, as shown below:

```
NAME          PCDVIEW
DESCRIPTION   'Photo-CD Viewer'
EXETYPE       WINDOWS
CODE          PRELOAD MOVEABLE
DATA          PRELOAD MOVEABLE MULTIPLE
SEGMENTS      WM__TEXT LOADONCALL
HEAPSIZE      8192
STACKSIZE     8192
```

and a project file, as shown in FIG. 5-9. If you're using something other than the Borland C++ for Windows integrated development environment, you should create an appropriate MAKE file rather than a project. Note that the project must include the PCDLIB.LIB library.

Much of the structure of PCDVIEW.CPP will look pretty familiar if you've worked your way through the earlier C language source files in this book. Note that the first call to the Photo-CD library is in the WinMain function. The PCDgetToolkitVersion function gets the revision level of the Photo-CD library itself. In fact, this isn't particularly useful information—like the BWCCGetVersion call, discussed in chapter 1, invoking this function makes sure that PCDLIB.DLL is available as soon as the PCDVIEW application comes on line.

5-7 The C language source listing for the Photo-CD viewer, PCDVIEW.CPP.

```
/*

    PCD Viewer
    Copyright (c) 1993 Alchemy Mindworks Inc.
*/

#include <windows.h>
#include <stdio.h>
#include <stdlib.h>
#include <dir.h>
#include <ctype.h>
#include <alloc.h>
#include <string.h>
#include <io.h>
#include <bwcc.h>
#include <dos.h>
#include <errno.h>
#include <math.h>
#include <time.h>
#include <pcdlib.h>

#define say(s)      MessageBox(NULL,s,"Yo...",MB_OK | MB_ICONSTOP);
#define saynumber(f,s)    {char b[128]; sprintf((LPSTR)b,(LPSTR)f,s); \
                MessageBox(NULL,b,"Debug Message",MB_OK | MB_ICONSTOP); }

#define ItemName(item,string)    { dlgH=GetDlgItem(hwnd,item); \
                                SetWindowText(dlgH,(LPSTR)string); }
#define ItemOn(item)     { dlgH=GetDlgItem(hwnd,item); EnableWindow(dlgH,TRUE); }
#define ItemOff(item)     { dlgH=GetDlgItem(hwnd,item); EnableWindow(dlgH,FALSE); }

#define STRINGSIZE              129         /* how big is a string? */

#define MAIN_LIST               201         /* objects in the main window */

#define MAIN_TITLE              301

#define MAIN_VIEW               102
#define MAIN_GETINFO            103
#define MAIN_ABOUT              105
#define MAIN_EXIT               107
#define MAIN_OPEN               108

#define MESSAGE_STRING          101         /* message box objects */

#define INFO_COPYRIGHT          101         /* get info box objects */
#define INFO_FILENAME           102
```

```
#define INFO_VERSION         103
#define INFO_MEDIA           104
#define INFO_SCANNER         105
#define INFO_SCANDATE        106
#define INFO_DIMENSIONS      107


#define INFO_THLEFT          10
#define INFO_THTOP           208


#define RGB_RED              0
#define RGB_GREEN            1
#define RGB_BLUE             2
#define RGB_SIZE             3


#ifndef max
#define max(a,b)        (((a)>(b))?(a):(b))
#endif
#ifndef min
#define min(a,b)        (((a)<(b))?(a):(b))
#endif


typedef struct {
    GLOBALHANDLE copyright;
    unsigned int number;
    PCDbitmapHdl thumbnail;
    PCDbitmapHdl bitmap;
    PCDpacInfoRec imageinfo;
    char filename[16];
    unsigned int width,depth,bits;
    RECT size;
    char palette[768];
    } FILEINFO;


/* prototypes */
DWORD FAR PASCAL SelectProc(HWND hwnd,WORD message,WORD wParam,LONG lParam);
DWORD FAR PASCAL AboutDlgProc(HWND hwnd,WORD message,WORD wParam,LONG lParam);
DWORD FAR PASCAL MessageDlgProc(HWND hwnd,WORD message,WORD wParam,LONG lParam);
DWORD FAR PASCAL InfoDlgProc(HWND hwnd,WORD message,WORD wParam,LONG lParam);

long FAR PASCAL PictureProc(HWND hwnd,unsigned int message,
                            unsigned int wParam,LONG lParam);


void ShowInfo(HWND hwnd,FILEINFO *fi);
void DoMessage(HWND hwnd,LPSTR message);
void lmemset(LPSTR s,int n,unsigned int size);
void ResetSelectorList(HWND hwnd,unsigned int listbox,unsigned int title,int pcd);
```

```
void FreeInfo(FILEINFO *fi);
void DrawPCDThumbnail(HWND hwnd,HDC hdc,int x,int y,FILEINFO *fi);
void SetImageInformation(FILEINFO far *fi);

int testdisk(int n);
int GetInfo(FILEINFO *fi,LPSTR path,unsigned int number);
int ViewFile(HWND hwnd,LPSTR path);

/* globals */
LPSTR messagehook;
char szAppName[]="PCDViewer";
char nocopyright[]=
     "No copyright information was found, or there was insufficient memory\r\n"
     "to load it. Check the \\PHOTO_CD\\RIGHTS subdirectory on your Photo-CD\r\n"
     "for text files which may contain copyright information.";
char norestriction[]="No copyright restriction exists for this image.";

HANDLE hInst;
char pcdpath[STRINGSIZE+1];
int PCDdrive=-1;

PCDoviewHdl PCDOhandle=NULL;

#pragma warn -par
int PASCAL WinMain(HANDLE hInstance,HANDLE hPrevInstance,
                   LPSTR lpszCmdParam,int nCmdShow)
{
    FARPROC dlgProc;
    unsigned short r;

    BWCCGetVersion();
    PCDgetToolkitVersion(&r);

    hInst=hInstance;

    dlgProc=MakeProcInstance((FARPROC)SelectProc,hInst);
    r=DialogBox(hInst,"MainScreen",NULL,dlgProc);

    FreeProcInstance(dlgProc);

    return(r);
}

DWORD FAR PASCAL SelectProc(HWND hwnd,WORD message,WORD wParam,LONG lParam)
{
```

```c
        FILEINFO fi;
        PAINTSTRUCT ps;
        static HICON hIcon;
        FARPROC lpfnDlgProc;
        POINT point;
        HWND dlgH;
        HMENU hmenu;
        char b[STRINGSIZE+1];
        long l;
        int i;

        switch(message) {
            case WM_CTLCOLOR:
                if(HIWORD(lParam)==CTLCOLOR_STATIC ||
                    HIWORD(lParam)==CTLCOLOR_DLG) {
                    SetBkColor(wParam,RGB(192,192,192));
                    SetTextColor(wParam,RGB(0,0,0));

                    ClientToScreen(hwnd,&point);
                    UnrealizeObject(GetStockObject(LTGRAY_BRUSH));
                    SetBrushOrg(wParam,point.x,point.y);

                    return((DWORD)GetStockObject(LTGRAY_BRUSH));

                }
                if(HIWORD(lParam)==CTLCOLOR_BTN) {
                    SetBkColor(wParam,RGB(192,192,192));
                    SetTextColor(wParam,RGB(0,0,0));

                    ClientToScreen(hwnd,&point);
                    UnrealizeObject(GetStockObject(BLACK_BRUSH));
                    SetBrushOrg(wParam,point.x,point.y);

                    return((DWORD)GetStockObject(BLACK_BRUSH));
                }
                break;
            case WM_SYSCOMMAND:
                switch(wParam & 0xfff0) {
                    case SC_CLOSE:
                        SendMessage(hwnd,WM_COMMAND,MAIN_EXIT,0L);
                        break;
                }
                break;
            case WM_INITDIALOG:
                hIcon=LoadIcon(hInst,szAppName);
                SetClassWord(hwnd,GCW_HICON,(WORD)hIcon);
```

```
        GetProfileString(szAppName,"CDROMdrive","~Unknown",b,STRINGSIZE);

        if(b[0] != '~') PCDdrive=toupper(b[0]);

        hmenu=GetMenu(hwnd);

        if(PCDdrive == -1) {
            ResetSelectorList(hwnd,MAIN_LIST,MAIN_TITLE,FALSE);
            ItemOff(MAIN_VIEW);
            ItemOff(MAIN_GETINFO);
            EnableMenuItem(hmenu,MAIN_OPEN,MF_ENABLED);
            EnableMenuItem(hmenu,MAIN_VIEW,MF_GRAYED);
            EnableMenuItem(hmenu,MAIN_GETINFO,MF_GRAYED);
        }
        else {
            setdisk(PCDdrive-'A');
            chdir("\\PHOTO_CD\\IMAGES");
            ResetSelectorList(hwnd,MAIN_LIST,MAIN_TITLE,TRUE);
            ItemOn(MAIN_VIEW);
            ItemOn(MAIN_GETINFO);
            EnableMenuItem(hmenu,MAIN_OPEN,MF_GRAYED);
            EnableMenuItem(hmenu,MAIN_VIEW,MF_ENABLED);
            EnableMenuItem(hmenu,MAIN_GETINFO,MF_ENABLED);
        }
        break;
    case WM_PAINT:
        BeginPaint(hwnd,&ps);
        EndPaint(hwnd,&ps);
        break;
    case WM_COMMAND:
        switch(wParam) {
            case MAIN_LIST:
                switch(HIWORD(lParam)) {
                    case LBN_DBLCLK:
                        if(DlgDirSelect(hwnd,b,MAIN_LIST)) {
                            i=toupper(b[0]);
                            if(!testdisk(i-'A')) {
                                wsprintf(b,"%c:\\PHOTO_CD\\OVERVIEW.PCD",i);
                                if(!access(b,0)) {
                                    PCDdrive=i;
                                    setdisk(i-'A');
                                    chdir("\\PHOTO_CD\\IMAGES");
                                    ResetSelectorList(hwnd,
                                        MAIN_LIST,MAIN_TITLE,TRUE);
```

```
                    hmenu=GetMenu(hwnd);
                    ItemOn(MAIN_VIEW);
                    ItemOn(MAIN_GETINFO);
                    EnableMenuItem(hmenu,
                        MAIN_VIEW,MF_ENABLED);
                    EnableMenuItem(hmenu,
                        MAIN_GETINFO,MF_ENABLED);
                }
                else {
                    DoMessage(hwnd,"The Photo-CD overview "
                                "was not found.");
                    ResetSelectorList(hwnd,
                        MAIN_LIST,MAIN_TITLE,FALSE);
                    PCDdrive=-1;

                    hmenu=GetMenu(hwnd);
                    ItemOn(MAIN_VIEW);
                    ItemOn(MAIN_GETINFO);
                    EnableMenuItem(hmenu,
                        MAIN_VIEW,MF_ENABLED);
                    EnableMenuItem(hmenu,
                        MAIN_GETINFO,MF_ENABLED);
                }
            }
            else DoMessage(hwnd,"That drive is off line. "
                "Please check to see that there's a disk in it.");
        }
        break;
    case LBN_SELCHANGE:
        break;

    }
    break;
case MAIN_OPEN:
    ResetSelectorList(hwnd,MAIN_LIST,MAIN_TITLE,FALSE);
    PCDdrive=-1;

    hmenu=GetMenu(hwnd);
    ItemOff(MAIN_VIEW);
    ItemOff(MAIN_GETINFO);
    EnableMenuItem(hmenu,MAIN_VIEW,MF_GRAYED);
    EnableMenuItem(hmenu,MAIN_GETINFO,MF_GRAYED);
    break;
case MAIN_GETINFO:
    if((l=SendDlgItemMessage(hwnd,MAIN_LIST,
        LB_GETCURSEL,0,0L)) != LB_ERR) {
```

```
                        SendDlgItemMessage(hwnd,MAIN_LIST,LB_GETTEXT,
                            (unsigned int)l,(DWORD)b);
                        if(GetInfo(&fi,b,(unsigned int)l)) {
                            ShowInfo(hwnd,&fi);
                            FreeInfo(&fi);
                        } else DoMessage(hwnd,"Error getting information");
                    }
                    break;
                case MAIN_VIEW:
                    if((l=SendDlgItemMessage(hwnd,MAIN_LIST,
                        LB_GETCURSEL,0,0L)) != LB_ERR) {
                        SendDlgItemMessage(hwnd,MAIN_LIST,LB_GETTEXT,
                            (unsigned int)l,(DWORD)b);
                        ViewFile(hwnd,b);
                    }
                    break;
                case MAIN_ABOUT:
                    if((lpfnDlgProc=MakeProcInstance((FARPROC)
                        AboutDlgProc,hInst)) != NULL) {
                        DialogBox(hInst,"AboutBox",hwnd,lpfnDlgProc);
                        FreeProcInstance(lpfnDlgProc);
                    }
                    break;
                case MAIN_EXIT:
                    if(PCDOhandle != NULL) PCDOclose(PCDOhandle);
                    FreeResource(hIcon);
                    PostQuitMessage(0);
                    break;
            }
            break;

    }

    return(FALSE);
}

DWORD FAR PASCAL AboutDlgProc(HWND hwnd,WORD message,WORD wParam,LONG lParam)
{
    POINT point;

    switch(message) {
        case WM_INITDIALOG:
            return(TRUE);
        case WM_CTLCOLOR:
            if(HIWORD(lParam)==CTLCOLOR_STATIC ||
```

```
                HIWORD(lParam)==CTLCOLOR_DLG) {
                    SetBkColor(wParam,RGB(192,192,192));
                    SetTextColor(wParam,RGB(0,0,0));

                    ClientToScreen(hwnd,&point);
                    UnrealizeObject(GetStockObject(LTGRAY_BRUSH));
                    SetBrushOrg(wParam,point.x,point.y);

                    return((DWORD)GetStockObject(LTGRAY_BRUSH));

                }
                if(HIWORD(lParam)==CTLCOLOR_BTN) {
                    SetBkColor(wParam,RGB(192,192,192));
                    SetTextColor(wParam,RGB(0,0,0));

                    ClientToScreen(hwnd,&point);
                    UnrealizeObject(GetStockObject(BLACK_BRUSH));
                    SetBrushOrg(wParam,point.x,point.y);

                    return((DWORD)GetStockObject(BLACK_BRUSH));
                }
                break;
            case WM_COMMAND:
                switch(wParam) {
                    case IDOK:
                        EndDialog(hwnd,wParam);
                        return(TRUE);
                }
                break;
        }

    return(FALSE);
}

void DoMessage(HWND hwnd,LPSTR message)
{
    FARPROC lpfnDlgProc;

    messagehook=message;

    if((lpfnDlgProc=MakeProcInstance((FARPROC)MessageDlgProc,hInst)) != NULL) {
        DialogBox(hInst,"MessageBox",hwnd,lpfnDlgProc);
        FreeProcInstance(lpfnDlgProc);
    }
}
```

5-7 Continued.

```
DWORD FAR PASCAL MessageDlgProc(HWND hwnd,WORD message,WORD wParam,LONG lParam)
{
    POINT point;
    HWND dlgH;

    switch(message) {
        case WM_INITDIALOG:
            dlgH=GetDlgItem(hwnd,MESSAGE_STRING);
            SetWindowText(dlgH,messagehook);
            return(TRUE);
        case WM_CTLCOLOR:
            if(HIWORD(lParam)==CTLCOLOR_STATIC ||
                HIWORD(lParam)==CTLCOLOR_DLG) {
                SetBkColor(wParam,RGB(192,192,192));
                SetTextColor(wParam,RGB(0,0,0));

                ClientToScreen(hwnd,&point);
                UnrealizeObject(GetStockObject(LTGRAY_BRUSH));
                SetBrushOrg(wParam,point.x,point.y);

                return((DWORD)GetStockObject(LTGRAY_BRUSH));

            }
            if(HIWORD(lParam)==CTLCOLOR_BTN) {
                SetBkColor(wParam,RGB(192,192,192));
                SetTextColor(wParam,RGB(0,0,0));

                ClientToScreen(hwnd,&point);
                UnrealizeObject(GetStockObject(BLACK_BRUSH));
                SetBrushOrg(wParam,point.x,point.y);

                return((DWORD)GetStockObject(BLACK_BRUSH));
            }
            break;
        case WM_COMMAND:
            switch(wParam) {
                case IDCANCEL:
                case IDOK:
                case IDYES:
                case IDNO:
                    EndDialog(hwnd,wParam);
                    return(TRUE);
            }
            break;
    }
```

```
        return(FALSE);
}

void lmemset(LPSTR s,int n,unsigned int size)
{
    unsigned int i;

    for(i=0;i<size;++i) *s++=n;
}

void ResetSelectorList(HWND hwnd,unsigned int listbox,unsigned int title,int pcd)
{
    HWND dlgH;
    HCURSOR hSaveCursor,hHourGlass;
    char b[128];

    hHourGlass=LoadCursor(NULL,IDC_WAIT);
    hSaveCursor=SetCursor(hHourGlass);

    dlgH=GetDlgItem(hwnd,listbox);

    if(pcd) {
        ItemName(title," Images");
        SendDlgItemMessage(hwnd,listbox,LB_RESETCONTENT,0,0L);

        SendMessage(dlgH,WM_SETREDRAW,FALSE,0L);

        lstrcpy(b,"*.PCD");
        SendDlgItemMessage(hwnd,listbox,LB_DIR,0x0000,(long )b);
        SendDlgItemMessage(hwnd,listbox,LB_SETCURSEL,0,0L);

        SendMessage(dlgH,WM_SETREDRAW,TRUE,0L);

        if(PCDOhandle != NULL) PCDOclose(PCDOhandle);

        if(PCDOopen((LPSTR)"\\PHOTO_CD\\OVERVIEW.PCD", &PCDOhandle)==pcdSuccess)
            PCDOsetFormat(PCDOhandle,PCD_PALETTE);
        else MessageBeep(0);
    }
    else {
        ItemName(title, "Drives");
        SendDlgItemMessage(hwnd,listbox,LB_RESETCONTENT,0,0L);

        SendMessage(dlgH,WM_SETREDRAW,FALSE,0L);

        lstrcpy(b,"*.PCD");
```

```
        SendDlgItemMessage(hwnd,listbox,LB_DIR,0xc010,(long )b);

        SendMessage(dlgH,WM_SETREDRAW,TRUE,0L);
    }
    SetCursor(hSaveCursor);
}


int testdisk(int n)
{
    FILE *fp;
    char b[32];
    int r;

    SetErrorMode(1);
    sprintf(b,"%c:\\TEMP.DAT",n+'A');
    if((fp=fopen(b,"r")) != NULL) fclose(fp);

    if(_doserrno==ENOPATH) r=1;
    else r=0;

    SetErrorMode(0);
    return(r);
}


int GetInfo(FILEINFO *fi,LPSTR path,unsigned int number)
{
    PCDphotoHdl PCDhandle;
    HCURSOR hSaveCursor,hHourGlass;
    char huge *p;
    char b[STRINGSIZE+1],s[STRINGSIZE+1];
    unsigned long l;
    int i,fh;

    hHourGlass=LoadCursor(NULL,IDC_WAIT);
    hSaveCursor=SetCursor(hHourGlass);

    lmemset((char *)fi,0,sizeof(FILEINFO));

    if(PCDopen(path,&PCDhandle)==pcdSuccess) {
        PCDreadImageInfo(PCDhandle,&fi->imageinfo);
        PCDgetSize(PCDhandle,&fi->size);
        PCDclose(PCDhandle);
    }

    if(fi->imageinfo.copyright) {
```

```
        wsprintf(s,"%.30s",(LPSTR)fi->imageinfo.copyrightFile);
        for(i=lstrlen(s)-1;s[i]==32 && i > 0;--i) s[i]=0;
        wsprintf(b,"\\PHOTO_CD\\RIGHTS\\%s",(LPSTR)s);
        if((fh=_open(b,OF_READ)) != -1) {
            l=_llseek(fh,0L,SEEK_END);
            _llseek(fh,0L,SEEK_SET);
            if((fi->copyright=GlobalAlloc(GMEM_MOVEABLE |
              GMEM_ZEROINIT,l)) != NULL) {
                if((p=GlobalLock(fi->copyright)) != NULL) _hread(fh,p,l);
                GlobalUnlock(fi->copyright);
            }
            _lclose(fh);
        }

        if(fi->copyright==NULL)  {
            if((fi->copyright=GlobalAlloc(GMEM_MOVEABLE | GMEM_ZEROINIT,
                (long)lstrlen(nocopyright)+16L)) != NULL) {
                if((p=GlobalLock(fi->copyright)) != NULL)
                  lstrcpy((LPSTR)p,nocopyright);
                GlobalUnlock(fi->copyright);
            }
        }
    }
    else {
        if(fi->copyright==NULL)  {
            if((fi->copyright=GlobalAlloc(GMEM_MOVEABLE | GMEM_ZEROINIT,
                (long)lstrlen(norestriction)+16L)) != NULL) {
                if((p=GlobalLock(fi->copyright)) != NULL)
                    lstrcpy((LPSTR)p,norestriction);
                GlobalUnlock(fi->copyright);
            }
        }
    }

    fi->number=number;

    if(PCDOsetSelect(PCDOhandle,number+1)==pcdSuccess) {
        PCDOsetResolution(PCDOhandle,PCD_BASE_OVER_64);
        PCDOloadImage(PCDOhandle, &fi->thumbnail);
    }

    lstrcpy(fi->filename,path);

    SetCursor(hSaveCursor);

    return(1);
```

```
}

void FreeInfo(FILEINFO *fi)
{
    if(fi->copyright != NULL) GlobalFree(fi->copyright);
    fi->copyright=NULL;
    if(fi->thumbnail != NULL) PCDfreeBitmap(fi->thumbnail);
    fi->thumbnail=NULL;
}


void ShowInfo(HWND hwnd,FILEINFO *fi)
{
    FARPROC lpfnDlgProc;

    messagehook=(LPSTR)fi;
    if((lpfnDlgProc=MakeProcInstance((FARPROC)InfoDlgProc,hInst)) != NULL) {
        DialogBox(hInst,"InfoBox",hwnd,lpfnDlgProc);
        FreeProcInstance(lpfnDlgProc);
    }
}

DWORD FAR PASCAL InfoDlgProc(HWND hwnd,WORD message,WORD wParam,LONG lParam)
{
    static FILEINFO *fi;
    HWND dlgH;
    POINT point;
    HDC hdc;
    PAINTSTRUCT ps;
    LPSTR p;
    char b[STRINGSIZE+1],s[STRINGSIZE+1];
    int i;

    switch(message) {
        case WM_INITDIALOG:
            fi=(FILEINFO *)messagehook;
            if((p=GlobalLock(fi->copyright)) != NULL) {
                ItemName(INFO_COPYRIGHT,p);
                GlobalUnlock(fi->copyright);
            }
            wsprintf(b,"FILE: %s",(LPSTR)fi->filename);
            ItemName(INFO_FILENAME,b);

            wsprintf(b,"VERSION: %u.%u",fi->imageinfo.version>>8,
                fi->imageinfo.version & 0x00ff);
            ItemName(INFO_VERSION,b);
```

```c
lstrcpy(b,"MEDIA TYPE: ");
switch(fi->imageinfo.mediaId) {
    case PCD_COLOR_NEGATIVE:
        lstrcat(b,"Colour negative");
        break;
    case PCD_COLOR_REVERSAL:
        lstrcat(b,"Colour reversal");
        break;
    case PCD_COLOR_HARDCOPY:
        lstrcat(b,"Colour hard copy");
        break;
    case PCD_THERMAL_HARDCOPY:
        lstrcat(b,"Thermal hard copy");
        break;
    case PCD_BW_NEGATIVE:
        lstrcat(b,"B/W negative");
        break;
    case PCD_BW_REVERSAL:
        lstrcat(b,"B/W reversal");
        break;
    case PCD_BW_HARDCOPY:
        lstrcat(b,"B/W hard copy");
        break;
    case PCD_INTERNEGATIVE:
        lstrcat(b,"Internegative");
        break;
    case PCD_SYNTHETIC_IMAGE:
        lstrcat(b,"Synthetic image");
        break;
    default:
        lstrcat(b,"Unknown");
        break;

}
ItemName(INFO_MEDIA,b);

wsprintf(s,"%.20s",(LPSTR)fi->imageinfo.scannerVendor);
for(i=lstrlen(s)-1;s[i]==32 && i > 0;--i) s[i]=0;

wsprintf(b,"SCANNER: %s %.16s",(LPSTR)s,
    (LPSTR)fi->imageinfo.scannerProdID);
ItemName(INFO_SCANNER,b);

wsprintf(b,"SCANNED: %24.24s",
    (LPSTR)ctime((const long *)&fi->imageinfo.scanTime));
ItemName(INFO_SCANDATE,b);
```

5-7 Continued.

```
            wsprintf(b,"DIMENSIONS: %u x %u",fi->size.right,fi->size.bottom);
            ItemName(INFO_DIMENSIONS,b);

            return(TRUE);
        case WM_CTLCOLOR:
            if(HIWORD(lParam)==CTLCOLOR_STATIC ||
                HIWORD(lParam)==CTLCOLOR_DLG) {
                SetBkColor(wParam,RGB(192,192,192));
                SetTextColor(wParam,RGB(0,0,0));

                ClientToScreen(hwnd,&point);
                UnrealizeObject(GetStockObject(LTGRAY_BRUSH));
                SetBrushOrg(wParam,point.x,point.y);

                return((DWORD)GetStockObject(LTGRAY_BRUSH));

            }
            if(HIWORD(lParam)==CTLCOLOR_BTN) {
                SetBkColor(wParam,RGB(192,192,192));
                SetTextColor(wParam,RGB(0,0,0));

                ClientToScreen(hwnd,&point);
                UnrealizeObject(GetStockObject(BLACK_BRUSH));
                SetBrushOrg(wParam,point.x,point.y);

                return((DWORD)GetStockObject(BLACK_BRUSH));
            }
            break;
        case WM_PAINT:
            hdc=BeginPaint(hwnd,&ps);
            DrawPCDThumbnail(hwnd,hdc,INFO_THLEFT,INFO_THTOP,fi);
            EndPaint(hwnd,&ps);
            break;
        case WM_COMMAND:
            switch(wParam) {
                case IDOK:
                    EndDialog(hwnd,wParam);
                    return(TRUE);
            }
            break;
    }

    return(FALSE);
}
```

```c
void DrawPCDThumbnail(HWND hwnd,HDC hdc,int x,int y,FILEINFO *fi)
{
    LPBITMAPINFO bmp;
    HCURSOR hSaveCursor,hHourGlass;
    LOGPALETTE *pLogPal;
    HANDLE hPal=NULL;
    LPSTR image;
    RGBQUAD far *palette;
    int i,j,n;
    unsigned int width,depth,bits;

    hHourGlass=LoadCursor(NULL,IDC_WAIT);
    hSaveCursor=SetCursor(hHourGlass);

    if((bmp=(LPBITMAPINFO)GlobalLock(fi->thumbnail)) != NULL) {
        width=(unsigned int)bmp->bmiHeader.biWidth;
        depth=(unsigned int)bmp->bmiHeader.biHeight;
        bits=bmp->bmiHeader.biBitCount;

        SelectObject(hdc,GetStockObject(BLACK_PEN));
        SelectObject(hdc,GetStockObject(WHITE_BRUSH));
        Rectangle(hdc,x-2,y-2,x+width+2,y+depth+2);

        n=1<<bits;
        j=min(n,256);

        palette=(RGBQUAD far *)((LPSTR)bmp+(unsigned int)bmp->bmiHeader.biSize);
        image=(LPSTR)bmp+(unsigned int)bmp->bmiHeader.biSize+(j*sizeof(RGBQUAD)));

        if((pLogPal=(LOGPALETTE *)malloc(sizeof(LOGPALETTE)+
           (j*sizeof(PALETTEENTRY)))) != NULL) {
            pLogPal->palVersion=0x0300;
            pLogPal->palNumEntries=j;

            for(i=0;i<j;i++) {
                pLogPal->palPalEntry[i].peRed=palette[i].rgbRed;
                pLogPal->palPalEntry[i].peGreen=palette[i].rgbGreen;
                pLogPal->palPalEntry[i].peBlue=palette[i].rgbBlue;
                pLogPal->palPalEntry[i].peFlags=0;
            }

            hPal=CreatePalette(pLogPal);
            free(pLogPal);

            SelectPalette(hdc,hPal,0);
            RealizePalette(hdc);
```

```
        }

        SetDIBitsToDevice(hdc,x,y,width,depth,
            0,0,0,depth,image,bmp,DIB_RGB_COLORS);

        if(hPal != NULL) DeleteObject(hPal);

        GlobalUnlock(fi->thumbnail);
    }

    SetCursor(hSaveCursor);
}

int ViewFile(HWND hwnd,LPSTR path)
{
    HCURSOR hSaveCursor,hHourGlass;
    FILEINFO fi;
    HWND childhwnd;
    MSG msg;
    WNDCLASS wndclass;
    PCDphotoHdl PCDhandle;
    char b[STRINGSIZE+1];

    hHourGlass=LoadCursor(NULL,IDC_WAIT);
    hSaveCursor=SetCursor(hHourGlass);

    if(PCDopen(path,&PCDhandle) != pcdSuccess) {
        SetCursor(hSaveCursor);
        DoMessage(hwnd,"Error opening the image");
        return(0);
    }

    PCDsetFormat(PCDhandle,PCD_PALETTE);
    PCDsetResolution(PCDhandle,PCD_BASE);
    PCDgetSize(PCDhandle,&fi.size);

    if(PCDloadImage(PCDhandle,NULL,&fi.bitmap) != pcdSuccess) {
        PCDclose(PCDhandle);
        SetCursor(hSaveCursor);
        DoMessage(hwnd,"Error loading the image");
        return(0);
    }

    SetCursor(hSaveCursor);
```

```
    messagehook=(LPSTR)&fi;
    wndclass.style=CS_HREDRAW | CS_VREDRAW;
    wndclass.lpfnWndProc=PictureProc;
    wndclass.cbClsExtra=0;
    wndclass.cbWndExtra=0;
    wndclass.hInstance=hInst;
    wndclass.hIcon=LoadIcon(NULL,IDI_APPLICATION);
    wndclass.hCursor=LoadCursor(NULL,IDC_ARROW);
    wndclass.hbrBackground=GetStockObject(BLACK_BRUSH);
    wndclass.lpszMenuName=NULL;
    wndclass.lpszClassName=szAppName;

    RegisterClass(&wndclass);

    wsprintf(b,"%s - (%u x %u)",(LPSTR)path,fi.size.right,fi.size.bottom);
    childhwnd = CreateWindow(szAppName,b,
        WS_POPUP | WS_CAPTION | WS_SYSMENU | WS_VSCROLL | WS_HSCROLL,
        CW_USEDEFAULT,CW_USEDEFAULT,CW_USEDEFAULT,CW_USEDEFAULT,
        hwnd,NULL,hInst,NULL);

    ShowWindow(childhwnd,SW_SHOWMAXIMIZED);
    UpdateWindow(childhwnd);

    while(GetMessage(&msg,NULL,0,0)) {
        TranslateMessage(&msg);
        DispatchMessage(&msg);
    }

    UnregisterClass(szAppName,hInst);

    PCDfreeBitmap(fi.bitmap);
    PCDclose(PCDhandle);
}

void SetImageInformation(FILEINFO far *fi)
{
    LPBITMAPINFO bmp;
    RGBQUAD far *palette;
    int i,j,n;

    if(fi->bitmap == NULL) return;

    if((bmp=(LPBITMAPINFO)GlobalLock(fi->bitmap)) != NULL) {
        fi->width=(unsigned int)bmp->bmiHeader.biWidth;
        fi->depth=(unsigned int)bmp->bmiHeader.biHeight;
        fi->bits=bmp->bmiHeader.biBitCount;
```

```
        n=1<<fi->bits;
        j=min(n,256);

        palette=(RGBQUAD far *)((LPSTR)bmp+(unsigned int)bmp->bmiHeader.biSize);

        for(i=0;i<j;i++) {
            fi->palette[i*RGB_SIZE+RGB_RED]=palette[i].rgbRed;
            fi->palette[i*RGB_SIZE+RGB_GREEN]=palette[i].rgbGreen;
            fi->palette[i*RGB_SIZE+RGB_BLUE]=palette[i].rgbBlue;
        }

        GlobalUnlock(fi->bitmap);
    }
}

long FAR PASCAL PictureProc(HWND hwnd,unsigned int message,
                            unsigned int wParam,LONG lParam)
{
    static FILEINFO far *fi;
    LPBITMAPINFO bmp;
    LOGPALETTE *pLogPal;
    HANDLE hPal=NULL;
    LPSTR image;
    RGBQUAD far *palette;
    HDC hdc;
    PAINTSTRUCT ps;
    RECT rect;
    static int vpos,hpos;
    int vsize,hsize,vjump,hjump;
    int i,j,n;

    switch (message) {
        case WM_VSCROLL:
            GetClientRect(hwnd,&rect);
            vsize=rect.bottom-rect.top;
            vjump=vsize/4;
            switch(wParam) {
                case SB_LINEUP:
                    vpos-=1;
                    break;
                case SB_LINEDOWN:
                    vpos+=1;
                    break;
                case SB_PAGEUP:
                    vpos-=vjump;
```

```
                break;
            case SB_PAGEDOWN:
                vpos+=vjump;
                break;
            case SB_THUMBPOSITION:
                vpos=LOWORD(lParam);
                break;
        }

        if(vpos < 0 || fi->depth < vsize) vpos=0;
        else if(vpos > (fi->depth-vsize)) vpos=fi->depth-vsize;

        if(vpos != GetScrollPos(hwnd,SB_VERT)) {
            SetScrollPos(hwnd,SB_VERT,vpos,TRUE);
            InvalidateRect(hwnd,NULL,FALSE);
        }
        return(0);
    case WM_HSCROLL:
        GetClientRect(hwnd,&rect);
        hsize=rect.right-rect.left;
        hjump=hsize/4;
        switch(wParam) {
            case SB_LINEUP:
                hpos-=1;
                break;
            case SB_LINEDOWN:
                hpos+=1;
                break;
            case SB_PAGEUP:
                hpos-=hjump;
                break;
            case SB_PAGEDOWN:
                hpos+=hjump;
                break;
            case SB_THUMBPOSITION:
                hpos=LOWORD(lParam);
                break;
        }

        if(hpos < 0 || fi->width < hsize) hpos=0;
        else if(hpos > (fi->width-hsize)) hpos=fi->width-hsize;

        if(hpos != GetScrollPos(hwnd,SB_HORZ)) {
            SetScrollPos(hwnd,SB_HORZ,hpos,TRUE);
            InvalidateRect(hwnd,NULL,FALSE);
        }
```

```
            return(0);
    case WM_CREATE:
        fi=(FILEINFO far *)messagehook;
        SetImageInformation(fi);
        vpos=hpos=0;
    case WM_SIZE:
        GetClientRect(hwnd,&rect);
        vsize=rect.bottom-rect.top;
        if(fi->depth > vsize)
            SetScrollRange(hwnd,SB_VERT,0,fi->depth-vsize,TRUE);
        else
            SetScrollRange(hwnd,SB_VERT,0,1,TRUE);
        hsize=rect.right-rect.left;
        if(fi->width > hsize)
            SetScrollRange(hwnd,SB_HORZ,0,fi->width-hsize,TRUE);
        else
            SetScrollRange(hwnd,SB_HORZ,0,1,TRUE);
        return(0);
    case WM_PAINT:
        hdc=BeginPaint(hwnd,&ps);

        if((bmp=(LPBITMAPINFO)GlobalLock(fi->bitmap)) != NULL) {

            n=1<<fi->bits;
            j=min(n,256);

            palette=(RGBQUAD far *)((LPSTR)bmp+
                (unsigned int)bmp->bmiHeader.biSize);
            image=(LPSTR)bmp+(unsigned int)bmp->bmiHeader.biSize+
                (j*sizeof(RGBQUAD));

            if((pLogPal=(LOGPALETTE *)malloc(sizeof(LOGPALETTE)+
                (j*sizeof(PALETTEENTRY)))) != NULL) {
                pLogPal->palVersion=0x0300;
                pLogPal->palNumEntries=j;

                for(i=0;i<j;i++) {
                    pLogPal->palPalEntry[i].peRed=palette[i].rgbRed;
                    pLogPal->palPalEntry[i].peGreen=palette[i].rgbGreen;
                    pLogPal->palPalEntry[i].peBlue=palette[i].rgbBlue;
                    pLogPal->palPalEntry[i].peFlags=0;
                }

                hPal=CreatePalette(pLogPal);
                free(pLogPal);
```

```
                SelectPalette(hdc,hPal,0);
                RealizePalette(hdc);
            }

            SetDIBitsToDevice(hdc,0,0,fi->width,fi->depth,
                hpos,-vpos,0,fi->depth,image,bmp,DIB_RGB_COLORS);

            if(hPal != NULL) DeleteObject(hPal);

            GlobalUnlock(fi->bitmap);
        } else MessageBeep(0);

        EndPaint(hwnd,&ps);
        return(0);
    case WM_DESTROY:
        PostQuitMessage(0);
        break;
    case WM_SYSCOMMAND:
        switch(wParam & 0xfff0) {
            case SC_CLOSE:
                SendMessage(hwnd,WM_DESTROY,0,0L);
                break;
        }
        break;

    }

    return(DefWindowProc(hwnd,message,wParam,lParam));
}
```

5-8 The resource script for the Photo-CD viewer, PCDVIEW.RC.

```
MainScreen DIALOG 117, 55, 156, 148
STYLE WS_POPUP ¦ WS_CAPTION ¦ WS_SYSMENU ¦ WS_MINIMIZEBOX
CAPTION "Photo-CD Viewer"
MENU MainMenu
BEGIN
  LISTBOX 201, 12, 20, 76, 120,
      LBS_NOTIFY ¦ WS_CHILD ¦ WS_VISIBLE ¦ WS_BORDER ¦ WS_VSCROLL
  LTEXT "", 301, 8, 8, 84, 8, WS_CHILD ¦ WS_VISIBLE ¦ WS_GROUP
  CONTROL "", -1, "BorShade", BSS_GROUP ¦ WS_CHILD ¦ WS_VISIBLE, 8, 16, 84, 128
  PUSHBUTTON "View", 102, 108, 44, 40, 20, WS_CHILD ¦ WS_VISIBLE ¦ WS_TABSTOP
  PUSHBUTTON "Get Info", 103, 108, 72, 40, 20, WS_CHILD ¦ WS_VISIBLE ¦ WS_TABSTOP
  PUSHBUTTON "Quit", 107, 108, 100, 40, 20, WS_CHILD ¦ WS_VISIBLE ¦ WS_TABSTOP
  CONTROL "", -1, "BorShade", BSS_VDIP ¦ WS_CHILD ¦ WS_VISIBLE, 100, 0, 1, 148
  DEFPUSHBUTTON "New PCD", 108, 108, 16, 40, 20, WS_CHILD ¦ WS_VISIBLE ¦ WS_TABSTOP
```

5-8 Continued.
```
END

MainMenu MENU
BEGIN
    POPUP "&File"
    BEGIN
        MENUITEM "&View", 102
        MENUITEM "&Get Info", 103
        MENUITEM "&Open Photo-CD", 108
        MENUITEM "&About", 105
        MENUITEM SEPARATOR
        MENUITEM "E&xit", 107
    END

END

AboutBox DIALOG 18, 18, 156, 104
STYLE WS_POPUP | WS_CAPTION
CAPTION "About PCD Viewer..."
BEGIN
  CONTROL "", 102, "BorShade", BSS_GROUP | WS_CHILD | WS_VISIBLE | WS_TABSTOP,
      8, 8, 140, 68
  LTEXT "PCD Viewer 1.0\nCopyright (c) 1993\nAlchemy Mindworks Inc.\n"
      "This program is part of the book Multimedia Programming for Windows by "
      "Steven William Rimmer, published by Windcrest (Book 4484).",
      -1, 12, 12, 128, 60, WS_CHILD | WS_VISIBLE | WS_GROUP
  DEFPUSHBUTTON "Ok", IDOK, 116, 80, 32, 20, WS_CHILD | WS_VISIBLE | WS_TABSTOP
END

MessageBox DIALOG 72, 72, 144, 80
STYLE DS_MODALFRAME | WS_POPUP | WS_CAPTION
CAPTION "Message"
BEGIN
  CONTROL "", 102, "BorShade", BSS_GROUP | WS_CHILD | WS_VISIBLE, 4, 8, 136, 44
  CTEXT "", 101, 8, 12, 128, 36, WS_CHILD | WS_VISIBLE | WS_GROUP
  DEFPUSHBUTTON "Ok", IDOK, 108, 56, 32, 20, WS_CHILD | WS_VISIBLE | WS_TABSTOP
END

PCDView ICON
BEGIN
    '00 00 01 00 01 00 20 20 10 00 00 00 00 00 E8 02'
    '00 00 16 00 00 00 28 00 00 00 20 00 00 00 40 00'
    '00 00 01 00 04 00 00 00 00 00 80 02 00 00 00 00'
    '00 00 00 00 00 00 00 00 00 00 00 00 00 00 00 00'
    '00 00 00 00 BF 00 00 BF 00 00 00 BF BF 00 BF 00'
```

```
'00 00 BF 00 BF 00 BF BF 00 00 C0 C0 C0 00 80 80'
'80 00 00 00 FF 00 00 FF 00 00 00 FF FF 00 FF 00'
'00 00 FF 00 FF 00 FF FF 00 00 FF FF FF 00 08 88'
'88 88 88 88 88 88 88 88 88 88 88 88 88 80 80 88'
'88 88 88 88 88 88 88 88 88 88 88 88 88 08 88 08'
'88 88 88 88 88 88 88 88 88 88 88 88 80 88 88 8A'
'BA AA AA AA BA BA AB AA AA AB AA AB A8 88 88 8A'
'AC CC CC AA AB BA AB AA B9 AA AA 9A A8 88 88 8A'
'CC CC CC CC AB BA AA BA AA BA AA AA A8 88 88 8C'
'CC CC CC CC CA AA BB AA BA AA AB AA B8 88 88 8C'
'FF FF FF FF CC AA AA AA BB CC CC AA B8 88 88 8F'
'FF FF FF FF CC CC CC CC CC CC CC CC C8 88 88 8F'
'FF F8 FF FF CC FC CC CC CC CC CC CC C8 88 88 8F'
'FF F8 8F FF FF FF FF FF CC CC FF FF F8 88 88 8F'
'FF FF 8F FF FF FF FF FF FF FF FF FF F8 88 88 8F'
'FF FF 88 8F FF FF FF FF FF FF FF FF F8 88 88 8F'
'FF FF F8 88 FF FF FF FF 88 88 FF FF F8 88 88 8F'
'FF FF FF 88 FF FF FF FF FF F8 88 8F F8 88 88 8F'
'FF FF FF 88 FF FF FF F8 FF FF FF 88 F8 88 88 8F'
'F8 FF FF F8 8F FF FF F8 88 FF FF F8 88 88 88 8F'
'F0 0F FF F8 8F FF FF F8 88 FF FF FF 88 88 88 8F'
'FF 0F FF FF 8F FF FF 88 88 8F FF FF 88 88 88 8F'
'88 B0 FF FF 8F FF FF 08 88 88 FF FF F8 88 88 88'
'8C CC 00 FF 88 FF F8 C0 08 88 8F FF F8 88 88 88'
'BC CC CB FF F8 FF 80 CC CC C0 88 FF F8 88 88 8C'
'CC CC B0 FF F8 F0 0C CC CC C0 88 8F F8 88 88 8C'
'CC CB CC B0 FF 0C CC CC CC CC 08 8F F8 88 88 8B'
'CC BC CC CB BF 0C CC CC CC CC C8 8F F8 88 88 8B'
'BB BC CC BC CB CC CC CC CC CC CC C8 F8 88 88 8B'
'BB BB CB CC CC CC CC CC CC CC CC CC F8 88 88 8B'
'BB BB BC CC CC CC CC CC CC CC CC CC 88 88 88 8B'
'BB BB CC BC CC CC CC CC CC CC CC CC C8 88 88 08'
'88 88 88 88 88 88 88 88 88 88 88 88 80 88 80 88'
'88 88 88 88 88 88 88 88 88 88 88 88 88 08 08 88'
'88 88 88 88 88 88 88 88 88 88 88 88 88 80 00 00'
'00 00 00 00 00 00 00 00 00 00 00 00 00 00 00 00'
'00 00 00 00 00 00 00 00 00 00 00 00 00 00 00 00'
'00 00 00 00 00 00 00 00 00 00 00 00 00 00 00 00'
'00 00 00 00 00 00 00 00 00 00 00 00 00 00 00 00'
'00 00 00 00 00 00 00 00 00 00 00 00 00 00 00 00'
'00 00 00 00 00 00 00 00 00 00 00 00 00 00 00 00'
'00 00 00 00 00 00 00 00 00 00 00 00 00 00 00 00'
'00 00 00 00 00 00 00 00 00 00 00 00 00 00 00'
```
END

InfoBox DIALOG 8, -12, 276, 168

```
STYLE DS_MODALFRAME | WS_POPUP | WS_CAPTION
CAPTION "GetInfo"
BEGIN
  DEFPUSHBUTTON "Ok", IDOK, 240, 140, 32, 20, WS_CHILD | WS_VISIBLE | WS_TABSTOP
  CONTROL "", 101, "EDIT", ES_LEFT | ES_MULTILINE | ES_AUTOVSCROLL | ES_READONLY |
    WS_CHILD | WS_VISIBLE | WS_BORDER | WS_VSCROLL | WS_TABSTOP, 4, 16, 268, 72
  LTEXT " Copyright message", -1, 4, 8, 268, 8, WS_CHILD | WS_VISIBLE | WS_GROUP
  CONTROL "", -1, "BorShade", BSS_HDIP | WS_CHILD | WS_VISIBLE, 0, 96, 276, 1
  LTEXT "", 102, 80, 104, 64, 8, WS_CHILD | WS_VISIBLE | WS_GROUP
  CONTROL "", 102, "BorShade", 3 | WS_CHILD | WS_VISIBLE, 68, 100, 2, 64
  LTEXT "", 104, 152, 104, 120, 8, WS_CHILD | WS_VISIBLE | WS_GROUP
  LTEXT "", 103, 80, 116, 64, 8, WS_CHILD | WS_VISIBLE | WS_GROUP
  LTEXT "", 105, 80, 128, 192, 8, WS_CHILD | WS_VISIBLE | WS_GROUP
  LTEXT "", 106, 152, 116, 120, 8, WS_CHILD | WS_VISIBLE | WS_GROUP
  LTEXT "", 107, 80, 140, 120, 8, WS_CHILD | WS_VISIBLE | WS_GROUP
END
```

The WM_INITDIALOG case of SelectProc does something that hasn't turned up in any of the previous applications in this book. It uses the Get-ProfileString function to fetch a line from your WIN.INI file. Specifically, it's looking for something like this:

```
[PCDViewer]
CDROMdrive=F
```

By default, PCDVIEW will come up with a list of drive letters in its list box, allowing you to select your CD-ROM drive from them. However, because most users get by with a single CD-ROM drive, the assignment of which doesn't usually change, you might want to install the previous section in your WIN.INI file, changing the second line to reflect the actual drive letter of your CD-ROM drive. If PCDVIEW finds this section in WIN.INI, it will automatically log in the drive for you, saving you a bit of clicking around.

The PCDVIEW application really does only two things of note, these being fetching information about a Photo-CD image and actually displaying one. These functions are initiated by the MAIN_GETINFO and MAIN_VIEW cases of the switch in SelectProc, respectively.

The GetInfo function, called from SelectProc, will load a FILEINFO structure with information about the currently selected Photo-CD image file—you can find a definition of a FILEINFO object at the top of PCD-VIEW.CPP. The function begins by opening the PCD file in question and fetching a PCDpacInfoRec object with information about it, as dealt with earlier in this chapter.

The PCDpacInfoRec object specifies whether there's a text file available to define the copyright restrictions of the image in question. If one exists, it's loaded into a buffer referenced by the copyright element if the FILEINFO object. If such a file can't be found, GetInfo will fill this buffer with some canned text to state either that the copyright text couldn't be loaded or that no copyright restrictions apply to the image.

Finally, GetInfo will fetch a thumbnail image for the PCD file in question and store it in a buffer referenced by the thumbnail element of the FILE-INFO object passed to it.

Once GetInfo is done, the ShowInfo function will set up a dialog box like the one in FIG. 5-5. The InfoDlgProc function handles messages for it. In fact, all its meaningful tasks take place in its WM_INITDIALOG case. Despite its size and complexity, the information dialog is actually a very simple structure. It merely formats the information in the FILEINFO object passed to ShowInfo and waits for someone to click on OK.

As in the earlier applications in this book, the messagehook object is used as an all-purpose pointer to pass data to the InfoDlgProc function. Note that when you're done with a FILEINFO object you should pass it to FreeInfo, as GetInfo will have allocated some buffers on its behalf.

The InfoDlgProc function calls DrawPCDThumbnail, which appears as the next function declaration in PCDVIEW.CPP. This rather extensive bit of code exists entirely to paint the thumbnail image in the information dialog box. Its workings were discussed in the previous chapter.

5-9 The project file for the Photo-CD viewer, PCDVIEW.PRJ.

The ViewFile function will accept a path to a Photo-CD image file, load it into memory, and display it. It selects 256-color, 512×768-resolution images at the moment, but you're free to change this if you like. The various PCD calls at the beginning of the function have all been dealt with in depth earlier in this chapter. When they're complete, the bitmap element of the FILEINFO object will reference a suitable Windows bitmap.

When ViewFile has loaded a Photo-CD image into memory, it will open a new window in which to display it by calling CreateWindow. The messages for the new window are handled by PictureProc. For the most part, Picture-Proc is responsible for repainting areas of the bitmap based on the positions of its scroll bars, something else that was dealt with in the previous chapter. You can double-click on the system menu icon in the upper left corner to close the image window.

The SetImageInformation function, called from PictureProc, fetches the image dimensions and palette colors from a device-independent bitmap.

Extending Photo-CD applications

As was noted earlier, this chapter's discussion of the Photo-CD library doesn't go into some of its more exotic facilities. You might want to explore them if you plan to write much more elaborate applications to deal with Photo-CD images.

Having said this, I should note that in writing the Photo-CD support for Graphic Workshop I found that most of the ancillary functions offered by the Photo-CD library—image transformations and exporting, for example—could typically be handled more rapidly and with greater flexibility by custom code. The image transformations are particularly slow and memory-hungry. There's a lot to be said for approaching the creation of a Photo-CD interface with a "snatch and grab" philosophy—get an image from the Photo-CD library and then have as little to do with it as possible.

Further, and perhaps in keeping with the current 0.6 revision level of the Photo-CD interface, there's a memory-allocation bug somewhere in the Kodak libraries as of this writing. Each time you load a Photo-CD image and have it dithered by the library—that is, if you call PCDloadImage or PCDgetBlock with the image format set to PCD_PALETTE—about 28 kilobytes worth of memory will be orphaned until your application terminates. Clearly, this isn't likely to cripple a system with several megabytes of memory on hand, but it's something to be aware of.

6
Playing MIDI files

"How can I be overdrawn when I still have checks?"

There's a distinction between sound and music, and while it might not be all that apparent if you listen to AM radio a lot, it matters to a computer. Sound, such as the sound in wave files, is basically just digitized data that makes no sense to a computer, per se. Your system will blast whatever is in a wave file out to your speakers and think no more of it.

By comparison, music—whether it's written down as a score or stored in machine-readable form—is actual information. While it's usual to think of music as that which emerges from a speaker, to a musician it's more like what appears in FIG. 6-1. The information in FIG. 6-1 is stored using a very old encoding scheme. You don't have to understand how it works to use the information in this chapter.

Even if you can't sight read music, it's pretty easy to understand what FIG. 6-1 is up to. The black dots on the staff represent the notes to be played. Notes are defined in discrete pitches, and as such the position of each black dot can be thought of as an index into a lookup table of notes. This is a bit simplistic, as sheet music can express a lot more than just the notes to be played, but it will do for this explanation.

The music in FIG. 6-1 is a fiddle tune—you can hear it played on the audio portion of the companion CD-ROM for this book. However, it could just as easily be played on a saxophone or a piano. The sheet music defines only which notes are to be played, not the instruments to be used to play them.

Loftus Jones

Allegretto

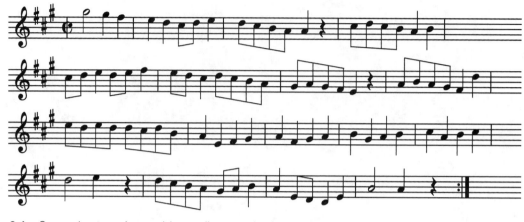

6-1 Some sheet music, an old encoding standard.

In practice, sheet music isn't quite as transparent as this. A complex work written for specific instruments will usually take into account the range and phrasing of the instruments. This matters less to the technology discussed in this chapter than it does to real instruments.

Quite a long time ago, back when digital synthesizers were first crawling out of their respective primordial swamps, a standard was devised to allow them to exchange note information. The musical instrument digital interface, or MIDI, meant that you could play the sounds of one synthesizer with the keyboard of another. Alternately, you could play the sounds of many synthesizers with a computer pretending to be a keyboard. The concept expanded—MIDI allows a keyboard synthesizer to be played through a guitar or a sax, for example, and for a computer to control not only the performance of music, but also things like stage lighting and mixdown.

The basis of MIDI is a standardized set of data blocks, or "messages" that tell any MIDI-compatible sound source which notes to play. In practice, these messages will also do things like tell a sound source how hard the keys of the keyboard have been struck, if a keyboard were involved at all, how long the sound should be sustained, and how long it should take to fade away.

In its initial form, MIDI information existed only in the cables that connected MIDI devices together. However, there's a lot to be said for storing MIDI information in a file. Given the facility to edit and play back stored MIDI files, a computer can become a sort of digital recording studio and musician's copyist—a word processor for music, in a sense. In fact, as is often the case when traditional paper functions find software equivalents, you can do things with MIDI files that typically can't be done, or done realistically, with conventional scores and human musicians.

There are, however, limitations to MIDI. For one thing, it's pretty well an instrumental medium—MIDI music doesn't include singing. The quality of instrumental MIDI music is limited by the quality of the music synthesizers of the device that play the music back, which varies enormously.

The first computer-basic MIDI music systems consisted of a computer driving an external synthesizer. If you have a sound card with MIDI support in your system, however, you'll have both these components in one box. A high-end sound card like the AudioMaster that was mentioned in the first chapter of this book will have an on-board MIDI synthesizer. Such cards can play MIDI music without requiring an external synthesizer.

One of the other limitations of MIDI as it was first implemented was that every synthesizer had a different set of "voices," or instrument sounds. In fact, most MIDI sound sources allowed their voices to be programmed, so that two examples of the same synthesizer would probably have different voices. This meant that if you scored a piece for three violins and cello, as played on your synthesizer, the odds were not particularly favorable that it would be played the same way on someone else's synthesizer.

The Windows multimedia extensions allow for MIDI music, which seems pretty obvious given the context of this chapter. In implementing MIDI for Windows, the multimedia extensions have provided it with several interesting new facets. The first is the same sort of device-independent approach to playing MIDI as turned up in chapter 2, in the discussion of playing wave files. You need not know anything about music, MIDI, or synthesizers to play MIDI files.

The second is something called the Windows MIDI mapper. This is a definition of standard instrument voices. No matter what sort of MIDI device is being driven by Windows—whether it's an external MIDI synthesizer or an internal sound card—playing music through the MIDI mapper will mean that the same voices are always available. They might not sound exactly the same, as differing synthesizers have differing capabilities, but they'll be reasonably close.

Using the MIDI mapper, a file that's scored for three violins and a cello won't unexpectedly play back in African log drums and a bassoon on some systems.

Under Windows, MIDI files are stored with the extension MID. Because MIDI music is just note data and other related information, rather than actual sampled sound, even fairly long scores with multiple parts don't usually result in particularly large files. Many of the problems that will crop up in the next chapter, when we deal with the enormity of Video For Windows files, never trouble MIDI data.

Advanced users of MIDI will look at the page count for this chapter and ask—typically in a loud, blustering voice—who it thinks it might be fooling. In its entirety, MIDI is a vast subject, rich with information, folklore, esoteric details, and all manner of flat-out lies. While you might find understanding MIDI to be fairly important if you actually want to write software to deal with the contents of MIDI files, using MIDI music in a Windows application doesn't really require that you do so.

This chapter deals with playing MIDI files, and will feature a brief excursion into their structures, but it won't get enmired in the workings of MIDI itself. A pretty substantial book could be written about this subject all by itself. Chances are, though, the aforementioned advanced users of MIDI would still ask who such a book thought it was fooling.

Playing MIDI music

If you've read the chapters of this book that deal with wave files and compact disc audio, you'll have encountered the MCI interface of the Windows multimedia extensions. The really powerful aspect of the MCI interface is that it rarely insists that you know very much about the files you're working with. As long as you're reasonably certain that what purports to be a MIDI file isn't really a digitized photograph of an albino Bengal tiger, the MCI interface will play its contents.

If you do get it wrong, the MCI interface will tell you so, without throwing protected-mode exceptions or other traditional forms of Windows complaints.

The MCI interface is very much into the idea of files as "black boxes," that is, data objects it must be able to understand but that software authors need not.

The following function is everything you'll need to play all four voices of Pachelbel's Canon, a Mozart requiem, the complete performance of Jethro Tull's "Thick as a Brick," or anything else you can find scored as a MIDI file. There are quite a few MIDI files in the \MIDI subdirectory of the companion CD-ROM for this book.

```
DWORD PlaySound(LPSTR path,HWND hwnd)
{
    MCI__OPEN__PARMS mciOpen;
    MCI__PLAY__PARMS mciPlay;
    char b[STRINGSIZE+1];
    unsigned long rtrn;

    mciOpen.wDeviceID=NULL;
    mciOpen.lpstrDeviceType="sequencer";
    mciOpen.lpstrElementName=path;
    if((rtrn=mciSendCommand(NULL,MCI__OPEN,MCI__OPEN__TYPE |
        MCI__OPEN__ELEMENT,(DWORD)(LPVOID)&mciOpen)) != 0L) {
        mciGetErrorString(rtrn,(LPSTR)b,STRINGSIZE);
```

```
        DoMessage(hwnd,b);
        return(OL);
    }

    soundID=mciOpen.wDeviceID;

    mciPlay.dwCallback=hwnd;
    if((rtrn=mciSendCommand(soundID,MCI__PLAY,MCI__NOTIFY,
        (DWORD)(LPVOID)&mciPlay)) != OL) {
        mciSendCommand(soundID,MCI__CLOSE,O,NULL);
        mciGetErrorString(rtrn,(LPSTR)b,STRINGSIZE);
        DoMessage(hwnd,b);
        return(OL);
    }

    return(1L);
}
```

The PlaySound function is agreeably simple, as is usually the case for things that call the MCI interface. Its path argument is the path to a MIDI file to be played. Its hwnd argument is a window handle. It assumes that there exists a global integer called soundID to store the driver identification value it fetches.

If you read through the section of chapter 2 that dealt with MCI calls to play wave files, this function should be pretty elementary. The first call to mciSendCommand opens a device called "sequencer", which is a MIDI driver. The second call plays the specified MIDI file though the device. The MCI interface will notify the window specified by hwnd when the music has finished playing by sending it an MM__MCINOTIFY message, as was discussed in chapter 2.

In order for this function to work, the MCI MIDI sequencer driver must be installed in your system. If you haven't done so previously, use the Control Panel of the Windows Program Manager to add it to your configuration. It's in the standard Windows driver list.

Understanding MIDI files

If you consult the Microsoft multimedia development kit's programmer's reference, you'll find that MIDI data is stored as RIFF files, just like wave files. In fact, this isn't exactly true—actually, it isn't true at all. The structure of MIDI files is quite a bit simpler. But beware Microsoft's documentation as it applies to MIDI. There are a few rather subtle mistakes in it.

Before you get into the grotty details of this section, it seems worth noting that you can skip it all with complete impunity. You need not know anything about how MIDI files are structured just to be able to play them back. If you do proceed, be warned that the nature of MIDI files is a bit perplexing, and that this section will omit much more than it includes, lest you find that you require the assistance of several friends to lift this book.

A MIDI file is comprised of variable-length chunks, much like RIFF files, although the chunk structure is quite a bit simpler. There are only two types of chunks in a MIDI file. Each MIDI file contains one header chunk and one or more track chunks. A header chunk has the following structure—sort of:

```
typedef struct {
    char MThd[4];
    unsigned long length;
    unsigned int format;
    unsigned int tracks;
    unsigned int division;
    } MIDIHEADER;
```

The MThd element of a MIDI file header will always contain the string "MThd". The remaining elements are not quite what they seem, as the byte orders of numbers in a MIDI file are stored in an order inverse to that of a PC's processor. The length value is the number of bytes in the header, minus the four bytes for the MThd string and the four bytes of the length value itself. The value of length should be six.

The format value defines the type of MIDI file involved. At present, there are three formats defined:

0   The file contains one multiple-channel music track.
1   The file contains one or more concurrent music tracks.
2   The file contains one or more sequentially independent single track patterns.

For the sake of this section, you can ignore the format value of a MIDI file header. You can also ignore the division value, which specifies the amount of time one musical element in the file—for example, a quarter note—will take.

To make reading the peculiar multiple-byte numbers in a MIDI file a bit more practical, let's define some functions to handle the task. To begin with, this function will read a single byte. It will also keep track of the number of bytes being read, the relevance of which will become apparent later on. All the file handling in this section will be performed with the standard C language streamed-file functions.

```
unsigned int Read8(FILE *fp,long *size)
{
    if(size != NULL) *size-=1;
        return(fgetc(fp));
}
```

This next function will read a sixteen-bit word from a MIDI file:

```
unsigned int Read16(FILE *fp,long *size)
{
    if(size != NULL) *size-=2;
    return((fgetc(fp) << 8) + fgetc(fp));
}
```

This function will read a long integer from a MIDI file:

```
unsigned long Read32(FILE *fp,long *size)
{
    if(size != NULL) *size-=4;
    return(((long)fgetc(fp) << 24) +
           ((long)fgetc(fp) << 16) +
           ((long)fgetc(fp) << 8) +
           ((long)fgetc(fp) ));
}
```

Finally, this function will read a variable-length number from a MIDI file. Variable-length numbers allow values to be stored in as many bytes as are required to contain them, without wasting any space. To read a variable-length number, you would fetch the first byte and test its high-order bit. If the high-order bit is clear, the whole number has been read. If it's set, clear the high-order bit, shift the number left by seven places, and repeat the procedure until a byte with a clear high- order bit is encountered.

```
unsigned long ReadVari(FILE *fp,long *size)
{
    long value;
    int c;

    c = fgetc(fp);
    if(size != NULL) *size-=1;
    value = (long)c;
    if(c & 0x80) {
        value &= 0x7fL;
        do {
            c=fgetc(fp);
            if(size != NULL) *size-=1;
            value=(value << 7)+(long)(c & 0x7f);
        } while(c & 0x80);
    }
    return(value);
}
```

Following the header of a MIDI file, there will be some track chunks, the number of chunks having been defined by the tracks element of the header. Each track consists of an identification string, a long integer defining its length and then one or more events. The header string is "MTrk".

A MIDI event can be one of a number of things. It can be a message to turn a particular note on or off, to change the voice being played by a particular channel, or to define something about the piece being played. While I won't get into all the subtlety and nuances of MIDI data here, the following information should give you an overview of the nature of MIDI.

Each MIDI event consists of a type byte followed by some data. The amount of data is determined by the type. A type byte consists of two nybbles. The high-order nybble defines the type and the low-order nybble defines the channel the event pertains to. MIDI allows for a maximum of 16 channels. In more traditional terms, this means that 16 distinct instruments can play at a time in a MIDI performance. Each instrument can play multiple notes at once, however, if your MIDI hardware allows for this.

Because MIDI synthesizers vary widely in their facilities, not all the event types mean exactly the same things to all synthesizers. Here are the event types:

80H	Turn a note off
90H	Turn a note on
A0H	Define the key pressure for a channel
B0H	Define a hardware-specific parameter for a channel
C0H	Change the voice for a channel
D0H	Set the aftertouch for a channel
E0H	Set the pitch bend for a channel
F7H	A system-exclusive message
FFH	A meta-event

Once again, I won't get too deeply into what all this means, as it's not really necessary in understanding MIDI to the extent that this chapter will deal with it.

System-exclusive events are messages that pertain only to specific MIDI devices. For example, a system-exclusive message would be used to program the way the voices in a Yamaha DX-7 synthesizer sounded. If it found its way to any other synthesizer, it would be ignored.

Meta-events are things that pertain to a piece as a whole, rather than to specific channels. The byte following the FFH byte of a meta-event defines what the data of the event pertains to. Here are the currently defined meta-events:

00H	The sequence number
01H	Some text
02H	A text copyright notice
03H	A text sequence or track name
04H	A text instrument name
05H	A text lyric, to be sung (if you like to sing to your computer)

06H	A text marker
07H	A text cue point
20H	A MIDI channel prefix
2FH	An end of track marker (every track ends with one of these)
51H	Set tempo
54H	Define the SMPTE offset
58H	Set the time signature
59H	Set the key signature
7FH	Sequencer-specific data

You'll be able to see how the data for some of these events is handled when you look at the MIDI file player later in this chapter.

With the fairly predictable structure of a MIDI file, it's possible to write a function to expand each of the events so it's readable in English. The Get Info function of the MIDI player, to be presented in a moment, does just that. The following is a listing of the header and the first two track chunks of the file AXEL_F.MID, from the companion CD-ROM for this book. This file contains the theme from *Beverly Hills Cop*.

```
MIDI FILE:          axel__f.mid
FORMAT:             1
TRACKS:             10
DIVISION:           96
```

```
SEQUENCE:           AXEL__F
INSTRUMENT:         Tempo/TimeSig
KEY SIGNATURE:      0 - MAJOR
TEMPO:              128000000
TIME SIGNATURE:     2/4
END OF TRACK
```

```
SEQUENCE:           SawWve/Clarinet/SqwWv
INSTRUMENT:         Roland SC-55
PROGRAM CHANGE:     program 81 - chan 0
NOTE ON:            note 64 - vel 95 - chan 0
NOTE ON:            note 64 - vel 0 - chan 0
NOTE ON:            note 67 - vel 95 - chan 0

NOTE ON:            note 66 - vel 0 - chan 0
NOTE ON:            note 64 - vel 95 - chan 0
NOTE ON:            note 64 - vel 0 - chan 0
END OF TRACK
```

The second track actually contains countless note on events, most of which have been excised in this example. Technically, a MIDI file should contain a note off for each note on. In many applications you'll find that this isn't the case, and that note off events occur only at the end of a piece. You'll probably need to refer to the reference listed at the end of this chapter to fully interpret the data in one of these listings.

There's one more thing to know about MIDI events. They each occupy a defined amount of time. The amount of time, the *delta time* in MIDI terms, is expressed as a variable-length number just before each event. I've ignored the delta-time values here, as they're not really relevant to listing a MIDI file's contents. You'll want to allow for them, however, if you write software to deal with MIDI directly.

The MIDIPLAY application

Figure 6-2 illustrates the main screen of MIDIPLAY—it should be somewhat familiar, looking as it does like most of the other players in this book. The MIDIPLAY software will allow you to play and get information about selected MIDI files. At present it allows you to play only one MIDI file at a time—if you'd like something to add to it, you might want to modify it to play multiple files, one after another, as was done with the compact disc audio player earlier in this book.

The complete C language source code for MIDIPLAY is illustrated in FIG. 6-3. In addition to MIDIPLAY.CPP, you'll need the MIDIPLAY.RC file, as shown in FIG. 6-4.

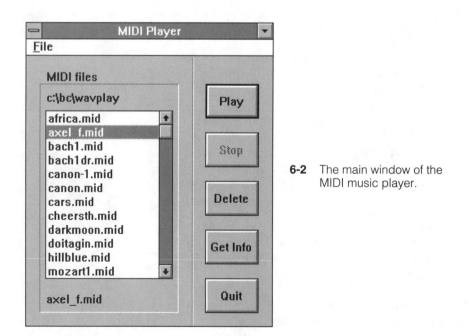

6-2 The main window of the MIDI music player.

Finally, you'll need a DEF file, as shown below, to complete the MIDIPLAY application:

```
NAME            MIDIPLAY
DESCRIPTION     'Midi Player'
EXETYPE         WINDOWS
CODE            PRELOAD MOVEABLE
DATA            PRELOAD MOVEABLE MULTIPLE
SEGMENTS        WM__TEXT LOADONCALL
HEAPSIZE        8192
STACKSIZE       8192
```

You'll also need a project file, as shown in FIG. 6-5, which can be replaced by a suitable MAKE file if you're not using the Borland C++ for Windows integrated development environment.

6-3 The C language source listing for the MIDI music player, MIDIPLAY.CPP.

```
/*
    Midi File Player
    Copyright (c) 1993 Alchemy Mindworks Inc.
*/
#include <windows.h>
#include <stdio.h>
#include <stdlib.h>
#include <dir.h>
#include <ctype.h>
#include <alloc.h>
#include <string.h>
#include <io.h>
#include <bwcc.h>
#include <dos.h>
#include <errno.h>
#include <math.h>
#include <mmsystem.h>

#define say(s)     MessageBox(NULL,s,"Yo...",MB_OK | MB_ICONSTOP);
#define saynumber(f,s)    {char b[128]; sprintf((LPSTR)b,(LPSTR)f,s); \
    MessageBox(NULL,b,"Debug Message",MB_OK | MB_ICONSTOP); }

#define ItemName(item,string)    { dlgH=GetDlgItem(hwnd,item); \
                                   SetWindowText(dlgH,(LPSTR)string); }
#define ItemOn(item)       { dlgH=GetDlgItem(hwnd,item); EnableWindow(dlgH,TRUE); }
#define ItemOff(item)      { dlgH=GetDlgItem(hwnd,item); EnableWindow(dlgH,FALSE); }

#define STRINGSIZE            128        /* how big is a string? */

#define MAIN_LIST            201         /* objects in the main window */
```

6-3 Continued.

```
#define MAIN_TEXT          202
#define MAIN_PATH          203


#define MAIN_PLAY          101         /* buttons and main menu items */
#define MAIN_STOP          102
#define MAIN_GETINFO       103
#define MAIN_DELETE        104
#define MAIN_ABOUT         105
#define MAIN_EXIT          107


#define INFO_LIST          101         /* objects in the Get Info box */


#define MESSAGE_STRING     101         /* message box object */


#define INFO_SIZE          4096L         /* size of information block */
#define EVENT_EXTRA        3


#define FILE_EXTENSION     "MID"        /* file extension? Could be... */

#ifndef max
#define max(a,b)           (((a)>(b))?(a):(b))
#endif
#ifndef min
#define min(a,b)           (((a)<(b))?(a):(b))
#endif


/* prototypes */
DWORD FAR PASCAL CapsDlgProc(HWND hwnd,WORD message,WORD wParam,LONG lParam);
DWORD FAR PASCAL SelectProc(HWND hwnd,WORD message,WORD wParam,LONG lParam);
DWORD FAR PASCAL AboutDlgProc(HWND hwnd,WORD message,WORD wParam,LONG lParam);
DWORD FAR PASCAL MessageDlgProc(HWND hwnd,WORD message,WORD wParam,LONG lParam);
DWORD FAR PASCAL InfoDlgProc(HWND hwnd,WORD message,WORD wParam,LONG lParam);
DWORD PlaySound(LPSTR path,HWND hwnd);

void ShowCurrentStats(HWND hwnd,unsigned int listbox,unsigned int textbox);
void ResetSelectorList(HWND hwnd,unsigned int listbox,unsigned int pathstring);
void DoMessage(HWND hwnd,LPSTR message);
void ShowInfo(HWND hwnd,GLOBALHANDLE h);
void lmemset(LPSTR s,int n,unsigned int size);
void Addline(LPSTR p,LPSTR b);
void ChannelMessage(int status,int c1,int c2,LPSTR p);
void AddMeta(LPSTR p,LPSTR msg,unsigned int type);

int DrawWave(HDC hdc,unsigned int x,unsigned int y,LPSTR filepath);
int testdisk(int n);
```

```
int lmemcmp(LPSTR d,LPSTR s,unsigned int size);
int YesNo(HWND hwnd,LPSTR message);

unsigned int Read8(FILE *fp,long *size);
unsigned int Read16(FILE *fp,long *size);
unsigned long Read32(FILE *fp,long *size);
unsigned long ReadVari(FILE *fp,long *size);

unsigned int Get16(LPSTR p);
unsigned long Get32(LPSTR p);

GLOBALHANDLE GetInfo(LPSTR b);
GLOBALHANDLE GetFileInfo(LPSTR b);

/* globals */

LPSTR messagehook;
char szFileSpec[145];
char bar[]="_____\n";
char szAppName[] = "MidiPlayer";
HANDLE hInst;

int soundID=-1;

#pragma warn -par
int PASCAL WinMain(HANDLE hInstance,HANDLE hPrevInstance,
                   LPSTR lpszCmdParam,int nCmdShow)
{
    FARPROC dlgProc;
    int r=0;

    BWCCGetVersion();

    hInst=hInstance;

    dlgProc=MakeProcInstance((FARPROC)SelectProc,hInst);
    r=DialogBox(hInst,"MainScreen",NULL,dlgProc);

    FreeProcInstance(dlgProc);

    return(r);
}

DWORD FAR PASCAL SelectProc(HWND hwnd,WORD message,WORD wParam,LONG lParam)
{
    MCI_GENERIC_PARMS mcigen;
```

6-3 Continued.

```
    HMENU hmenu;
    HWND dlgH;
    PAINTSTRUCT ps;
    HICON hIcon;
    FARPROC lpfnDlgProc;
    POINT point;
    GLOBALHANDLE h;
    char b[STRINGSIZE+1],s[STRINGSIZE+1];
    unsigned long l;
    unsigned int i;

    switch(message) {
        case MM_MCINOTIFY:
            mciSendCommand(LOWORD(lParam),MCI_CLOSE,MCI_WAIT,NULL);
            soundID=-1;
            ItemOn(MAIN_LIST);
            ItemOn(MAIN_PLAY);
            ItemOff(MAIN_STOP);
            ItemOn(MAIN_GETINFO);
            ItemOn(MAIN_DELETE);
            hmenu=GetMenu(hwnd);
            EnableMenuItem(hmenu,MAIN_PLAY,MF_ENABLED);
            EnableMenuItem(hmenu,MAIN_STOP,MF_GRAYED);
            EnableMenuItem(hmenu,MAIN_GETINFO,MF_ENABLED);
            EnableMenuItem(hmenu,MAIN_DELETE,MF_ENABLED);
            break;
        case WM_CTLCOLOR:
            if(HIWORD(lParam)==CTLCOLOR_STATIC ||
               HIWORD(lParam)==CTLCOLOR_DLG) {
                SetBkColor(wParam,RGB(192,192,192));
                SetTextColor(wParam,RGB(0,0,0));

                ClientToScreen(hwnd,&point);
                UnrealizeObject(GetStockObject(LTGRAY_BRUSH));
                SetBrushOrg(wParam,point.x,point.y);

                return((DWORD)GetStockObject(LTGRAY_BRUSH));

            }
            if(HIWORD(lParam)==CTLCOLOR_BTN) {
                SetBkColor(wParam,RGB(192,192,192));
                SetTextColor(wParam,RGB(0,0,0));

                ClientToScreen(hwnd,&point);
                UnrealizeObject(GetStockObject(BLACK_BRUSH));
```

```
                SetBrushOrg(wParam,point.x,point.y);

                return((DWORD)GetStockObject(BLACK_BRUSH));
            }
            break;
    case WM_SYSCOMMAND:
        switch(wParam & 0xfff0) {
            case SC_CLOSE:
                SendMessage(hwnd,WM_COMMAND,MAIN_EXIT,0L);
                break;
        }
        break;
    case WM_INITDIALOG:
        hIcon=LoadIcon(hInst,szAppName);
        SetClassWord(hwnd,GCW_HICON,(WORD)hIcon);
        ResetSelectorList(hwnd,MAIN_LIST,MAIN_PATH);
        if((l=SendDlgItemMessage(hwnd,MAIN_LIST,LB_GETCURSEL,0,0L)) != LB_ERR) {
            SendDlgItemMessage(hwnd,MAIN_LIST,LB_GETTEXT,
              (unsigned int)l,(DWORD)b);
            if(b[0] != '[') {
                ItemName(MAIN_TEXT,b);
            }
            else {
                ItemName(MAIN_TEXT," ");
            }
        }

        ItemOff(MAIN_STOP);
        hmenu=GetMenu(hwnd);
        EnableMenuItem(hmenu,MAIN_STOP,MF_GRAYED);
        break;
    case WM_PAINT:
        BeginPaint(hwnd,&ps);
        EndPaint(hwnd,&ps);
        break;
    case WM_COMMAND:
        switch(wParam) {
            case MAIN_LIST:
                switch(HIWORD(lParam)) {
                    case LBN_DBLCLK:
                        if(DlgDirSelect(hwnd,b,MAIN_LIST)) {
                            i=lstrlen(b);
                            if(b[i-1]=='\\') {
                                b[i-1]=0;
                                chdir(b);
                            }
```

```
                            else {
                                if(!testdisk(b[0]-'A'))
                                    setdisk(toupper(b[0])-'A');
                                else DoMessage(hwnd,"That drive is off line. "
                                    "Please check to see that "
                                    "there's a disk in it.");
                            }
                            ResetSelectorList(hwnd,MAIN_LIST,MAIN_PATH);
                        }
                        else {
                            SendMessage(hwnd,WM_COMMAND,MAIN_PLAY,0L);
                        }
                        break;
                case LBN_SELCHANGE:
                    if(!DlgDirSelect(hwnd,b,MAIN_LIST)) {
                        ItemName(MAIN_TEXT,b);
                    }
                    else {
                        ItemName(MAIN_TEXT," ");
                    }
                    break;

        }
        break;
    case MAIN_STOP:
        if(soundID != -1) {
            mcigen.dwCallback=hwnd;
            mciSendCommand(soundID,MCI_STOP,MCI_NOTIFY | MCI_WAIT,
                (DWORD)(LPVOID)&mcigen);
        }
        break;
    case MAIN_DELETE:
        if((l=SendDlgItemMessage(hwnd,MAIN_LIST,
            LB_GETCURSEL,0,0L)) != LB_ERR) {
            SendDlgItemMessage(hwnd,MAIN_LIST,LB_GETTEXT,
                (unsigned int)l,(DWORD)b);
            if(b[0] != '[') {
                wsprintf(s,"Do you want to delete %s?",(LPSTR)b);
                    if(YesNo(hwnd,s)) {
                    remove(b);
                    SendDlgItemMessage(hwnd,MAIN_LIST,LB_DELETESTRING,
                        (unsigned int)l,0L);
                    }
            }
        }
    }
```

```
            break;
        case MAIN_PLAY:
            if((l=SendDlgItemMessage(hwnd,MAIN_LIST,
               LB_GETCURSEL,0,0L)) != LB_ERR) {
                SendDlgItemMessage(hwnd,MAIN_LIST,LB_GETTEXT,
                    (unsigned int)l,(DWORD)b);
                if(b[0] != '[') {
                    if(PlaySound((LPSTR)b,hwnd)) {
                        ItemOff(MAIN_LIST);
                        ItemOff(MAIN_PLAY);
                        ItemOn(MAIN_STOP);
                        ItemOff(MAIN_GETINFO);
                        ItemOff(MAIN_DELETE);
                        hmenu=GetMenu(hwnd);
                        EnableMenuItem(hmenu,MAIN_PLAY,MF_GRAYED);
                        EnableMenuItem(hmenu,MAIN_STOP,MF_ENABLED);
                        EnableMenuItem(hmenu,MAIN_GETINFO,MF_GRAYED);
                        EnableMenuItem(hmenu,MAIN_DELETE,MF_GRAYED);
                    }
                }
            }
            break;
        case MAIN_GETINFO:
            if((l=SendDlgItemMessage(hwnd,MAIN_LIST,
               LB_GETCURSEL,0,0L)) != LB_ERR) {
                SendDlgItemMessage(hwnd,MAIN_LIST,LB_GETTEXT,
                    (unsigned int)l,(DWORD)b);
                if(b[0] != '[') {
                    if((h=GetInfo(b)) != NULL ) {
                        ShowInfo(hwnd,h);
                        GlobalFree(h);
                    } else DoMessage(hwnd,"Error reading file");
                }
            }
            break;
        case MAIN_ABOUT:
            if((lpfnDlgProc=MakeProcInstance((FARPROC)
              AboutDlgProc,hInst)) != NULL) {
                DialogBox(hInst,"AboutBox",hwnd,lpfnDlgProc);
                FreeProcInstance(lpfnDlgProc);
            }
            break;
        case MAIN_EXIT:
            SendMessage(hwnd,WM_COMMAND,MAIN_STOP,0L);
            PostQuitMessage(0);
            break;
```

```
            }
            break;

    }

    return(FALSE);
}

DWORD PlaySound(LPSTR path,HWND hwnd)
{
    MCI_OPEN_PARMS mciOpen;
    MCI_PLAY_PARMS mciPlay;
    char b[STRINGSIZE+1];
    unsigned long rtrn;

    mciOpen.wDeviceID=NULL;
    mciOpen.lpstrDeviceType="sequencer";
    mciOpen.lpstrElementName=path;
    if((rtrn=mciSendCommand(NULL,MCI_OPEN,MCI_OPEN_TYPE | MCI_OPEN_ELEMENT,
      (DWORD)(LPVOID)&mciOpen)) != 0L) {
        mciGetErrorString(rtrn,(LPSTR)b,STRINGSIZE);
        DoMessage(hwnd,b);
        return(0L);
    }

    soundID=mciOpen.wDeviceID;

    mciPlay.dwCallback=hwnd;
    if((rtrn=mciSendCommand(soundID,MCI_PLAY,MCI_NOTIFY,
      (DWORD)(LPVOID)&mciPlay)) != 0L) {
        mciSendCommand(soundID,MCI_CLOSE,0,NULL);
        mciGetErrorString(rtrn,(LPSTR)b,STRINGSIZE);
        DoMessage(hwnd,b);
        return(0L);
    }

    return(1L);
}

DWORD FAR PASCAL AboutDlgProc(HWND hwnd,WORD message,WORD wParam,LONG lParam)
{
    static HANDLE sound;
    static LPSTR psound;
    HANDLE handle;
    POINT point;
```

```
switch(message) {
    case WM_INITDIALOG:
        if((handle=FindResource(hInst,"Hello",RT_RCDATA)) != NULL) {
            if((sound=LoadResource(hInst,handle)) != NULL) {
                if((psound=LockResource(sound)) != NULL)
                    sndPlaySound(psound,SND_ASYNC | SND_MEMORY | SND_NOSTOP);
            }
        }
        return(TRUE);
    case WM_CTLCOLOR:
        if(HIWORD(lParam)==CTLCOLOR_STATIC ||
           HIWORD(lParam)==CTLCOLOR_DLG) {
            SetBkColor(wParam,RGB(192,192,192));
            SetTextColor(wParam,RGB(0,0,0));

            ClientToScreen(hwnd,&point);
            UnrealizeObject(GetStockObject(LTGRAY_BRUSH));
            SetBrushOrg(wParam,point.x,point.y);

            return((DWORD)GetStockObject(LTGRAY_BRUSH));

        }
        if(HIWORD(lParam)==CTLCOLOR_BTN) {
            SetBkColor(wParam,RGB(192,192,192));
            SetTextColor(wParam,RGB(0,0,0));

            ClientToScreen(hwnd,&point);
            UnrealizeObject(GetStockObject(BLACK_BRUSH));
            SetBrushOrg(wParam,point.x,point.y);

            return((DWORD)GetStockObject(BLACK_BRUSH));
        }
        break;
    case WM_COMMAND:
        switch(wParam) {
            case IDOK:
                if(psound != NULL) UnlockResource(sound);
                if(sound != NULL) FreeResource(sound);
                sndPlaySound(NULL,SND_SYNC);
                EndDialog(hwnd,wParam);
                return(TRUE);
        }
        break;
}

return(FALSE);
```

```
}

int YesNo(HWND hwnd,LPSTR message)
{
    FARPROC lpfnDlgProc;
    int r;

    messagehook=message;

    if((lpfnDlgProc=MakeProcInstance((FARPROC)MessageDlgProc,hInst)) != NULL) {
        r=DialogBox(hInst,"YesNoBox",hwnd,lpfnDlgProc);
        FreeProcInstance(lpfnDlgProc);
    }
    if(r==IDYES) return(1);
    else return(0);
}

void DoMessage(HWND hwnd,LPSTR message)
{
    FARPROC lpfnDlgProc;

    messagehook=message;

    if((lpfnDlgProc=MakeProcInstance((FARPROC)MessageDlgProc,hInst)) != NULL) {
        DialogBox(hInst,"MessageBox",hwnd,lpfnDlgProc);
        FreeProcInstance(lpfnDlgProc);
    }
}

void ShowCaps(HWND hwnd)
{
    FARPROC lpfnDlgProc;

    if((lpfnDlgProc=MakeProcInstance((FARPROC)CapsDlgProc,hInst)) != NULL) {
        DialogBox(hInst,"CapsBox",hwnd,lpfnDlgProc);
        FreeProcInstance(lpfnDlgProc);
    }
}

DWORD FAR PASCAL MessageDlgProc(HWND hwnd,WORD message,WORD wParam,LONG lParam)
{
    POINT point;
    HWND dlgH;

    switch(message) {
```

```
        case WM_INITDIALOG:
            dlgH=GetDlgItem(hwnd,MESSAGE_STRING);
            SetWindowText(dlgH,messagehook);
            return(TRUE);
        case WM_CTLCOLOR:
            if(HIWORD(lParam)==CTLCOLOR_STATIC ||
                HIWORD(lParam)==CTLCOLOR_DLG) {
                SetBkColor(wParam,RGB(192,192,192));
                SetTextColor(wParam,RGB(0,0,0));

                ClientToScreen(hwnd,&point);
                UnrealizeObject(GetStockObject(LTGRAY_BRUSH));
                SetBrushOrg(wParam,point.x,point.y);

                return((DWORD)GetStockObject(LTGRAY_BRUSH));

            }
            if(HIWORD(lParam)==CTLCOLOR_BTN) {
                SetBkColor(wParam,RGB(192,192,192));
                SetTextColor(wParam,RGB(0,0,0));

                ClientToScreen(hwnd,&point);
                UnrealizeObject(GetStockObject(BLACK_BRUSH));
                SetBrushOrg(wParam,point.x,point.y);

                return((DWORD)GetStockObject(BLACK_BRUSH));
            }
            break;
        case WM_COMMAND:
            switch(wParam) {
                case IDCANCEL:
                case IDOK:
                case IDYES:
                case IDNO:
                    EndDialog(hwnd,wParam);
                    return(TRUE);
            }
            break;
    }

    return(FALSE);
}

DWORD FAR PASCAL CapsDlgProc(HWND hwnd,WORD message,WORD wParam,LONG lParam)
{
    POINT point;
```

```
    switch(message) {
        case WM_INITDIALOG:
            return(TRUE);
        case WM_CTLCOLOR:
            if(HIWORD(lParam)==CTLCOLOR_STATIC ||
                HIWORD(lParam)==CTLCOLOR_DLG) {
                SetBkColor(wParam,RGB(192,192,192));
                SetTextColor(wParam,RGB(0,0,0));

                ClientToScreen(hwnd,&point);
                UnrealizeObject(GetStockObject(LTGRAY_BRUSH));
                SetBrushOrg(wParam,point.x,point.y);

                return((DWORD)GetStockObject(LTGRAY_BRUSH));

            }
            if(HIWORD(lParam)==CTLCOLOR_BTN) {
                SetBkColor(wParam,RGB(192,192,192));
                SetTextColor(wParam,RGB(0,0,0));

                ClientToScreen(hwnd,&point);
                UnrealizeObject(GetStockObject(BLACK_BRUSH));
                SetBrushOrg(wParam,point.x,point.y);

                return((DWORD)GetStockObject(BLACK_BRUSH));
            }
            break;
        case WM_COMMAND:
            switch(wParam) {
                case IDOK:
                    EndDialog(hwnd,wParam);
                    return(TRUE);
            }
            break;
    }

    return(FALSE);
}

int testdisk(int n)
{
    FILE *fp;
    char b[32];
    int r;
```

```
    SetErrorMode(1);
    sprintf(b,"%c:\\TEMP.DAT",n+'A');
    if((fp=fopen(b,"r")) != NULL) fclose(fp);

    if(_doserrno==ENOPATH) r=1;
    else r=0;

    SetErrorMode(0);
    return(r);
}

void lmemset(LPSTR s,int n,unsigned int size)
{
    unsigned int i;

    for(i=0;i<size;++i) *s++=n;
}

int lmemcmp(LPSTR d,LPSTR s,unsigned int size)
{
    unsigned int i;

    for(i=0;i<size;++i) {
        if(*d++ != *s++) return(1);
    }
    return(0);
}

void ResetSelectorList(HWND hwnd,unsigned int listbox,unsigned int pathstring)
{
    HWND dlgH;
    HCURSOR hSaveCursor,hHourGlass;
    char b[145];

    hHourGlass=LoadCursor(NULL,IDC_WAIT);
    hSaveCursor=SetCursor(hHourGlass);

    dlgH=GetDlgItem(hwnd,listbox);

    SendDlgItemMessage(hwnd,listbox,LB_RESETCONTENT,0,0L);
    getcwd(b,64);
    AnsiLower(b);
    SetDlgItemText(hwnd,pathstring,b);

    SendMessage(dlgH,WM_SETREDRAW,FALSE,0L);
```

```
    lstrcpy(b,"*.");
    lstrcat(b,FILE_EXTENSION);
    SendDlgItemMessage(hwnd,listbox,LB_DIR,0x0000,(long )b);

    lstrcpy(b,"*.*");
    SendDlgItemMessage(hwnd,listbox,LB_DIR,0xc010,(long )b);

    SendDlgItemMessage(hwnd,listbox,LB_SETCURSEL,0,0L);

    SendMessage(dlgH,WM_SETREDRAW,TRUE,0L);

    SetCursor(hSaveCursor);
}

GLOBALHANDLE GetInfo(LPSTR path)
{
    GLOBALHANDLE h;
    HCURSOR hSaveCursor,hHourGlass;

    hHourGlass=LoadCursor(NULL,IDC_WAIT);
    hSaveCursor=SetCursor(hHourGlass);

    h=GetFileInfo(path);

    SetCursor(hSaveCursor);

    return(h);
}

GLOBALHANDLE GetFileInfo(LPSTR path)
{
    static int chantype[] = {
        0, 0, 0, 0, 0, 0, 0, 0,
        2, 2, 2, 2, 1, 1, 2, 0
    };

    FILE *fp;
    GLOBALHANDLE h;
    LPSTR p;
    unsigned long ct,lookfor;
    long size,oldsize,pos;
    char b[STRINGSIZE+1];
    unsigned int c,i,c1,c2,tracks,tr;
    int syscont,status,running,needed,type,nomerge;
```

```c
if((h=GlobalAlloc(GMEM_MOVEABLE | GMEM_ZEROINIT,
    (long)(INFO_SIZE+STRINGSIZE+1)))==NULL) return(0);

if((p=GlobalLock(h))==NULL) {
    GlobalFree(h);
    return(0);
}

wsprintf(b,"MIDI FILE:\t\t %s\n",(LPSTR)path);
Addline(p,b);

lstrcpy(b,path);

if((fp=fopen(b,"rb"))==NULL) {
    GlobalUnlock(h);
    GlobalFree(h);
    return(NULL);
}

if(fread(b,1,4,fp) != 4) {
    GlobalUnlock(h);
    GlobalFree(h);
    fclose(fp);
    return(NULL);
}

if(memcmp(b,"MThd",4)) {
    GlobalUnlock(h);
    GlobalFree(h);
    fclose(fp);
    return(NULL);
}

size=Read32(fp,NULL);

pos=ftell(fp);

wsprintf(b,"FORMAT:\t\t\t %u\n",Read16(fp,NULL));
Addline(p,b);

wsprintf(b,"TRACKS:\t\t\t %u\n",(tracks=Read16(fp,NULL)));
Addline(p,b);

wsprintf(b,"DIVISION:\t\t %u\n",Read16(fp,NULL));
Addline(p,b);
```

6-3 Continued.

```
Addline(p,bar);

fseek(fp,pos+size,SEEK_SET);

for(tr=0;tr<tracks;++tr) {

    ct=0L;
    syscont=status=running=nomerge=0;

    if(fread(b,1,4,fp) != 4) {
        GlobalUnlock(h);
        fclose(fp);
        return(h);
    }

    if(memcmp(b,"MTrk",4)) {
        GlobalUnlock(h);
        fclose(fp);
        return(h);
    }

    oldsize=size=Read32(fp,&size);

    pos=ftell(fp);

    while(size > 0L && !ferror(fp)) {
        ct+=ReadVari(fp,&size);
        c=Read8(fp,&size);

        if(syscont && c != 0xf7) {
            Addline(p,"Bad file - expected continuation of system exclusive\n");
            GlobalUnlock(h);
            fclose(fp);
            return(h);
        }

        if((c & 0x80)==0) {
            if(!status) {
                Addline(p,"Bad file - unexpected running status\n");
                GlobalUnlock(h);
                fclose(fp);
                return(h);
            }
            running=1;
        }
```

```
else {
    status = c;
    running = 0;
}

needed=chantype[(status>>4) & 0x0f];

if(needed) {
    if(running) c1 = c;
    else c1 = Read8(fp,&size);

    if(needed > 1) c2=Read8(fp,&size);
    ChannelMessage(status,c1,c2,p);
    continue;;
}

switch(c) {
    case 0xff:
        type=Read8(fp,&size);
        lookfor=size-ReadVari(fp,&size);
        b[0]=0;
        i=0;
        while(size > lookfor) {
            c=Read8(fp,&size);
            if(i < STRINGSIZE) b[i++]=c;
        }
        b[i]=0;
        AddMeta(p,b,type);
        break;

    case 0xf0:
        lookfor = size-ReadVari(fp,&size);
        while(size > lookfor) c=Read8(fp,&size);
        if(c==0xf7 || nomerge==0) {

        }
        else syscont=1;
    case 0xf7:
        lookfor = size-ReadVari(fp,&size);
        while(size > lookfor) c=Read8(fp,&size);

        if(syscont && c ==0xf7) syscont=0;
        break;
    default:
        Addline(p,"Bad file - unexpected message");
        GlobalUnlock(h);
```

```
                        fclose(fp);
                        return(h);
                }
        }

        Addline(p,bar);

        fseek(fp,pos+oldsize,SEEK_SET);
    }

    GlobalUnlock(h);
    fclose(fp);
    return(h);

}

void ShowInfo(HWND hwnd,GLOBALHANDLE h)
{
    FARPROC lpfnDlgProc;

    messagehook=(LPSTR)(DWORD)h;
    if((lpfnDlgProc=MakeProcInstance((FARPROC)InfoDlgProc,hInst)) != NULL) {
        DialogBox(hInst,"InfoBox",hwnd,lpfnDlgProc);
        FreeProcInstance(lpfnDlgProc);
    }
}

DWORD FAR PASCAL InfoDlgProc(HWND hwnd,WORD message,WORD wParam,LONG lParam)
{
    GLOBALHANDLE h;
    HWND dlgH;
    POINT point;
    PAINTSTRUCT ps;
    LPSTR p;
    char b[STRINGSIZE+1];
    int i;

    switch(message) {
        case WM_INITDIALOG:
            h=(GLOBALHANDLE)messagehook;

            if((p=GlobalLock(h)) != NULL) {
                while(*p) {
                    while(*p=='\n') ++p;
                    for(i=0;*p != 0 && *p != '\n' && i < STRINGSIZE;++i)
```

```
                        b[i]=*p++;
                    b[i]=0;

                SendDlgItemMessage(hwnd,INFO_LIST,LB_INSERTSTRING,-1,(long)b);
                }
            GlobalUnlock(h);
        } else ItemName(INFO_LIST,"Error locking information");

        return(TRUE);
    case WM_CTLCOLOR:
        if(HIWORD(lParam)==CTLCOLOR_STATIC ||
           HIWORD(lParam)==CTLCOLOR_DLG) {
            SetBkColor(wParam,RGB(192,192,192));
            SetTextColor(wParam,RGB(0,0,0));

            ClientToScreen(hwnd,&point);
            UnrealizeObject(GetStockObject(LTGRAY_BRUSH));
            SetBrushOrg(wParam,point.x,point.y);

            return((DWORD)GetStockObject(LTGRAY_BRUSH));

        }
        if(HIWORD(lParam)==CTLCOLOR_BTN) {
            SetBkColor(wParam,RGB(192,192,192));
            SetTextColor(wParam,RGB(0,0,0));

            ClientToScreen(hwnd,&point);
            UnrealizeObject(GetStockObject(BLACK_BRUSH));
            SetBrushOrg(wParam,point.x,point.y);

            return((DWORD)GetStockObject(BLACK_BRUSH));
        }
        break;
    case WM_PAINT:
        BeginPaint(hwnd,&ps);
        EndPaint(hwnd,&ps);
        break;
    case WM_COMMAND:
        switch(wParam) {
            case IDOK:
                EndDialog(hwnd,wParam);
                return(TRUE);
        }
        break;
}
```

6-3 Continued.

```
    return(FALSE);
}

void Addline(LPSTR p,LPSTR b)
{

    if(((unsigned long)lstrlen(p)+(unsigned long)lstrlen(b)+STRINGSIZE+1) <
       (unsigned int)INFO_SIZE)
         lstrcat(p,b);
}

unsigned int Read8(FILE *fp,long *size)
{
    if(size != NULL) *size-=1;
    return(fgetc(fp));
}

unsigned int Read16(FILE *fp,long *size)
{
    if(size != NULL) *size-=2;
    return((fgetc(fp) <<8) + fgetc(fp));
}

unsigned long Read32(FILE *fp,long *size)
{
    if(size != NULL) *size-=4;
    return(((long)fgetc(fp) << 24) +
           ((long)fgetc(fp) << 16) +
           ((long)fgetc(fp) << 8) +
           ((long)fgetc(fp) ));
}

unsigned long ReadVari(FILE *fp,long *size)
{
    long value;
    int c;

    c = fgetc(fp);
    if(size != NULL) *size-=1;
    value = (long)c;
    if(c & 0x80) {
        value &= 0x7fL;
        do {
            c=fgetc(fp);
            if(size != NULL) *size-=1;
```

```
                value=(value << 7)+(long)(c & 0x7f);
        } while(c & 0x80);
    }
    return(value);
}

void ChannelMessage(int status,int c1,int c2,LPSTR p)
{
    char b[STRINGSIZE+1];
    int chan;

    chan=status & 0x0f;

    switch(status & 0xf0) {
        case 0x80:
            sprintf(b,"NOTE OFF:\t\t note %u - vel %u - chan %u\n",c1,c2,chan);
            break;
        case 0x90:
            sprintf(b,"NOTE ON:\t\t note %u - vel %u - chan %u\n",c1,c2,chan);
            break;
        case 0xa0:
            sprintf(b,"KEY PRESSURE:\t\t ctrl %u - val %u - chan %u\n",c1,c2,chan);
            break;
        case 0xb0:
            sprintf(b,"PARAMETER:\t\t p1 %u - p2 %u - chan %u\n",c1,c2,chan);
            break;
        case 0xc0:
            sprintf(b,"PROGRAM CHANGE:\t program %u - chan %u\n",c1,chan);
            break;
        case 0xd0:
            sprintf(b,"AFTERTOUCH:\t val %u - chan %u\n",c1,chan);
            break;
        case 0xe0:
            sprintf(b,"PITCH BEND:\t\t ctrl %u - val %u - chan %u\n",c1,chan);
            break;
    }

    Addline(p,b);
}

void AddMeta(LPSTR p,LPSTR msg,unsigned int type)
{
    char mm[2][6]={"MAJOR","MINOR"};
    char b[2*STRINGSIZE+1];

    switch(type) {
```

```
    case 0x00:
        wsprintf(b,"SEQUENCE NUMBER:\t %u\n",Get16(msg));
        break;
    case 0x01:
        wsprintf(b,"TEXT:\t\t\t %s\n",(LPSTR)msg);
            break;
    case 0x02:
        wsprintf(b,"COPYRIGHT:\t %s\n",(LPSTR)msg);
        break;
    case 0x03:
        wsprintf(b,"SEQUENCE:\t\t %s\n",(LPSTR)msg);
        break;
    case 0x04:
        wsprintf(b,"INSTRUMENT:\t\t %s\n",(LPSTR)msg);
        break;
    case 0x05:
        wsprintf(b,"LYRIC:\t %s\n",(LPSTR)msg);
        break;
    case 0x06:
        wsprintf(b,"MARKER:\t %s\n",(LPSTR)msg);
        break;
    case 0x07:
        wsprintf(b,"CUE POINT:\t %s\n",(LPSTR)msg);
        break;
    case 0x20:
        wsprintf(b,"CHANNEL PREFIX:\t %u\n",Get16(msg));
        break;
    case 0x2f:
        wsprintf(b,"END OF TRACK\n");
        break;
    case 0x51:
        wsprintf(b,"TEMPO:\t\t\t %lu\n",Get32(msg));
        break;
    case 0x58:
        wsprintf(b,"TIME SIGNATURE:\t\t %u/%u\n",msg[1],msg[0]);
        break;
    case 0x59:
        sprintf(b,"KEY SIGNATURE:\t\t %u - %s\n",msg[0],mm[msg[1] & 0x0001]);
        break;
    case 0x7f:
        break;
    }
    Addline(p,b);

}
```

```
unsigned int Get16(LPSTR p)
{
    return(((p[0] & 0x00ff) << 8) + (p[1] & 0x00ff));
}

unsigned long Get32(LPSTR p)
{
    return(
        (((long)(p[0] & 0x00ff)) << 24) +
        (((long)(p[1] & 0x00ff)) << 16) +
        (((long)(p[2] & 0x00ff)) << 8) +
        (long)(p[3] & 0x00ff));
}
```

6-4 The resource script for the MIDI music player, MIDIPLAY.RC.

```
MainScreen DIALOG 9, 24, 148, 156
STYLE WS_POPUP | WS_CAPTION | WS_SYSMENU | WS_MINIMIZEBOX
CAPTION "MIDI Player"
MENU MainMenu
BEGIN
  CONTROL "", 201, "LISTBOX", LBS_STANDARD | WS_CHILD | WS_VISIBLE, 12, 32, 76, 100
  LTEXT " MIDI files", -1, 8, 8, 84, 8, WS_CHILD | WS_VISIBLE | WS_GROUP
  CONTROL "", -1, "BorShade", BSS_GROUP | WS_CHILD | WS_VISIBLE, 8, 16, 84, 132
  LTEXT "", 202, 12, 136, 76, 8, WS_CHILD | WS_VISIBLE | WS_GROUP
  LTEXT "", 203, 12, 20, 75, 8, WS_CHILD | WS_VISIBLE | WS_GROUP
  CONTROL "", 204, "BorShade", 3 | WS_CHILD | WS_VISIBLE, 100, 0, 1, 156
  DEFPUSHBUTTON "Play", 101, 108, 16, 32, 20, WS_CHILD | WS_VISIBLE | WS_TABSTOP
  PUSHBUTTON "Stop", 102, 108, 44, 32, 20, WS_CHILD | WS_VISIBLE | WS_TABSTOP
  PUSHBUTTON "Delete", 104, 108, 72, 32, 20, WS_CHILD | WS_VISIBLE | WS_TABSTOP
  PUSHBUTTON "Get Info", 103, 108, 100, 32, 20, WS_CHILD | WS_VISIBLE | WS_TABSTOP
  PUSHBUTTON "Quit", 107, 108, 128, 32, 20, WS_CHILD | WS_VISIBLE | WS_TABSTOP
END

MainMenu MENU
BEGIN
    POPUP "&File"
    BEGIN
        MENUITEM "&Play", 101
        MENUITEM "&Stop", 102
        MENUITEM "&Get Info", 103
        MENUITEM "&Delete", 104
        MENUITEM "&About", 105
        MENUITEM SEPARATOR
        MENUITEM "E&xit", 107
    END
```

6-4 Continued.

```
END


AboutBox DIALOG 18, 18, 156, 104
STYLE WS_POPUP | WS_CAPTION
CAPTION "About MIDI Player..."
BEGIN
  CONTROL "", 102, "BorShade",
    BSS_GROUP | WS_CHILD | WS_VISIBLE | WS_TABSTOP, 8, 8, 140, 68
  LTEXT "MIDI Player 1.0\nCopyright (c) 1993\nAlchemy Mindworks Inc.\n"
    "This program is part of the book Multimedia Programming for Windows by "
    "Steven William Rimmer, published by Windcrest (Book 4484).",
    -1, 12, 12, 128, 60, WS_CHILD | WS_VISIBLE | WS_GROUP
  DEFPUSHBUTTON "Ok", IDOK, 116, 80, 32, 20, WS_CHILD | WS_VISIBLE | WS_TABSTOP
END


MessageBox DIALOG 72, 72, 144, 84
STYLE DS_MODALFRAME | WS_POPUP | WS_CAPTION
CAPTION "Message"
BEGIN
  CONTROL "", 102, "BorShade", BSS_GROUP | WS_CHILD | WS_VISIBLE, 4, 8, 136, 40
  CTEXT "", 101, 8, 12, 128, 32, WS_CHILD | WS_VISIBLE | WS_GROUP
  DEFPUSHBUTTON "Ok", IDOK, 108, 56, 32, 20, WS_CHILD | WS_VISIBLE | WS_TABSTOP
END


MidiPlayer ICON
BEGIN
    '00 00 01 00 01 00 20 20 10 00 00 00 00 00 E8 02'
    '00 00 16 00 00 00 28 00 00 00 20 00 00 00 40 00'
    '00 00 01 00 04 00 00 00 00 00 80 02 00 00 00 00'
    '00 00 00 00 00 00 00 00 00 00 00 00 00 00 00 00'
    '00 00 00 00 80 00 00 80 00 00 00 80 80 00 80 00'
    '00 00 80 00 80 00 80 80 00 00 80 80 80 00 C0 C0'
    'C0 00 00 00 FF 00 00 FF 00 00 00 FF FF 00 FF 00'
    '00 00 FF 00 FF 00 FF FF 00 00 FF FF FF 00 A0 00'
    '00 00 00 00 00 00 00 00 00 00 00 00 00 00 AA 00'
    '00 00 00 00 00 00 00 00 00 00 00 00 00 00 AA 22'
    '22 22 22 22 22 22 22 22 22 22 22 22 22 00 AA 22'
    '22 22 20 00 00 02 22 22 22 22 22 22 22 00 AA 22'
    '22 20 00 00 00 00 02 22 22 22 22 22 22 00 AA 22'
    '22 00 00 00 00 00 00 22 22 22 22 22 22 00 AA 22'
    '20 00 00 00 00 00 00 02 22 22 22 22 22 00 AA 22'
    '20 00 00 00 00 00 00 02 22 22 22 22 22 00 AA 22'
    '20 00 00 00 00 00 00 02 22 22 22 22 22 00 AA 22'
    '20 00 00 00 00 00 00 02 22 22 22 22 22 00 AA 22'
    '22 00 00 00 00 00 00 02 22 22 22 22 22 00 AA 22'
```

```
'22 20 00 00 00 00 02 02 22 22 22 22 22 00 AA 22'
'22 22 20 00 00 02 22 02 22 22 22 22 22 00 AA 22'
'22 22 22 22 22 22 22 02 22 22 22 22 22 00 AA 22'
'22 22 22 22 22 22 22 02 22 22 22 22 22 00 AA 22'
'22 22 22 22 22 22 22 02 22 22 22 20 22 00 AA 22'
'22 22 22 22 22 22 22 02 22 22 22 00 22 00 AA 22'
'22 22 22 22 22 22 22 02 22 22 22 00 22 00 AA 22'
'22 22 22 22 22 22 22 02 22 22 20 00 22 00 AA 22'
'22 22 22 22 22 22 22 02 22 22 00 00 22 00 AA 22'
'22 22 22 22 22 22 22 02 22 20 00 02 22 00 AA 22'
'22 22 22 22 22 22 22 02 20 00 00 02 22 00 AA 22'
'22 22 22 22 22 22 22 00 00 00 00 22 22 00 AA 22'
'22 22 22 22 22 22 22 00 00 00 02 22 22 00 AA 22'
'22 22 22 22 22 22 22 00 00 00 22 22 22 00 AA 22'
'22 22 22 22 22 22 22 00 00 02 22 22 22 00 AA 22'
'22 22 22 22 22 22 22 00 00 22 22 22 22 00 AA 22'
'22 22 22 22 22 22 22 00 02 22 22 22 22 00 AA 22'
'22 22 22 22 22 22 22 02 22 22 22 22 22 00 AA 22'
'22 22 22 22 22 22 22 22 22 22 22 22 22 00 AA AA'
'AA AA AA AA AA AA AA AA AA AA AA AA AA A0 AA AA'
'AA AA AA AA AA AA AA AA AA AA AA AA AA AA 00 00'
'00 00 00 00 00 00 00 00 00 00 00 00 00 00 00 00'
'00 00 00 00 00 00 00 00 00 00 00 00 00 00 00 00'
'00 00 00 00 00 00 00 00 00 00 00 00 00 00 00 00'
'00 00 00 00 00 00 00 00 00 00 00 00 00 00 00 00'
'00 00 00 00 00 00 00 00 00 00 00 00 00 00 00 00'
'00 00 00 00 00 00 00 00 00 00 00 00 00 00 00 00'
'00 00 00 00 00 00 00 00 00 00 00 00 00 00 00 00'
'00 00 00 00 00 00 00 00 00 00 00 00 00 00 00 00'
'00 00 00 00 00 00 00 00 00 00 00 00 00 00 00'
END


InfoBox DIALOG 11, 36, 292, 152
STYLE DS_MODALFRAME | WS_POPUP | WS_CAPTION
CAPTION "Information"
BEGIN
  DEFPUSHBUTTON "Ok", IDOK, 252, 128, 32, 20, WS_CHILD | WS_VISIBLE | WS_TABSTOP
  CONTROL "", 101, "LISTBOX",
    LBS_NOTIFY | LBS_USETABSTOPS | WS_CHILD | WS_VISIBLE | WS_BORDER | WS_VSCROLL,
    8, 8, 276, 112
END
YesNoBox DIALOG 72, 72, 144, 64
STYLE DS_MODALFRAME | WS_POPUP | WS_CAPTION
CAPTION "Message"
BEGIN
  CONTROL "", 102, "BorShade", BSS_GROUP | WS_CHILD | WS_VISIBLE, 4, 8, 136, 28
  CTEXT "", 101, 8, 12, 128, 20, WS_CHILD | WS_VISIBLE | WS_GROUP
```

```
DEFPUSHBUTTON "Yes", IDYES, 108, 40, 32, 20, WS_CHILD | WS_VISIBLE | WS_TABSTOP
    PUSHBUTTON "No", IDNO, 68, 40, 32, 20, WS_CHILD | WS_VISIBLE | WS_TABSTOP
END
```

6-5 The project file for the MIDI music player, MIDIPLAY.PRJ.

The PlaySound function in MIDIPLAY was discussed earlier in this chapter—what there was of it to discuss. In most applications involving MIDI files, this is all of MIDIPLAY you're likely to require. Note that you must have an MM__MCINOTIFY case in the message handler that will receive the message sent from the MCI interface when the MIDI file played by PlaySound terminates, as dealt with in chapter 2 of this book.

The GetFileInfo function of MIDIPLAY faces a rather more complex problem than the functions to get information for the other file types discussed in this book. A MIDI file listing can get pretty large, and it doesn't lend itself to a fixed data structure. As such, GetFileInfo allocates a large buffer and then proceeds to add text strings to it until it's full.

The size of the text buffer GetFileInfo uses is defined at the top of MIDIPLAY.CPP as INFO__SIZE. You can increase the size of this value if you like, although if you do it will take longer for GetFileInfo to complete its task. As it's currently configured, GetFileInfo will display the header and the first track or two of a MIDI file, which is typically where the interesting events are. Following this, you'll usually find little more than rolling hills and plummeting gorges of note data, which isn't all that useful.

Each time a string is to be added to the text buffer, it's handled by calling the Addline function, which checks to see if there's room in the buffer for the new string, and appends it to the existing text if there is. Each line is separated by a newline character.

The bulk of GetFileInfo handles unpacking a MIDI file's chunks. It begins by reading the header, which verifies the nature of the file and provides it with a total count for the number of track chunks to be read. The large for loop handles the tracks themselves.

In reading a track chunk, GetFileInfo reads its identification string and size. The size is stored twice—once in size, which will be decremented as the bytes of the chunk are read and once as oldsize, which will be used to locate the next chunk. In theory, one chunk should follow another immediately, but it's more reliable to locate a subsequent chunk based on the specified size of the chunk preceding it.

A chunk consists of as many events as will fit in size bytes, which is what the while loop in GetFileInfo keeps track of. Before reading each event, the ReadVari function is called to dispense with the delta-time value that precedes it. The Read8 function fetches the event-type byte.

System-exclusive messages can be split over multiple events—the syscont flag keeps track of this condition. Assuming that GetFileInfo is not in the midst of reading through a long system-exclusive message, it begins to decode the type byte.

The chantype array defines the number of bytes of data that accompany each of the event types in a MIDI file. When the appropriate number of bytes has been read, the ChannelMessage function is called to expand the data into something readable and add it to the text buffer.

System exclusive messages and meta-events are handled by the latter part of the while loop, in the switch statement. If a meta-event is encountered, its data is read into a buffer and the AddMeta function is called to decode it.

When a complete track has been unpacked—as indicated by the size value reaching zero—the while loop terminates and the next track is located.

The ShowInfo function opens the Information dialog, as shown in FIG. 6-6, and displays the text buffer created by GetFileInfo in its list-box control.

The Information dialog is managed by InfoDlgProc. You can see how the strings of the GetFileInfo text buffer are extracted and added to the list-box control in the WM__INITDIALOG case of its main switch statement. The rest of the function does what all the dialog handlers in this book have done—it makes the background of the box gray and waits for someone to come along and hit the OK button.

Information	
MIDI FILE:	axel_f.mid
FORMAT:	1
TRACKS:	10
DIVISION:	96
SEQUENCE:	AXEL_F
INSTRUMENT:	Tempo/TimeSig
KEY SIGNATURE:	0 - MAJOR
TEMPO:	128000000
TIME SIGNATURE:	2/4
END OF TRACK	
SEQUENCE:	SawWve/Clarinet/SqwWv
INSTRUMENT:	Roland SC-55

6-6 The Information dialog from the MIDI music player.

More MIDI

If you'll be creating multimedia applications that play instrumental music, there's a lot to be said for handling it with MIDI rather than as digitized wave files. The relative size of the files involved is among the best arguments for doing so, of course. In addition, MIDI music will typically sound cleaner and more professional, especially if you don't have the facilities of a sound studio to record your tracks.

You can obtain complete documentation for MIDI and MIDI files by contacting:

> The International MIDI Association
> 5316 West 57th St.
> Los Angeles, CA 90056
> (310) 649-6434

The code in the GetFileInfo function in this chapter is based on MIDIFILE.C, by Michael Czeiszperger, and can be found in the public domain.

7
Viewing Video for Windows AVI files

"Dreadfully sorry . . . I thought it was set on stun."

Video for Windows seems very much like a brilliant solution in search of a problem to solve. While its technology is interesting and seems potentially useful, it has a number of notable catches. Not the least of these is that you have to come up with a reason to want to see little movie clips appear in application windows on your screen.

Actually, some of the hardware limitations of the medium might be more troubling still. The AVI files (AVI stands for *audio visual interface*) that store Video for Windows movies run to enormity, even for for movies that don't play long enough to make it as brief commercials. The Video for Windows package comes with a wealth of example movies, but it requires a CD-ROM to store them.

This, in turn, could present some problems if you don't have a CD-ROM drive with a very high transfer rate. Some of the larger movies involved must be copied to a hard drive to be played, as they can't be read from a CD-ROM quickly enough. I'll get into this in greater detail later in this chapter.

In addition to requiring a lot of storage to use, Video for Windows needs a fast computer on which to run. A 66-megahertz '486 system with local bus video would suit it ideally. In fact, most '486 systems—of any speed and with any Super VGA display card—will run Video for Windows movies reasonably well. Lesser hardware will produce less convincing movies. Microsoft recommends a 16-megahertz '386 machine as the lower limit of hardware to handle Video for Windows.

The impressive aspect of Video for Windows—especially if you want to write applications to play its AVI files—is that it's quite well executed, fairly seamless in the way it integrates into other software, and capable of dealing with a wide variety of system hardware—even fairly old, ugly computers covered with dust and warts. As with much of Windows in general, it will work better with more capable equipment, but it won't entirely fail to work even if it's run on a relative antique.

Many software authors will have noticed Video for Windows in passing in the new products column of a magazine, and not thought of it since. To get a better feel for exactly what it's up to, you might want to install the AVIPLAY application from the \APPS directory of the companion CD-ROM for this book and play a few of the example movies from the \AVI directory. You must also install the AVI driver, as will be discussed in a moment.

Figure 7-1 illustrates AVIPLAY in action. The small window is a Video for Windows movie. This figure was captured from an 800×600-pixel screen. While you can have larger movie windows, there's a catch involved.

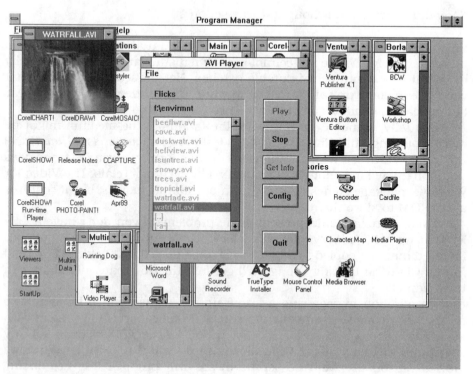

7-1 The Video For Windows player in action.

The catch in using Video for Windows is similar to the one mentioned earlier in this book in discussing animation—Video for Windows is essentially an animation protocol. Larger objects require more processor resources to animate. This means that it will take longer to move each frame of the animation from your hard drive—or wherever it resides—to your screen. If the time involved is long enough, your computer won't be able to run a Video for Windows movie at its intended speed. The AVI driver handles this by skipping frames in the movie being played, so while the action doesn't necessarily slow down, it does get jumpier.

A system with a slower processor or with less memory available might produce fairly erratic, unconvincing video for this reason. You can create AVI files with large movies in them—that is, with movies that occupy larger windows than the ones in FIG. 7-2—but you might find that your hardware really isn't up to running them.

All these limitations aside, integrating Video for Windows files into your own Windows multimedia applications can be very eye-catching. The typically static aspect of Windows, wherein only the mouse cursor moves, makes animated elements particularly noticeable.

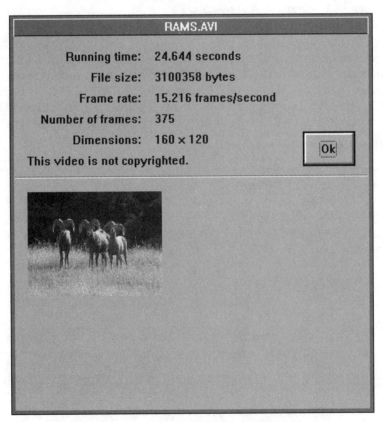

7-2 The Information dialog from the Video For Windows player.

This chapter will look at the techniques for playing back AVI files, as well as a few forays into their structure. There's quite a bit more you can do with them, although many of the additional applications are somewhat exotic. Despite their rather leading-edge qualities, Video for Windows AVI files are surprisingly easy to work with, and there are few variations on what you can use them for.

In working with AVI files, be warned that as of this writing there are numerous subtle errors in the Video for Windows manual as it deals with the MCI commands used to play them. All the code examples in this chapter have been compiled and run—in cases where they seem to disagree with the Video for Windows documentation, trust this book.

Finally, while the obvious manifestation of playing Video for Windows files will be a window with some video in it, you should also keep in mind that AVI files typically have digitized sound tracks along with their pictures. If you play an AVI file on a system with a sound card installed in it—and if you remember to turn on your speakers—you'll hear the sound it contains as well.

Playing AVI files

The process of playing AVI files is decidedly uncomplicated—experienced Windows programmers might wonder at first if some of the code has been left out of the example AVI player to be dealt with later in this chapter.

To begin with, in order to play AVI files you must have the AVI driver installed in Windows. The driver file is called MCIAVI.DRV, and must be located in the \WINDOWS\SYSTEM directory of your hard drive. It should also be listed in the [MCI] section of your SYSTEM.INI file, like this:

```
AVIVideo=mciavi.drv
```

The driver will be installed automatically if you install Video for Windows. You can do it yourself through the Windows Control Panel if you're using the driver from the companion CD-ROM for this book. It's in the \APPS directory.

Most AVI functions can be handled through calls to the MCI interface. For example, here's everything you'd have to do to play an AVI file:

```
DWORD PlayFlick(LPSTR path,HWND hwnd)
{
    MCI__DGV__OPEN__PARMS mciopen;
    MCI__DGV__PLAY__PARMS mciplay;
    MCI__GENERIC__PARMS mcigen;
    DWORD rtrn;
    char b[STRINGSIZE+1];

    mciopen.lpstrDeviceType="avivideo";
    mciopen.lpstrElementName=path;
```

```
if((rtrn=mciSendCommand(0,MCI__OPEN,MCI__OPEN__TYPE |
    MCI__OPEN__ELEMENT,(DWORD)(LPVOID)&mciopen)) != 0L) {
        mciGetErrorString(rtrn,(LPSTR)b,STRINGSIZE);
        DoMessage(hwnd,b);
        return(0L);
}

videoID=mciopen.wDeviceID;

mciplay.dwCallback=(DWORD)hwnd;
if((rtrn=mciSendCommand(videoID,MCI__PLAY,MCI__NOTIFY,
    (DWORD)(LPVOID)&mciplay)) != 0L) {
        mciSendCommand(videoID,MCI__CLOSE,0,NULL);
        mciGetErrorString(rtrn,(LPSTR)b,STRINGSIZE);
        DoMessage(hwnd,b);
        return(0L);
}

return(1L);
}
```

In this example of the PlayFlick function, the path argument is a path to the AVI file to be played. The hwnd argument is a window handle. There should be a global integer called videoID defined somewhere to hold the driver ID value returned by the MCI__OPEN call.

Much of the code in PlayFlick will be familiar if you've had a look at the compact disc audio player or the MCI version of the wave file player earlier in this book. There are two distinctions to note—the MCI device in question is called "avivideo" and a few of the data structures involved are specific to AVI files. The definitions for these additional structures are in a file called DIGITALV.H, in the \WINVIDEO\INCLUDE directory. While you don't need the complete Video for Windows package to play Video for Windows AVI files, you will require it to compile the AVIPLAY application from this chapter.

The first call to mciSendCommand opens the avivideo device and returns an ID value for it. The second call plays the AVI file passed to it. As with playing wave files and compact disc audio, the MCI interface will notify the window of your choice when the AVI file being played has terminated by sending an MM__MCINOTIFY message to it.

Having executed the second call to mciSendCommand, a window will appear on your screen, video will display in it, and the accompanying sound track will play through your sound card if you have one.

You might find it useful to be able to modify characteristics of the window in which an AVI file is playing. You can do this by having the MCI interface return an HWND to the window in which an AVI file is playing. For example, you could use this handle to reposition a window. Here's how to fetch the handle:

```
MCI__DGV__STATUS__PARMS mcistat;

if((rtrn=mciSendCommand(videoID,MCI__STATUS,MCI__DGV__STATUS__HWND,
    (DWORD)(LPVOID)&mcistat)) != 0L) {
        mciGetErrorString(rtrn,(LPSTR)b,STRINGSIZE);
        DoMessage(hwnd,b);
        return(0L);
}
```

Having executed this bit of code, the HWND for the window referenced by the videoID value returned when you opened the "avivideo" device will be in the dwReturn element of the mcistat object.

Note that in most of the MCI calls that have to do with playing AVI files the parameter blocks are specialized—for example, MCI_DGV_STATUS_PARMS rather than the MCI_STATUS_PARMS object used for compact disc audio or playing wave files. It's important to keep track of these and use them where they're expected, as they typically have different internal structures. The Video for Windows manual lists the MCI calls that are relevant to playing AVI files in its appendix F.

As with the other applications in this book that use MCI calls, you should have a case in the message handler of the window that will receive notification of the termination of the AVI file being played to respond to it. In its simplest form, it looks like this:

```
case MM__MCINOTIFY:
    mciSendCommand(LOWORD(lParam),MCI__CLOSE,MCI__WAIT,NULL);
    videoID=-1;
    break;
```

The low-order word of the lParam argument to the function handler of the window in question is the ID value of the driver—in this example, it should be the same as the one in videoID. The call to sendMciCommand will close the driver and wait until the close operation is complete before it returns.

You can terminate an AVI file that's playing in one of two ways. Either double-click on the system menu of the window that contains it or issue this MCI call:

```
MCI__GENERIC__PARMS mcigen;

mciSendCommand(videoID,MCI__STOP,
    MCI__NOTIFY | MCI__WAIT,(DWORD)(LPVOID)&mcigen);
```

The MCI_STOP command will cause an MM_MCINOTIFY message to be sent to the destination window for the driver specified by videoID, just as if the movie had ended on its own.

There are no external buffers to free in playing an AVI file—all the storage allocated by the driver when it was opened is deallocated when the MCI_CLOSE call is issued.

Getting information about AVI files

It seems rather a shame that there aren't defined text chunks in AVI files—they could be called "credits." Mind, the subroutines for a Video for Windows movie would probably be the gaffer and the key grip.

As with playing wave files, getting information about the movie in an AVI file requires a foray into the structure of the files themselves. Like wave files, an AVI movie is actually a RIFF file—you might want to have a look at the discussion of RIFF files in chapter 2 if you haven't done so previously.

The structure of AVI files is rather more complex than that of a simple wave file. Fortunately, it's not necessary to really get into the grotty details of one. There's a single data structure of interest if you'd like to know the basic parameters of an AVI file, and it's relatively easy to find. This is the complete structure of an AVI file:

```
RIFF('AVI'
    LIST('hdrl'
        avih(<MainAVIHeader>)
        LIST ('strl'
            strh(<Stream header>)
            strf(<Stream format>)
            ... additional header data
    LIST('movi'
        { LIST('rec'
                SubChunk...
              )
            ¦ SubChunk } ...
    )
    [ <AVIIndex> ]
)
```

Note that this is how Microsoft expresses it—it's not calculated to be immediately fathomable. You can find out most of the interesting things about an AVI file by fetching the object called <MainAVIHeader> in the preceding diagram. This is what it looks like:

```
typedef struct {
    DWORD dwMicroSecPerFrame;
    DWORD dwMaxBytesPerSec;
    DWORD dwPaddingGranularity;
    DWORD dwFlags;
    DWORD dwTotalFrames;
    DWORD dwInitialFrames;
    DWORD dwStreams;
    DWORD dwSuggestedBufferSize;
    DWORD dwWidth;
    DWORD dwHeight;
```

```
        DWORD dwScale;
        DWORD dwRate;
        DWORD dwStart;
        DWORD dwLength;
        } MAINAVIHEADER;
```

Not all the fields in a MAINAVIHEADER object are of immediate use. The dwMicroSecPerFrame element defines the time in microseconds each frame in the movie should remain visible until it's superseded. The dwTotal-Frames value specifies the actual number of frames in the movie. The dwWidth and dwHeight elements specify the size of the rectangle in pixels that the movie will occupy. The dwLength value defines the total playing time.

You can fetch the MAINAVIHEADER object of an AVI file by descending into the file and locating a LIST chunk having the fccType element 'hdrl'. Having done so, find a subchunk having the chunk ID 'avih'. Then read sizeof (MAINAVIHEADER) bytes into a MAINAVIHEADER object. Here is a function to perform this bit of chainsaw juggling:

```
HMMIO h;
MMCKINFO mmParent,mmSub,mmSubSub;
MAINAVIHEADER avi;

if((h=mmioOpen(path,NULL,MMIO__READ)) == NULL) {
    DoMessage(hwnd,"Error opening file");
    return(0);
}

mmParent.fccType=mmioFOURCC('A','V','I',' ');
if(mmioDescend(h,(LPMMCKINFO)&mmParent,NULL,MMIO__FINDRIFF)) {
    mmioClose(h,0);
    DoMessage(hwnd,"Error finding AVI chunk");
    return(0);
}

mmSub.fccType=mmioFOURCC('h','d','r','l');
if(mmioDescend(h,(LPMMCKINFO)&mmSub,
    (LPMMCKINFO)&mmParent,MMIO__FINDLIST)) {
        DoMessage(hwnd,"Error finding hdrl chunk");
        mmioClose(h,0);
        return(0);
}

mmSubSub.ckid=mmioFOURCC('a','v','i','h');
if(mmioDescend(h,(LPMMCKINFO)&mmSubSub,
    (LPMMCKINFO)&mmSub,MMIO__FINDCHUNK)) {
        DoMessage(hwnd,"Error finding avih chunk");
        mmioClose(h,0);
```

```
            return(0);
    }

    n=min((unsigned int)mmSub.cksize,sizeof(MAINAVIHEADER));
    if(mmioRead(h,(LPSTR)&avi,n) != n) {
        DoMessage(hwnd,"Error reading header chunk");
        mmioClose(h,0);
        return(0);
    }

    mmioClose(h,0);
    return(1);
```

Let's look at how to format this data in a useful way in the AVIPLAY application, to be discussed in a moment. Figure 7-2 illustrates the file information dialog from AVIPLAY.

The largest part of the information box in FIG. 7-2 is occupied by a bitmapped image of the first frame in the AVI file under scrutiny. Managing this seems as if it should entail a lot more searching about with RIFF chunks, LISTs, and other demons of the multimedia development kit. In fact, it's exceedingly easy to arrive at, as there's actually an MCI call to handle it. This is a function to display the first frame of an AVI file. It's typically called from the WM_PAINT message handler of the window in which to display the frame.

```
    int ShowFrame(LPSTR path,HDC hdc)
    {
        MCI_DGV_OPEN_PARMS mciopen;
        MCI_DGV_UPDATE_PARMS mciupdate;
        int id;

        mciopen.lpstrDeviceType="avivideo";
        mciopen.lpstrElementName=path;
        if(mciSendCommand(0,MCI_OPEN,MCI_OPEN_TYPE |
            MCI_OPEN_ELEMENT,(DWORD)(LPVOID)&mciopen) != 0L) {
                return(0);
        }

        id=mciopen.wDeviceID;

        mciupdate.hDC=hdc;
        mciupdate.rc.left=0;
        mciupdate.rc.top=0;
        mciupdate.rc.right=(unsigned int)width;
        mciupdate.rc.bottom=(unsigned int)depth;

        if(mciSendCommand(id,MCI_UPDATE,MCI_DGV_UPDATE_HDC |
            MCI_DGV_UPDATE_PAINT,(DWORD)(LPVOID)&mciupdate) != 0L) {
                mciSendCommand(id,MCI_CLOSE,0,NULL);
```

```
                return(0);
        }

        mciSendCommand(id,MCI__CLOSE,0,NULL);

        return(1);
}
```

In this example, the width and depth values are assumed to have been loaded with the actual width and depth of the frame to be displayed, presumably as found through a previous call to get the MAINAVIHEADER header object for the file. The hdc argument is the device context handle returned by BeginPaint, and the path argument specifies the AVI file to be read. This code will display the frame in the upper left corner of the window in question—there's a more practical application of it in AVIPLAY itself.

The AVIPLAY application

The AVI file player that generated FIG. 7-1 is no more complicated than the other MCI-based applications discussed in this book. It will allow you to select a file and get information about it or play it. You can also configure the playback parameters once the movie starts rolling by clicking on its Config button.

The complete C language source code for AVIPLAY is illustrated in FIG. 7-3. In addition to AVIPLAY.CPP, you'll need the AVIPLAY.RC file, as shown in FIG. 7-4.

7-3 The C language source listing for the Video For Windows movie player, AVIPLAY.CPP.

```
/*

    Video for Windows Player
    Copyright (c) 1993 Alchemy Mindworks Inc.

*/

#include <windows.h>
#include <stdio.h>
#include <stdlib.h>
#include <dir.h>
#include <ctype.h>
#include <alloc.h>
#include <string.h>
#include <io.h>
#include <bwcc.h>
#include <dos.h>
#include <errno.h>
```

```
#include <math.h>
#include <mmsystem.h>
#include <mciavi.h>          /* in \WINVIDEO\INCLUDE */
#include <digitalv.h>         /* in \WINVIDEO\INCLUDE */

#define say(s)     MessageBox(NULL,s,"Yo...",MB_OK | MB_ICONSTOP);
#define saynumber(f,s)    {char b[128]; sprintf((LPSTR)b,(LPSTR)f,s); \
    MessageBox(NULL,b,"Debug Message",MB_OK | MB_ICONSTOP); }

#define ItemName(item,string)    { dlgH=GetDlgItem(hwnd,item); \
                                   SetWindowText(dlgH,(LPSTR)string); }
#define ItemOn(item)        { dlgH=GetDlgItem(hwnd,item); EnableWindow(dlgH,TRUE); }
#define ItemOff(item)       { dlgH=GetDlgItem(hwnd,item); EnableWindow(dlgH,FALSE); }

#define FILE_EXTENSION     "AVI"        /* file extension? Could be... */

#define STRINGSIZE         129         /* how big is a string? */

#define MAIN_PLAY          101         /* buttons and main menu items */
#define MAIN_STOP          102
#define MAIN_GETINFO       103
#define MAIN_CONFIG        104
#define MAIN_ABOUT         105
#define MAIN_EXIT          107

#define MAIN_LIST          201
#define MAIN_STATUS        202
#define MAIN_PATH          203

#define INFO_RUNTIME       101         /* resources in the Get Info box */
#define INFO_FILESIZE      102
#define INFO_FRAMERATE     103
#define INFO_FRAMECOUNT    104
#define INFO_DIMENSIONS    105
#define INFO_COPYRIGHT     106

#define INFO_FRAMELEFT     16          /* where the example frame will appear */
#define INFO_FRAMETOP      180

#define MESSAGE_STRING     101         /* message box object */

#ifndef max
#define max(a,b)           (((a)>(b))?(a):(b))
```

7-3 Continued.
```
#endif
#ifndef min
#define min(a,b)          (((a)<(b))?(a):(b))
#endif

#define AVIF_HASINDEX        0x00000010L
#define AVIF_MUSTUSEINDEX    0x00000020L
#define AVIF_ISINTERLEAVED   0x00000100L
#define AVIF_WASCAPTUREFILE  0x00010000L
#define AVIF_COPYRIGHTED     0x00020000L

typedef struct {
    DWORD dwMicroSecPerFrame;
    DWORD dwMaxBytesPerSec;
    DWORD dwPaddingGranularity;
    DWORD dwFlags;
    DWORD dwTotalFrames;
    DWORD dwInitialFrames;
    DWORD dwStreams;
    DWORD dwSuggestedBufferSize;
    DWORD dwWidth;
    DWORD dwHeight;
    DWORD dwScale;
    DWORD dwRate;
    DWORD dwStart;
    DWORD dwLength;
    } MAINAVIHEADER;

typedef struct {
    char filename[STRINGSIZE+1];
    unsigned long filesize;
    MAINAVIHEADER avi;
    } FLICK;

/* prototypes */
long FAR PASCAL WaitProc(HWND hwnd,unsigned int message,
                         unsigned int wParam,LONG lParam);
DWORD FAR PASCAL SelectProc(HWND hwnd,WORD message,WORD wParam,LONG lParam);
DWORD FAR PASCAL AboutDlgProc(HWND hwnd,WORD message,WORD wParam,LONG lParam);
DWORD FAR PASCAL MessageDlgProc(HWND hwnd,WORD message,WORD wParam,LONG lParam);
DWORD FAR PASCAL InfoDlgProc(HWND hwnd,WORD message,WORD wParam,LONG lParam);
DWORD PlayFlick(LPSTR path,HWND hwnd);

int testdisk(int n);
int GetInfo(FLICK *flick,LPSTR path,HWND hwnd);
```

```c
int ShowFrame(LPSTR path,HDC hdc,FLICK far *flick);

void ShowInfo(HWND hwnd,FLICK far *flick);

void Config(HWND hwnd);
void DoMessage(HWND hwnd,LPSTR message);
void lmemset(LPSTR s,int n,unsigned int size);

void ResetSelectorList(HWND hwnd,unsigned int listbox,unsigned int pathstring);

/* globals */
LPSTR messagehook;

char stopped[]=" Stay tuned";
char szAppName[] = "AVIPlayer";
HANDLE hInst;

int videoID=-1;

#pragma warn -par
int PASCAL WinMain(HANDLE hInstance,HANDLE hPrevInstance,
                   LPSTR lpszCmdParam,int nCmdShow)
{
    FARPROC dlgProc;
    int r=0;

    BWCCGetVersion();

    hInst=hInstance;

    dlgProc=MakeProcInstance((FARPROC)SelectProc,hInst);
    r=DialogBox(hInst,"MainScreen",NULL,dlgProc);

    FreeProcInstance(dlgProc);

    return(r);
}
#pragma warn +par

DWORD FAR PASCAL SelectProc(HWND hwnd,WORD message,WORD wParam,LONG lParam)
{
    MCI_GENERIC_PARMS mcigen;
    PAINTSTRUCT ps;
    static HICON hIcon;
    FARPROC lpfnDlgProc;
    POINT point;
```

```
        HWND dlgH;
        HMENU hmenu;
        static FLICK flick;
        char b[STRINGSIZE+1];
        unsigned long l;
        int i;

        switch(message) {
            case MM_MCINOTIFY:
                mciSendCommand(LOWORD(lParam),MCI_CLOSE,MCI_WAIT,NULL);
                videoID=-1;
                ItemOn(MAIN_LIST);
                ItemOn(MAIN_PLAY);
                ItemOn(MAIN_GETINFO);
                ItemOff(MAIN_STOP);
                ItemOff(MAIN_CONFIG);
                hmenu=GetMenu(hwnd);
                EnableMenuItem(hmenu,MAIN_PLAY,MF_ENABLED);
                EnableMenuItem(hmenu,MAIN_GETINFO,MF_ENABLED);
                EnableMenuItem(hmenu,MAIN_STOP,MF_GRAYED);
                EnableMenuItem(hmenu,MAIN_CONFIG,MF_GRAYED);
                    ItemName(MAIN_STATUS,stopped);
                break;
            case WM_CTLCOLOR:
                if(HIWORD(lParam)==CTLCOLOR_STATIC ||
                   HIWORD(lParam)==CTLCOLOR_DLG) {
                    SetBkColor(wParam,RGB(192,192,192));
                    SetTextColor(wParam,RGB(0,0,0));

                    ClientToScreen(hwnd,&point);
                    UnrealizeObject(GetStockObject(LTGRAY_BRUSH));
                    SetBrushOrg(wParam,point.x,point.y);

                    return((DWORD)GetStockObject(LTGRAY_BRUSH));

                }
                if(HIWORD(lParam)==CTLCOLOR_BTN) {
                    SetBkColor(wParam,RGB(192,192,192));
                    SetTextColor(wParam,RGB(0,0,0));

                    ClientToScreen(hwnd,&point);
                    UnrealizeObject(GetStockObject(BLACK_BRUSH));
                    SetBrushOrg(wParam,point.x,point.y);

                    return((DWORD)GetStockObject(BLACK_BRUSH));
```

```
        }
        break;
case WM_SYSCOMMAND:
    switch(wParam & 0xfff0) {
        case SC_CLOSE:
            SendMessage(hwnd,WM_COMMAND,MAIN_EXIT,0L);
            break;
    }
    break;
case WM_INITDIALOG:
    hIcon=LoadIcon(hInst,szAppName);
    SetClassWord(hwnd,GCW_HICON,(WORD)hIcon);
    ResetSelectorList(hwnd,MAIN_LIST,MAIN_PATH);

    ItemOff(MAIN_STOP);
    ItemOff(MAIN_CONFIG);
    hmenu=GetMenu(hwnd);
    EnableMenuItem(hmenu,MAIN_STOP,MF_GRAYED);
    EnableMenuItem(hmenu,MAIN_CONFIG,MF_GRAYED);

    ItemName(MAIN_STATUS,stopped);

    break;
case WM_PAINT:
    BeginPaint(hwnd,&ps);
    EndPaint(hwnd,&ps);
    break;
case WM_COMMAND:
    switch(wParam) {
        case MAIN_LIST:
            switch(HIWORD(lParam)) {
                case LBN_DBLCLK:
                    if(DlgDirSelect(hwnd,b,MAIN_LIST)) {
                        i=lstrlen(b);
                        if(b[i-1]=='\\') {
                            b[i-1]=0;
                            chdir(b);
                        }
                        else {
                            if(!testdisk(b[0]-'A'))
                                setdisk(toupper(b[0])-'A');
                            else DoMessage(hwnd,
                                "That drive is off line. "
                                "Please check to see that "
                                "there's a disk in it.");
                        }
```

```
                            ResetSelectorList(hwnd,MAIN_LIST,MAIN_PATH);
                    }
                else SendMessage(hwnd,WM_COMMAND,MAIN_PLAY,0L);
                break;
            case LBN_SELCHANGE:
                break;


        }
        break;

    case MAIN_STOP:
        if(videoID != -1) {
            mcigen.dwCallback=hwnd;
            mciSendCommand(videoID,MCI_STOP,MCI_NOTIFY |
                MCI_WAIT,(DWORD)(LPVOID)&mcigen);
        }
        break;
    case MAIN_PLAY:
        if((l=SendDlgItemMessage(hwnd,MAIN_LIST,
            LB_GETCURSEL,0,0L)) != LB_ERR) {
            SendDlgItemMessage(hwnd,MAIN_LIST,LB_GETTEXT,
                (unsigned int)l,(DWORD)b);
            if(b[0] != '[') {
                if(PlayFlick(b,hwnd)) {
                    ItemName(MAIN_STATUS,b);

                    ItemOff(MAIN_LIST);
                    ItemOff(MAIN_PLAY);
                    ItemOff(MAIN_GETINFO);
                    ItemOn(MAIN_STOP);
                    ItemOn(MAIN_CONFIG);
                    hmenu=GetMenu(hwnd);
                    EnableMenuItem(hmenu,MAIN_PLAY,MF_GRAYED);
                    EnableMenuItem(hmenu,MAIN_GETINFO,MF_GRAYED);
                    EnableMenuItem(hmenu,MAIN_STOP,MF_ENABLED);
                    EnableMenuItem(hmenu,MAIN_CONFIG,MF_ENABLED);
                }
            }
        }
        break;
    case MAIN_CONFIG:
        Config(hwnd);
        break;
    case MAIN_GETINFO:
        if((l=SendDlgItemMessage(hwnd,MAIN_LIST,
```

```
                              LB_GETCURSEL,0,0L)) != LB_ERR) {
                           SendDlgItemMessage(hwnd,MAIN_LIST,
                             LB_GETTEXT,(unsigned int)l,(DWORD)b);
                           if(b[0] != '[') {
                                 if(GetInfo(&flick,b,hwnd)) {
                                      ShowInfo(hwnd,&flick);
                                 }
                           }
                        }
                        break;
                  case MAIN_ABOUT:
                     if((lpfnDlgProc=MakeProcInstance((FARPROC)
                       AboutDlgProc,hInst)) != NULL) {
                          DialogBox(hInst,"AboutBox",hwnd,lpfnDlgProc);
                          FreeProcInstance(lpfnDlgProc);
                     }
                     break;
                  case MAIN_EXIT:
                     SendMessage(hwnd,WM_COMMAND,MAIN_STOP,0L);
                     FreeResource(hIcon);
                     PostQuitMessage(0);
                     break;
            }
            break;

    }

    return(FALSE);
}

DWORD PlayFlick(LPSTR path,HWND hwnd)
{
    MCI_DGV_OPEN_PARMS mciopen;
    MCI_DGV_PLAY_PARMS mciplay;
    MCI_GENERIC_PARMS mcigen;
    DWORD rtrn;
    char b[STRINGSIZE+1];

    if(videoID != -1) {
        mcigen.dwCallback=hwnd;
        mciSendCommand(videoID,MCI_STOP,0,(DWORD)(LPVOID)&mcigen);
        videoID=-1;
    }

    mciopen.lpstrDeviceType="avivideo";
    mciopen.lpstrElementName=path;
```

```
    if((rtrn=mciSendCommand(O,MCI_OPEN,MCI_OPEN_TYPE |
      MCI_OPEN_ELEMENT,(DWORD)(LPVOID)&mciopen)) != OL) {
        mciGetErrorString(rtrn,(LPSTR)b,STRINGSIZE);
        DoMessage(hwnd,b);
        return(OL);
    }

    videoID=mciopen.wDeviceID;

    mciplay.dwCallback=(DWORD)hwnd;
    if((rtrn=mciSendCommand(videoID,MCI_PLAY,MCI_NOTIFY,
      (DWORD)(LPVOID)&mciplay)) != OL) {
        mciSendCommand(videoID,MCI_CLOSE,O,NULL);
        mciGetErrorString(rtrn,(LPSTR)b,STRINGSIZE);
        DoMessage(hwnd,b);
        return(OL);
    }

    return(1L);
}

void Config(HWND hwnd)
{
    MCI_GENERIC_PARMS mcigen;
    DWORD rtrn;
    char b[STRINGSIZE+1];

    mcigen.dwCallback=hwnd;
    if((rtrn=mciSendCommand(videoID,MCI_CONFIGURE,MCI_WAIT,
      (DWORD)(LPVOID)&mcigen)) != OL) {
        mciGetErrorString(rtrn,(LPSTR)b,STRINGSIZE);
        DoMessage(hwnd,b);
    }
}

int GetInfo(FLICK *flick,LPSTR path,HWND hwnd)
{
    struct ffblk fb;
    HMMIO h;
    MMCKINFO mmParent,mmSub,mmSubSub;
    unsigned int n;

    lmemset((LPSTR)flick,O,sizeof(FLICK));

    lstrcpy(flick->filename,path);
```

```
        if(findfirst(flick->filename,&fb,0)) {
            DoMessage(hwnd,"Error finding file");
            return(0);
        }
        flick->filesize=fb.ff_fsize;

        strupr(flick->filename);

        if((h=mmioOpen(path,NULL,MMIO_READ)) == NULL) {
            DoMessage(hwnd,"Error opening file");
            return(0);
        }

        mmParent.fccType=mmioFOURCC('A','V','I',' ');
        if(mmioDescend(h,(LPMMCKINFO)&mmParent,NULL,MMIO_FINDRIFF)) {
            mmioClose(h,0);
            DoMessage(hwnd,"Error finding AVI chunk");
            return(0);
        }

        mmSub.fccType=mmioFOURCC('h','d','r','l');
        if(mmioDescend(h,(LPMMCKINFO)&mmSub,(LPMMCKINFO)&mmParent,MMIO_FINDLIST)) {
            DoMessage(hwnd,"Error finding hdrl chunk");
            mmioClose(h,0);
            return(0);
        }

        mmSubSub.ckid=mmioFOURCC('a','v','i','h');
        if(mmioDescend(h,(LPMMCKINFO)&mmSubSub,(LPMMCKINFO)&mmSub,MMIO_FINDCHUNK)) {
            DoMessage(hwnd,"Error finding avih chunk");
            mmioClose(h,0);
            return(0);
        }

        n=min((unsigned int)mmSub.cksize,sizeof(MAINAVIHEADER));
        if(mmioRead(h,(LPSTR)&flick->avi,n) != n) {
            DoMessage(hwnd,"Error reading header chunk");
            mmioClose(h,0);
            return(0);
        }

        mmioClose(h,0);
        return(1);
}

int ShowFrame(LPSTR path,HDC hdc,FLICK far *flick)
```

```
{
    MCI_DGV_OPEN_PARMS mciopen;
    MCI_DGV_UPDATE_PARMS mciupdate;
    int id;

    mciopen.lpstrDeviceType="avivideo";
    mciopen.lpstrElementName=path;
    if(mciSendCommand(0,MCI_OPEN,MCI_OPEN_TYPE |
      MCI_OPEN_ELEMENT,(DWORD)(LPVOID)&mciopen) != 0L) {
        return(0);
    }

    id=mciopen.wDeviceID;

    mciupdate.hDC=hdc;
    mciupdate.rc.left=0;
    mciupdate.rc.top=0;
    mciupdate.rc.right=(unsigned int)flick->avi.dwWidth;
    mciupdate.rc.bottom=(unsigned int)flick->avi.dwHeight;

    SetWindowOrg(hdc,-INFO_FRAMELEFT,-INFO_FRAMETOP);

    if(mciSendCommand(id,MCI_UPDATE,MCI_DGV_UPDATE_HDC |
      MCI_DGV_UPDATE_PAINT,(DWORD)(LPVOID)&mciupdate) != 0L) {
        mciSendCommand(id,MCI_CLOSE,0,NULL);
        return(0);
    }

    mciSendCommand(id,MCI_CLOSE,0,NULL);

    return(1);
}

DWORD FAR PASCAL AboutDlgProc(HWND hwnd,WORD message,WORD wParam,LONG lParam)
{
    POINT point;

    switch(message) {
        case WM_INITDIALOG:
            return(TRUE);
        case WM_CTLCOLOR:
            if(HIWORD(lParam)==CTLCOLOR_STATIC ||
              HIWORD(lParam)==CTLCOLOR_DLG) {
                SetBkColor(wParam,RGB(192,192,192));
                SetTextColor(wParam,RGB(0,0,0));
```

```
                ClientToScreen(hwnd,&point);
                UnrealizeObject(GetStockObject(LTGRAY_BRUSH));
                SetBrushOrg(wParam,point.x,point.y);

                return((DWORD)GetStockObject(LTGRAY_BRUSH));

            }
            if(HIWORD(lParam)==CTLCOLOR_BTN) {
                SetBkColor(wParam,RGB(192,192,192));
                SetTextColor(wParam,RGB(0,0,0));

                ClientToScreen(hwnd,&point);
                UnrealizeObject(GetStockObject(BLACK_BRUSH));
                SetBrushOrg(wParam,point.x,point.y);

                return((DWORD)GetStockObject(BLACK_BRUSH));
            }
            break;
        case WM_COMMAND:
            switch(wParam) {
                case IDOK:
                    EndDialog(hwnd,wParam);
                    return(TRUE);
            }
            break;
    }

    return(FALSE);
}

void DoMessage(HWND hwnd,LPSTR message)
{
    FARPROC lpfnDlgProc;

    messagehook=message;

    if((lpfnDlgProc=MakeProcInstance((FARPROC)MessageDlgProc,hInst)) != NULL) {
        DialogBox(hInst,"MessageBox",hwnd,lpfnDlgProc);
        FreeProcInstance(lpfnDlgProc);
    }
}

DWORD FAR PASCAL MessageDlgProc(HWND hwnd,WORD message,WORD wParam,LONG lParam)
{
    POINT point;
    HWND dlgH;
```

```
switch(message) {
    case WM_INITDIALOG:
        dlgH=GetDlgItem(hwnd,MESSAGE_STRING);
        SetWindowText(dlgH,messagehook);
        return(TRUE);
    case WM_CTLCOLOR:
        if(HIWORD(lParam)==CTLCOLOR_STATIC ||
            HIWORD(lParam)==CTLCOLOR_DLG) {
            SetBkColor(wParam,RGB(192,192,192));
            SetTextColor(wParam,RGB(0,0,0));

            ClientToScreen(hwnd,&point);
            UnrealizeObject(GetStockObject(LTGRAY_BRUSH));
            SetBrushOrg(wParam,point.x,point.y);

            return((DWORD)GetStockObject(LTGRAY_BRUSH));

        }
        if(HIWORD(lParam)==CTLCOLOR_BTN) {
            SetBkColor(wParam,RGB(192,192,192));
            SetTextColor(wParam,RGB(0,0,0));

            ClientToScreen(hwnd,&point);
            UnrealizeObject(GetStockObject(BLACK_BRUSH));
            SetBrushOrg(wParam,point.x,point.y);

            return((DWORD)GetStockObject(BLACK_BRUSH));
        }
        break;
    case WM_COMMAND:
        switch(wParam) {
            case IDCANCEL:
            case IDOK:
            case IDYES:
            case IDNO:
                EndDialog(hwnd,wParam);
                return(TRUE);
        }
        break;
}

return(FALSE);
}

void lmemset(LPSTR s,int n,unsigned int size)
```

```c
{
    unsigned int i;

    for(i=0;i<size;++i) *s++=n;
}

void ResetSelectorList(HWND hwnd,unsigned int listbox,unsigned int pathstring)
{
    HWND dlgH;
    HCURSOR hSaveCursor,hHourGlass;
    char b[145];

    hHourGlass=LoadCursor(NULL,IDC_WAIT);
    hSaveCursor=SetCursor(hHourGlass);

    dlgH=GetDlgItem(hwnd,listbox);

    SendDlgItemMessage(hwnd,listbox,LB_RESETCONTENT,0,0L);
    getcwd(b,64);
    AnsiLower(b);
    SetDlgItemText(hwnd,pathstring,b);

    SendMessage(dlgH,WM_SETREDRAW,FALSE,0L);

    lstrcpy(b,"*.");
    lstrcat(b,FILE_EXTENSION);
    SendDlgItemMessage(hwnd,listbox,LB_DIR,0x0000,(long )b);

    lstrcpy(b,"*.*");
    SendDlgItemMessage(hwnd,listbox,LB_DIR,0xc010,(long )b);

    SendDlgItemMessage(hwnd,listbox,LB_SETCURSEL,0,0L);

    SendMessage(dlgH,WM_SETREDRAW,TRUE,0L);

    SetCursor(hSaveCursor);
}

int testdisk(int n)
{
    FILE *fp;
    char b[32];
    int r;

    SetErrorMode(1);
    sprintf(b,"%c:\\TEMP.DAT",n+'A');
```

```
    if((fp=fopen(b,"r")) != NULL) fclose(fp);

    if(_doserrno==ENOPATH) r=1;
    else r=0;

    SetErrorMode(0);
    return(r);
}

void ShowInfo(HWND hwnd,FLICK far *flick)
{
    FARPROC lpfnDlgProc;

    messagehook=(LPSTR)flick;
    if((lpfnDlgProc=MakeProcInstance((FARPROC)InfoDlgProc,hInst)) != NULL) {
        DialogBox(hInst,"InfoBox",hwnd,lpfnDlgProc);
        FreeProcInstance(lpfnDlgProc);
    }
}

DWORD FAR PASCAL InfoDlgProc(HWND hwnd,WORD message,WORD wParam,LONG lParam)
{
    FLICK far *flick;
    HDC hdc;
    HWND dlgH;
    POINT point;
    PAINTSTRUCT ps;
    unsigned long l;
    char b[STRINGSIZE+1];

    switch(message) {
        case WM_INITDIALOG:
            flick=(FLICK far *)messagehook;

            l=flick->avi.dwMicroSecPerFrame * flick->avi.dwTotalFrames / 1000L;

            wsprintf(b,"%u.%03.3u seconds",
                (unsigned int)(l/1000L),
                (unsigned int)(l%1000L));
            ItemName(INFO_RUNTIME,b);

            wsprintf(b,"%lu bytes",flick->filesize);
            ItemName(INFO_FILESIZE,b);

            l=1000000000L/flick->avi.dwMicroSecPerFrame;
```

```
            wsprintf(b,"%u.%03.3u frames/second",
                (unsigned int)(1/1000L),
                (unsigned int)(1%1000L));
        ItemName(INFO_FRAMERATE,b);

            wsprintf(b,"%lu",flick->avi.dwTotalFrames);
        ItemName(INFO_FRAMECOUNT,b);

            wsprintf(b,"%u x %u",
                (unsigned int)flick->avi.dwWidth,
                (unsigned int)flick->avi.dwHeight);
        ItemName(INFO_DIMENSIONS,b);

            if(flick->avi.dwFlags & AVIF_COPYRIGHTED) {
                ItemName(INFO_COPYRIGHT,"This video is copyrighted.");
            }
            else {
                ItemName(INFO_COPYRIGHT,"This video is not copyrighted.");
            }

            SetWindowText(hwnd,(LPSTR)flick->filename);

            return(TRUE);
        case WM_CTLCOLOR:
            if(HIWORD(lParam)==CTLCOLOR_STATIC ||
               HIWORD(lParam)==CTLCOLOR_DLG) {
                SetBkColor(wParam,RGB(192,192,192));
                SetTextColor(wParam,RGB(0,0,0));

                ClientToScreen(hwnd,&point);
                UnrealizeObject(GetStockObject(LTGRAY_BRUSH));
                SetBrushOrg(wParam,point.x,point.y);

                return((DWORD)GetStockObject(LTGRAY_BRUSH));

            }
            if(HIWORD(lParam)==CTLCOLOR_BTN) {
                SetBkColor(wParam,RGB(192,192,192));
                SetTextColor(wParam,RGB(0,0,0));

                ClientToScreen(hwnd,&point);
                UnrealizeObject(GetStockObject(BLACK_BRUSH));
                SetBrushOrg(wParam,point.x,point.y);

                return((DWORD)GetStockObject(BLACK_BRUSH));
            }
```

7-3 Continued.

```
                break;
        case WM_PAINT:
            hdc=BeginPaint(hwnd,&ps);
            flick=(FLICK far *)messagehook;
            ShowFrame(flick->filename,hdc,flick);
             EndPaint(hwnd,&ps);
            break;
        case WM_COMMAND:
            switch(wParam) {
                case IDOK:
                    EndDialog(hwnd,wParam);
                    return(TRUE);
            }
            break;
    }


    return(FALSE);
}
```

7-4 The resource script for the Video For Windows movie player, AVIPLAY.RC.

```
MainScreen DIALOG 117, 55, 148, 156
STYLE WS_POPUP | WS_CAPTION | WS_SYSMENU | WS_MINIMIZEBOX
CAPTION "AVI Player"
MENU MainMenu
BEGIN
  CONTROL "", 201, "LISTBOX", LBS_STANDARD | WS_CHILD | WS_VISIBLE, 12, 32, 76, 100
  LTEXT " Flicks", -1, 8, 8, 84, 8, WS_CHILD | WS_VISIBLE | WS_GROUP
  CONTROL "", -1, "BorShade", BSS_GROUP | WS_CHILD | WS_VISIBLE, 8, 16, 84, 132
  DEFPUSHBUTTON "Play", 101, 108, 16, 32, 20, WS_CHILD | WS_VISIBLE | WS_TABSTOP
  PUSHBUTTON "Stop", 102, 108, 40, 32, 20, WS_CHILD | WS_VISIBLE | WS_TABSTOP
  PUSHBUTTON "Quit", 107, 108, 128, 32, 20, WS_CHILD | WS_VISIBLE | WS_TABSTOP
  CONTROL "", -1, "BorShade", BSS_VDIP | WS_CHILD | WS_VISIBLE, 100, 0, 1, 156
  LTEXT "", 202, 12, 136, 76, 8, WS_CHILD | WS_VISIBLE | WS_GROUP
  PUSHBUTTON "Config", 104, 108, 88, 32, 20, WS_CHILD | WS_VISIBLE | WS_TABSTOP
  PUSHBUTTON "Get Info", 103, 108, 64, 32, 20, WS_CHILD | WS_VISIBLE | WS_TABSTOP
  LTEXT "", 203, 12, 20, 76, 8, WS_CHILD | WS_VISIBLE | WS_GROUP
END

MainMenu MENU
BEGIN
    POPUP "&File"
    BEGIN
        MENUITEM "&Play", 101
        MENUITEM "&Stop", 102
```

```
          MENUITEM "&Get Info", 103
          MENUITEM "&Config", 104
          MENUITEM "&About", 105
          MENUITEM SEPARATOR
          MENUITEM "E&xit", 107
     END

END


AboutBox DIALOG 18, 18, 156, 104
STYLE WS_POPUP | WS_CAPTION
CAPTION "About AVI Player..."
BEGIN
   CONTROL "", 102, "BorShade",
       BSS_GROUP | WS_CHILD | WS_VISIBLE | WS_TABSTOP, 8, 8, 140, 68
   CTEXT "AVI Player 1.0\nCopyright (c) 1993\nAlchemy Mindworks Inc.\n"
        "This program is part of the book Multimedia Programming for Windows "
        "by Steven William Rimmer, published by Windcrest (Book 4484).",
        -1, 12, 12, 128, 60, WS_CHILD | WS_VISIBLE | WS_GROUP
   DEFPUSHBUTTON "Ok", IDOK, 116, 80, 32, 20, WS_CHILD | WS_VISIBLE | WS_TABSTOP
END


MessageBox DIALOG 72, 72, 144, 80
STYLE DS_MODALFRAME | WS_POPUP | WS_CAPTION
CAPTION "Message"
BEGIN
   CONTROL "", 102, "BorShade", BSS_GROUP | WS_CHILD | WS_VISIBLE, 4, 8, 136, 44
   CTEXT "", 101, 8, 12, 128, 36, WS_CHILD | WS_VISIBLE | WS_GROUP
   DEFPUSHBUTTON "Ok", IDOK, 108, 56, 32, 20, WS_CHILD | WS_VISIBLE | WS_TABSTOP
END


AVIPlayer ICON
BEGIN
    '00 00 01 00 01 00 20 20 10 00 00 00 00 00 E8 02'
    '00 00 16 00 00 00 28 00 00 00 20 00 00 00 40 00'
    '00 00 01 00 04 00 00 00 00 00 80 02 00 00 00 00'
    '00 00 00 00 00 00 00 00 00 00 00 00 00 00 00 00'
    '00 00 00 00 BF 00 00 BF 00 00 00 BF BF 00 BF 00'
    '00 00 BF 00 BF 00 BF BF 00 00 C0 C0 C0 00 80 80'
    '80 00 00 00 FF 00 00 FF 00 00 00 FF FF 00 FF 00'
    '00 00 FF 00 FF 00 FF FF 00 00 FF FF FF 00 FF FF'
    'FF FF FF FF FF FF FF FF FF FF FF FF FF FF FF FF'
    'FF FF FF F0 FF 07 77 77 77 77 77 77 0F F0 FF FF'
    'FF FF FF F0 FF 07 77 77 77 77 77 77 0F F0 FF FF'
    'FF FF FF F0 00 07 77 77 77 77 77 77 00 00 FF FF'
    'FF FF FF F0 00 07 77 77 77 77 77 77 00 00 FF FF'
```

```
'FF FF FF F0 FF 00 00 00 00 00 00 00 0F F0 FF FF'
'FF FF FF F0 FF 07 77 77 77 77 77 77 0F F0 FF FF'
'FF FF FF F0 00 07 77 77 77 77 77 77 00 00 FF FF'
'FF FF FF F0 00 08 88 88 77 77 87 77 00 00 0F F0'
'77 77 77 70 FF 08 88 88 88 88 87 77 0F F0 07 70'
'00 00 00 00 00 00 00 88 08 88 87 77 0F F0 00 00'
'F7 F7 7F 77 77 77 70 00 08 88 87 77 00 00 00 00'
'FF 77 F7 F7 7F 77 70 00 08 88 87 77 00 00 0F F0'
'FF FF 77 7F 77 F7 70 FF 08 88 87 77 0F F0 0F F0'
'FF 7F FF F7 F7 77 F0 FF 0F FF FF FF FF FF 00 00'
'FF F7 F7 7F 77 F7 70 00 0F FF FF FF FF FF 00 00'
'FF FF 7F F7 F7 77 70 00 0F FF FF FF FF FF 0F F0'
'FF F7 FF 7F 77 7F 70 FF 0F FF FF FF FF FF 0F F0'
'FF FF F7 F7 F7 F7 70 FF 0F FF FF FF FF FF 00 00'
'FF FF FF FF FF 7F 70 00 0F FF FF FF FF FF 00 00'
'FF FF FF FF FF FF F0 00 0F FF FF FF FF FF 0F F0'
'00 00 00 00 00 00 00 FF 0F FF FF FF FF FF FF FF'
'FF FF FF FF FF FF FF FF FF FF FF FF FF FF FF FF'
'FF FF FF F0 00 07 77 77 77 77 77 77 00 00 FF FF'
'FF FF FF F0 00 07 77 77 77 77 77 77 00 00 FF FF'
'FF FF FF F0 FF 07 77 77 77 77 77 77 0F F0 FF FF'
'FF FF FF F0 FF 07 77 77 77 77 77 77 0F F0 FF FF'
'FF FF FF F0 00 07 77 77 77 77 77 77 00 00 FF FF'
'FF FF FF F0 00 07 77 77 77 77 77 77 00 00 FF FF'
'FF FF FF F0 FF 07 77 77 77 77 77 77 0F F0 FF FF'
'FF FF FF FF FF FF FF FF FF FF FF FF FF FF FF FF'
'FF FF FF FF FF FF FF FF FF FF FF FF FF FF 00 00'
'00 00 00 00 00 00 00 00 00 00 00 00 00 00 00 00'
'00 00 00 00 00 00 00 00 00 00 00 00 00 00 00 00'
'00 00 00 00 00 00 00 00 00 00 00 00 00 00 00 00'
'00 00 00 00 00 00 00 00 00 00 00 00 00 00 00 00'
'00 00 00 00 00 00 00 00 00 00 00 00 00 00 00 00'
'00 00 00 00 00 00 00 00 00 00 00 00 00 00 00 00'
'00 00 00 00 00 00 00 00 00 00 00 00 00 00 00 00'
'00 00 00 00 00 00 00 00 00 00 00 00 00 00 00'
END


InfoBox DIALOG 18, 18, 212, 216
STYLE DS_MODALFRAME | WS_POPUP | WS_CAPTION
CAPTION "Information"
BEGIN
  DEFPUSHBUTTON "Ok", IDOK, 172, 56, 32, 20, WS_CHILD | WS_VISIBLE | WS_TABSTOP
  RTEXT "Running time:", -1, 8, 8, 68, 8,
      SS_RIGHT | WS_CHILD | WS_VISIBLE | WS_GROUP
  RTEXT "File size:", -1, 8, 20, 68, 8,
```

```
    SS_RIGHT | WS_CHILD | WS_VISIBLE | WS_GROUP
RTEXT "Frame rate:", -1, 8, 32, 68, 8,
    SS_RIGHT | WS_CHILD | WS_VISIBLE | WS_GROUP
RTEXT "Number of frames:", -1, 8, 44, 68, 8,
    SS_RIGHT | WS_CHILD | WS_VISIBLE | WS_GROUP
LTEXT "", 101, 84, 8, 92, 8, WS_CHILD | WS_VISIBLE | WS_GROUP
LTEXT "", 102, 84, 20, 92, 8, WS_CHILD | WS_VISIBLE | WS_GROUP
LTEXT "", 103, 84, 32, 92, 8, WS_CHILD | WS_VISIBLE | WS_GROUP
LTEXT "", 104, 84, 44, 48, 8, WS_CHILD | WS_VISIBLE | WS_GROUP
RTEXT "Dimensions:", -1, 8, 56, 68, 8,
    SS_RIGHT | WS_CHILD | WS_VISIBLE | WS_GROUP
LTEXT "", 105, 84, 56, 48, 8, WS_CHILD | WS_VISIBLE | WS_GROUP
LTEXT "", 106, 8, 68, 124, 8, WS_CHILD | WS_VISIBLE | WS_GROUP
CONTROL "", 107, "BorShade", 2 | WS_CHILD | WS_VISIBLE, 0, 81, 212, 2
END
```

Finally, you'll need a project and a DEF file to complete the AVIPLAY application. The project file, shown in FIG. 7-5, can be replaced by a suitable MAKE file if you're not using the Borland C++ for Windows integrated development environment. The DEF file, AVIPLAY.DEF, is as follows:

```
NAME         aviPLAY
DESCRIPTION  'AVI Player'
EXETYPE      WINDOWS
CODE         PRELOAD MOVEABLE
DATA         PRELOAD MOVEABLE MULTIPLE
SEGMENTS     WM_TEXT LOADONCALL
HEAPSIZE     8192
STACKSIZE    8192
```

There's little that's really remarkable about AVIPLAY—it's really just the code discussed earlier in this chapter with enough glue around it to turn it into a complete application. Note that you must modify the Directories field of your compiler setup to include the MCIAVI.H and DIGITALV.H files in \WINVIDEO\INCLUDE. These files assume that MMSYSTEM.H was included previously. The INFO_FRAMELEFT and INFO_FRAMETOP constants define the location of the example frame in the file-information box.

The list of AVIF flag constants and MAINAVIHEADER values are defined in AVIPLAY.CPP. They're actually available in a file called AVI_RIFF.H, but it's not included in the Video for Windows package. I happened upon it on CompuServe. In any case, the definitions in AVI_RIFF.H are a bit awkward—it's simpler to use these items as they're illustrated here.

The AVIF constants represent flags that can be used to test the dwFlags value of a MAINAVIHEADER object. Not all of them are immediately useful—in most cases the conditions they pertain to will matter only if you have cause to bypass the MCI functions and write your own low-level AVI player, a task of some enormity.

The AVIF_HASINDEX flag indicates that there's an 'idx1' chunk at the end of an AVI file, that is, an index of the contents of the file. The AVIF_MUSTUSEINDEX flag specifies that the index must be used to determine how the file is to be played. Neither of these things is relevant to the code in this chapter.

The AVIF_ISINTERLEAVED flag indicates that the AVI file in question is interleaved, something else that MCI takes care of for you. The AVIF_WASCAPTUREFILE flag indicates that the AVI file being read was used to capture real-time video.

Finally, the AVIF_COPYRIGHTED flag will be set if the AVI file being read contains copyrighted video, something you might want to keep track of in an application that deals with Video for Windows movies.

The other data structure defined in AVIPLAY.CPP is a FLICK, which is an internal notation for the objects that define an AVI file, much as FILEINFO has been used in previous chapters of this book.

The SelectProc function of AVIPLAY dispatches the various functions of the application, as well as handling MM_MCINOTIFY messages returned by the AVI player function. It's pretty well identical to the equiva-

7-5 The project file for the Video For Windows movie player, AVIPLAY.PRJ.

lent functions in the other examples of MCI-based programs in this book—and, in fact, much of its code was lifted from them.

The principal functions of AVIPLAY—PlayFlick and GetInfo—have been discussed at length earlier in this chapter. The GetInfo function fetches the file size in bytes in addition to plumbing the catacombs of RIFF chunks in the AVI file it's presented with.

Note that the ShowFrame function, while essentially similar to the one discussed in the previous section, uses a call to SetWindowOrg to position the example frame, so it will draw somewhere other than in the upper left corner of the window it updates. It's called from InfoDlgProc at the bottom of the listing, which is also responsible for formatting the data in a FLICK object to make it intelligible.

You could certainly add a few more values to the information InfoDl-gProc displays, although the remaining elements in a MAINAVIHEADER are probably of questionable importance to most users of AVI files.

It's a wrap

While the applications of AVI movies are still arguably a matter for imagination and grand designs, neither the software to work with them nor the hardware to create and play them need be particularly exotic. While Microsoft recommends the rather expensive Intel Indeo board for creating AVI files, there are alternatives that won't do in your Visa card to quite the same extent. I use a Digital Vision ComputerEyes RT board, quite an inexpensive real-time digitizer, with pretty respectable results.

Index

About the author

When I'm not writing computer books, I write books. These other books are about as far removed from computer books as they can get, I imagine. The novels I write have thus far all been set in infrequently visited bits of Britain, mostly Wales and Scotland. I'm not certain what "genre" they'd fall into—they're typically concerned with witchcraft and fertility magic and such. That's real witchcraft, as opposed to Hollywood/Stephen King witchcraft. I'm pretty certain they're not horror novels, in any case. (There are those, of course, who will consider the phrase *real witchcraft* to be a contradiction in terms.)

My first novel was *Coven*, published by Ballantine a few years ago. My two most recent books are currently with my agent, who's questing after a publisher for them. I think the hot topic for publishers this season is royal divorces . . . and I can't quite figure a way to work them into a novel.

One of the curious things about writing computer books is that everyone seems to think I write science fiction on the side. I'm not certain why this is—I rarely have any patience for it. A quick stroll through the science fiction section of most book stores suggests that half the books in the field are novelizations of episodes of Star Trek and the other half are works of would-be latter-day J.R.R. Tolkien.

One of the hardships of writing the sort of fiction I do is having to go over to Wales or Scotland every summer to do some research. This involves grueling afternoons and evenings spent in sundry pubs downing the local ale, tortuous walks through various towns and villages, and so on. The things one does for art frequently transcend the limits of human endurance . . . although I feel I'll manage to press on.

When I really can't face either computer books or lurid novels of debauchery, lust, and pagan excess, I play guitar in a band called Loftus. We started out doing traditional Irish instrumental music, although we've since diversified into bits of Breton and Elizabethan music and even a few left-over medieval tunes. The band's name is derived from the name of one of the Turlough Carolan's fiddle tunes, "Loftus Jones."

I feel moved to point out that there's a distinction between traditional Irish music and the music that's traditionally played in pseudo-Irish bars on St. Patrick's day, when the beer has been dyed green. The latter group includes such favorites as "Danny Boy," "Black Velvet Band," and so on. I suspect that if any of the member of Loftus were to suggest playing one of these, it would be regarded as grounds for impeachment. Loftus will, of course, be appearing in the otherwise unused tracks of the CD-ROM that accompanies this book.

I'm not certain what else I do that would constitute a hobby. Megan thinks I collect cars as a sort of pastime. I'm not certain I'd agree with this. For example, Clive Cussler, who wrote *Raise the Titanic* and several other novels, has 86 of them. I have—I believe—only three. I used to build instruments for a while, until the cost of the wood involved in doing so made collecting cars cheaper.

CD-ROM WARRANTY

This software is protected by both United States copyright law and international copyright treaty provision. You must treat this software just like a book. By saying "just like a book," McGraw-Hill means, for example, that this software may be used by any number of people and may be freely moved from one computer location to another, so long as there is no possibility of its being used at one location or on one computer while it also is being used at another. Just as a book cannot be read by two different people in two different places at the same time, neither can the software be used by two different people in two different places at the same time (unless, of course, McGraw-Hill's copyright is being violated).

LIMITED WARRANTY

Windcrest/McGraw-Hill takes great care to provide you with top-quality software, thoroughly checked to prevent virus infections. McGraw-Hill warrants the physical CD-ROM contained herein to be free of defects in materials and workmanship for a period of sixty days from the purchase date. If McGraw-Hill receives written notification within the warranty period of defects in materials or workmanship, and such notification is determined by McGraw-Hill to be correct, McGraw-Hill will replace the defective CD-ROM. Send requests to:

> Customer Service
> Windcrest/McGraw-Hill
> 13311 Monterey Lane
> Blue Ridge Summit, PA 17294-0850

The entire and exclusive liability and remedy for breach of this Limited Warranty shall be limited to replacement of a defective CD-ROM and shall not include or extend to any claim for or right to cover any other damages, including but not limited to, loss of profit, data, or use of the software, or special, incidental, or consequential damages or other similar claims, even if McGraw-Hill has been specifically advised of the possibility of such damages. In no event will McGraw-Hill's liability for any damages to you or any other person ever exceed the lower of suggested list price or actual price paid for the license to use the software, regardless of any form of the claim.

MCGRAW-HILL, INC. SPECIFICALLY DISCLAIMS ALL OTHER WARRANTIES, EXPRESS OR IMPLIED, INCLUDING, BUT NOT LIMITED TO, ANY IMPLIED WARRANTY OF MERCHANTABILITY OR FITNESS FOR A PARTICULAR PURPOSE.

Specifically, McGraw-Hill makes no representation or warranty that the software is fit for any particular purpose and any implied warranty of merchantability is limited to the sixty-day duration of the Limited Warranty covering the physical CD-ROM only (and not the software) and is otherwise expressly and specifically disclaimed.

This limited warranty gives you specific legal rights; you may have others which may vary from state to state. Some states do not allow the exclusion of incidental or consequential damages, or the limitation on how long an implied warranty lasts, so some of the above may not apply to you.

Among the directories of this included CD-ROM, you'll find the following:

- The source code for all the example applications in this book.
- The executable files for all the applications in this book.
- Graphic Workshop for Windows, to help you with the graphics.
- About twenty megabytes worth of public-domain wave files.
- About twenty megabytes worth of public-domain MIDI files.
- About twenty megabytes worth of public-domain graphics.
- Some Kodak Photo-CD images.
- Several Video for Windows clips.
- Half an hour with Loftus.

For more information, see chapter 1 of this book, under the section *Companion CD-ROM: The biggest disk I could find.*

IMPORTANT

Read the CD-ROM Warranty terms on the previous page before opening the envelope. Opening the envelope constitutes acceptance of these terms and renders this entire package nonreturnable except for replacement in kind due to material defects.
